TABLE OF CONTENTS

TABLE OF CONTENTS

MEMOIRS OF THE LIFE

OF

SIR WALTER SCOTT

CHAPTER I

MEMOIR OF THE EARLY LIFE OF SIR WALTER SCOTT, WRITTEN BY HIMSELF

ASHESTIEL, April 26, 1808.

THE present age has discovered a desire, or rather a rage, for literary anecdote and private history, that may be well permitted to alarm one who has engaged in a certain degree the attention of the public. That I have had more than my own share of popularity, my contemporaries will be as ready to admit as I am to confess that its measure has exceeded not only my hopes, but my merits, and even wishes. I may be therefore permitted, without an extraordinary degree of vanity, to take the precaution of recording a few leading circumstances (they do not merit the name of events) of a very quiet and uniform life — that, should my literary reputation survive my temporal existence, the public may know from good authority all that they are entitled to know of an individual who has contributed to their amusement.

From the lives of some poets a most important moral lesson may doubtless be derived, and few sermons can be read with so much profit as the Memoirs of Burns, of Chatterton, or of Savage. Were I conscious of anything peculiar in my own moral character which could render such development necessary or useful, I would as readily consent to it as I would bequeath my body to dissection, if the operation could tend to point out the nature and the means of curing any peculiar malady. But as my habits of thinking and acting, as well as my rank in society, were fixed long before I had attained, or even pretended to, any poetical reputation,[1] and as it produced, when acquired, no remarkable change upon either, it is hardly to be expected that much information can be derived from minutely investigating frailties, follies, or vices, not very different in number or degree from those of other men in my situation. As I have not been blessed with the talents of Burns or Chatterton, I have been happily exempted from the influence of their violent passions, exasperated by the struggle of feelings which rose up against the unjust decrees of fortune. Yet, although I cannot tell of difficulties vanquished, and distance of rank annihilated by the strength of genius, those who shall hereafter read this little Memoir may find in it some hints to be improved, for the regulation of their own minds, or the training those of others.

Every Scottishman has a pedigree. It is a national prerogative as unalienable as his pride and his poverty. My birth was neither distinguished nor sordid. According to the prejudices of my country, it was esteemed

---

[1] I do not mean to say that my success in literature has not led me to mix familiarly in society much above my birth and original pretensions, since I have been readily received in the first circles in Britain. But there is a certain intuitive knowledge of the world, to which most well-educated Scotchmen are early trained, that prevents them from being much dazzled by this species of elevation. A man who to good nature adds the general rudiments of good breeding, provided he rest contented with a simple and unaffected manner of behaving and expressing himself, will never be ridiculous in the best society, and so far as his talents and information permit, may be an agreeable part of the company. I have therefore never felt much elevated, nor did I experience any violent change in situation, by the passport which my poetical character afforded me into higher company than my birth warranted. — (1826.)

gentle, as I was connected, though remotely, with ancient families both by my father's and mother's side. My father's grandfather was Walter Scott, well known in Teviotdale by the surname of *Beardie*. He was the second son of Walter Scott, first Laird of Raeburn, who was third son of Sir William Scott, and the grandson of Walter Scott, commonly called in tradition *Auld Watt*, of Harden. I am therefore lineally descended from that ancient chieftain, whose name I have made to ring in many a ditty, and from his fair dame, the Flower of Yarrow — no bad genealogy for a Border minstrel. *Beardie*, my great-grandfather aforesaid, derived his cognomen from a venerable beard, which he wore unblemished by razor or scissors, in token of his regret for the banished dynasty of Stuart. It would have been well that his zeal had stopped there. But he took arms, and intrigued in their cause, until he lost all he had in the world, and, as I have heard, run a narrow risk of being hanged, had it not been for the interference of Anne, Duchess of Buccleuch and Monmouth. Beardie's elder brother, William Scott of Raeburn, my great-grand-uncle, was killed about the age of twenty-one, in a duel with Pringle of Crichton, grandfather of the present Mark Pringle of Clifton. They fought with swords, as was the fashion of the time, in a field near Selkirk, called from the catastrophe the *Raeburn Meadow-spot*. Pringle fled from Scotland to Spain, and was long a captive and slave in Barbary. *Beardie* became, of course, *Tutor of Raeburn*, as the old Scottish phrase called him — that is, guardian to his infant nephew, father of the present Walter Scott of Raeburn. He also managed the estates of Makerstoun, being nearly related to that family by his mother, Isobel MacDougal. I suppose he had some allowance for his care in either case, and subsisted upon that and the fortune which he had by his wife, a Miss Campbell of Silvercraigs, in the west, through which connection my father used to *call cousin*, as they say,

with the Campbells of Blythswood. Beardie was a man
of some learning, and a friend of Dr. Pitcairn, to whom
his politics probably made him acceptable. They had a
Tory or Jacobite club in Edinburgh, in which the conversation is said to have been maintained in Latin. Old
Beardie died in a house, still standing, at the northeast
entrance to the Churchyard of Kelso, about . . . [No-
vember 3, 1729.]

He left three sons. The eldest, Walter, had a family,
of which any that now remain have been long settled in
America: — the male heirs are long since extinct. The
third was William, father of James Scott, well known in
India as one of the original settlers of Prince of Wales
Island: — he had, besides, a numerous family both of
sons and daughters, and died at Lasswade, in Mid-
Lothian, about . . .

The second, Robert Scott, was my grandfather. He
was originally bred to the sea; but, being shipwrecked
near Dundee in his trial voyage, he took such a sincere
dislike to that element, that he could not be persuaded to
a second attempt. This occasioned a quarrel between
him and his father, who left him to shift for himself.
Robert was one of those active spirits to whom this was
no misfortune. He turned Whig upon the spot, and
fairly abjured his father's politics and his learned poverty. His chief and relative, Mr. Scott of Harden, gave
him a lease of the farm of Sandy-Knowe, comprehending
the rocks in the centre of which Smailholm or Sandy-
Knowe Tower is situated. He took for his shepherd
an old man called Hogg, who willingly lent him, out of
respect to his family, his whole savings, about £30, to
stock the new farm. With this sum, which it seems was
at the time sufficient for the purpose, the master and
servant set off to purchase a stock of sheep at Whit-
sun-Tryste, a fair held on a hill near Wooler in Northumberland. The old shepherd went carefully from drove
to drove, till he found a *hirsel* likely to answer their pur-

pose, and then returned to tell his master to come up and conclude the bargain. But what was his surprise to see him galloping a mettled hunter about the racecourse, and to find he had expended the whole stock in this extraordinary purchase! — Moses's bargain of green spectacles did not strike more dismay into the Vicar of Wakefield's family than my grandfather's rashness into the poor old shepherd. The thing, however, was irretrievable, and they returned without the sheep. In the course of a few days, however, my grandfather, who was one of the best horsemen of his time, attended John Scott of Harden's hounds on this same horse, and displayed him to such advantage that he sold him for double the original price. The farm was now stocked in earnest; and the rest of my grandfather's career was that of successful industry. He was one of the first who were active in the cattle trade, afterwards carried to such extent between the Highlands of Scotland and the leading counties in England, and by his droving transactions acquired a considerable sum of money. He was a man of middle stature, extremely active, quick, keen, and fiery in his temper, stubbornly honest, and so distinguished for his skill in country matters that he was the general referee in all points of dispute which occurred in the neighborhood. His birth being admitted as *gentle* gave him access to the best society in the county, and his dexterity in country sports, particularly hunting, made him an acceptable companion in the field as well as at the table.[1]

Robert Scott of Sandy-Knowe married, in 1728, Barbara Haliburton, daughter of Thomas Haliburton of Newmains, an ancient and respectable family in Berwickshire. Among other patrimonial possessions, they enjoyed the part of Dryburgh, now the property of the Earl of Buchan, comprehending the ruins of the Abbey.

---

[1] The present Lord Haddington, and other gentlemen conversant with the south country, remember my grandfather well. He was a fine, alert figure, and wore a jockey cap over his gray hair. — (1826.)

My grand-uncle, Robert Haliburton, having no male heirs, this estate, as well as the representation of the family, would have devolved upon my father, and indeed old Newmains had settled it upon him; but this was prevented by the misfortunes of my grand-uncle, a weak, silly man, who engaged in trade, for which he had neither stock nor talents, and became bankrupt. The ancient patrimony was sold for a trifle (about £3000), and my father, who might have purchased it with ease, was dissuaded by my grandfather, who at that time believed a more advantageous purchase might have been made of some lands which Raeburn thought of selling. And thus we have nothing left of Dryburgh, although my father's maternal inheritance, but the right of stretching our bones where mine may perhaps be laid ere any eye but my own glances over these pages.

Walter Scott, my father, was born in 1729, and educated to the profession of a Writer to the Signet. He was the eldest of a large family, several of whom I shall have occasion to mention with a tribute of sincere gratitude. My father was a singular instance of a man rising to eminence in a profession for which nature had in some degree unfitted him. He had indeed a turn for labor, and a pleasure in analyzing the abstruse feudal doctrines connected with conveyancing, which would probably have rendered him unrivalled in the line of a special pleader, had there been such a profession in Scotland; but in the actual business of the profession which he embraced, in that sharp and intuitive perception which is necessary in driving bargains for himself and others, in availing himself of the wants, necessities, caprices, and follies of some, and guarding against the knavery and malice of others, Uncle Toby himself could not have conducted himself with more simplicity than my father. Most attorneys have been suspected, more or less justly, of making their own fortune at the expense of their clients — my father's fate was to vindicate his calling from the stain in one instance, for in many cases his clients contrived to ease him of considerable sums. Many worshipful and be-knighted names occur to my memory, who did him the honor to run in his debt to the amount of thousands, and to pay him with a lawsuit, or a commission of bankruptcy, as the case happened. But they are gone to a different accounting, and it would be ungenerous to visit their disgrace upon their descendants. My father was wont also to give openings, to those who were pleased to take them, to pick a quarrel with him. He had a zeal for his clients which was almost ludicrous: far from coldly discharging the duties of his employment towards them, he thought for them, felt for their honor as for his own, and rather risked disobliging them than neglecting anything to which he conceived their duty bound them. If there was an old mother or aunt to be maintained, he was, I am afraid, too apt to administer to their necessities from what the young heir had destined exclusively to his pleasures. This ready discharge of obligations which the Civilians tell us are only natural and not legal, did not, I fear, recommend him to his employers. Yet his practice was, at one period of his life, very extensive. He understood his business theoretically, and was early introduced to it by a partnership with George Chalmers, Writer to the Signet, under whom he had served his apprenticeship.

His person and face were uncommonly handsome, with an expression of sweetness of temper, which was not fallacious; his manners were rather formal, but full of genuine kindness, especially when exercising the duties of hospitality. His general habits were not only temperate, but severely abstemious; but upon a festival occasion, there were few whom a moderate glass of wine exhilarated to such a lively degree. His religion, in which he was devoutly sincere, was Calvinism of the strictest kind, and his favorite study related to church history. I suspect the good old man was often engaged with Knox and

Spottiswoode's folios, when, immured in his solitary room, he was supposed to be immersed in professional researches. In his political principles he was a steady friend to freedom, with a bias, however, to the monarchical part of our constitution, which he considered as peculiarly exposed to danger during the later years of his life. He had much of ancient Scottish prejudice respecting the forms of marriages, funerals, christenings, and so forth, and was always vexed at any neglect of etiquette upon such occasions. As his education had not been upon an enlarged plan, it could not be expected that he should be an enlightened scholar, but he had not passed through a busy life without observation; and his remarks upon times and manners often exhibited strong traits of practical though untaught philosophy. Let me conclude this sketch, which I am unconscious of having overcharged, with a few lines written by the late Mrs. Cockburn[1] upon the subject. They made one among a set of poetical characters which were given as toasts among a few friends; and we must hold them to contain a striking likeness, since the original was recognized so soon as they were read aloud: —

> " To a thing that's uncommon —
> A youth of discretion,
> Who, though vastly handsome,
> Despises flirtation:
> To the friend in affliction,
> The heart of affection,
> Who may hear the last trump
> Without dread of detection."

In [April, 1758] my father married Anne Rutherford, eldest daughter of Dr. John Rutherford, professor of medicine in the University of Edinburgh. He was one of those pupils of Boerhaave, to whom the school of medicine in our northern metropolis owes its rise, and a man

[1] Mrs. Cockburn (born Miss Rutherford of Fairnalie) was the authoress of the beautiful song —

> " I have seen the smiling
> Of fortune beguiling." — (1826.)

distinguished for professional talent, for lively wit, and for literary acquirements. Dr. Rutherford was twice married. His first wife, of whom my mother is the sole surviving child, was a daughter of Sir John Swinton of Swinton, a family which produced many distinguished warriors during the Middle Ages, and which, for antiquity and honorable alliances, may rank with any in Britain. My grandfather's second wife was Miss Mackay, by whom he had a second family, of whom are now (1808) alive, Dr. Daniel Rutherford, professor of botany in the University of Edinburgh, and Misses Janet and Christian Rutherford, amiable and accomplished women.

My father and mother had a very numerous family, no fewer, I believe, than twelve children, of whom many were highly promising, though only five survived very early youth. My eldest brother (that is, the eldest whom I remember to have seen) was Robert Scott, so called after my uncle, of whom I shall have much to say hereafter. He was bred in the King's service, under Admiral, then Captain William Dickson, and was in most of Rodney's battles. His temper was bold and haughty, and to me was often checkered with what I felt to be capricious tyranny. In other respects I loved him much, for he had a strong turn for literature, read poetry with taste and judgment, and composed verses himself, which had gained him great applause among his messmates. Witness the following elegy upon the supposed loss of the vessel, composed the night before Rodney's celebrated battle of April the 12th, 1782. It alludes to the various amusements of his mess: —

> " No more the geese shall cackle on the poop,
>   No more the bagpipe through the orlop sound,
>   No more the midshipmen, a jovial group,
>   Shall toast the girls, and push the bottle round.
> In death's dark road at anchor fast they stay,
>   Till Heaven's loud signal shall in thunder roar ;
>   Then starting up, all hands shall quick obey,
>   Sheet home the topsail, and with speed unmoor."

Robert sung agreeably — (a virtue which was never seen in me) — understood the mechanical arts, and when in good humor, could regale us with many a tale of bold adventure and narrow escapes. When in bad humor, however, he gave us a practical taste of what was then man-of-war's discipline, and kicked and cuffed without mercy. I have often thought how he might have distinguished himself, had he continued in the navy until the present times, so glorious for nautical exploit. But the Peace of Paris [Versailles, 1783] cut off all hopes of promotion for those who had not great interest; and some disgust which his proud spirit had taken at harsh usage from a superior officer, combined to throw poor Robert into the East India Company's service, for which his habits were ill adapted. He made two voyages to the East, and died a victim to the climate in . . .

John Scott, my second brother, is about three years older than me. He addicted himself to the military service, and is now brevet-major in the 73rd regiment.[1]

I had an only sister, Anne Scott, who seemed to be from her cradle the butt for mischance to shoot arrows at. Her childhood was marked by perilous escapes from the most extraordinary accidents. Among others, I remember an iron-railed door leading into the area in the centre of George's Square being closed by the wind, while her fingers were betwixt the hasp and staple. Her hand was thus locked in, and must have been smashed to pieces, had not the bones of her fingers been remarkably slight and thin. As it was, the hand was cruelly mangled. On another occasion she was nearly drowned in a pond, or old quarry hole, in what was then called Brown's Park, on the south side of the square. But the most unfortunate accident, and which, though it happened while

---

[1] He was this year made major of the second battalion, by the kind intercession of Mr. Canning at the War Office — 1809. He retired from the army, and kept house with my mother. His health was totally broken, and he died, yet a young man, on 8th May, 1816. — (1826.)

she was only six years old, proved the remote cause of her death, was her cap accidentally taking fire. The child was alone in the room, and before assistance could be obtained, her head was dreadfully scorched. After a lingering and dangerous illness, she recovered — but never to enjoy perfect health. The slightest cold occasioned swellings in her face, and other indications of a delicate constitution. At length, in [1801], poor Anne was taken ill, and died after a very short interval. Her temper, like that of her brothers, was peculiar, and in her, perhaps, it showed more odd, from the habits of indulgence which her nervous illnesses had formed. But she was at heart an affectionate and kind girl, neither void of talent nor of feeling, though living in an ideal world which she had framed to herself by the force of imagination. Anne was my junior by about a year.

A year lower in the list was my brother Thomas Scott, who is still alive.[1]

Last, and most unfortunate of our family, was my youngest brother, Daniel. With the same aversion to labor, or rather, I should say, the same determined indolence that marked us all, he had neither the vivacity of intellect which supplies the want of diligence, nor the pride which renders the most detested labor better than dependence or contempt. His career was as unfortunate as might be augured from such an unhappy combination; and after various unsuccessful attempts to establish himself in life, he died on his return from the West Indies, in [July, 1806].

[1] Poor Tom, a man of infinite humor and excellent parts, pursued for some time my father's profession; but he was unfortunate, from engaging in speculations respecting farms and matters out of the line of his proper business. He afterwards became paymaster of the 70th regiment, and died in Canada. Tom married Elizabeth, a daughter of the family of M'Culloch of Ardwell, an ancient Galwegian stock, by whom he left a son, Walter Scott, now second lieutenant of engineers in the East India Company's service, Bombay — and three daughters; Jessie, married to Lieutenant-Colonel Huxley; 2. Anne; 3. Eliza — the two last still unmarried. — (1826.)

Having premised so much of my family, I return to my own story. I was born, as I believe, on the 15th August, 1771, in a house belonging to my father, at the head of the College Wynd. It was pulled down, with others, to make room for the northern front of the new College. I was an uncommonly healthy child, but had nearly died in consequence of my first nurse being ill of a consumption, a circumstance which she chose to conceal, though to do so was murder to both herself and me. She went privately to consult Dr. Black, the celebrated professor of chemistry, who put my father on his guard. The woman was dismissed, and I was consigned to a healthy peasant, who is still alive to boast of her *laddie* being what she calls *a grand gentleman*.[1] I showed every sign of health and strength until I was about eighteen months old. One night, I have been often told, I showed great reluctance to be caught and put to bed, and, after being chased about the room, was apprehended, and consigned to my dormitory with some difficulty. It was the last time I was to show such personal agility. In the morning I was discovered to be affected with the fever which often accompanies the cutting of large teeth. It held me three days. On the fourth, when they went to bathe me as usual, they discovered that I had lost the power of my right leg. My grandfather, an excellent anatomist as well as physician, the late worthy Alexander Wood, and many others of the most respectable of the faculty, were consulted. There appeared to be no dislocation or sprain; blisters and other topical remedies were applied in vain.[2] When the efforts of regular physicians had been exhausted without the slightest success, my anxious parents, during the course of many years, eagerly grasped at every prospect of cure which was held out by the promise of empirics, or of ancient ladies or gentle-

---

[1] She died in 1810. — (1826.)

[2] [Regarding this illness, see a medical note by Dr. Creighton to the article, "Scott," in the *Encyclopædia Britannica*.]

men who conceived themselves entitled to recommend various remedies, some of which were of a nature sufficiently singular. But the advice of my grandfather, Dr. Rutherford, that I should be sent to reside in the country, to give the chance of natural exertion, excited by free air and liberty, was first resorted to; and before I have the recollection of the slightest event, I was, agreeably to this friendly counsel, an inmate in the farmhouse of Sandy-Knowe.

An odd incident is worth recording. It seems my mother had sent a maid to take charge of me, that I might be no inconvenience in the family. But the damsel sent on that important mission had left her heart behind her, in the keeping of some wild fellow, it is likely, who had done and said more to her than he was like to make good. She became extremely desirous to return to Edinburgh, and as my mother made a point of her remaining where she was, she contracted a sort of hatred at poor me, as the cause of her being detained at Sandy-Knowe. This rose, I suppose, to a sort of delirious affection, for she confessed to old Alison Wilson, the housekeeper, that she had carried me up to the Craigs, meaning, under a strong temptation of the Devil, to cut my throat with her scissors, and bury me in the moss. Alison instantly took possession of my person, and took care that her confidant should not be subject to any farther temptation so far as I was concerned. She was dismissed, of course, and I have heard became afterwards a lunatic.

It is here at Sandy-Knowe, in the residence of my paternal grandfather, already mentioned, that I have the first consciousness of existence; and I recollect distinctly that my situation and appearance were a little whimsical. Among the odd remedies recurred to to aid my lameness, some one had recommended that so often as a sheep was killed for the use of the family, I should be stripped, and swathed up in the skin, warm as it was flayed from the

carcase of the animal.   In this Tartar-like habiliment I
well remember lying upon the floor of the little parlor in
the farmhouse, while my grandfather, a venerable old
man with white hair, used every excitement to make me
try to crawl.   I also distinctly remember the late Sir
George MacDougal of Makerstoun, father of the present
Sir Henry Hay MacDougal, joining in this kindly attempt.   He was, God knows how,[1] a relation of ours,
and I still recollect him in his old-fashioned military
habit (he had been colonel of the Greys), with a small
cocked hat, deeply laced, an embroidered scarlet waistcoat, and a light-colored coat, with milk-white locks tied
in a military fashion, kneeling on the ground before me,
and dragging his watch along the carpet to induce me to
follow it.   The benevolent old soldier and the infant
wrapped in his sheepskin would have afforded an odd
group to uninterested spectators.   This must have happened about my third year, for Sir George MacDougal
and my grandfather both died shortly after that period.

My grandmother continued for some years to take
charge of the farm, assisted by my father's second brother, Mr. Thomas Scott, who resided at Crailing, as
factor or land steward for Mr. Scott of Danesfield, then
proprietor of that estate.[2]   This was during the heat of
the American war, and I remember being as anxious on
my uncle's weekly visits (for we heard news at no other

[1] He was a second cousin of my grandfather's. Isobel MacDougal, wife
of Walter, the first Laird of Raeburn, and mother of Walter Scott, called
Beardie, was grand-aunt, I take it, to the late Sir George MacDougal.
There was always great friendship between us and the Makerstoun family. It singularly happened, that at the burial of the late Sir Henry Mac-
Dougal, my cousin William Scott younger of Raeburn, and I myself, were
the nearest blood relations present, although our connection was of so old
a date, and ranked as pall-bearers accordingly. — (1826.)

[2] My uncle afterwards resided at Elliston, and then took from Mr.
Cornelius Elliot the estate of Woollee. Finally he retired to Monklaw in
the neighborhood of Jedburgh, where he died, 1823, at the advanced age
of ninety years, and in full possession of his faculties. It was a fine thing
to hear him talk over the change of the country which he had witnessed.
— (1826.)

time) to hear of the defeat of Washington, as if I had had some deep and personal cause of antipathy to him. I know not how this was combined with a very strong prejudice in favor of the Stuart family, which I had originally imbibed from the songs and tales of the Jacobites. This latter political propensity was deeply confirmed by the stories told in my hearing of the cruelties exercised in the executions at Carlisle, and in the Highlands, after the battle of Culloden. One or two of our own distant relations had fallen on that occasion, and I remember of detesting the name of Cumberland with more than infant hatred. Mr. Curle, farmer at Yetbyre, husband of one of my aunts, had been present at their execution; and it was probably from him that I first heard these tragic tales which made so great an impression on me. The local information, which I conceive had some share in forming my future taste and pursuits, I derived from the old songs and tales which then formed the amusement of a retired country family. My grandmother, in whose youth the old Border depredations were matter of recent tradition, used to tell me many a tale of Watt of Harden, Wight Willie of Aikwood, Jamie Telfer of the fair Dodhead, and other heroes — merry men all, of the persuasion and calling of Robin Hood and Little John. A more recent hero, but not of less note, was the celebrated *Diel of Littledean*, whom she well remembered, as he had married her mother's sister. Of this extraordinary person I learned many a story, grave and gay, comic and warlike. Two or three old books which lay in the window seat were explored for my amusement in the tedious winter days. Automathes and Ramsay's Tea-Table Miscellany were my favorites, although at a later period an odd volume of Josephus's Wars of the Jews divided my partiality.

My kind and affectionate aunt, Miss Janet Scott, whose memory will ever be dear to me, used to read these works to me with admirable patience, until I could repeat long passages by heart. The ballad of Hardyknute I was early master of, to the great annoyance of almost our only visitor, the worthy clergyman of the parish, Dr. Duncan, who had not patience to have a sober chat interrupted by my shouting forth this ditty. Methinks I now see his tall, thin, emaciated figure, his legs cased in clasped gambadoes, and his face of a length that would have rivalled the Knight of La Mancha's, and hear him exclaiming, "One may as well speak in the mouth of a cannon as where that child is." With this little acidity, which was natural to him, he was a most excellent and benevolent man, a gentleman in every feeling, and altogether different from those of his order who cringe at the tables of the gentry, or domineer and riot at those of the yeomanry. In his youth he had been chaplain in the family of Lord Marchmont — had seen Pope — and could talk familiarly of many characters who had survived the Augustan age of Queen Anne. Though valetudinary, he lived to be nearly ninety, and to welcome to Scotland his son, Colonel William Duncan, who, with the highest character for military and civil merit, had made a considerable fortune in India. In [1795], a few days before his death, I paid him a visit, to inquire after his health. I found him emaciated to the last degree, wrapped in a tartan night-gown, and employed with all the activity of health and youth in correcting a history of the Revolution, which he intended should be given to the public when he was no more. He read me several passages with a voice naturally strong, and which the feelings of an author then raised above the depression of age and declining health. I begged him to spare this fatigue, which could not but injure his health. His answer was remarkable. "I know," he said, "that I cannot survive a fortnight — and what signifies an exertion that can at worst only accelerate my death a few days?" I marvelled at the composure of this reply, for his appearance sufficiently vouched the truth of his prophecy, and rode home to my uncle's (then my abode), musing what there could be in the spirit of authorship that could inspire its votaries with the courage of martyrs. He died within less than the period he assigned — with which event I close my digression.

I was in my fourth year when my father was advised that the Bath waters might be of some advantage to my lameness. My affectionate aunt, although such a journey promised to a person of her retired habits anything but pleasure or amusement, undertook as readily to accompany me to the wells of Bladud as if she had expected all the delight that ever the prospect of a watering-place held out to its most impatient visitants. My health was by this time a good deal confirmed by the country air, and the influence of that imperceptible and unfatiguing exercise to which the good sense of my grandfather had subjected me; for when the day was fine, I was usually carried out and laid down beside the old shepherd, among the crags or rocks round which he fed his sheep. The impatience of a child soon inclined me to struggle with my infirmity, and I began by degrees to stand, to walk, and to run. Although the limb affected was much shrunk and contracted, my general health, which was of more importance, was much strengthened by being frequently in the open air, and, in a word, I, who in a city had probably been condemned to hopeless and helpless decrepitude, was now a healthy, high-spirited, and, my lameness apart, a sturdy child — *non sine diis animosus infans.*

We went to London by sea, and it may gratify the curiosity of minute biographers to learn that our voyage was performed in the Duchess of Buccleuch, Captain Beatson, master. At London we made a short stay, and saw some of the common shows exhibited to strangers. When, twenty-five years afterwards, I visited the Tower of London and Westminster Abbey, I was astonished to find how accurate my recollections of these celebrated places of visitation proved to be, and I have ever since trusted more implicitly to my juvenile reminiscences. At Bath, where I lived about a year, I went through all the usual discipline of the pump-room and baths, but I believe without the least advantage to my lameness. During my residence at Bath, I acquired the rudiments of reading at a day-school, kept by an old dame near our lodgings, and I had never a more regular teacher, although I think I did not attend her a quarter of a year. An occasional lesson from my aunt supplied the rest. Afterwards, when grown a big boy, I had a few lessons from Mr. Stalker of Edinburgh, and finally from the Rev. Mr. Cleeve. But I never acquired a just pronunciation, nor could I read with much propriety.

In other respects my residence at Bath is marked by very pleasing recollections. The venerable John Home, author of Douglas, was then at the watering-place, and paid much attention to my aunt and to me. His wife, who has survived him, was then an invalid, and used to take the air in her carriage on the Downs, when I was often invited to accompany her. But the most delightful recollections of Bath are dated after the arrival of my uncle, Captain Robert Scott, who introduced me to all the little amusements which suited my age, and above all, to the theatre. The play was As You Like It; and the witchery of the whole scene is alive in my mind at this moment. I made, I believe, noise more than enough, and remember being so much scandalized at the quarrel between Orlando and his brother in the first scene, that I screamed out, "A'n't they brothers?" A few weeks' residence at home convinced me, who had till then been an only child in the house of my grandfather, that a quarrel between brothers was a very natural event.

The other circumstances I recollect of my residence in Bath are but trifling, yet I never recall them without a feeling of pleasure. The beauties of the parade (which of them I know not), with the river Avon winding around it, and the lowing of the cattle from the opposite hills, are warm in my recollection, and are only rivalled by the splendors of a toy-shop somewhere near the Orange Grove. I had acquired, I know not by what means, a kind of superstitious terror for statuary of all kinds. No ancient Iconoclast or modern Calvinist could have looked on the outside of the Abbey church (if I mistake not, the principal church at Bath is so called) with more horror than the image of Jacob's Ladder, with all its angels, presented to my infant eye. My uncle effectually combated my terrors, and formally introduced me to a statue of Neptune, which perhaps still keeps guard at the side of the Avon, where a pleasure boat crosses to Spring Gardens.

After being a year at Bath, I returned first to Edinburgh, and afterwards for a season to Sandy-Knowe; — and thus the time whiled away till about my eighth year, when it was thought sea bathing might be of service to my lameness.

For this purpose, still under my aunt's protection, I remained some weeks at Prestonpans, a circumstance not worth mentioning, excepting to record my juvenile intimacy with an old military veteran, Dalgetty by name, who had pitched his tent in that little village, after all his campaigns, subsisting upon an ensign's half-pay, though called by courtesy a Captain. As this old gentleman, who had been in all the German wars, found very few to listen to his tales of military feats, he formed a sort of alliance with me, and I used invariably to attend him for the pleasure of hearing those communications. Sometimes our conversation turned on the American war, which was then raging. It was about the time of Burgoyne's unfortunate expedition, to which my Captain and I augured different conclusions. Somebody had showed me a map of North America, and, struck with the rugged appearance of the country, and the quantity of lakes, I expressed some doubts on the subject of the

General's arriving safely at the end of his journey, which
were very indignantly refuted by the Captain. The
news of the Saratoga disaster, while it gave me a little
triumph, rather shook my intimacy with the veteran.[1]

[1] Besides this veteran, I found another ally at Prestonpans, in the person of George Constable, an old friend of my father's, educated to the
law, but retired upon his independent property, and generally residing
near Dundee. He had many of those peculiarities of temper which long
afterwards I tried to develop in the character of Jonathan Oldbuck. It is
very odd, that though I am unconscious of anything in which I strictly
copied the *manners* of my old friend, the resemblance was nevertheless
detected by George Chalmers, Esq., solicitor, London, an old friend, both
of my father and Mr. Constable, and who affirmed to my late friend, Lord
Kinnedder, that I must needs be the author of *The Antiquary*, since he
recognized the portrait of George Constable. But my friend George was
not so decided an enemy to womankind as his representative Monkbarns.
On the contrary, I rather suspect that he had a *tendresse* for my Aunt
Jenny, who even then was a most beautiful woman, though somewhat
advanced in life. To the close of her life, she had the finest eyes and
teeth I ever saw, and though she could be sufficiently sharp when she had
a mind, her general behavior was genteel and ladylike. However this
might be, I derived a great deal of curious information from George Constable, both at this early period, and afterwards. He was constantly phi-
landering about my aunt, and of course very kind to me. He was the
first person who told me about Falstaff and Hotspur, and other characters
in Shakespeare. What idea I annexed to them I know not; but I must
have annexed some, for I remember quite well being interested on the
subject. Indeed, I rather suspect that children derive impulses of a powerful and important kind in hearing things which they cannot entirely
comprehend; and therefore, that to write *down* to children's understanding is a mistake : set them on the scent, and let them puzzle it out. To
return to George Constable, I knew him well at a much later period. He
used always to dine at my father's house of a Sunday, and was authorized
to turn the conversation out of the austere and Calvinistic tone, which it
usually maintained on that day, upon subjects of history or auld langsyne.
He remembered the forty-five, and told many excellent stories, all with a
strong dash of a peculiar caustic humor.

George's sworn ally as a brother antiquary was John Davidson, then
Keeper of the Signet ; and I remember his flattering and compelling me
to go to dine there. A writer's apprentice with the Keeper of the Signet,
whose least officer kept us in order ! — It was an awful event. Thither,
however, I went with some secret expectation of a scantling of good
claret. Mr. D. had a son whose taste inclined him to the army, to which
his father, who had designed him for the Bar, gave a most unwilling consent. He was at this time a young officer, and he and I, leaving the two
seniors to proceed in their chat as they pleased, never once opened our
mouths either to them or each other. The Pragmatic Sanction happened

From Prestonpans I was transported back to my father's house in George's Square, which continued to be my most established place of residence, until my marriage in 1797. I felt the change from being a single indulged brat, to becoming a member of a large family, very severely; for under the gentle government of my kind grandmother, who was meekness itself, and of my aunt, who, though of an higher temper, was exceedingly attached to me, I had acquired a degree of license which could not be permitted in a large family. I had sense enough, however, to bend my temper to my new circumstances; but such was the agony which I internally experienced, that I have guarded against nothing more in the education of my own family, than against their acquiring habits of self-willed caprice and domination. I found much consolation during this period of mortification in the partiality of my mother. She joined to a light and happy temper of mind a strong turn to study poetry and works of imagination. She was sincerely devout, but her religion was, as became her sex, of a cast less austere than my father's. Still, the discipline of the Presbyterian Sabbath was severely strict, and I think injudiciously so. Although Bunyan's Pilgrim, Gessner's Death of Abel, Rowe's Letters, and one or two other books, which, for that reason, I still have a favor for, were admitted to relieve the gloom of one dull sermon succeeding to another — there was far too much tedium annexed to the duties of the day; and in the end it did none of us any good.

My week-day tasks were more agreeable. My lame-

---

unfortunately to become the theme of their conversation, when Constable said in jest, " Now, John, I'll wad you a plack that neither of these two lads ever heard of the Pragmatic Sanction." — ' Not heard of the Pragmatic Sanction ! " said John Davidson ; " I would like to see that ; " and with a voice of thunder he asked his son the fatal question. As young D. modestly allowed he knew nothing about it, his father drove him from the table in a rage, and I absconded during the confusion ; nor could Constable ever bring me back again to his friend Davidson's. — (1826.)

ness and my solitary habits had made me a tolerable
reader, and my hours of leisure were usually spent in
reading aloud to my mother Pope's translation of Homer,
which, excepting a few traditionary ballads, and the
songs in Allan Ramsay's Evergreen, was the first poetry
which I perused. My mother had good natural taste
and great feeling: she used to make me pause upon those
passages which expressed generous and worthy sentiments, and if she could not divert me from those which
were descriptive of battle and tumult, she contrived at
least to divide my attention between them. My own
enthusiasm, however, was chiefly awakened by the wonderful and the terrible — the common taste of children,
but in which I have remained a child even unto this day.
I got by heart, not as a task, but almost without intending it, the passages with which I was most pleased, and
used to recite them aloud, both when alone and to others
— more willingly, however, in my hours of solitude, for
I had observed some auditors smile, and I dreaded ridicule at that time of life more than I have ever done
since.

In [1778] I was sent to the second class of the Grammar School, or High School of Edinburgh, then taught
by Mr. Luke Fraser, a good Latin scholar and a very
worthy man.[1] Though I had received, with my brothers,
in private, lessons of Latin from Mr. James French,
now a minister of the Kirk of Scotland, I was nevertheless rather behind the class in which I was placed both
in years and in progress. This was a real disadvantage,
and one to which a boy of lively temper and talents ought
to be as little exposed as one who might be less expected
to make up his leeway, as it is called. The situation
has the unfortunate effect of reconciling a boy of the

---

[1] [Lord Cockburn, in his *Life of Jeffrey*, quotes with approval Scott's
commendation of Mr. Fraser, and adds, that this teacher had the singular good fortune to turn out from three successive classes Walter Scott,
Francis Jeffrey, and Henry Brougham.]

former character (which in a posthumous work I may claim for my own) to holding a subordinate station among his class-fellows — to which he would otherwise affix disgrace. There is, also, from the constitution of the High School, a certain danger not sufficiently attended to. The boys take precedence in their *places*, as they are called, according to their merit, and it requires a long while, in general, before even a clever boy, if he falls behind the class, or is put into one for which he is not quite ready, can force his way to the situation which his abilities really entitle him to hold. But, in the mean while, he is necessarily led to be the associate and companion of those inferior spirits with whom he is placed; for the system of precedence, though it does not limit the general intercourse among the boys, has nevertheless the effect of throwing them into clubs and coteries, according to the vicinity of the seats they hold. A boy of good talents, therefore, placed even for a time among his inferiors, especially if they be also his elders, learns to participate in their pursuits and objects of ambition, which are usually very distinct from the acquisition of learning; and it will be well if he does not also imitate them in that indifference which is contented with bustling over a lesson so as to avoid punishment, without affecting superiority or aiming at reward. It was probably owing to this circumstance that, although at a more advanced period of life I have enjoyed considerable facility in acquiring languages, I did not make any great figure at the High School — or, at least, any exertions which I made were desultory and little to be depended on.

Our class contained some very excellent scholars. The first *Dux* was James Buchan, who retained his honored place, almost without a day's interval, all the while we were at the High School. He was afterwards at the head of the medical staff in Egypt, and in exposing himself to the plague infection, by attending the hospitals there, displayed the same well-regulated and gentle, yet determined, perseverance which placed him most worthily at the head of his schoolfellows, while many lads of livelier parts and dispositions held an inferior station. The next best scholars (*sed longo intervallo*) were my friend David Douglas, the heir and *élève* of the celebrated Adam Smith, and James Hope, now a Writer to the Signet, both since well known and distinguished in their departments of the law. As for myself, I glanced like a meteor from one end of the class to the other, and commonly disgusted my kind master as much by negligence and frivolity, as I occasionally pleased him by flashes of intellect and talent. Among my companions my good-nature and a flow of ready imagination rendered me very popular. Boys are uncommonly just in their feelings, and at least equally generous. My lameness, and the efforts which I made to supply that disadvantage, by making up in address what I wanted in activity, engaged the latter principle in my favor; and in the winter play hours, when hard exercise was impossible, my tales used to assemble an admiring audience round Lucky Brown's fireside, and happy was he that could sit next to the inexhaustible narrator. I was also, though often negligent of my own task, always ready to assist my friends, and hence I had a little party of stanch partisans and adherents, stout of hand and heart, though somewhat dull of head — the very tools for raising a hero to eminence. So, on the whole, I made a brighter figure in the *yards* than in the *class*.[1]

---

[1] I read not long since, in that authentic record called the *Percy Anecdotes*, that I had been educated at Musselburgh school, where I had been distinguished as an absolute dunce ; only Dr. Blair, seeing farther into the millstone, had pronounced there was fire in it. I never was at Musselburgh school in my life, and though I have met Dr. Blair at my father's and elsewhere, I never had the good fortune to attract his notice, to my knowledge. Lastly, I was never a dunce, nor thought to be so, but an incorrigibly idle imp, who was always longing to do something else than what was enjoined him. — (1826.)

My father did not trust our education solely to our High School lessons. We had a tutor at home, a young man of an excellent disposition, and a laborious student. He was bred to the Kirk, but unfortunately took such a very strong turn to fanaticism, that he afterwards resigned an excellent living in a seaport town, merely because he could not persuade the mariners of the guilt of setting sail of a Sabbath, — in which, by the bye, he was less likely to be successful, as, *cœteris paribus*, sailors, from an opinion that it is a fortunate omen, always choose to weigh anchor on that day. The calibre of this young man's understanding may be judged of by this anecdote; but in other respects he was a faithful and active instructor; and from him chiefly I learned writing and arithmetic. I repeated to him my French lessons, and studied with him my themes in the classics, but not classically. I also acquired, by disputing with him (for this he readily permitted), some knowledge of school divinity and church history, and a great acquaintance in particular with the old books describing the early history of the Church of Scotland, the wars and sufferings of the Covenanters, and so forth. I, with a head on fire for chivalry, was a Cavalier; my friend was a Roundhead: I was a Tory, and he was a Whig. I hated Presbyterians, and admired Montrose with his victorious Highlanders; he liked the Presbyterian Ulysses, the dark and politic Argyle: so that we never wanted subjects of dispute; but our disputes were always amicable. In all these tenets there was no real conviction on my part, arising out of acquaintance with the views or principles of either party; nor had my antagonist address enough to turn the debate on such topics. I took up my politics at that period, as King Charles II. did his religion, from an idea that the Cavalier creed was the more gentlemanlike persuasion of the two.

After having been three years under Mr. Fraser, our class was, in the usual routine of the school, turned over to Dr. Adam, the Rector. It was from this respectable man that I first learned the value of the knowledge I had hitherto considered only as a burdensome task. It was the fashion to remain two years at his class, where we read Cæsar, and Livy, and Sallust, in prose; Virgil, Horace, and Terence, in verse. I had by this time mastered, in some degree, the difficulties of the language, and began to be sensible of its beauties. This was really gathering grapes from thistles; nor shall I soon forget the swelling of my little pride when the Rector pronounced, that though many of my schoolfellows understood the Latin better, *Gualterus Scott* was behind few in following and enjoying the author's meaning. Thus encouraged, I distinguished myself by some attempts at poetical versions from Horace and Virgil. Dr. Adam used to invite his scholars to such essays, but never made them tasks. I gained some distinction upon these occasions, and the Rector in future took much notice of me; and his judicious mixture of censure and praise went far to counterbalance my habits of indolence and inattention. I saw I was expected to do well, and I was piqued in honor to vindicate my master's favorable opinion. I climbed, therefore, to the first form; and, though I never made a first-rate Latinist, my schoolfellows, and what was of more consequence, I myself, considered that I had a character for learning to maintain. Dr. Adam, to whom I owed so much, never failed to remind me of my obligations when I had made some figure in the literary world. He was, indeed, deeply imbued with that fortunate vanity which alone could induce a man who has arms to pare and burn a muir, to submit to the yet more toilsome task of cultivating youth. As Catholics confide in the imputed righteousness of their saints, so did the good old Doctor plume himself upon the success of his scholars in life, all of which he never failed (and often justly) to claim as the creation, or at least the fruits, of his early instructions. He remembered the fate of every

boy at his school during the fifty years he had superintended it, and always traced their success or misfortunes
entirely to their attention or negligence when under his
care. His "noisy mansion," which to others would have
been a melancholy bedlam, was the pride of his heart;
and the only fatigues he felt, amidst din and tumult, and
the necessity of reading themes, hearing lessons, and
maintaining some degree of order at the same time, were
relieved by comparing himself to Cæsar, who could dictate to three secretaries at once; — so ready is vanity to
lighten the labors of duty.

It is a pity that a man so learned, so admirably
adapted for his station, so useful, so simple, so easily
contented, should have had other subjects of mortification. But the magistrates of Edinburgh, not knowing
the treasure they possessed in Dr. Adam, encouraged a
savage fellow, called Nicol, one of the undermasters, in
insulting his person and authority. This man was an
excellent classical scholar, and an admirable convivial
humorist (which latter quality recommended him to the
friendship of Burns); but worthless, drunken, and in-
humanly cruel to the boys under his charge. He carried
his feud against the Rector within an inch of assassination,
for he waylaid and knocked him down in the dark. The
favor which this worthless rival obtained in the town
council led to other consequences, which for some time
clouded poor Adam's happiness and fair fame. When
the French Revolution broke out, and parties ran high
in approving or condemning it, the Doctor incautiously
joined the former. This was very natural, for as all his
ideas of existing governments were derived from his experience of the town council of Edinburgh, it must be
admitted they scarce brooked comparison with the free
states of Rome and Greece, from which he borrowed his
opinions concerning republics. His want of caution in
speaking on the political topics of the day lost him the
respect of the boys, most of whom were accustomed to

hear very different opinions on those matters in the bosom of their families. This, however (which was long after my time), passed away with other heats of the period, and the Doctor continued his labors till about a year since, when he was struck with palsy while teaching his class. He survived a few days, but becoming delirious before his dissolution, conceived he was still in school, and after some expressions of applause or censure, he said, "But it grows dark — the boys may dismiss," — and instantly expired.[1]

From Dr. Adam's class I should, according to the usual routine, have proceeded immediately to college. But, fortunately, I was not yet to lose, by a total dismission from constraint, the acquaintance with the Latin which I had acquired. My health had become rather delicate from rapid growth, and my father was easily persuaded to allow me to spend half a year at Kelso with my kind aunt, Miss Janet Scott, whose inmate I again became. It was hardly worth mentioning that I had frequently visited her during our short vacations.

At this time she resided in a small house, situated very pleasantly in a large garden, to the eastward of the churchyard of Kelso, which extended down to the Tweed. It was then my father's property, from whom it was afterwards purchased by my uncle. My grandmother was now dead, and my aunt's only companion, besides an old maid-servant, was my cousin, Miss Barbara Scott, now Mrs. Meik. My time was here left entirely to my own disposal, excepting for about four hours in the day, when I was expected to attend the Grammar School of

---

[1] [On December 27, 1809, a few days after Dr. Adam's death, Scott writes to Mrs. Thomas Scott : "Poor old Dr. Adam died last week after a very short illness, which first affected him in school. He was light-headed, and continued to speak as in the class until the very last, when, having been silent for many hours, he said, ' That Horace was very well said ; *you* did not do it so well ; ' then added faintly, ' But it grows dark, very dark, the boys may dismiss,' and with these striking words he expired." — *Familiar Letters*, vol. i. p. 154.]

the village. The teacher at that time was Mr. Lancelot
Whale, an excellent classical scholar, a humorist, and a
worthy man. He had a supreme antipathy to the puns
which his very uncommon name frequently gave rise to;
insomuch, that he made his son spell the word *Wale*,
which only occasioned the young man being nicknamed
the Prince of Wales by the military mess to which he
belonged. As for Whale, senior, the least allusion to
Jonah, or the terming him an odd fish, or any similar
quibble, was sure to put him beside himself. In point
of knowledge and taste he was far too good for the situation he held, which only required that he should give his
scholars a rough foundation in the Latin language. My
time with him, though short, was spent greatly to my
advantage and his gratification. He was glad to escape
to Persius and Tacitus from the eternal Rudiments and
Cornelius Nepos; and as perusing these authors with one
who began to understand them was to him a labor of
love, I made considerable progress under his instructions.
I suspect, indeed, that some of the time dedicated to me
was withdrawn from the instruction of his more regular
scholars; but I was as grateful as I could be. I acted as
usher, and heard the inferior classes, and I spouted the
speech of Galgacus at the public examination, which did
not make the less impression on the audience that few of
them probably understood one word of it.

In the mean while my acquaintance with English literature was gradually extending itself. In the intervals of
my school hours I had always perused with avidity such
books of history or poetry or voyages and travels as
chance presented to me — not forgetting the usual, or
rather ten times the usual, quantity of fairy tales, Eastern
stories, romances, etc. These studies were totally un-
regulated and undirected. My tutor thought it almost
a sin to open a profane play or poem; and my mother,
besides that she might be in some degree trammelled by
the religious scruples which he suggested, had no longer

the opportunity to hear me read poetry as formerly. I found, however, in her dressing-room (where I slept at one time) some odd volumes of Shakespeare, nor can I easily forget the rapture with which I sat up in my shirt reading them by the light of a fire in her apartment, until the bustle of the family rising from supper warned me it was time to creep back to my bed, where I was supposed to have been safely deposited since nine o'clock. Chance, however, threw in my way a poetical preceptor. This was no other than the excellent and benevolent Dr. Blacklock, well known at that time as a literary character. I know not how I attracted his attention, and that of some of the young men who boarded in his family; but so it was that I became a frequent and favored guest. The kind old man opened to me the stores of his library, and through his recommendation I became intimate with Ossian and Spenser. I was delighted with both, yet I think chiefly with the latter poet. The tawdry repetitions of the Ossianic phraseology disgusted me rather sooner than might have been expected from my age. But Spenser I could have read forever. Too young to trouble myself about the allegory, I considered all the knights and ladies and dragons and giants in their outward and exoteric sense, and God only knows how delighted I was to find myself in such society. As I had always a wonderful facility in retaining in my memory whatever verses pleased me, the quantity of Spenser's stanzas which I could repeat was really marvellous. But this memory of mine was a very fickle ally, and has through my whole life acted merely upon its own capricious motion, and might have enabled me to adopt old Beattie of Meikledale's answer, when complimented by a certain reverend divine on the strength of the same faculty:— "No, sir," answered the old Borderer, "I have no command of my memory. It only retains what hits my fancy; and probably, sir, if you were to preach to me for two hours, I would not be able when you fin-

ished to remember a word you had been saying." My
memory was precisely of the same kind: it seldom failed
to preserve most tenaciously a favorite passage of poetry,
a playhouse ditty, or, above all, a Border-raid ballad;
but names, dates, and the other technicalities of history,
escaped me in a most melancholy degree. The philosophy of history, a much more important subject, was also
a sealed book at this period of my life; but I gradually
assembled much of what was striking and picturesque in
historical narrative; and when, in riper years, I attended
more to the deduction of general principles, I was furnished with a powerful host of examples in illustration of
them. I was, in short, like an ignorant gamester, who
kept a good hand until he knew how to play it.

I left the High School, therefore, with a great quantity
of general information, ill arranged, indeed, and collected
without system, yet deeply impressed upon my mind;
readily assorted by my power of connection and memory,
and gilded, if I may be permitted to say so, by a vivid
and active imagination. If my studies were not under
any direction at Edinburgh, in the country, it may be
well imagined, they were less so. A respectable subscription library, a circulating library of ancient standing, and some private book-shelves, were open to my
random perusal, and I waded into the stream like a blind
man into a ford, without the power of searching my way,
unless by groping for it. My appetite for books was as
ample and indiscriminating as it was indefatigable, and
I since have had too frequently reason to repent that few
ever read so much, and to so little purpose.

Among the valuable acquisitions I made about this
time was an acquaintance with Tasso's Jerusalem Delivered, through the flat medium of Mr. Hoole's translation. But above all, I then first became acquainted with
Bishop Percy's Reliques of Ancient Poetry. As I had
been from infancy devoted to legendary lore of this
nature, and only reluctantly withdrew my attention, from

the scarcity of materials and the rudeness of those which I possessed, it may be imagined, but cannot be described, with what delight I saw pieces of the same kind which had amused my childhood, and still continued in secret the Delilahs of my imagination, considered as the subject of sober research, grave commentary, and apt illustration, by an editor who showed his poetical genius was capable of emulating the best qualities of what his pious labor preserved. I remember well the spot where I read these volumes for the first time. It was beneath a huge platanus-tree, in the ruins of what had been intended for an old-fashioned arbor in the *garden* I have mentioned. The summer day sped onward so fast that, notwithstanding the sharp appetite of thirteen, I forgot the hour of dinner, was sought for with anxiety, and was still found entranced in my intellectual banquet. To read and to remember was in this instance the same thing, and henceforth I overwhelmed my schoolfellows, and all who would hearken to me, with tragical recitations from the ballads of Bishop Percy. The first time, too, I could scrape a few shillings together, which were not common occurrences with me, I bought unto myself a copy of these beloved volumes; nor do I believe I ever read a book half so frequently, or with half the enthusiasm. About this period, also, I became acquainted with the works of Richardson, and those of Mackenzie — (whom in later years I became entitled to call my friend) — with Fielding, Smollett, and some others of our best novelists.

To this period, also, I can trace distinctly the awaking of that delightful feeling for the beauties of natural objects which has never since deserted me. The neighborhood of Kelso, the most beautiful, if not the most romantic village in Scotland, is eminently calculated to awaken these ideas. It presents objects, not only grand in themselves, but venerable from their association. The meeting of two superb rivers, the Tweed and the Teviot, both renowned in song — the ruins of an ancient abbey — the

more distant vestiges of Roxburgh Castle — the modern
mansion of Fleurs, which is so situated as to combine the
ideas of ancient baronial grandeur with those of modern
taste — are in themselves objects of the first class; yet
are so mixed, united, and melted among a thousand other
beauties of a less prominent description, that they harmonize into one general picture, and please rather by
unison than by concord. I believe I have written unin-
telligibly upon this subject, but it is fitter for the pencil
than the pen. The romantic feelings which I have described as predominating in my mind, naturally rested
upon and associated themselves with these grand features
of the landscape around me; and the historical incidents,
or traditional legends connected with many of them, gave
to my admiration a sort of intense impression of reverence, which at times made my heart feel too big for its
bosom. From this time the love of natural beauty, more
especially when combined with ancient ruins, or remains
of our fathers' piety or splendor, became with me an in-
satiable passion, which, if circumstances had permitted,
I would willingly have gratified by travelling over half
the globe.

I was recalled to Edinburgh about the time when the
College meets, and put at once to the Humanity class,
under Mr. Hill, and the first Greek class, taught by Mr.
Dalzell. The former held the reins of discipline very
loosely, and though beloved by his students, for he was
a good-natured man as well as a good scholar, he had
not the art of exciting our attention as well as liking.
This was a dangerous character with whom to trust one
who relished labor as little as I did, and amid the riot
of his class I speedily lost much of what I had learned
under Adam and Whale. At the Greek class, I might
have made a better figure, for Professor Dalzell maintained a great deal of authority, and was not only himself
an admirable scholar, but was always deeply interested
in the progress of his students. But here lay the vil-

lainy. Almost all my companions who had left the High
School at the same time with myself had acquired a smattering of Greek before they came to College. I, alas,
had none; and finding myself far inferior to all my fellow-students, I could hit upon no better mode of vindi-
cating my equality than by professing my contempt for
the language, and my resolution not to learn it. A youth
who died early, himself an excellent Greek scholar, saw
my negligence and folly with pain, instead of contempt.
He came to call on me in George's Square, and pointed
out in the strongest terms the silliness of the conduct I
had adopted, told me I was distinguished by the name of
the *Greek Blockhead*, and exhorted me to redeem my
reputation while it was called to-day. My stubborn
pride received this advice with sulky civility; the birth
of my Mentor (whose name was Archibald, the son of an
innkeeper) did not, as I thought in my folly, authorize
him to intrude upon me his advice. The other was not
sharp-sighted, or his consciousness of a generous intention overcame his resentment. He offered me his daily
and nightly assistance, and pledged himself to bring me
forward with the foremost of my class. I felt some
twinges of conscience, but they were unable to prevail
over my pride and self-conceit. The poor lad left me
more in sorrow than in anger, nor did we ever meet
again. All hopes of my progress in the Greek were now
over; insomuch that when we were required to write
essays on the authors we had studied, I had the audacity
to produce a composition in which I weighed Homer
against Ariosto, and pronounced him wanting in the
balance. I supported this heresy by a profusion of bad
reading and flimsy argument. The wrath of the Professor was extreme, while at the same time he could not
suppress his surprise at the quantity of out-of-the-way
knowledge which I displayed. He pronounced upon me
the severe sentence — that dunce I was, and dunce was
to remain — which, however, my excellent and learned

friend lived to revoke over a bottle of Burgundy, at our literary Club at Fortune's, of which he was a distinguished member.

Meanwhile, as if to eradicate my slightest tincture of Greek, I fell ill during the middle of Mr. Dalzell's second class, and migrated a second time to Kelso — where I again continued a long time reading what and how I pleased, and of course reading nothing but what afforded me immediate entertainment. The only thing which saved my mind from utter dissipation was that turn for historical pursuit, which never abandoned me even at the idlest period. I had forsworn the Latin classics for no reason I know of, unless because they were akin to the Greek; but the occasional perusal of Buchanan's history, that of Matthew Paris, and other monkish chronicles, kept up a kind of familiarity with the language even in its rudest state. But I forgot the very letters of the Greek alphabet; a loss never to be repaired, considering what that language is, and who they were who employed it in their compositions.

About this period — or soon afterwards — my father judged it proper I should study mathematics, a study upon which I entered with all the ardor of novelty. My tutor was an aged person, Dr. MacFait, who had in his time been distinguished as a teacher of this science. Age, however, and some domestic inconveniences, had diminished his pupils, and lessened his authority amongst the few who remained. I think that, had I been more fortunately placed for instruction, or had I had the spur of emulation, I might have made some progress in this science, of which, under the circumstances I have mentioned, I only acquired a very superficial smattering.

In other studies I was rather more fortunate. I made some progress in Ethics under Professor John Bruce, and was selected, as one of his students whose progress he approved, to read an essay before Principal Robertson.

I was farther instructed in Moral Philosophy at the class of Mr. Dugald Stewart, whose striking and impressive eloquence riveted the attention even of the most volatile student. To sum up my academical studies, I attended the class of History, then taught by the present Lord Woodhouselee, and, as far as I remember, no others, excepting those of the Civil and Municipal Law. So that, if my learning be flimsy and inaccurate, the reader must have some compassion even for an idle workman, who had so narrow a foundation to build upon. If, however, it should ever fall to the lot of youth to peruse these pages — let such a reader remember that it is with the deepest regret that I recollect in my manhood the opportunities of learning which I neglected in my youth; that through every part of my literary career I have felt pinched and hampered by my own ignorance; and that I would at this moment give half the reputation I have had the good fortune to acquire, if by doing so I could rest the remaining part upon a sound foundation of learning and science.

I imagine my father's reason for sending me to so few classes in the College was a desire that I should apply myself particularly to my legal studies. He had not determined whether I should fill the situation of an Advocate or a Writer; but judiciously considering the technical knowledge of the latter to be useful at least, if not essential, to a barrister, he resolved I should serve the ordinary apprenticeship of five years to his own profession. I accordingly entered into indentures with my father about 1785–86, and entered upon the dry and barren wilderness of forms and conveyances.

I cannot reproach myself with being entirely an idle apprentice — far less, as the reader might reasonably have expected,

> "A clerk foredoom'd my father's soul to cross."

The drudgery, indeed, of the office I disliked, and the

confinement I altogether detested; but I loved my father, and I felt the rational pride and pleasure of rendering myself useful to him. I was ambitious also; and among my companions in labor, the only way to gratify ambition was to labor hard and well. Other circumstances reconciled me in some measure to the confinement. The allowance for copy-money furnished a little fund for the *menus plaisirs* of the circulating library and the theatre; and this was no trifling incentive to labor. When actually at the oar, no man could pull it harder than I, and I remember writing upwards of 120 folio pages with no interval either for food or rest. Again, the hours of attendance on the office were lightened by the power of choosing my own books, and reading them in my own way, which often consisted in beginning at the middle or the end of a volume. A deceased friend, who was a fellow-apprentice with me, used often to express his surprise that, after such a hop-step-and-jump perusal, I knew as much of the book as he had been able to acquire from reading it in the usual manner. My desk usually contained a store of most miscellaneous volumes, especially works of fiction of every kind, which were my supreme delight. I might except novels, unless those of the better and higher class; for though I read many of them, yet it was with more selection than might have been expected. The whole Jemmy and Jenny Jessamy tribe I abhorred, and it required the art of Burney, or the feeling of Mackenzie, to fix my attention upon a domestic tale. But all that was adventurous and romantic I devoured without much discrimination, and I really believe I have read as much nonsense of this class as any man now living. Everything which touched on knight-errantry was particularly acceptable to me, and I soon attempted to imitate what I so greatly admired. My efforts, however, were in the manner of the tale-teller, not of the bard.

My greatest intimate, from the days of my school-tide,

was Mr. John Irving, now a Writer to the Signet. We lived near each other, and by joint agreement were wont, each of us, to compose a romance for the other's amusement. These legends, in which the martial and the miraculous always predominated, we rehearsed to each other during our walks, which were usually directed to the most solitary spots about Arthur's Seat and Salisbury Crags. We naturally sought seclusion, for we were conscious no small degree of ridicule would have attended our amusement, if the nature of it had become known. Whole holidays were spent in this singular pastime, which continued for two or three years, and had, I believe, no small effect in directing the turn of my imagination to the chivalrous and romantic in poetry and prose.

Meanwhile, the translations of Mr. Hoole having made me acquainted with Tasso and Ariosto, I learned from his notes on the latter, that the Italian language contained a fund of romantic lore. A part of my earnings was dedicated to an Italian class which I attended twice a week, and rapidly acquired some proficiency. I had previously renewed and extended my knowledge of the French language, from the same principle of romantic research. Tressan's romances, the Bibliothèque Bleue, and Bibliothèque de Romans, were already familiar to me, and I now acquired similar intimacy with the works of Dante, Boiardo, Pulci, and other eminent Italian authors. I fastened also, like a tiger, upon every collection of old songs or romances which chance threw in my way, or which my scrutiny was able to discover on the dusty shelves of James Sibbald's circulating library in the Parliament Square. This collection, now dismantled and dispersed, contained at that time many rare and curious works, seldom found in such a collection. Mr. Sibbald himself, a man of rough manners but of some taste and judgment, cultivated music and poetry, and in his shop I had a distant view of some literary characters, besides the privilege of ransacking the stores of old French and Italian books, which were in little demand among the bulk of his subscribers. Here I saw the unfortunate Andrew Macdonald, author of Vimonda; and here, too, I saw at a distance the boast of Scotland, Robert Burns. Of the latter I shall presently have occasion to speak more fully.

I am inadvertently led to confound dates while I talk of this remote period, for, as I have no notes, it is impossible for me to remember with accuracy the progress of studies, if they deserve the name, so irregular and miscellaneous. But about the second year of my apprenticeship my health, which, from rapid growth and other causes, had been hitherto rather uncertain and delicate, was affected by the breaking of a blood-vessel. The regimen I had to undergo on this occasion was far from agreeable. It was spring, and the weather raw and cold, yet I was confined to bed with a single blanket, and bled and blistered till I scarcely had a pulse left. I had all the appetite of a growing boy, but was prohibited any sustenance beyond what was absolutely necessary for the support of nature, and that in vegetables alone. Above all, with a considerable disposition to talk, I was not permitted to open my lips without one or two old ladies who watched my couch being ready at once to souse upon me,

" imposing silence with a stilly sound."[1]

My only refuge was reading and playing at chess. To the romances and poetry, which I chiefly delighted in, I had always added the study of history, especially as connected with military events. I was encouraged in this latter study by a tolerable acquaintance with geography, and by the opportunities I had enjoyed while with Mr. MacFait to learn the meaning of the more ordinary terms of fortification. While, therefore, I lay in this dreary and silent solitude, I fell upon the resource of illustrat-

[1] [Home's *Douglas*.]

ing the battles I read of by the childish expedient of
arranging shells, and seeds, and pebbles, so as to represent encountering armies. Diminutive cross-bows were
contrived to mimic artillery, and with the assistance of
a friendly carpenter I contrived to model a fortress,
which, like that of Uncle Toby, represented whatever
place happened to be uppermost in my imagination. I
fought my way thus through Vertot's Knights of Malta
— a book which, as it hovered between history and romance, was exceedingly dear to me; and Orme's interesting and beautiful History of Indostan, whose copious
plans, aided by the clear and luminous explanations of
the author, rendered my imitative amusement peculiarly
easy. Other moments of these weary weeks were spent
in looking at the Meadow Walks, by assistance of a combination of mirrors so arranged that, while lying in bed,
I could see the troops march out to exercise, or any other
incident which occurred on that promenade.

After one or two relapses, my constitution recovered
the injury it had sustained, though for several months
afterwards I was restricted to a severe vegetable diet.
And I must say, in passing, that though I gained health
under this necessary restriction, yet it was far from being
agreeable to me, and I was affected whilst under its influence with a nervousness which I never felt before or since.
A disposition to start upon slight alarms — a want of de-
cision in feeling and acting, which has not usually been
my failing — an acute sensibility to trifling inconveniences
— and an unnecessary apprehension of contingent misfortunes, rise to my memory as connected with my vegetable
diet, although they may very possibly have been entirely
the result of the disorder and not of the cure. Be this as
it may, with this illness I bade farewell both to disease
and medicine; for since that time, till the hour I am now
writing, I have enjoyed a state of the most robust health,
having only had to complain of occasional headaches or
stomachic affections when I have been long without taking

exercise, or have lived too convivially — the latter having been occasionally, though not habitually, the error of my youth, as the former has been of my advanced life.

My frame gradually became hardened with my constitution, and being both tall and muscular, I was rather disfigured than disabled by my lameness. This personal disadvantage did not prevent me from taking much exercise on horseback, and making long journeys on foot, in the course of which I often walked from twenty to thirty miles a day. A distinct instance occurs to me. I remember walking with poor James Ramsay, my fellow-apprentice, now no more, and two other friends, to breakfast at Prestonpans. We spent the forenoon in visiting the ruins at Seton, and the field of battle at Preston — dined at Prestonpans on *tiled haddocks* very sumptuously — drank half a bottle of port each, and returned in the evening. This could not be less than thirty miles, nor do I remember being at all fatigued upon the occasion.

These excursions on foot or horseback formed by far my most favorite amusement. I have all my life delighted in travelling, though I have never enjoyed that pleasure upon a large scale. It was a propensity which I sometimes indulged so unduly as to alarm and vex my parents. Wood, water, wilderness itself, had an inexpressible charm for me, and I had a dreamy way of going much farther than I intended, so that unconsciously my return was protracted, and my parents had sometimes serious cause of uneasiness. For example, I once set out with Mr. George Abercromby [1] (the son of the immortal General), Mr. William Clerk, and some others, to fish in the lake above Howgate, and the stream which descends from it into the Esk. We breakfasted at Howgate, and fished the whole day; and while we were on our return next morning, I was easily seduced by William Clerk, then a great intimate, to visit Pennycuik-house, the seat of his family. Here he and John Irving, and I for their sake,

[1] Now Lord Abercromby. — (1826.)

were overwhelmed with kindness by the late Sir John
Clerk and his lady, the present Dowager Lady Clerk.
The pleasure of looking at fine pictures, the beauty of the
place, and the flattering hospitality of the owners, drowned
all recollection of home for a day or two. Meanwhile
our companions, who had walked on without being aware
of our digression, returned to Edinburgh without us, and
excited no small alarm in my father's household. At
length, however, they became accustomed to my esca-
pades. My father used to protest to me on such occasions
that he thought I was born to be a strolling pedlar; and
though the prediction was intended to mortify my conceit,
I am not sure that I altogether disliked it. I was now
familiar with Shakespeare, and thought of Autolycus's
song —

> "Jog on, jog on, the foot-path way,
>   And merrily hent the stile-a :
> A merry heart goes all the day,
>   Your sad tires in a mile-a."

My principal object in these excursions was the pleasure of seeing romantic scenery, or what afforded me at
least equal pleasure, the places which had been distinguished by remarkable historical events. The delight
with which I regarded the former, of course had general
approbation, but I often found it difficult to procure sympathy with the interest I felt in the latter. Yet to me,
the wandering over the field of Bannockburn was the
source of more exquisite pleasure than gazing upon the
celebrated landscape from the battlements of Stirling
castle. I do not by any means infer that I was dead to
the feeling of picturesque scenery; on the contrary, few
delighted more in its general effect. But I was unable
with the eye of a painter to dissect the various parts of
the scene, to comprehend how the one bore upon the other,
to estimate the effect which various features of the view
had in producing its leading and general effect. I have
never, indeed, been capable of doing this with precision

or nicety, though my latter studies have led me to amend
and arrange my original ideas upon the subject. Even
the humble ambition, which I long cherished, of making
sketches of those places which interested me, from a defect of eye or of hand was totally ineffectual. After long
study and many efforts, I was unable to apply the elements of perspective or of shade to the scene before me,
and was obliged to relinquish in despair an art which I
was most anxious to practise. But show me an old castle
or a field of battle, and I was at home at once, filled it
with its combatants in their proper costume, and overwhelmed my hearers by the enthusiasm of my description.
In crossing Magus Moor, near St. Andrews, the spirit
moved me to give a picture of the assassination of the
Archbishop of St. Andrews to some fellow-travellers with
whom I was accidentally associated, and one of them,
though well acquainted with the story, protested my narrative had frightened away his night's sleep. I mention
this to show the distinction between a sense of the picturesque in action and in scenery. If I have since been
able in poetry to trace with some success the principles
of the latter, it has always been with reference to its
general and leading features, or under some alliance with
moral feeling; and even this proficiency has cost me
study. — Meanwhile I endeavored to make amends for
my ignorance of drawing, by adopting a sort of technical
memory respecting the scenes I visited. Wherever I
went, I cut a piece of a branch from a tree — these constituted what I called my log-book; and I intended to
have a set of chessmen out of them, each having reference to the place where it was cut — as the kings from
Falkland and Holy-Rood; the queens from Queen Mary's
yew-tree at Crookston; the bishops from abbeys or epis-
copal palaces; the knights from baronial residences; the
rooks from royal fortresses; and the pawns generally
from places worthy of historical note. But this whimsical design I never carried into execution.

With music it was even worse than with painting. My mother was anxious we should at least learn Psalmody; but the incurable defects of my voice and ear soon drove my teacher to despair.[1] It is only by long practice that I have acquired the power of selecting or distinguishing melodies; and although now few things delight or affect me more than a simple tune sung with feeling, yet I am sensible that even this pitch of musical taste has only been gained by attention and habit, and, as it were, by my feeling of the words being associated with the tune. I have, therefore, been usually unsuccessful in composing words to a tune, although my friend, Dr. Clarke, and other musical composers, have sometimes been able to make a happy union between their music and my poetry.

In other points, however, I began to make some amends for the irregularity of my education. It is well known that in Edinburgh one great spur to emulation among youthful students is in those associations called *literary societies*, formed not only for the purpose of debate, but of composition. These undoubtedly have some disadvantages, where a bold, petulant, and disputatious temper happens to be combined with considerable information and talent. Still, however, in order to such a

---

[1] The late Alexander Campbell, a warm-hearted man, and an enthusiast in Scottish music, which he sang most beautifully, had this ungrateful task imposed on him. He was a man of many accomplishments, but dashed with a *bizarrerie* of temper which made them useless to their proprietor. He wrote several books — as a *Tour in Scotland*, etc.; — and he made an advantageous marriage, but fell nevertheless into distressed circumstances, which I had the pleasure of relieving, if I could not remove. His sense of gratitude was very strong, and showed itself oddly in one respect. He would never allow that I had a bad ear; but contended, that if I did not understand music, it was because I did not choose to learn it. But when he attended us in George's Square, our neighbor, Lady Cumming, sent to beg the boys might not be all flogged precisely at the same hour, as, though she had no doubt the punishment was deserved, the noise of the concord was really dreadful. Robert was the only one of our family who could sing, though my father was musical, and a performer on the violoncello at the *gentlemen's concerts*. — (1826.)

person being actually spoiled by his mixing in such debates, his talents must be of a very rare nature, or his effrontery must be proof to every species of assault; for there is generally, in a well-selected society of this nature, talent sufficient to meet the forwardest, and satire enough to penetrate the most undaunted. I am particularly obliged to this sort of club for introducing me about my seventeenth year into the society which at one time I had entirely dropped; for, from the time of my illness at college, I had had little or no intercourse with any of my class-companions, one or two only excepted. Now, however, about 1788, I began to feel and take my ground in society. A ready wit, a good deal of enthusiasm, and a perception that soon ripened into tact and observation of character, rendered me an acceptable companion to many young men whose acquisitions in philosophy and science were infinitely superior to anything I could boast.

In the business of these societies — for I was a member of more than one successively — I cannot boast of having made any great figure. I never was a good speaker unless upon some subject which strongly animated my feelings; and, as I was totally unaccustomed to composition, as well as to the art of generalizing my ideas upon any subject, my literary essays were but very poor work. I never attempted them unless when compelled to do so by the regulations of the society, and then I was like the Lord of Castle Rackrent, who was obliged to cut down a tree to get a few fagots to boil the kettle; for the quantity of ponderous and miscellaneous knowledge, which I really possessed on many subjects, was not easily condensed, or brought to bear upon the object I wished particularly to become master of. Yet there occurred opportunities when this odd lumber of my brain, especially that which was connected with the recondite parts of history, did me, as Hamlet says, "yeoman's service." My memory of events was like one of the large, old-fashioned stone-cannons of the Turks — very difficult to load

well and discharge, but making a powerful effect when
by good chance any object did come within range of its
shot. Such fortunate opportunities of exploding with
effect maintained my literary character among my companions, with whom I soon met with great indulgence and
regard. The persons with whom I chiefly lived at this
period of my youth were William Clerk, already mentioned; James Edmonstoune, of Newton; George Abercromby; Adam Ferguson, son of the celebrated Professor Ferguson, and who combined the lightest and most
airy temper with the best and kindest disposition; John
Irving, already mentioned; the Honorable Thomas Douglas, now Earl of Selkirk; David Boyle,[1] — and two or
three others, who sometimes plunged deeply into politics
and metaphysics, and not unfrequently "doffed the world
aside, and bid it pass."

Looking back on these times, I cannot applaud in all
respects the way in which our days were spent. There
was too much idleness, and sometimes too much conviviality: but our hearts were warm, our minds honorably
bent on knowledge and literary distinction; and if I,
certainly the least informed of the party, may be permitted to bear witness, we were not without the fair and
creditable means of attaining the distinction to which we
aspired. In this society I was naturally led to correct
my former useless course of reading; for — feeling myself greatly inferior to my companions in metaphysical
philosophy and other branches of regular study — I
labored, not without some success, to acquire at least
such a portion of knowledge as might enable me to maintain my rank in conversation. In this I succeeded pretty
well; but unfortunately then, as often since through my
life, I incurred the deserved ridicule of my friends from
the superficial nature of my acquisitions, which being,
in the mercantile phrase, *got up* for society, very often
proved flimsy in the texture; and thus the gifts of an

[1] Now Lord Justice-Clerk. — (1826.)

uncommonly retentive memory and acute powers of perception were sometimes detrimental to their possessor by encouraging him to a presumptuous reliance upon them.

Amidst these studies, and in this society, the time of my apprenticeship elapsed; and in 1790, or thereabouts, it became necessary that I should seriously consider to which department of the law I was to attach myself. My father behaved with the most parental kindness. He offered, if I preferred his own profession, immediately to take me into partnership with him, which, though his business was much diminished, still afforded me an immediate prospect of a handsome independence. But he did not disguise his wish that I should relinquish this situation to my younger brother, and embrace the more ambitious profession of the Bar. I had little hesitation in making my choice — for I was never very fond of money; and in no other particular do the professions admit of a comparison. Besides, I knew and felt the inconveniences attached to that of a Writer; and I thought (like a young man) many of them were "ingenio non subeunda meo." The appearance of personal dependence which that profession requires was disagreeable to me; the sort of connection between the client and the attorney seemed to render the latter more subservient than was quite agreeable to my nature; and, besides, I had seen many sad examples, while overlooking my father's business, that the utmost exertions, and the best meant services, do not secure the *man of business*, as he is called, from great loss, and most ungracious treatment on the part of his employers. The Bar, though I was conscious of my deficiencies as a public speaker, was the line of ambition and liberty; it was that also for which most of my contemporary friends were destined. And, lastly, although I would willingly have relieved my father of the labors of his business, yet I saw plainly we could not have agreed on some particulars if we had attempted to conduct it together, and that I should disappoint his expectations if I did not turn to the Bar. So to that object my studies were directed with great ardor and perseverance during the years 1789, 1790, 1791, 1792.

In the usual course of study, the Roman or Civil Law was the first object of my attention — the second, the Municipal Law of Scotland. In the course of reading on both subjects, I had the advantage of studying in conjunction with my friend William Clerk, a man of the most acute intellects and powerful apprehension, and who, should he ever shake loose the fetters of indolence by which he has been hitherto trammelled, cannot fail to be distinguished in the highest degree. We attended the regular classes of both laws in the University of Edinburgh. The Civil Law chair, now worthily filled by Mr. Alexander Irving, might at that time be considered as in *abeyance*, since the person by whom it was occupied had never been fit for the situation, and was then almost in a state of dotage. But the Scotch Law lectures were those of Mr. David Hume, who still continues to occupy that situation with as much honor to himself as advantage to his country. I copied over his lectures twice with my own hand, from notes taken in the class; and when I have had occasion to consult them, I can never sufficiently admire the penetration and clearness of conception which were necessary to the arrangement of the fabric of law, formed originally under the strictest influence of feudal principles, and innovated, altered, and broken in upon by the change of times, of habits, and of manners, until it resembles some ancient castle, partly entire, partly ruinous, partly dilapidated, patched and altered during the succession of ages by a thousand additions and combinations, yet still exhibiting, with the marks of its antiquity, symptoms of the skill and wisdom of its founders, and capable of being analyzed and made the subject of a methodical plan by an architect who can understand the various styles of the different ages in which it was subjected to alteration. Such an architect has Mr.

Hume been to the law of Scotland, neither wandering into fanciful and abstruse disquisitions, which are the more proper subject of the antiquary, nor satisfied with presenting to his pupils a dry and undigested detail of the laws in their present state, but combining the past state of our legal enactments with the present, and tracing clearly and judiciously the changes which took place, and the causes which led to them.

Under these auspices I commenced my legal studies. A little parlor was assigned me in my father's house, which was spacious and convenient, and I took the exclusive possession of my new realms with all the feelings of novelty and liberty. Let me do justice to the only years of my life in which I applied to learning with stern, steady, and undeviating industry. The rule of my friend Clerk and myself was that we should mutually qualify ourselves for undergoing an examination upon certain points of law every morning in the week, Sundays excepted. This was at first to have taken place alternately at each other's houses, but we soon discovered that my friend's resolution was inadequate to severing him from his couch at the early hour fixed for this exercitation. Accordingly I agreed to go every morning to his house, which, being at the extremity of Prince's Street, New Town, was a walk of two miles. With great punctuality, however, I beat him up to his task every morning before seven o'clock, and in the course of two summers, we went, by way of question and answer, through the whole of Heineccius's Analysis of the Institutes and Pandects, as well as through the smaller copy of Erskine's Institutes of the Law of Scotland. This course of study enabled us to pass with credit the usual trials, which, by the regulations of the Faculty of Advocates, must be undergone by every candidate for admission into their body. My friend William Clerk and I passed these ordeals on the same days — namely, the Civil Law trial on the [30th June, 1791], and the Scots Law trial on the

[6th July, 1792]. On the [11th July, 1792], we both assumed the gown with all its duties and honors.

My progress in life during these two or three years had been gradually enlarging my acquaintance, and facilitating my entrance into good company. My father and mother, already advanced in life, saw little society at home, excepting that of near relations, or upon particular occasions, so that I was left to form connections in a great measure for myself. It is not difficult for a youth with a real desire to please and be pleased, to make his way into good society in Edinburgh — or indeed anywhere; and my family connections, if they did not greatly further, had nothing to embarrass my progress. I was a gentleman, and so welcome anywhere, if so be I could behave myself, as Tony Lumpkin says, "in a concatenation accordingly."

CHAPTER II

Sir Walter Scott opens his brief account of his ancestry with a playful allusion to a trait of national character, which has, time out of mind, furnished merriment to the neighbors of the Scotch; but the zeal of pedigree was deeply rooted in himself, and he would have been the last to treat it with serious disparagement. It has often been exhibited under circumstances sufficiently grotesque; but it has lent strength to many a good impulse, sustained hope and self-respect under many a difficulty and distress, armed heart and nerve to many a bold and resolute struggle for independence; and prompted also many a generous act of assistance, which under its influence alone could have been accepted without any feeling of degradation.

He speaks modestly of his own descent; for, while none of his predecessors had ever sunk below the situation and character of a gentleman, he had but to go three or four generations back, and thence, as far as they could be followed, either on the paternal or maternal side, they were to be found moving in the highest ranks of our baronage. When he fitted up, in his later years, the beautiful hall of Abbotsford, he was careful to have the armorial bearings of his forefathers blazoned in due order on the compartments of its roof; and there are few in Scotland, under the titled nobility, who could trace their blood to so many stocks of historical distinction.

In the Minstrelsy of the Scottish Border, and Notes to The Lay of the Last Minstrel, the reader will find sundry notices of the "Bauld Rutherfords that were sae stout," and the Swintons of Swinton in Berwickshire, the two nearest houses on the maternal side. An illustrious old warrior of the latter family, Sir John Swinton, extolled by Froissart, is the hero of the dramatic sketch, Halidon Hill; and it is not to be omitted, that through the Swintons Sir Walter Scott could trace himself to William Alexander, Earl of Stirling, the poet and dramatist.[1] His respect for the worthy barons of Newmains and Dryburgh, of whom, in right of his father's mother, he was the representative, and in whose venerable sepulchre his remains now rest, was testified by his Memorials of the Haliburtons, a small volume printed (for private circulation only) in the year 1820. His own male ancestors of the family of Harden, whose lineage is traced by Douglas in his Baronage of Scotland back to the middle of the fourteenth century, when they branched off from the great blood of Buccleuch, have been so largely celebrated in his various writings, that I might perhaps content myself with a general reference to those pages, their only imperishable monument. The antique splendor of the ducal house itself has been dignified to all Europe by the pen of its remote descendant; but it may be doubted whether his genius could have been adequately developed, had he not attracted, at an early and critical period, the kindly recognition and support of the Buccleuchs.

The race had been celebrated, however, long before

[1] On Sir Walter's copy of *Recreations with the Muses, by William, Earl of Stirling*, 1637, there is the following MS. note: — "Sir William Alexander, sixth Baron of Menstrie, and first Earl of Stirling, the friend of Drummond of Hawthornden and Ben Jonson, died in 1640. His eldest son, William, Viscount Canada, died before his father, leaving one son and three daughters by his wife, Lady Margaret Douglas, eldest daughter of William, first Marquis of Douglas. Margaret, the second of these daughters, married Sir Robert Sinclair of Longformacus in the Merse, to whom she bore two daughters, Anne and Jean. Jean Sinclair, the younger daughter, married Sir John Swinton of Swinton; and Jean Swinton, her eldest daughter, was the grandmother of the proprietor of this volume."

his day, by a minstrel of its own; nor did he conceal his belief that he owed much to the influence exerted over his juvenile mind by the rude but enthusiastic clan-poetry of old *Satchells*, who describes himself *on his title-page* as

> " Captain Walter Scot, an old Souldier and no Scholler,
>   And one that can write nane,
>   But just the Letters of his Name."

His True History of several honourable Families of the Right Honourable Name of Scot, in the Shires of Roxburgh and Selkirk, and others adjacent, gathered out of Ancient Chronicles, Histories, and Traditions of our Fathers, includes, among other things, a string of complimentary rhymes addressed to the first Laird of Raeburn; and the copy which had belonged to that gentleman was in all likelihood about the first book of verses that fell into the poet's hand.[1] How continually its

---

[1] His family well remember the delight which he expressed on receiving, in 1818, a copy of this first edition, a small dark quarto of 1688, from his friend Constable. He was breakfasting when the present was delivered, and said, " This is indeed the resurrection of an old ally — I mind *spelling* these lines." He read aloud the jingling epistle to his own great-great-grandfather, which, like the rest, concludes with a broad hint, that as the author had neither lands nor flocks — " no estate left except his designation " — the more fortunate kinsman who enjoyed, like Jason of old, a fair share of *fleeces*, might do worse than bestow on him some of King James's *broad pieces*. On rising from table, Sir Walter immediately wrote as follows on the blank leaf opposite to poor Satchells' honest title-page —

> " I, Walter Scott of Abbotsford, a poor scholar, no soldier, but a soldier's lover,
>   In the style of my namesake and kinsman do hereby discover,
>   That I have written the twenty-four letters twenty-four million times over ;
>   And to every true-born Scott I do wish as many golden pieces
>   As ever were hairs in Jason's and Medea's golden fleeces."

The rarity of the original edition of Satchells is such, that the copy now at Abbotsford was the only one Mr. Constable had ever seen — and no wonder, for the author's *envoy* is in these words : —

> " Begone, my book, stretch forth thy wings and fly
>   Amongst the nobles and gentility ;
>   Thou 'rt not to sell to scavengers and clowns,
>   But given to worthy persons of renown.
>   The number 's few I 've printed, in regard
>   My charges have been great, and I hope reward ;
>   I caus'd not print many above twelve score,
>   And the printers are engaged that they shall print no more."

wild and uncouth doggerel was on his lips to his latest day all his familiars can testify; and the passages which he quoted with the greatest zest were those commemorative of two ancient worthies, both of whom had had to contend against physical misfortune similar to his own. The former of these, according to Satchells, was the immediate founder of the branch originally designed of Sinton, afterwards of Harden: —

> " It is four hundred winters past in order
> Since that Buccleuch was Warden in the Border;
> A son he had at that same tide,
> Which was so lame could neither run nor ride.
> John, this lame son, if my author speaks true,
> He sent him to St. Mungo's in Glasgu,
> Where he remained a scholar's time,
> Then married a wife according to his mind. . . .
> And betwixt them twa was procreat
> Headshaw, Askirk, Sinton, and Glack."

But, if the scholarship of *John the Lamiter* furnished his descendant with many a mirthful allusion, a far greater favorite was the memory of *William the Boltfoot*, who followed him in the sixth generation: —

> " The Laird and Lady of Harden
> Betwixt them procreat was a son
> Called William Boltfoot of Harden."

The emphasis with which this next line was quoted I can never forget: —

> " *He did survive to be* A MAN."

He was, in fact, one of the "prowest knights" of the whole genealogy — a fearless horseman and expert spearman, renowned and dreaded; and I suppose I have heard Sir Walter repeat a dozen times, as he was dashing into the Tweed or Ettrick, "rolling red from brae to brae," a stanza from what he called an old ballad, though it was most likely one of his own early imitations: —

> " To tak the foord he aye was first,
> Unless the English loons were near;
> Plunge vassal than, plunge horse and man,
> Auld Boltfoot rides into the rear."

"From childhood's earliest hour," says the poet in one of his last Journals, "I have rebelled against external circumstances." How largely the traditional famousness of the stalwart *Boltfoot* may have helped to develop this element of his character, I do not pretend to say; but I cannot avoid regretting that Lord Byron had not discovered such another "Deformed Transformed" among his own chivalrous progenitors.

So long as Sir Walter retained his vigorous habits, he used to make an autumnal excursion, with whatever friend happened to be his guest at the time, to the tower of Harden, the *incunabula* of his race. A more picturesque scene for the fastness of a lineage of Border marauders could not be conceived; and so much did he delight in it, remote and inaccessible as its situation is, that, in the earlier part of his life, he had nearly availed himself of his kinsman's permission to fit up the dilapidated *peel* for his summer residence. Harden (the ravine of hares) is a deep, dark, and narrow glen, along which a little mountain brook flows to join the river Borthwick, itself a tributary of the Teviot. The castle is perched on the brink of the precipitous bank, and from the ruinous windows you look down into the crows' nests on the summits of the old mouldering elms, that have their roots on the margin of the stream far below: —

> " Where Bortha hoarse, that loads the meads with sand,
> Rolls her red tide to Teviot's western strand,
> Through slaty hills, whose sides are shagged with thorn,
> Where springs in scattered tufts the dark-green corn,
> Towers wood-girt Harden far above the vale,
> And clouds of ravens o'er the turrets sail.
> A hardy race who never shrunk from war,
> The Scott, to rival realms a mighty bar,
> Here fixed his mountain home ; — a wide domain,
> And rich the soil, had purple heath been grain ;
> But what the niggard ground of wealth denied,
> From fields more bless'd his fearless arm supplied." [1]

[1] Leyden, the author of these beautiful lines, has borrowed, as *The Lay of the Last Minstrel* did also, from one of Satchells's primitive couplets —

> " If heather-tops had been corn of the best,
> Then Buccleugh mill had gotten a noble grist."

It was to this wild retreat that the Harden of The Lay of the Last Minstrel, the Auld Wat of a hundred Border ditties, brought home, in 1567, his beautiful bride, Mary Scott, "the Flower of Yarrow," whose grace and gentleness have lived in song along with the stern virtues of her lord. She is said to have chiefly owed her celebrity to the gratitude of an English captive, a beautiful child, whom she rescued from the tender mercies of Wat's moss-troopers, on their return from a foray into Cumberland. The youth grew up under her protection, and is believed to have been the composer both of the words and the music of many of the best old songs of the Border. As Leyden says,

> " His are the strains whose wandering echoes thrill
>   The shepherd lingering on the twilight hill,
>   When evening brings the merry folding hours,
>   And sun-eyed daisies close their winking flowers.
>   He lived o'er Yarrow's Flower to shed the tear,
>   To strew the holly leaves o'er Harden's bier ;
>   But none was found above the minstrel's tomb,
>   Emblem of peace, to bid the daisy bloom.
>   He, nameless as the race from which he sprung,
>   Saved other names, and left his own unsung."

We are told that when the last bullock which Auld Wat had provided from the English pastures was consumed, the Flower of Yarrow placed on her table a dish containing a pair of clean spurs; a hint to the company that they must bestir themselves for their next dinner. Sir Walter adds, in a note to the Minstrelsy, "Upon one occasion when the village herd was driving out the cattle to pasture, the old laird heard him call loudly to drive out Harden's cow. ' Harden's *cow!* ' echoed the affronted chief; ' is it come to that pass? By my faith they shall soon say Harden's *kye* ' (cows). Accordingly, he sounded his bugle, set out with his followers, and next day returned with *a bow of kye, and a bassen'd* (brindled) *bull*. On his return with this gallant prey, he passed a very large haystack. It occurred to the provident laird that this would be extremely convenient to fodder his new stock of cattle; but as no means of transporting it were obvious, he was fain to take leave of it with the apostrophe, now become proverbial — ' *By my saul, had ye but four feet, ye should not stand lang there.*' In short, as Froissart says of a similar class of feudal robbers, nothing came amiss to them that was not *too heavy or too hot.*"

Another striking chapter in the genealogical history belongs to the marriage of Auld Wat's son and heir, afterwards Sir William Scott of Harden, distinguished by the early favor of James VI., and severely fined for his loyalty under the usurpation of Cromwell. The period of this gentleman's youth was a very wild one in that district. The Border clans still made war on each other occasionally, much in the fashion of their forefathers; and the young and handsome heir of Harden, engaging in a foray upon the lands of Sir Gideon Murray of Elibank, treasurer-depute of Scotland, was overpowered by that baron's retainers, and carried in shackles to his castle, now a heap of ruins, on the banks of the Tweed. Elibank's "doomtree" extended its broad arms close to the gates of his fortress, and the indignant laird was on the point of desiring his prisoner to say a last prayer, when his more considerate dame interposed milder counsels, suggesting that the culprit was born to a good estate, and that they had three unmarried daughters. Young Harden, not, it is said, without hesitation, agreed to save his life by taking the plainest of the three off their hands, and the contract of marriage, executed instantly on the parchment of a drum, is still in the charter-chest of his noble representative.

Walter Scott, the third son of this couple, was the first Laird of Raeburn, already alluded to as one of the patrons of Satchells. He married Isabel Macdougal, daughter of Macdougal of Makerstoun — a family of great antiquity and distinction in Roxburghshire, of whose blood, through various alliances, the poet had a large share in his veins. Raeburn, though the son and brother of two steady Cavaliers, and married into a family of the same political creed, became a Whig, and at last a Quaker; and the reader will find, in one of the notes to The Heart of Mid-Lothian, a singular account of the persecution to which this backsliding exposed him at the hands of both his own and his wife's relations. He was incarcerated (A. D. 1665), first at Edinburgh and then at Jedburgh, by order of the Privy Council — his children were forcibly taken from him, and a heavy sum was levied on his estate yearly, for the purposes of their education beyond the reach of his perilous influence. "It appears," says Sir Walter, in a MS. memorandum now before me, "that the Laird of Makerstoun, his brother-in-law, joined with Raeburn's own elder brother, Harden, in this singular persecution, as it will now be termed by Christians of all persuasions. It was observed by the people that the male line of the second Sir William of Harden became extinct in 1710, and that the representation of Makerstoun soon passed into the female line. They assigned as a cause, that when the wife of Raeburn found herself deprived of her husband, and refused permission even to see her children, she pronounced a malediction on her husband's brother as well as on her own, and prayed that a male of their body might not inherit their property."

The MS. adds, "of the first Raeburn's two sons it may be observed that, thanks to the discipline of the Privy Council, they were both good scholars." Of these sons, Walter, the second, was the poet's great-grandfather, the enthusiastic Jacobite of the autobiographical fragment, — who is introduced,

> " With amber beard and flaxen hair,
> And reverend apostolic air,"

in the epistle prefixed to the sixth canto of Marmion. A

good portrait of Bearded Wat, painted for his friend
Pitcairn, was presented by the Doctor's grandson, the
Earl of Kellie, to the father of Sir Walter. It is now
at Abbotsford; and shows a considerable resemblance to
the poet. Some verses addressed to the original by his
kinsman Walter Scott of Harden are given in one of
the Notes to Marmion. The old gentleman himself is
said to have written verses occasionally, both English
and Latin ; but I never heard more than the burden
of a drinking-song —

> " Barba crescat, barba crescat,
> Donec carduus revirescat." [1]

Scantily as the worthy Jacobite seems to have been
provided with this world's goods, he married the daughter of a gentleman of good condition, "through whom,"
says the MS. memorandum already quoted, "his descendants have inherited a connection with some honorable
branches of the *Slioch nan Diarmid*, or Clan of Campbell." To this connection Sir Walter owed, as we shall
see hereafter, many of those early opportunities for studying the manners of the Highlanders, to which the world
are indebted for Waverley, Rob Roy, and The Lady of
the Lake.

Robert Scott, the son of Beardie, formed also an hon-

---

[1] Since this book was first published, I have seen in print *A Poem on
the Death of Master Walter Scott, who died at Kelso, November 3, 1729,* written, it is said, by Sir William Scott of Thirlestane, Bart., the male ancestor of Lord Napier. It has these lines : —

> " His converse breathed the Christian. On his tongue
> The praises of religion ever hung ;
> Whence it appeared he did on solid ground
> Commend the pleasures which himself had found. . . .
> His venerable mien and goodly air
> Fix on our hearts impressions strong and fair.
> Full seventy years had shed their silvery glow
> Around his locks, and made his beard to grow ;
> That decent beard, which in becoming grace
> Did spread a reverend honor on his face," etc. — (1838.)

orable alliance.   His father-in-law, Thomas Haliburton,[1] the last but one of the "good lairds of Newmains," entered his marriage as follows in the domestic record, which Sir Walter's pious respect induced him to have printed nearly a century afterwards:— "My second daughter Barbara is married to Robert Scott, son to Walter Scott, uncle to Raeburn, upon this sixteen day of July, 1728, at my house of Dryburgh, by Mr. James Innes, minister of Mertoun, their mothers being cousings; may the blessing of the Lord rest upon them, and make them comforts to each other and to all their relations;" to which the editor of the Memorials adds this note — "May God grant that the prayers of the excellent persons who have passed away may avail for the benefit of those who succeed them! — *Abbotsford*, Nov., 1824."

I need scarcely remind the reader of the exquisite description of the poet's grandfather, in the Introduction to the third canto of Marmion —

> —— " the thatched mansion's gray-hair'd sire,
> Wise without learning, plain and good,
> And sprung of Scotland's gentler blood ;

[1] " From the genealogical deduction in the Memorials, it appears that the Haliburtons of Newmains were descended from and represented the ancient and once powerful family of Haliburton of Mertoun, which became extinct in the beginning of the eighteenth century.   The first of this latter family possessed the lands and barony of Mertoun by a charter granted by Archibald, Earl of Douglas and Lord of Galloway (one of those tremendous lords whose coronets counterpoised the Scottish crown), to Henry de Haliburton, whom he designates as his standard-bearer, on account of his service to the earl in England.   On this account the Haliburtons of Mertoun and those of Newmains, in addition to the arms borne by the Haliburtons of Dirleton (the ancient chiefs of that once great and powerful, but now almost extinguished name) — viz. *or*, on a bend *azure*, three mascles of the first — gave the distinctive bearing of a buckle of the second in the sinister canton.   These arms still appear on various old tombs in the abbeys of Melrose and Dryburgh, as well as on their house at Dryburgh, which was built in 1572." — *MS. Memorandum*, 1820.   Sir Walter was served heir to these Haliburtons soon after the date of this Memorandum, and thenceforth quartered the arms above described with those of his paternal family.

> Whose eye, in age quick, clear, and keen,
> Showed what in youth its glance had been;
> Whose doom discording neighbors sought,
> Content with equity unbought."

In the Preface to Guy Mannering, we have an anecdote of Robert Scott in his earlier days: "My grandfather, while riding over Charterhouse Moor, then a very extensive common, fell suddenly among a large band of gypsies, who were carousing in a hollow surrounded by bushes. They instantly seized on his bridle with shouts of welcome, exclaiming that they had often dined at his expense, and he must now stay and share their cheer. My ancestor was a little alarmed, for he had more money about his person than he cared to risk in such society. However, being naturally a bold, lively spirited man, he entered into the humor of the thing, and sat down to the feast, which consisted of all the varieties of game, poultry, pigs, and so forth, that could be collected by a wide and indiscriminate system of plunder. The dinner was a very merry one, but my relative got a hint from some of the older gypsies, just when ' the mirth and fun grew fast and furious,' and mounting his horse accordingly, he took a French leave of his entertainers." His grandson might have reported more than one scene of the like sort in which he was himself engaged, while hunting the same district, not in quest of foxes or of cattle sales, like the Goodman of Sandy-Knowe, but of ballads for the Minstrelsy. Gypsy stories, as we are told in the same Preface, were frequently in the mouth of the old man when his face "brightened at the evening fire," in the days of the poet's childhood. And he adds that, "as Dr. Johnson had a shadowy recollection of Queen Anne as a stately lady in black, adorned with diamonds," so his own memory was haunted with "a solemn remembrance of a woman of more than female height, dressed in a long red cloak, who once made her appearance beneath the thatched roof of Sandy-Knowe, commenced acquaintance by giving him an apple, and whom he looked on, nevertheless, with as much awe as the future doctor, High Church and Tory as he was doomed to be, could look upon the Queen." This was Madge Gordon, granddaughter of Jean Gordon, the prototype of Meg Merrilies.

Of Robert of Sandy-Knowe, also, there is a very tolerable portrait at Abbotsford, and the likeness of the poet to his grandfather must have forcibly struck every one who has seen it. Indeed, but for its wanting some inches in elevation of forehead — (a considerable want, it must be allowed) — the picture might be mistaken for one of Sir Walter Scott. The keen, shrewd expression of the eye, and the remarkable length and compression of the upper lip, bring him exactly before me as he appeared when entering with all the zeal of a professional agriculturist into the merits of a pit of marle discovered at Abbotsford. Had the old man been represented with his cap on his head, the resemblance to one particular phasis of the most changeful of countenances would have been perfect.

Robert Scott had a numerous progeny, and Sir Walter has intimated his intention of recording several of them "with a sincere tribute of gratitude" in the contemplated prosecution of his autobiography. Two of the younger sons were bred to the naval service of the East India Company; one of whom died early and unmarried; the other was the excellent Captain Robert Scott, of whose kindness to his nephew some particulars are given in the Ashestiel fragment, and more will occur hereafter. Another son, Thomas, followed the profession of his father with ability, and retired in old age upon a handsome independence, acquired by his industrious exertions. He was twice married, — first to his near relation, a daughter of Raeburn; and secondly to Miss Rutherford of Know-South, the estate of which respectable family is now possessed by his son Charles Scott, an amiable and

high-spirited gentleman, who was always a special favorite with his eminent kinsman. The death of Thomas Scott is thus recorded in one of the MS. notes on his nephew's own copy of the Haliburton Memorials: —
"The said Thomas Scott died at Monklaw, near Jedburgh, at two of the clock, 27th January, 1823, in the 90th year of his life, and fully possessed of all his faculties. He read till nearly the year before his death; and being a great musician on the Scotch pipes, had, when on his deathbed, a favorite tune played over to him by his son James, that he might be sure he left him in full possession of it. After hearing it, he hummed it over himself, and corrected it in several of the notes. The air was that called Sour Plums in Galashiels. When barks and other tonics were given him during his last illness, he privately spat them into his handkerchief, saying, as he had lived all his life without taking doctor's drugs, he wished to die without doing so."

I visited this old man two years before his death, in company with Sir Walter, and thought him about the most venerable figure I had ever set my eyes on — tall and erect, with long flowing tresses of the most silvery whiteness, and stockings rolled up over his knees, after the fashion of three generations back. He sat reading his Bible without spectacles, and did not, for a moment, perceive that any one had entered his room, but on recognizing his nephew he rose, with cordial alacrity, kissing him on both cheeks, and exclaiming, "God bless thee, Walter, my man! thou hast risen to be great, but thou wast always good." His remarks were lively and sagacious, and delivered with a touch of that humor which seems to have been shared by most of the family. He had the air and manner of an ancient gentleman, and must in his day have been eminently handsome. I saw more than once, about the same period, this respectable man's sister, who had married her cousin Walter, Laird of Raeburn — thus adding a new link to the closeness of the family connection. She also must have been, in her youth, remarkable for personal attractions; as it was, she dwells on my memory as the perfect picture of an old Scotch lady, with a great deal of simple dignity in her bearing, but with the softest eye, and the sweetest voice, and a charm of meekness and gentleness about every look and expression; all which contrasted strikingly enough with the stern dry aspect and manners of her husband, a right descendant of the moss-troopers of Harden, who never seemed at his ease but on horseback, and continued to be the boldest fox-hunter of the district, even to the verge of eighty. The poet's aunt spoke her native language pure and undiluted, but without the slightest tincture of that vulgarity which now seems almost unavoidable in the oral use of a dialect so long banished from courts, and which has not been avoided by any modern writer who has ventured to introduce it, with the exception of Scott, and I may add, speaking generally, of Burns. Lady Raeburn, as she was universally styled, may be numbered with those friends of early days whom her nephew has alluded to in one of his prefaces, as preserving what we may fancy to have been the old Scotch of Holyrood.

The particulars which I have been setting down may help English readers to form some notion of the structure of society in those southern districts of Scotland. When Satchells wrote, he boasted that Buccleuch could summon to his banner one hundred lairds, all of his own name, with ten thousand more — landless men, but still of the same blood. The younger sons of these various lairds were, through many successive generations, portioned off with fragments of the inheritance, until such subdivision could be carried no farther, and then the cadet, of necessity, either adopted the profession of arms, in some foreign service very frequently, or became a cultivator on the estate of his own elder brother, of the chieftain of his branch, or of the great chief and patriarchal protector of the whole clan. Until the commerce of Eng-

land and, above all, the military and civil services of the
English colonies were thrown open to the enterprise of
the Scotch, this system of things continued entire. It
still remained in force to a considerable extent at the
time when the Goodman of Sandy-Knowe was establishing his children in the world — and I am happy to say,
that it is far from being abolished even at the present
day. It was a system which bound together the various
classes of the rural population in bonds of mutual love
and confidence: the original community of lineage was
equally remembered on all sides; the landlord could
count for more than his rent on the tenant, who regarded
him rather as a father or an elder brother, than as one
who owed his superiority to mere wealth; and the farmer
who, on fit occasions, partook on equal terms of the chase
and the hospitality of his landlord, went back with content and satisfaction to the daily labors of a vocation
which he found no one disposed to consider as derogating
from his gentle blood. Such delusions, if delusions they
were, held the natural arrogance of riches in check,
taught the poor man to believe that in virtuous poverty
he had nothing to blush for, and spread over the whole
being of the community the gracious spirit of a primitive
humanity.

Walter Scott, the eldest son of Robert of Sandy-
Knowe, appears to have been the first of the family that
ever adopted a town life, or anything claiming to be
classed among the learned professions. His branch of
the law, however, could not in those days be advantageously prosecuted without extensive connections in the
country; his own were too respectable not to be of much
service to him in his calling, and they were cultivated
accordingly. His professional visits to Roxburghshire
and Ettrick Forest were, in his vigorous life, very frequent; and though he was never supposed to have any
tincture either of romance or poetry in his composition,
he retained to the last a warm affection for his native dis-

trict, with a certain reluctant flavor of the old feelings and prejudices of the Borderer. I have little to add to Sir Walter's short and respectful notice of his father, except that I have heard it confirmed by the testimony of many less partial observers. According to every account, he was a most just, honorable, conscientious man; only too high of spirit for some parts of his business. "He passed from the cradle to the grave," says a surviving relation, "without making an enemy or losing a friend. He was a most affectionate parent, and if he discouraged, rather than otherwise, his son's early devotion to the pursuits which led him to the height of literary eminence, it was only because he did not understand what such things meant, and considered it his duty to keep his young man to that path in which good sense and industry might, humanly speaking, be thought sure of success."

Sir Walter's mother was short of stature, and by no means comely, at least after the days of her early youth. She had received, as became the daughter of an eminently learned physician, the best sort of education then bestowed on young gentlewomen in Scotland. The poet, speaking of Mrs. Euphemia Sinclair, the mistress of the school at which his mother was reared, to the ingenious local antiquary, Mr. Robert Chambers, said that "she must have been possessed of uncommon talents for education, as all her young ladies were, in after-life, fond of reading, wrote and spelled admirably, were well acquainted with history and the belles-lettres, without neglecting the more homely duties of the needle and accompt book; and perfectly well-bred in society." Mr. Chambers adds: "Sir W. further communicated that his mother, and many others of Mrs. Sinclair's pupils, were sent afterwards *to be finished off* by the Honorable Mrs. Ogilvie, a lady who trained her young friends to a style of manners which would now be considered intolerably stiff. Such was the effect of this early training upon the mind of Mrs. Scott, that even when she approached her eightieth year, she took as much care to avoid touching her chair with her back as if she had still been under the stern eye of Mrs. Ogilvie." [1] The physiognomy of the poet bore, if their portraits may be trusted, no resemblance to either of his parents.

Mr. Scott was nearly thirty years of age when he married, and six children, born to him between 1759 and 1766, all perished in infancy. [2] A suspicion that the close situation of the College Wynd had been unfavorable to the health of his family was the motive that induced him to remove to the house which he ever afterwards occupied in George's Square. [3] This removal took place shortly after the poet's birth; and the children born subsequently were in general healthy. Of a family of twelve, of whom six lived to maturity, not one now survives; nor have any of them left descendants, except Sir Walter himself, and his next and dearest brother, Thomas Scott.

He says that his consciousness of existence dated from Sandy-Knowe; and how deep and indelible was the impression which its romantic localities had left on his imagination, I need not remind the readers of Marmion and The Eve of St. John. On the summit of the Crags

[1] See Chambers's *Traditions of Edinburgh*, vol. ii. pp. 127–131. The functions here ascribed to Mrs. Ogilvie may appear to modern readers little consistent with her rank. Such things, however, were not uncommon in those days in poor old Scotland. Ladies with whom I have conversed in my youth well remembered an *Honorable Mrs. Maitland* who practised the obstetric art in the Cowgate.

[2] In Sir Walter Scott's desk, after his death, there was found a little packet containing six locks of hair, with this inscription in the handwriting of his mother : —

" 1. Anne Scott, born March 10, 1759.
    2. Robert Scott, born August 22, 1760.
    3. John Scott, born November 28, 1761.
    4. Robert Scott, born June 7, 1763.
    5. Jean Scott, born March 27, 1765.
    6. Walter Scott, born August 30, 1766.

" All these are dead, and none of my present family was born till some time afterwards."

[3] [No. 25.]

which overhang the farmhouse stands the ruined tower of
Smailholme, the scene of that fine ballad; and the view
from thence takes in a wide expanse of the district in
which, as has been truly said, every field has its battle,
and every rivulet its song: —

> "That lady sat in mournful mood,
> Looked over hill and vale,
> O'er Tweed's fair flood, and Mertoun's wood,
> And all down Teviotdale." —

Mertoun, the principal seat of the Harden family, with
its noble groves; nearly in front of it, across the Tweed,
Lessudden, the comparatively small but still venerable
and stately abode of the Lairds of Raeburn; and the
hoary Abbey of Dryburgh, surrounded with yew-trees as
ancient as itself, seem to lie almost below the feet of the
spectator. Opposite him rise the purple peaks of Eildon,
the traditional scene of Thomas the Rhymer's interview
with the Queen of Faerie; behind are the blasted peel
which the seer of Ercildoune himself inhabited, " the
Broom of the Cowdenknowes," the pastoral valley of the
Leader, and the bleak wilderness of Lammermoor. To
the eastward, the desolate grandeur of Hume Castle
breaks the horizon, as the eye travels towards the range
of the Cheviot. A few miles westward, Melrose, "like
some tall rock with lichens grey," appears clasped amidst
the windings of the Tweed; and the distance presents the
serrated mountains of the Gala, the Ettrick, and the
Yarrow, all famous in song. Such were the objects that
had painted the earliest images on the eye of the last and
greatest of the Border Minstrels.

As his memory reached to an earlier period of childhood than that of almost any other person, so assuredly
no poet has given to the world a picture of the dawning
feelings of life and genius, at once so simple, so beautiful, and so complete, as that of his epistle to William
Erskine, the chief literary confidant and counsellor of his
prime of manhood.

" Whether an impulse that has birth
Soon as the infant wakes on earth,
One with our feelings and our powers,
And rather part of us than ours;
Or whether fitlier term'd the sway
Of habit, formed in early day,
Howe'er derived, its force confest
Rules with despotic sway the breast.
And drags us on by viewless chain,
While taste and reason plead in vain. . . .
Thus, while I ape the measure wild
Of tales that charm'd me yet a child,
Rude though they be, still with the chime
Return the thoughts of early time,
And feelings rous'd in life's first day,
Glow in the line and prompt the lay.
Then rise those crags, that mountain tower
Which charm'd my fancy's wakening hour.
It was a barren scene and wild
Where naked cliffs were rudely piled;
But ever and anon between
Lay velvet tufts of loveliest green;
And well the lonely infant knew
Recesses where the wall-flower grew,
And honey-suckle loved to crawl
Up the low crag and ruin'd wall.
I deem'd such nooks the sweetest shade
The sun in all its round surveyed;
And still I thought that shattered tower
The mightiest work of human power,
And marvelled as the aged hind,
With some strange tale bewitch'd my mind,
Of forayers who, with headlong force,
Down from that strength had spurr'd their horse,
Their southern rapine to renew,
Far in the distant Cheviots blue,
And home returning, fill'd the hall
With revel, wassail-rout, and brawl.
Methought that still with trump and clang
The gateway's broken arches rang;
Methought grim features, seam'd with scars,
Glared through the windows' rusty bars;
And ever, by the winter hearth,
Old tales I heard of woe or mirth,
Of lovers' slights, of ladies' charms,
Of witches' spells, of warriors' arms —
Of patriot battles won of old
By Wallace Wight and Bruce the Bold —

> Of later fields of feud and fight,
> When, pouring from their Highland height,
> The Scottish clans, in headlong sway,
> Had swept the scarlet ranks away.
> While stretched at length upon the floor,
> Again I fought each combat o'er,
> Pebbles and shells, in order laid,
> The mimic ranks of war displayed,
> And onward still the Scottish Lion bore,
> And still the scattered Southron fled before." [1]

There are still living in that neighborhood two old women who were in the domestic service of Sandy-Knowe when the lame child was brought thither in the third year of his age. One of them, Tibby Hunter, remembers his coming well; and that "he was a sweet-tempered bairn, a darling with all about the house." The young ewe-milkers delighted, she says, to carry him about on their backs among the crags; and he was "very gleg (quick) at the uptake, and soon kenned every sheep and lamb by headmark as well as any of them." His great pleasure, however, was in the society of the "aged hind," recorded in the epistle to Erskine. "Auld Sandy Ormistoun," called, from the most dignified part of his function, "the Cow-bailie," had the chief superintendence of the flocks that browsed upon "the velvet tufts of loveliest green." If the child saw him in the morning, he could not be satisfied unless the old man would set him astride on his shoulder, and take him to keep him company as he lay watching his charge.

> " Here was poetic impulse given
> By the green hill and clear blue heaven."

The Cow-bailie blew a particular note on his whistle, which signified to the maid-servants in the house below when the little boy wished to be carried home again. He told his friend, Mr. Skene of Rubislaw, when spending a summer day in his old age among these well-remembered crags, that he delighted to roll about on the grass all day long in the midst of the flock, and that "the sort

---

[1] [*Poetical Works*, Cambridge Edition, p. 108.]

of fellowship he thus formed with the sheep and lambs had impressed his mind with a degree of affectionate feeling towards them which had lasted throughout life." There is a story of his having been forgotten one day among the knolls when a thunderstorm came on; and his aunt, suddenly recollecting his situation, and running out to bring him home, is said to have found him lying on his back, clapping his hands at the lightning, and crying out, "Bonny! bonny!" at every flash.

I find the following marginal note on his copy of Allan Ramsay's Tea-Table Miscellany (edition 1724): "This book belonged to my grandfather, Robert Scott, and out of it I was taught Hardiknute by heart before I could read the ballad myself. It was the first poem I ever learnt — the last I shall ever forget." According to Tibby Hunter, he was not particularly fond of his book, embracing every pretext for joining his friend the Cowbailie out of doors; but "Miss Jenny was a grand hand at keeping him to the bit, and by degrees he came to read brawly." [1] An early acquaintance of a higher class, Mrs. Duncan, the wife of the present excellent minister of Mertoun, informs me, that though she was younger than Sir Walter, she has a dim remembrance of the interior of Sandy-Knowe — "Old Mrs. Scott sitting, with her spinning-wheel, at one side of the fire, in a *clean clean* parlor; the grandfather, a good deal failed, in his elbow-chair opposite; and the little boy lying on the carpet, at the old man's feet, listening to the Bible, or whatever good book Miss Jenny was reading to them." [2]

---

[1] This old woman still possesses "the *banes*" (bones) — that is to say, the boards — of a Psalm-book, which Master Walter gave her at Sandy-Knowe. "He chose it," she says, "of a very large print, that I might be able to read it when I was *very auld — forty year auld*; but the bairns pulled the leaves out langsyne."

[2] [In writing of his little grandson's earliest lessons, Scott recalls these days in a letter to Lockhart (March 3, 1826) : —

"I rejoice to hear of Johnnie's grand flip towards instruction. I hope Mrs. Mactavish, whom I like not the worse, you may be sure, for her name, will be mild in her rule, and let him listen to reading a good deal

Robert Scott died before his grandson was four years
of age; and I heard him mention when he was an old
man that he distinctly remembered the writing and seal-
ing of the funeral letters, and all the ceremonial of the
melancholy procession as it left Sandy-Knowe. I shall
conclude my notices of the residence at Sandy-Knowe
with observing that in Sir Walter's account of the
friendly clergyman who so often sat at his grandfather's
fireside, we cannot fail to trace many features of the se-
cluded divine in the novel of St. Ronan's Well.

I have nothing to add to what he has told us of that
excursion to England which interrupted his residence at
Sandy-Knowe for about a twelvemonth, except that I
had often been astonished, long before I read his auto-
biographic fragment, with the minute recollection he
seemed to possess of all the striking features of the city
of Bath, which he had never seen again since he quitted
it before he was six years of age. He has himself
alluded, in his Memoir, to the lively recollection he
retained of his first visit to the theatre, to which his
Uncle Robert carried him to witness a representation of
As You Like It. In his review of the Life of John
Kemble, written in 1826, he has recorded that impression more fully, and in terms so striking, that I must
copy them in this place: —

" There are few things which those gifted with any degree of
imagination recollect with a sense of more anxious and mysteri-
ous delight than the first dramatic representation which they
have witnessed. The unusual form of the house, filled with such

without cramming the alphabet and grammar down the poor child's throat.
I cannot at this moment tell how or when I learned to read, but it was
by fits and snatches, as one aunt or another in the old rumble-tumble
farmhouses could give me a lesson, and I am sure it increased my love
and habit of reading more than the austerities of a school could have
done. I gave trouble, I believe, in wishing to be taught, and in self-defence gradually acquired the mystery myself. Johnnie is infirm a little,
though not so much so as I was, and often he has brought back to my recollection the days of my own childhood. I hope he will be twice any good
that was in me, with less carelessness." — Lang's *Life of Lockhart*, vol. i.
p. 397.]

groups of crowded spectators, themselves forming an extraordinary spectacle to the eye which has never witnessed it before, yet all intent upon that wide and mystic curtain, whose dusky undulations permit us now and then to discern the momentary glitter of some gaudy form, or the spangles of some sandalled foot, which trips lightly within : Then the light, brilliant as that of day ; then the music, which, in itself a treat sufficient in every other situation, our inexperience mistakes for the very play we came to witness ; then the slow rise of the shadowy curtain, disclosing, as if by actual magic, a new land, with woods, and mountains, and lakes, lighted, it seems to us, by another sun, and inhabited by a race of beings different from ourselves, whose language is poetry, — whose dress, demeanor, and sentiments seem something supernatural, — and whose whole actions and discourse are calculated not for the ordinary tone of everyday life, but to excite the stronger and more powerful faculties — to melt with sorrow, overpower with terror, astonish with the marvellous, or convulse with irresistible laughter : — all these wonders stamp indelible impressions on the memory. Those mixed feelings, also, which perplex us between a sense that the scene is but a plaything, and an interest which ever and anon surprises us into a transient belief that that which so strongly affects us cannot be fictitious ; those mixed and puzzling feelings, also, are exciting in the highest degree. Then there are the bursts of applause, like distant thunder, and the permission afforded to clap our little hands, and add our own scream of delight to a sound so commanding. All this, and much, much more, is fresh in our memory, although, when we felt these sensations, we looked on the stage which Garrick had not yet left. It is now a long while since ; yet we have not passed many hours of such unmixed delight, and we still remember the sinking lights, the dispersing crowd, with the vain longings which we felt that the music would again sound, the magic curtain once more arise, and the enchanting dream recommence ; and the astonishment with which we looked upon the apathy of the elder part of our company, who, having the means, did not spend every evening in the theatre." [1]

Probably it was this performance that first tempted

him to open the page of Shakespeare. Before he returned
to Sandy-Knowe, assuredly, notwithstanding the modest
language of his autobiography, the progress which had
been made in his intellectual education was extraordinary; and it is impossible to doubt that his hitherto
almost sole tutoress, Miss Jenny Scott, must have been
a woman of tastes and acquirements very far above what
could have been often found among Scotch ladies, of any
but the highest class at least, in that day. In the winter
of 1777, she and her charge spent some few weeks — not
happy weeks, the Memoir hints them to have been —
in George's Square, Edinburgh; and it so happened,
that during this little interval, Mr. and Mrs. Scott received in their domestic circle a guest capable of appre-
ciating, and, fortunately for us, of recording in a very
striking manner the remarkable development of young
Walter's faculties. Mrs. Cockburn, mentioned by him
in his Memoir as the authoress of the modern Flowers
of the Forest, born a Rutherford, of Fairnalie, in Selkirkshire, was distantly related to the poet's mother,
with whom she had through life been in habits of intimate friendship. This accomplished woman was staying
at Ravelston, in the vicinity of Edinburgh, a seat of the
Keiths of Dunnottar, nearly related to Mrs. Scott, and to
herself. With some of that family she spent an evening
in George's Square. She chanced to be writing next day
to Dr. Douglas, the well-known and much respected
minister of her native parish, Galashiels; and her letter,
of which the Doctor's son has kindly given me a copy,
contains the following passage: —

"Edinburgh, Saturday night, 15th of ' the gloomy month when the
people of England hang and drown themselves.'

. . . "I last night supped in Mr. Walter Scott's. He has
the most extraordinary genius of a boy I ever saw. He was
reading a poem to his mother when I went in. I made him
read on; it was the description of a shipwreck. His passion
rose with the storm. He lifted his eyes and hands. ' There's

the mast gone,' says he ; ' crash it goes ! — they will all perish ! ' After his agitation, he turns to me. ' That is too melancholy,' says he ; ' I had better read you something more amusing.' I preferred a little chat, and asked his opinion of Milton and other books he was reading, which he gave me wonderfully. One of his observations was, ' How strange it is that Adam, just new come into the world, should know everything — that must be the poet's fancy,' says he. But when he was told he was created perfect by God, he instantly yielded. When taken to bed last night, he told his aunt he liked that lady. ' What lady ? ' says she. ' Why, Mrs. Cockburn ; for I think she is a virtuoso like myself.' ' Dear Walter,' says Aunt Jenny, ' what is a virtuoso ? ' ' Don't ye know ? Why, it 's one who wishes and will know everything.' [1] — Now, sir, you will think this a very silly story. Pray, what age do you suppose this boy to be ? Name it now, before I tell you. Why, twelve or fourteen. No such thing ; he is not quite six years old.[2] He has a lame leg, for which he was a year at Bath, and has acquired the perfect English accent, which he has not lost since he came, and he reads like a Garrick. You will allow this an uncommon exotic."

Some particulars in Mrs. Cockburn's account appear considerably at variance with what Sir Walter has told us respecting his own boyish proficiency — especially in the article of pronunciation. On that last head, however, Mrs. Cockburn was not, probably, a very accurate judge ; all that can be said is, that if at this early period he had acquired anything which could be justly described

---

[1] It may amuse my reader to recall, by the side of Scott's early definition of "a virtuoso," the lines in which Akenside has painted that character — lines which might have been written for a description of the Author of *Waverley* : —

> " He knew the various modes of ancient times,
> Their arts and fashions of each various guise ;
> Their weddings, funerals, punishments of crimes ;
> Their strength, their learning eke, and rarities.
> Of old habiliment, each sort and size,
> Male, female, high and low, to him were known ;
> Each gladiator's dress, and stage disguise,
> With learned clerkly phrase he could have shown."

[2] He was, in fact, six years and three months old before this letter was written.

as an English accent, he soon lost, and never again recovered, what he had thus gained from his short residence at Bath. In after-life his pronunciation of words, considered separately, was seldom much different from that of a well-educated Englishman of his time; but he used many words in a sense which belonged to Scotland, not to England, and the tone and accent remained broadly Scotch, though, unless in the *burr*, which no doubt smacked of the country bordering on Northumberland, there was no *provincial* peculiarity about his utterance. He had strong powers of mimicry — could talk with a peasant quite in his own style, and frequently in general society introduced rustic *patois*, northern, southern, or midland, with great truth and effect; but these things were inlaid dramatically, or playfully, upon his narrative. His exquisite taste in this matter was not less remarkable in his conversation than in the prose of his Scotch novels.

Another lady, nearly connected with the Keiths of Ravelston, has a lively recollection of young Walter, when paying a visit much about the same period to his kind relation,[1] the mistress of that picturesque old mansion, which furnished him in after-days with many of the features of his Tully-Veolan, and whose venerable gardens, with their massive hedges of yew and holly, he always considered as the ideal of the art. The lady, whose letter I have now before me, says she distinctly remembers the sickly boy sitting at the gate of the house with his attendant, when a poor mendicant approached, old and woe-begone, to claim the charity which none asked for in vain at Ravelston. When the man was retiring, the servant remarked to Walter that he ought to be thankful to Providence for having placed him above the want and misery he had been contemplating. The child looked up with a half-wistful, half-incredulous

---

[1] Mrs. Keith of Ravelston was born a Swinton of Swinton, and sister to Sir Walter's maternal grandmother.

expression, and said, "*Homer was a beggar!*" "How do you know that?" said the other. "Why, don't you remember," answered the little virtuoso, "that

> ' Seven *Roman* cities strove for Homer dead,
> Through which the living Homer begged his bread ? ' "

The lady smiled at the "*Roman* cities," — but already

> " Each blank in faithless memory void
> The poet's glowing thought supplied."

It was in this same year, 1777, that he spent some time at Prestonpans; made his first acquaintance with George Constable, the original of his Monkbarns; explored the field where Colonel Gardiner received his death-wound, under the learned guidance of Dalgetty; and marked the spot "where the grass long grew rank and green, distinguishing it from the rest of the field,"[1] above the grave of poor Balmawhapple.

His Uncle Thomas, whom I have described as I saw him in extreme old age at Monklaw, had the management of the farm affairs at Sandy-Knowe, when Walter returned thither from Prestonpans; he was a kind-hearted man, and very fond of the child. Appearing on his return somewhat strengthened, his uncle promoted him from the Cow-bailie's shoulder to a dwarf of the Shetland race, not so large as many a Newfoundland dog. This creature walked freely into the house, and was regularly fed from the boy's hand. He soon learned to sit her well, and often alarmed Aunt Jenny, by cantering over the rough places about the tower. In the evening of his life, when he had a grandchild afflicted with an infirmity akin to his own, he provided him with a little mare of the same breed, and gave her the name of *Marion*, in memory of this early favorite.

[1] *Waverley*, chap. xlvii. note.

CHAPTER III

THE report of Walter's progress in horsemanship
probably reminded his father that it was time he should
be learning other things beyond the department either of
Aunt Jenny or Uncle Thomas, and after a few months he
was recalled to Edinburgh. But extraordinary as was
the progress he had by this time made in that self-educa-
tion which alone is of primary consequence to spirits of
his order, he was found too deficient in lesser matters to
be at once entered in the High School. Probably his
mother dreaded, and deferred as long as she could, the
day when he should be exposed to the rude collision of
a crowd of boys. At all events he was placed first in a
little private school kept by one Leechman in Bristo
Port; and then, that experiment not answering expectation, under the domestic tutorage of Mr. James French,
afterwards minister of East Kilbride in Lanarkshire.
This respectable man considered him fit to join Luke
Fraser's class in October, 1778.

His own account of his progress at this excellent seminary is, on the whole, very similar to what I have received from some of his surviving schoolfellows. His
quick apprehension and powerful memory enabled him,
at little cost of labor, to perform the usual routine of
tasks, in such a manner as to keep him generally "in a
decent place" (so he once expressed it to Mr. Skene)
"about the middle of the class; with which," he contin-

ued, "I was the better contented, that it chanced to be near the fire."[1]   Mr. Fraser was, I believe, more zealous in enforcing attention to the technicalities of grammar, than to excite curiosity about historical facts, or imagination to strain after the flights of a poet.   There is no evidence that Scott, though he speaks of him as his "kind master," in remembrance probably of sympathy for his physical infirmities, ever attracted his special notice with reference to scholarship; but Adam, the Rector, into whose class he passed in October, 1782, was, as his situation demanded, a teacher of a more liberal caste; and though never, even under his guidance, did Walter fix and concentrate his ambition so as to maintain an eminent place, still the vivacity of his talents was observed, and the readiness of his memory in particular was so often displayed, that (as Mr. Irving, his chosen friend of that day, informs me) the Doctor "would constantly refer to him for dates, the particulars of battles, and other remarkable events alluded to in Horace, or whatever author the boys were reading, and used to call him the historian of the class."   No one who has read, as few have not, Dr. Adam's interesting work on Roman Antiquities will doubt the author's capacity for stimulating such a mind as young Scott's.

He speaks of himself as occasionally "glancing like a meteor from the bottom to the top of the form."   His schoolfellow, Mr. Claud Russell, remembers that he once made a great leap in consequence of the stupidity of some laggard on what is called the *dult's* (dolt's) bench, who being asked, on boggling at *cum*, "what part of speech is *with?*" answered, "*a substantive.*"   The Rector, after a moment's pause, thought it worth while to ask his *dux* — "Is *with* ever a substantive?" but all were

[1] According to Mr. Irving's recollections, Scott's place, after the first winter, was usually between the 7th and the 15th from the top of the class. He adds, " Dr. James Buchan was always the *dux;* David Douglas (Lord Reston) *second;* and the present Lord Melville *third.*"

silent until the query reached Scott, then near the bottom
of the class, who instantly responded by quoting a verse of
the book of Judges: — "And Samson said unto Delilah,
If they bind me with seven green *withs* that were never
dried, then shall I be weak, and as another man." [1]
Another upward movement, accomplished in a less laudable manner, but still one strikingly illustrative of his
ingenious resources, I am enabled to preserve through
the kindness of a brother poet and esteemed friend, to
whom Sir Walter himself communicated it in the melancholy twilight of his bright day.

Mr. Rogers says — "Sitting one day alone with him
in your house, in the Regent's Park — (it was the day
but one before he left it to embark at Portsmouth for
Malta) — I led him, among other things, to tell me once
again a story of himself, which he had formerly told me,
and which I had often wished to recover. When I returned home, I wrote it down, as nearly as I could, in
his own words; and here they are. The subject is an
achievement worthy of Ulysses himself, and such as
many of his schoolfellows could, no doubt, have related
of him; but I fear I have done it no justice, though the
story is so very characteristic that it should not be lost.
The inimitable manner in which he told it — the glance
of the eye, the turn of the head, and the light that played
over his faded features, as, one by one, the circumstances
came back to him, accompanied by a thousand boyish
feelings, that had slept perhaps for years — there is no
language, not even his own, could convey to you; but you
can supply them. Would that others could do so, who
had not the good fortune to know him! — The memorandum (Friday, October 21, 1831) is as follows: —

"There was a boy in my class at school, who stood
always at the top,[2] nor could I with all my efforts sup-

---

[1] Chap. xvi. verse 7.

[2] Mr. Irving inclines to think that this incident must have occurred
during Scott's attendance on Luke Fraser, not after he went to Dr. Adam;
and he also suspects that the boy referred to sat at the top, not of the
class, but of Scott's own bench or division of the class.

plant him. Day came after day, and still he kept his place, do what I would; till at length I observed that, when a question was asked him, he always fumbled with his fingers at a particular button in the lower part of his waistcoat. To remove it, therefore, became expedient in my eyes; and in an evil moment it was removed with a knife. Great was my anxiety to know the success of my measure; and it succeeded too well. When the boy was again questioned, his fingers sought again for the button, but it was not to be found. In his distress he looked down for it; it was to be seen no more than to be felt. He stood confounded, and I took possession of his place; nor did he ever recover it, or ever, I believe, suspect who was the author of his wrong. Often in after-life has the sight of him smote me as I passed by him; and often have I resolved to make him some reparation; but it ended in good resolutions. Though I never renewed my acquaintance with him, I often saw him, for he filled some inferior office in one of the courts of law at Edinburgh. Poor fellow! I believe he is dead; he took early to drinking."

The autobiography tells us that his translations in verse from Horace and Virgil were often approved by Dr. Adam. One of these little pieces, written in a weak boyish scrawl, within pencilled marks still visible, had been carefully preserved by his mother; it was found folded up in a cover inscribed by the old lady — "*My Walter's first lines*, 1782."

> " In awful ruins Ætna thunders nigh,
> And sends in pitchy whirlwinds to the sky
> Black clouds of smoke, which, still as they aspire,
> From their dark sides there bursts the glowing fire ;
> At other times huge balls of fire are toss'd,
> That lick the stars, and in the smoke are lost :
> Sometimes the mount, with vast convulsions torn,
> Emits huge rocks, which instantly are borne
> With loud explosions to the starry skies,
> The stones made liquid as the huge mass flies,
> Then back again with greater weight recoils,
> While Ætna thundering from the bottom boils."

I gather from Mr. Irving that these lines were considered as the second best set of those produced on the occasion — Colin Mackenzie of Portmore, through life Scott's dear friend, carrying off the premium.

In his Introduction to the Lay, he alludes to an original effusion of these "schoolboy days," prompted by a thunderstorm, which he says "was much approved of, until a malevolent critic sprung up in the shape of an apothecary's blue-buskined wife, who affirmed that my most sweet poetry was copied from an old magazine. I never" (he continues) "forgave the imputation, and even now I acknowledge some resentment against the poor woman's memory. She indeed accused me unjustly when she said I had stolen my poem ready made; but as I had, like most premature poets, copied all the words and ideas of which my verses consisted, she was so far right. I made one or two faint attempts at verse after I had undergone this sort of daw-plucking at the hands of the apothecary's wife, but some friend or other always advised me to put my verses into the fire; and, like Dorax in the play, I submitted, though with a swelling heart." These lines, and another short piece "On the Setting Sun," were lately found wrapped up in a cover, inscribed by Dr. Adam, "Walter Scott, July, 1783," and have been kindly transmitted to me by the gentleman who discovered them.

ON A THUNDERSTORM.

" Loud o'er my head though awful thunders roll,
    And vivid lightnings flash from pole to pole,
    Yet 't is thy voice, my God, that bids them fly,
    Thy arm directs those lightnings through the sky.
    Then let the good thy mighty name revere,
    And hardened sinners thy just vengeance fear."

ON THE SETTING SUN.

" Those evening clouds, that setting ray
    And beauteous tints, serve to display
    Their great Creator's praise ;
    Then let the short-lived thing call'd man,

Whose life's comprised within a span,
To Him his homage raise.

" We often praise the evening clouds,
And tints so gay and bold,
But seldom think upon our God,
Who tinged these clouds with gold ! " [1]

It must, I think, be allowed that these lines, though of the class to which the poet himself modestly ascribes them, and not to be compared with the efforts of Pope, still less of Cowley at the same period, show, nevertheless, praiseworthy dexterity for a boy of twelve.

The fragment tells us that on the whole he was "more distinguished in *the yards* (as the High School playground was called) than in *the class;*" and this, not less than the intellectual advancement which years before had excited the admiration of Mrs. Cockburn, was the natural result of his lifelong "rebellion against external circumstances." He might now with very slender exertion have been the *dux* of his form; but if there was more difficulty, there was also more to whet his ambition, in the attempt to overcome the disadvantages of his physical misfortune, and in spite of them assert equality with the best of his compeers on the ground which they considered as the true arena of honor. He told me, in walking through these same *yards* forty years afterwards, that he had scarcely made his first appearance there, before some dispute arising, his opponent remarked that "there was no use to hargle-bargle with a cripple;" upon which he replied, that if he might fight *mounted*, he would try his hand with any one of his inches. "An elder boy," said he, "who had perhaps been chuckling over our friend

---

[1] I am obliged for these little memorials to the Rev. W. Steven of Rotterdam, author of an interesting book on the history of the branch of the Scotch Church long established in Holland, and still flourishing under the protection of the enlightened government of that country. Mr. Steven found them in the course of his recent researches, undertaken with a view to some memoirs of the High School of Edinburgh, at which he had received his own early education.

Roderick Random when his mother supposed him to be in full cry after Pyrrhus or Porus, suggested that the two little tinklers might be lashed front to front upon a deal board — and — 'O gran bontà de' cavalier antichi ' — the proposal being forthwith agreed to, I received my first bloody nose in an attitude which would have entitled me, in the blessed days of personal cognizances, to assume that of a *lioncel seiant gules*. My pugilistic trophies here," he continued, "were all the results of such *sittings in banco*." Considering his utter ignorance of fear, the strength of his chest and upper limbs, and that the scientific part of pugilism never flourished in Scotland, I dare say these trophies were not few.

The mettle of the High School boys, however, was principally displayed elsewhere than in their own *yards;* and Sir Walter has furnished us with ample indications of the delight with which he found himself at length capable of rivalling others in such achievements as required the exertion of active locomotive powers. Speaking of some scene of his infancy in one of his latest tales, he says — "Every step of the way after I have passed through the green already mentioned " (probably the *Meadows* behind George's Square) "has for me something of an early remembrance. There is the stile at which I can recollect a cross child's-maid upbraiding me with my infirmity as she lifted me coarsely and carelessly over the flinty steps which my brothers traversed with shout and bound. I remember the *suppressed bitterness* of the moment, and, conscious of my own infirmity, the envy with which I regarded the easy movements and elastic steps of my more happily formed brethren. Alas! " he adds, "these goodly barks have all perished in life's wide ocean, and only that which seemed, as the naval phrase goes, so little seaworthy, has reached the port when the tempest is over." How touching to compare with this passage that in which he records his pride in being found before he left the High School one of the boldest and nimblest climbers of "the kittle nine stanes," a passage of difficulty which might puzzle a chamois-hunter of the Alps, its steps, "few and far between," projected high in air from the precipitous black granite of the Castle rock. But climbing and fighting could sometimes be combined, and he has in almost the same page dwelt upon perhaps the most favorite of all these juvenile exploits — namely, "the manning of the Cow-gate Port," — in the season when snowballs could be employed by the young scorners of discipline for the annoyance of the Town-guard. To understand fully the feelings of a High School boy of that day with regard to those ancient Highlanders, who then formed the only police of the city of Edinburgh, the reader must consult the poetry of the scapegrace Fergusson. It was in defi-ance of their Lochaber axes that the Cowgate Port was manned — and many were the occasions on which its de-fence presented a formidable mimicry of warfare. "The gateway," Sir Walter adds, "is now demolished, and probably most of its garrison lie as low as the fortress! To recollect that I, however naturally disqualified, was one of these juvenile dreadnoughts, is a sad reflection for one who cannot now step over a brook without assist-ance."

I am unwilling to swell this narrative by extracts from Scott's published works, but there is one juvenile exploit told in the General Preface to the Waverley Novels, which I must crave leave to introduce here in his own language, because it is essentially necessary to complete our notion of his schoolboy life and character. "It is well known," he says, "that there is little boxing at the Scottish schools. About forty or fifty years ago, how-ever, a far more dangerous mode of fighting, in parties or factions, was permitted in the streets of Edinburgh, to the great disgrace of the police, and danger of the parties concerned. These parties were generally formed from the quarters of the town in which the combatants resided, those of a particular square or district fighting against those of an adjoining one. Hence it happened that the children of the higher classes were often pitted against those of the lower, each taking their side according to the residence of their friends. So far as I recollect, however, it was unmingled either with feelings of democracy or aristocracy, or indeed with malice or ill-will of any kind towards the opposite party. In fact, it was only a rough mode of play. Such contests were, however, maintained with great vigor with stones, and sticks, and fisticuffs, when one party dared to charge, and the other stood their ground. Of course, mischief sometimes happened; boys are said to have been killed at these *bickers*, as they were called, and serious accidents certainly took place, as many contemporaries can bear witness.

"The author's father residing in George's Square, in the southern side of Edinburgh, the boys belonging to that family, with others in the square, were arranged into a sort of company, to which a lady of distinction presented a handsome set of colors.[1] Now, this company or regiment, as a matter of course, was engaged in weekly warfare with the boys inhabiting the Cross-causeway, Bristo-Street, the Potterrow — in short, the neighboring suburbs. These last were chiefly of the lower rank, but hardy loons, who threw stones to a hair's-breadth, and were very rugged antagonists at close quarters. The skirmish sometimes lasted for a whole evening, until one party or the other was victorious, when, if ours were successful, we drove the enemy to their quarters, and were usually chased back by the reinforcement of bigger lads who came to their assistance. If, on the contrary, we were pursued, as was often the case, into the precincts of our square, we were in our turn supported by our elder brothers, domestic servants, and similar auxiliaries. It followed, from our frequent opposition to each other,

[1] This young patroness was the Duchess-Countess of Sutherland.

that, though not knowing the names of our enemies, we were yet well acquainted with their appearance, and had nicknames for the most remarkable of them. One very active and spirited boy might be considered as the principal leader in the cohort of the suburbs. He was, I suppose, thirteen or fourteen years old, finely made, tall, blue-eyed, with long fair hair, the very picture of a youthful Goth. This lad was always first in the charge, and last in the retreat — the Achilles at once and Ajax of the Cross-causeway. He was too formidable to us not to have a cognomen, and, like that of a knight of old, it was taken from the most remarkable part of his dress, being a pair of old green livery breeches, which was the principal part of his clothing; for, like Pentapolin, according to Don Quixote's account, Green-breeks, as we called him, always entered the battle with bare arms, legs, and feet.

"It fell, that once upon a time when the combat was at its thickest, this plebeian champion headed a charge so rapid and furious, that all fled before him. He was several paces before his comrades, and had actually laid his hands upon the patrician standard, when one of our party, whom some misjudging friend had entrusted with a *couteau de chasse*, or hanger, inspired with a zeal for the honor of the corps, worthy of Major Sturgeon himself, struck poor Green-breeks over the head, with strength sufficient to cut him down. When this was seen, the casualty was so far beyond what had ever taken place before, that both parties fled different ways, leaving poor Green-breeks, with his bright hair plentifully dabbled in blood, to the care of the watchman, who (honest man) took care not to know who had done the mischief. The bloody hanger was thrown into one of the Meadow ditches, and solemn secrecy was sworn on all hands; but the remorse and terror of the actor were beyond all bounds, and his apprehensions of the most dreadful character. The wounded hero was for a few days in the

Infirmary, the case being only a trifling one. But though inquiry was strongly pressed on him, no argument could make him indicate the person from whom he had received the wound, though he must have been perfectly well known to him. When he recovered and was dismissed, the author and his brothers opened a communication with him, through the medium of a popular gingerbread baker, of whom both parties were customers, in order to tender a subsidy in the name of smart-money. The sum would excite ridicule were I to name it; but sure I am that the pockets of the noted Green-breeks never held as much money of his own. He declined the remittance, saying that he would not sell his blood; but at the same time reprobated the idea of being an informer, which he said was *clam*, that is, base or mean. With much urgency, he accepted a pound of snuff for the use of some old woman — aunt, grandmother, or the like — with whom he lived. We did not become friends, for the *bickers* were more agreeable to both parties than any more pacific amusement; but we conducted them ever after under mutual assurances of the highest consideration for each other." Sir Walter adds — "Of five brothers, all healthy and promising in a degree far beyond one whose infancy was visited by personal infirmity, and whose health after this period seemed long very precarious, I am, nevertheless, the only survivor. The best loved, and the best deserving to be loved, who had destined this incident to be the foundation of a literary composition, died ' before his day,' in a distant and foreign land; and trifles assume an importance not their own when connected with those who have been loved and lost."

During some part of his attendance on the High School, young Walter spent one hour daily at a small separate seminary of writing and arithmetic, kept by one Morton, where, as was, and I suppose continues to be, the custom of Edinburgh, young girls came for instruc-

tion as well as boys; and one of Mr. Morton's female
pupils has been kind enough to set down some little reminiscences of Scott, who happened to sit at the same desk
with herself. They appear to me the more interesting,
because the lady had no acquaintance with him in the
course of his subsequent life. Her nephew, Mr. James
(the accomplished author of Richelieu), to whose friendship I owe her communication, assures me, too, that he
had constantly heard her tell the same things in the very
same way, as far back as his own memory reaches, many
years before he had ever seen Sir Walter, or his aunt
could have dreamt of surviving to assist in the biography
of his early days.

"He attracted," Mrs. Churnside says, "the regard and
fondness of all his companions, for he was ever rational,
fanciful, lively, and possessed of that urbane gentleness
of manner which makes its way to the heart. His imagination was constantly at work, and he often so engrossed
the attention of those who learnt with him, that little
could be done — Mr. Morton himself being forced to
laugh as much as the little scholars at the odd turns and
devices he fell upon; for he did nothing in the ordinary
way, but, for example, even when he wanted ink to his
pen, would get up some ludicrous story about sending his
doggie to the mill again. He used also to interest us in
a more serious way, by telling us the *visions*, as he called
them, which he had lying alone on the floor or sofa, when
kept from going to church on a Sunday by ill health.
Child as I was, I could not help being highly delighted
with his description of the glories he had seen — his misty
and sublime sketches of the regions above, which he had
visited in his trance. Recollecting these descriptions,
radiant and not gloomy as they were, I have often thought
since that there must have been a bias in his mind to superstition — the marvellous seemed to have such power
over him, though the mere offspring of his own imagination, that the expression of his face, habitually that of

genuine benevolence, mingled with a shrewd innocent humor, changed greatly while he was speaking of these things, and showed a deep intenseness of feeling, as if he were awed even by his own recital. . . . I may add, that in walking he used always to keep his eyes turned downwards as if thinking, but with a pleasing expression of countenance, as if enjoying his thoughts. Having once known him, it was impossible ever to forget him. In this manner, after all the changes of a long life, he constantly appears as fresh as yesterday to my mind's eye."

This beautiful extract needs no commentary. I may as well, however, bear witness, that exactly as the schoolboy still walks before her "mind's eye," his image rises familiarly to mine, who never saw him until he was past the middle of life: that I trace in every feature of her delineation the same gentleness of aspect and demeanor which the presence of the female sex, whether in silk or in russet, ever commanded in the man; and that her description of the change on his countenance when passing from the "doggie of the mill" to the dream of Paradise is a perfect picture of what no one that has heard him recite a fragment of high poetry, in the course of table talk, can ever forget. Strangers may catch some notion of what fondly dwells on the memory of every friend, by glancing from the conversational bust of Chantrey to the first portrait by Raeburn, which represents the Last Minstrel as musing in his prime within sight of Hermitage.

I believe it was about this time that, as he expresses it in one of his latest works, "the first images of horror from the scenes of real life were stamped upon his mind," by the tragical death of his great-aunt, Mrs. Margaret Swinton. This old lady, whose extraordinary nerve of character he illustrates largely in the introduction to the story of Aunt Margaret's Mirror, was now living with one female attendant, in a small house not far from Mr. Scott's residence in George's Square. The maid-servant,

in a sudden access of insanity, struck her mistress to
death with a coal-axe, and then rushed furiously into the
street with the bloody weapon in her hand, proclaiming
aloud the horror she had perpetrated. I need not dwell
on the effects which must have been produced in a virtuous and affectionate circle by this shocking incident.
The old lady had been tenderly attached to her nephew.
"She was," he says, "our constant resource in sickness,
or when we tired of noisy play, and closed round her to
listen to her tales."

It was at this same period that Mr. and Mrs. Scott
received into their house, as tutor for their children, Mr.
James Mitchell, of whom the Ashestiel Memoir gives us
a description, such as I could not have presented had he
been still alive. Mr. Mitchell was living, however, at
the time of his pupil's death, and I am now not only at
liberty to present Scott's unmutilated account of their
intercourse, but enabled to give also the most simple and
characteristic narrative of the other party. I am sure no
one, however nearly related to Mr. Mitchell, will now
complain of seeing his keen-sighted pupil's sketch placed
by the side, as it were, of the fuller portraiture drawn by
the unconscious hand of the amiable and worthy man
himself. The following is an extract from Mr. Mitchell's
MS., entitled "Memorials of the most remarkable occurrences and transactions of my life, drawn up in the hope
that, when I shall be no more, they may be read with
profit and pleasure by my children." The good man was
so kind as to copy out one chapter for my use, as soon as
he heard of Sir Walter Scott's death. He was then, and
had for many years been, minister of a Presbyterian
chapel at Wooler, in Northumberland, to which situation
he had retired on losing his benefice at Montrose, in consequence of the Sabbatarian scruples alluded to in Scott's
Autobiography.

"In 1782," says Mr. Mitchell, "I became a tutor in Mr.
Walter Scott's family. He was a Writer to the Signet in

George's Square, Edinburgh.　Mr. Scott was a fine-looking man, then a little past the meridian of life, of dignified, yet agreeable manners.　His business was extensive.　He was a man of tried integrity, of strict morals, and had a respect for religion and its ordinances.　The church the family attended was the Old Greyfriars, of which the celebrated Doctors Robertson and Erskine were the ministers.　Thither went Mr. and Mrs. Scott every Sabbath, when well and at home, attended by their fine young family of children, and their domestic servants — a sight so amiable and exemplary as often to excite in my breast a glow of heartfelt satisfaction.　According to an established and laudable practice in the family, the heads of it, the children, and servants, were assembled on Sunday evenings in the drawing-room, and examined on the Church Catechism and sermons they had heard delivered during the course of the day; on which occasions I had to perform the part of chaplain, and conclude with prayer.　From Mrs. Scott I learned that Mr. Scott was one that had not been seduced from the paths of virtue; but had been enabled to venerate good morals from his youth.　When he first came to Edinburgh to follow out his profession, some of his schoolfellows, who, like him, had come to reside in Edinburgh, attempted to unhinge his principles, and corrupt his morals; but when they found him resolute, and unshaken in his virtuous dispositions, they gave up the attempt; but, instead of abandoning him altogether, they thought the more of him, and honored him with their confidence and patronage; which is certainly a great inducement to young men in the outset of life to act a similar part.

" After having heard of his inflexible adherence to the cause of virtue in his youth, and his regular attendance on the ordinances of religion in after-life, we will not be surprised to be told that he bore a sacred regard for the Sabbath, nor at the following anecdote illustrative of it.　An opulent farmer of East Lothian had employed Mr. Scott as his agent, in a cause depending before the Court of Session.　Having a curiosity to see something in the papers relative to the process, which were deposited in Mr. Scott's hands, this worldly man came into Edinburgh on a Sunday to have an inspection of them.　As there was no immediate necessity for this measure, Mr. Scott asked the farmer if an ordinary week-day would not answer equally well. The farmer was not willing to take this advice, but insisted on the production of his papers. Mr. Scott then delivered them to him, saying, it was not his practice to engage in secular business on the Sabbath, and that he would have no difficulty in Edinburgh to find some of his profession who would have none of his scruples. No wonder such a man was confided in, and greatly honored in his professional line. — All the poor services I did to his family were more than repaid by the comfort and honor I had by being in the family, the pecuniary remuneration I received, and particularly by his recommendation of me, some time afterwards, to the Magistrates and Town Council of Montrose, when there was a vacancy, and this brought me on the carpet, which, as he said, was all he could do, as the settlement would ultimately hinge on a popular election.

" Mrs. Scott was a wife in every respect worthy of such a husband. Like her partner, she was then a little past the meridian of life, of a prepossessing appearance, amiable manners, of a cultivated understanding, affectionate disposition, and fine taste. She was both able and disposed to soothe her husband's mind under the asperities of business, and to be a rich blessing to her numerous progeny. But what constituted her distinguishing ornament was that she was sincerely religious. Some years previous to my entrance into the family, I understood from one of the servants she had been under deep religious concern about her soul's salvation, which had ultimately issued in a conviction of the truth of Christianity, and in the enjoyment of its divine consolations. She liked Dr. Erskine's sermons ; but was not fond of the Principal's, however rational, eloquent, and well composed, and would, if other things had answered, have gone, when he preached, to have heard Dr. Davidson. Mrs. Scott was a descendant of Dr. Daniel Rutherford, a professor in the Medical School of Edinburgh, and one of those eminent men, who, by learning and professional skill, brought it to the high pitch of celebrity to which it has attained. He was an excellent linguist, and, according to the custom of the times, delivered his prelections to the students in Latin. Mrs. Scott told me, that, when prescribing to his patients, it was his custom to offer up at the same time a prayer for the accompanying blessing of heaven ; a laudable practice, in which, I fear, he has not been generally imitated by those of his profession.

" Mr. Scott's family consisted of six children, all of which were at home except the eldest, who was an officer in the army ; and as they were of an age fit for instruction, they were all committed to my superintendence, which, in dependence on God, I exercised with an earnest and faithful regard to their temporal and spiritual good. As the most of them were under public teachers, the duty assigned me was mainly to assist them in the prosecution of their studies. In all the excellencies, whether as to temper, conduct, talents natural or acquired, which any of the children individually possessed, to Master Walter, since the celebrated Sir Walter, must a decided preference be ascribed. Though, like the rest of the children, placed under my tuition, the conducting of his education comparatively cost me but little trouble, being, by the quickness of his intellect, tenacity of memory, and diligent application to his studies, generally equal of himself to the acquisition of those tasks I or others prescribed to him. So that Master Walter might be regarded not so much as a pupil of mine, but as a friend and companion, and, I may add, as an assistant also ; for, by his example and admonitions, he greatly strengthened my hands, and stimulated my other pupils to industry and good behavior. I seldom had occasion all the time I was in the family to find fault with him even for trifles, and only once to threaten serious castigation, of which he was no sooner aware than he suddenly sprung up, threw his arms about my neck, and kissed me. It is hardly needful to state, that now the intended castigation was no longer thought of. By such generous and noble conduct, my displeasure was in a moment converted into esteem and admiration ; my soul melted into tenderness, and I was ready to mingle my tears with his. Some incidents in reference to him in that early period, and some interesting and useful conversations I had with him, then deeply impressed on my mind, and which the lapse of near half a century has not yet obliterated, afforded no doubtful presage of his future greatness and celebrity. On my going into the family, as far as I can judge, he might be in his twelfth or thirteenth year, a boy in the rector's class. However elevated above the other boys in genius, though generally in the list of the duxes, he was seldom, as far as I recollect, the leader of the school : nor need this be deemed surprising, as it has often been observed that boys of original genius have been outstripped, by those that were far inferior to themselves, in the acquisition of the dead languages. Dr. Adam, the rector, celebrated for his knowledge of the Latin language, was deservedly held by Mr. Walter in high admiration and regard ; of which the following anecdote may be adduced as a proof. In the High School, as is well known, there are four masters and a rector. The classes of those masters the rector in rotation inspects, and in the mean time the master, whose school is examined, goes in to take care of the rector's. One of the masters, on account of some grudge, had rudely assaulted and injured the venerable rector one night in the High School Wynd. The rector's scholars, exasperated at the outrage, at the instigation of Master Walter, determined on revenge, and which was to be executed when this obnoxious master should again come to teach the class. When this occurred, the task the class had prescribed to them was that passage in the Æneid of Virgil, where the Queen of Carthage interrogates the court as to the stranger that had come to her habitation —

' Quis novus hic hospes successit sedibus nostris ? ' [1]

Master Walter, having taken a piece of paper, inscribed upon it these words, substituting *vanus* for *novus*, and pinned it to the tail of the master's coat, and turned him into ridicule by raising the laugh of the whole school against him. Though this juvenile action could not be justified on the footing of Christian principles, yet certainly it was so far honorable that it was not a dictate of personal revenge, but that it originated in respect for a worthy and injured man, and detestation of one whom he looked upon as a bad character.

" One forenoon, on coming from the High School, he said he wished to know my opinion as to his conduct in a matter he should state to me. When passing through the High School Yards, he found a half-guinea piece on the ground. Instead of appropriating this to his own use, a sense of honesty led him to look around, and on doing so he espied a countryman, whom he suspected to be the proprietor. Having asked the man if he

---

[1] This transposition of *hospes* and *nostris* sufficiently confirms his pupil's statement that Mr. Mitchell " superintended his classical themes, but not classically." The " obnoxious master " alluded to was Burns's friend Nicoll, the hero of the song —

" Willie brewed a peck o' maut,
And Rob and Allan cam' to see," etc.

had lost anything, he searched his pockets, and then replied that he had lost half-a-guinea. Master Walter with pleasure presented him with his lost treasure. In this transaction, his ingenuity in finding out the proper owner, and his integrity in restoring the property, met my most cordial approbation.

"When in church, Master Walter had more of a soporific tendency than the rest of my young charge. This seemed to be constitutional. He needed one or other of the family to arouse him, and from this it might be inferred that he would cut a poor figure on the Sabbath evening when examined about the sermons. But what excited the admiration of the family was, that none of the children, however wakeful, could answer as he did. The only way that I could account for this was, that when he heard the text, and divisions of the subject, his good sense, memory, and genius, supplied the thoughts which would occur to the preacher.

"On one occasion, in the dining-room, when, according to custom, he was reading some author in the time of relaxation from study, I asked him how he accounted for the superiority of knowledge he possessed above the rest of the family. His reply was : — Some years ago he had been attacked by a swelling in one of his ankles, which confined him to the house, and prevented him taking amusement and exercise, and which was the cause of his lameness. As under this ailment he could not romp with his brothers and the other young people in the green in George's Square, he found himself compelled to have recourse to some substitute for the juvenile amusements of his comrades, and this was reading. So that, to what he no doubt accounted a painful dispensation of Providence, he probably stood indebted for his future celebrity. When it was understood I was to leave the family, Master Walter told me that he had a small present to give me, to be kept as a memorandum of his friendship. and that it was of little value : 'But you know, Mr. Mitchell,' said he, 'that presents are not to be estimated according to their intrinsic value, but according to the intention of the donor.' This was his Adam's Grammar, which had seen hard service in its day, and had many animals and inscriptions on its margins. This, to my regret, is no longer to be found in my collection of books, nor do I know what has become of it.

"Since leaving the family, although no stranger to the widely spreading fame of Sir Walter, I have had few opportunities of personal intercourse with him. When minister in the second charge of the Established Church at Montrose, he paid me a visit, and spent a night with me — few visits have been more gratifying. He was then on his return from Aberdeen, where he, as an advocate, had attended the Court of Justiciary in its northern circuit. Nor was his attendance in this court his sole object: another, and perhaps the principal, was, as he stated to me, to collect in his excursion ancient ballads and traditional stories about fairies, witches, and ghosts. Such intelligence proved to me as an electrical shock ; and as I then sincerely regretted, so do I still, that Sir Walter's precious time was so much devoted to the *dulce*, rather than the *utile* of composition, and that his great talent should have been wasted on such subjects. At the same time I feel happy to qualify this censure, as I am generally given to understand that his Novels are of a more pure and unexceptionable nature than characterizes writings of a similar description ; while at the same time his pen has been occupied in the production of works of a better and nobler order. Impressed with the conviction that he would one day arrive at honor and influence in his native country, I endeavored to improve the occasion of his visit to secure his patronage in behalf of the strict and evangelical party in the Church of Scotland, in exerting himself to induce patrons to grant to the Christian people liberty to elect their own pastors in cases of vacancy. His answer struck me much: it was — ' Nay, nay, Mr. Mitchell, I'll not do that; for if that were to be done, I and the like of me would have no life with such as you ; ' from which I inferred he thought that, were the evangelical clergy to obtain the superiority, they would introduce such strictness of discipline as would not quadrate with the ideas of that party called *the moderate* in the Church of Scotland, whose views, I presume, Sir Walter had now adopted. Some, however, to whom I have mentioned Sir Walter's reply, have suggested that I had misunderstood his meaning, and that what he said was not in earnest, but in jocularity and good-humor. This may be true, and certainly is a candid interpretation. As to the ideal beings already mentioned as the subject of his inquiries, my materials were too scanty to afford him much information."

Notwithstanding the rigidly Presbyterian habits which this chronicle describes with so much more satisfaction than the corresponding page in the Ashestiel Memoir, I am reminded, by a communication already quoted from a lady of the Ravelston family, that Mrs. Scott, who had, she says, "a turn for literature quite uncommon among the ladies of the time," encouraged her son in his passion for Shakespeare; that his plays, and the Arabian Nights, were often read aloud in the family circle by Walter, "and served to spend many a happy evening hour;" nay, that, however good Mitchell may have frowned at such a suggestion, even Mr. Scott made little objection to his children, and some of their young friends, getting up private theatricals occasionally in the dining-room after the lessons of the day were over. The lady adds, that Walter was always the manager, and had the whole charge of the affair, and that the favorite piece used to be Jane Shore, in which he was the Hastings, his sister the Alicia. I have heard from another friend of the family that Richard III. also was attempted, and that Walter took the part of the Duke of Gloucester, observing that "the limp would do well enough to represent the hump."

A story which I have seen in print, about his partaking in the dancing lessons of his brothers, I do not believe. But it was during Mr. Mitchell's residence in the family that they all made their unsuccessful attempts in the art of music, under the auspices of poor *Allister* Campbell — the Editor of Albyn's Anthology.

Mr. Mitchell appears to have terminated his superintendence before Walter left Dr. Adam, and in the interval between this and his entrance at College, he spent some time with his aunt, who now inhabited a cottage at Kelso; but the Memoir, I suspect, gives too much extension to that residence — which may be accounted for by his blending with it a similar visit which he paid to the same place during his College vacation of the next year.

Some of the features of Miss Jenny's abode at Kelso are alluded to in the Memoir, but the fullest description of it occurs in his Essay on Landscape Gardening (1828), where, talking of grounds laid out in the *Dutch taste*, he says: — "Their rarity *now* entitles them to some care as a species of antiques, and unquestionably they give character to some snug, quiet, and sequestered situations, which would otherwise have no marked feature of any kind. I retain an early and pleasing recollection of the seclusion of such a scene. A small cottage, adjacent to a beautiful village, the habitation of an ancient maiden lady, was for some time my abode. It was situated in a garden of seven or eight acres, planted about the beginning of the eighteenth century by one of the Millars, related to the author of the Gardeners' Dictionary, or, for aught I know, by himself. It was full of long, straight walks, between hedges of yew and hornbeam, which rose tall and close on every side. There were thickets of flowery shrubs, a bower, and an arbor, to which access was obtained through a little maze of contorted walks calling itself a labyrinth. In the centre of the bower was a splendid Platanus, or Oriental plane — a huge hill of leaves — one of the noblest specimens of that regularly beautiful tree which I remember to have seen. In different parts of the garden were fine ornamental trees, which had attained great size, and the orchard was filled with fruit-trees of the best description. There were seats, and hilly walks, and a banqueting house. I visited this scene lately, after an absence of many years. Its air of retreat, the seclusion which its alleys afforded, was entirely gone; the huge Platanus had died, like most of its kind, in the beginning of this century; the hedges were cut down, the trees stubbed up, and the whole character of the place so destroyed that I was glad when I could leave it." It was under this Platanus that Scott first devoured Percy's Reliques. I remember well being with him, in 1820 or 1821, when he revisited the favorite scene, and the sadness of his looks when he discovered that the "huge hill of leaves" was no more.

To keep up his scholarship while inhabiting *the garden*, he attended daily, as he informs us, the public school of Kelso, and here he made his first acquaintance with a family, two members of which were intimately connected with the most important literary transactions of his after-life — James Ballantyne, the printer of almost all his works, and his brother John, who had a share in the publication of many of them. Their father was a respectable tradesman in this pretty town. The elder of the brothers, who did not long survive his illustrious friend, was kind enough to make an exertion on behalf of this work, while stretched on the bed from which he never rose, and dictated a valuable paper of *memoranda*, from which I shall here introduce my first extract: —

"I think," says James Ballantyne, "it was in the year 1783 that I first became acquainted with Sir Walter Scott, then a boy about my own age, at the Grammar School of Kelso, of which Mr. Lancelot Whale was the Rector. The impression left by his manners was, even at that early period, calculated to be deep, and I cannot recall any other instance in which the man and the boy continued to resemble each other so much and so long. Walter Scott was not a constant schoolfellow at this seminary ; he only attended it for a few weeks during the vacation of the Edinburgh High School. He was then, as he continued during all his after-life to be, devoted to antiquarian lore, and was certainly the best story-teller I had ever heard, either then or since. He soon discovered that I was as fond of listening as he himself was of relating; and I remember it was a thing of daily occurrence, that after he had made himself master of his own lesson, I, alas, being still sadly to seek in mine, he used to whisper to me, ' Come, slink over beside me, Jamie, and I 'll tell you a story.' I well recollect that he had a form, or seat, appropriated to himself, the particular reason of which I cannot tell, but he was always treated with a peculiar degree of respect, not by the boys of the different classes merely, but by the venerable Master Lancelot himself, who, an absent, grotesque being, betwixt six and seven feet high, was nevertheless an admirable scholar, and sure to be delighted to find any one so well qualified to sympathize with him as young Walter Scott ; and the affectionate gratitude of the young pupil was never intermitted, so long as his venerable master continued to live. I may mention, in passing, that old Whale bore, in many particulars, a strong resemblance to Dominie Sampson, though, it must be admitted, combining more gentlemanly manners with equal classical lore, and, on the whole, being a much superior sort of person. In the intervals of school hours, it was our constant practice to walk together by the banks of the Tweed, our employment continuing exactly the same, for his stories seemed to be quite inexhaustible. This intercourse continued during the summers of the years 1783–84, but was broken off in 1785–86, when I went into Edinburgh to College."

Perhaps the separate seat assigned to Walter Scott by the Kelso schoolmaster was considered due to him as a temporary visitor from the great Edinburgh seminary. Very possibly, however, the worthy Mr. Whale thought of nothing but protecting his solitary student of Persius and Tacitus from the chances of being jostled among the adherents of Ruddiman and Cornelius Nepos.

Another of his Kelso schoolfellows was Robert Waldie (son of Mr. Waldie of Henderside), and to this connection he owed, both while quartered in the garden, and afterwards at Rosebank, many kind attentions, of which he ever preserved a grateful recollection, and which have left strong traces on every page of his works in which he has occasion to introduce the Society of Friends. This young companion's mother, though always called in the neighborhood "Lady Waldie," belonged to that community; and the style of life and manners depicted in the household of Joshua Geddes of Mount Sharon and his amiable sister, in some of the sweetest chapters of Redgauntlet, is a slightly decorated edition of what he wit-

nessed under her hospitable roof. He records, in a note
to the novel, the "liberality and benevolence" of this
"kind old lady" in allowing him to "rummage at pleasure, and carry home any volumes he chose of her small
but valuable library;" annexing only the condition that
he should "take at the same time some of the tracts
printed for encouraging and extending the doctrines of
her own sect. She did not," he adds, "even exact any
assurance that I would read these performances, being
too justly afraid of involving me in a breach of promise,
but was merely desirous that I should have the chance of
instruction within my reach, in case whim, curiosity, or
accident, might induce me to have recourse to it." I
remember the pleasure with which he read, late in life,
Rome in the Nineteenth Century, an ingenious work produced by one of Mrs. Waldie's granddaughters, and how
comically he pictured the alarm with which his ancient
friend would have perused some of its delineations of the
high places of Popery.

I shall be pardoned for adding a marginal note written,
apparently late in Scott's life, on his copy of a little forgotten volume, entitled Trifles in Verse, by a Young
Soldier. "In 1783," he says, "or about that time, I
remember John Marjoribanks, a smart recruiting officer
in the village of Kelso, the Weekly Chronicle of which
he filled with his love verses. His Delia was a Miss
Dickson, daughter of a shopkeeper in the same village —
his Gloriana a certain prudish old maiden lady, benempt
Miss Goldie; I think I see her still, with her thin arms
sheathed in scarlet gloves, and crossed like two lobsters
in a fishmonger's stand. Poor Delia was a very beautiful girl, and not more conceited than a be-rhymed miss
ought to be. Many years afterwards I found the Kelso
belle, thin and pale, her good looks gone, and her smart
dress neglected, governess to the brats of a Paisley manu-
facturer. I ought to say there was not an atom of scandal
in her flirtation with the young military poet. The

bard's fate was not much better; after some service in India and elsewhere, he led a half-pay life about Edinburgh, and died there. There is a tenuity of thought in what he has written, but his verses are usually easy, and I like them because they recall my schoolboy days, when I thought him a Horace, and his Delia a goddess."

CHAPTER IV

ILLUSTRATIONS OF THE AUTOBIOGRAPHY CONTINUED. —
ANECDOTES OF SCOTT'S COLLEGE LIFE

1783–1786

ON returning to Edinburgh, and entering the College, in November, 1783, Scott found himself once more in the fellowship of all his intimates of the High School; of whom, besides those mentioned in the autobiographical fragment, he speaks in his diaries with particular affection of Sir William Rae, Bart., David Monypenny (afterwards Lord Pitmilly), Thomas Tod, W. S., Sir Archibald Campbell of Succoth, Bart., all familiar friends of his through manhood, — and the Earl of Dalhousie,[1] whom, on meeting with him after a long separation in the evening of life, he records as still being, and having always been, "the same manly and generous character that all about him loved as the *Lordie Ramsay* of the Yards." The chosen companion, however, continued to be for some time Mr. John Irving — his suburban walks with whom have been recollected so tenderly, both in the Memoir of 1808, and in the Preface to Waverley of 1829. It will interest the reader to compare with those beautiful descriptions the following extract from a letter with which Mr. Irving has favored me: —

"Every Saturday, and more frequently during the vacations, we used to retire, with three or four books from the circulating library, to Salisbury Crags, Arthur's Seat, or Blackford Hill, and read them together. He

---

[1] George, ninth Earl of Dalhousie, highly distinguished in the military annals of his time, died on the 21st March, 1838, in his 68th year.

read faster than I, and had, on this account, to wait a
little at finishing every two pages, before turning the
leaf. The books we most delighted in were romances of
knight-errantry; the Castle of Otranto, Spenser, Ariosto,
and Boiardo were great favorites. We used to climb up
the rocks in search of places where we might sit sheltered
from the wind; and the more inaccessible they were, the
better we liked them. He was very expert at climbing.
Sometimes we got into places where we found it difficult
to move either up or down, and I recollect it being proposed, on several occasions, that I should go for a ladder
to see and extricate him; but I never had any need really
to do so, for he always managed somehow either to get
down or ascend to the top. The number of books we
thus devoured was very great. I forgot great part of
what I read; but my friend, notwithstanding he read
with such rapidity, remained, to my surprise, master of it
all, and could even weeks or months afterwards repeat a
whole page in which anything had particularly struck him
at the moment. After we had continued this practice of
reading for two years or more together, he proposed that
we should recite to each other alternately such adventures
of knight-errants as we could ourselves contrive; and we
continued to do so a long while. He found no difficulty
in it, and used to recite for half an hour or more at a
time, while I seldom continued half that space. The
stories we told were, as Sir Walter has said, intermin-
able — for we were unwilling to have any of our favorite
knights killed. Our passion for romance led us to learn
Italian together; after a time we could both read it with
fluency, and we then copied such tales as we had met with
in that language, being a continued succession of battles
and enchantments. He began early to collect old ballads, and as my mother could repeat a great many, he
used to come and learn those she could recite to him. He
used to get all the copies of these ballads he could, and
select the best."

These, no doubt, were among the germs of the collection of ballads in six little volumes, which, from the handwriting, had been begun at this early period, and which is still preserved at Abbotsford. And it appears that at least as early a date must be ascribed to another collection of little humorous stories in prose, the *Penny Chap-books*, as they are called, still in high favor among the lower classes in Scotland, which stands on the same shelf. In a letter of 1830 [1] he states that he had bound up things of this kind to the extent of several volumes, before he was ten years old.

Although the Ashestiel Memoir mentions so very lightly his boyish addiction to verse, and the rebuke which his vein received from the apothecary's blue-buskined wife as having been followed by similar treatment on the part of others, I am inclined to believe that while thus devouring, along with his young friend, the stories of Italian romance, he essayed, from time to time, to weave some of their materials into rhyme; — nay, that he must have made at least one rather serious effort of this kind, as early as the date of these rambles to the Salisbury Crags. I have found among his mother's papers a copy of verses, headed, "*Lines to Mr. Walter Scott — on reading his poem of Guiscard and Matilda, inscribed to Miss Keith of Ravelston.*" There is no date; but I conceive the lines bear internal evidence of having been written when he was very young — not, I should suppose, above fourteen or fifteen at most. I think it also certain that the writer was a woman; and have almost as little doubt that they came from the pen of his old admirer, Mrs. Cockburn. They are as follows: —

> " If such the accents of thy early youth
>   When playful fancy holds the place of truth ;
>   If so divinely sweet thy numbers flow,
>   And thy young heart melts with such tender woe ;

[1] See Strang's *Germany in 1831*, vol. i. p. 265.

What praise, what admiration shall be thine,
When sense mature with science shall combine
To raise thy genius, and thy taste refine !

" Go on, dear youth, the glorious path pursue
Which bounteous Nature kindly smooths for you ;
Go, bid the seeds her hand hath sown arise,
By timely culture, to their native skies ;
Go, and employ the poet's heavenly art,
Not merely to delight, but mend the heart.
Than other poets happier mayst thou prove,
More blest in friendship, fortunate in love,
Whilst Fame, who longs to make true merit known,
Impatient waits, to claim thee as her own.

"Scorning the yoke of prejudice and pride,
Thy tender mind let truth and reason guide ;
Let meek humility thy steps attend,
And firm integrity, youth's surest friend.
So peace and honor all thy hours shall bless,
And conscious rectitude each joy increase ;
A nobler meed be thine than empty praise —
Heaven shall approve thy life, and Keith thy lays." [1]

At the period to which I refer these verses, Scott's
parents still continued to have some expectations of curing his lameness, and Mr. Irving remembers to have
often assisted in applying the electrical apparatus, on
which for a considerable time they principally rested their
hopes. There is an allusion to these experiments in Scott's
autobiographical fragment, but I have found a fuller
notice on the margin of his copy of the Guide to Health,
Beauty, Riches, and Longevity, as Captain Grose chose
to entitle an amusing collection of quack advertisements.

"The celebrated Dr. Graham," says the annotator,
"was an empiric of some genius and great assurance. In

[1] [Miss Fleming, in her contribution to Dr. John Brown's memorial of
her sister Marjorie, says that these verses were written by her aunt, Mrs.
Keir, after meeting the boy poet at Ravelston. Another aunt was the
wife of Scott's kinsman, Mr. William Keith of Corstorphine Hill, and it
was at her house, 1, North Charlotte Street, that Sir Walter came to know
familiarly her delightful little niece, during her long visits to Edinburgh.
These ladies and Mrs. Fleming were the daughters of Dr. James Rae. —
See Marjorie Fleming.]

fact, he had a dash of madness in his composition. He had a fine electrical apparatus, and used it with skill. I myself, amongst others, was subjected to a course of electricity under his charge. I remember seeing the old Earl of Hopetoun seated in a large armchair, and hung round with a collar, and a belt of magnets, like an Indian chief. After this, growing quite wild, Graham set up his *Temple of Health*, and lectured on *the Celestial Bed*. He attempted a course of these lectures at Edinburgh, and as the Magistrates refused to let him do so, he libelled them in a series of advertisements, the flights of which were infinitely more absurd and exalted than those which Grose has collected. In one tirade (long in my possession), he declared that ' he looked down upon them ' (the Magistrates) ' as the sun in his meridian glory looks down on the poor, feeble, stinking glimmer of an expiring farthing candle, or as G— himself, in the plenitude of his omnipotence, may regard the insolent bouncings of a few refractory maggots in a rotten cheese.' Graham was a good-looking man; he used to come to the Greyfriars' Church in a suit of white and silver, with a chapeau-bras, and his hair marvellously dressed into a sort of double toupee, which divided upon his head like the two tops of Parnassus. Mrs. Macaulay, the historianess, married his brother. Lady Hamilton is said to have first enacted his Goddess of Health, being at this time a *fille de joie* of great celebrity.[1] The Temple of Health dwindled into a sort of obscene *hell*, or gambling house. In a quarrel which took place there, a poor young man was run into the bowels with a red-hot poker, of which injury he died. The mob vented their fury on the house, and the Magistrates, somewhat of the latest, shut up the exhibition. A quantity of glass and crystal trumpery, the remains of the splendid apparatus, was sold on the South Bridge for next to nothing. Graham's

---

[1] Lord Nelson's connection with this lady will preserve her celebrity. In Kay's *Edinburgh Portraits* the reader will find more about Dr. Graham.

next receipt was *the earth-bath*, with which he wrought some cures; but that also failing, he was, I believe, literally starved to death."

Graham's earth-bath, too, was, I understand, tried upon Scott, but his was not one of the cases, if any such there were, in which it worked a cure. He, however, improved about this time greatly in his general health and strength, and Mr. Irving, in accordance with the statement in the Memoir, assures me that while attending the early classes at the College the young friends extended their walks, so as to visit in succession all the old castles within eight or ten miles of Edinburgh. "Sir Walter," he says, "was specially fond of Rosslyn. We frequently walked thither before breakfast — after breakfasting there, walked all down the river side to Lasswade — and thence home to town before dinner. He used generally to rest one hand upon my shoulder when we walked together, and leaned with the other on a stout stick."

The love of picturesque scenery, and especially of feudal castles, with which the vicinity of Edinburgh is plentifully garnished, awoke, as the Memoir tells us, the desire of being able to use the pencil. Mr. Irving says — "I attended one summer a class of drawing along with him, but although both fond of it, we found it took up so much time that we gave this up before we had made much progress." In one of his later diaries, Scott himself gives the following more particular account of this matter: —

"I took lessons of oil-painting in youth from a little Jew animalcule — a smouch called Burrell — a clever, sensible creature though. But I could make no progress either in painting or drawing. Nature denied me the correctness of eye and neatness of hand. Yet I was very desirous to be a draughtsman at least — and labored harder to attain that point than at any other in my recollection to which I did not make some approaches. Bur-

rell was not useless to me altogether neither. He was
a Prussian, and I got from him many a long story of the
battles of Frederick, in whose armies his father had been
a commissary, or perhaps a spy. I remember his picturesque account of seeing a party of the *black hussars*
bringing in some forage carts which they had taken from
a body of the Cossacks, whom he described as lying on
the top of the carts of hay mortally wounded, and, like
the dying gladiator, eyeing their own blood as it ran
down through the straw."

A year or two later Scott renewed his attempt. "I
afterwards," he says, "took lessons from Walker, whom
we used to call *Blue Beard*. He was one of the most
conceited persons in the world, but a good teacher; one
of the ugliest countenances he had that need be exhibited
— enough, as we say, to *spean weans*. The man was
always extremely precise in the quality of everything
about him; his dress, accommodations, and everything
else. He became insolvent, poor man, and, for some
reason or other, I attended the meeting of those concerned in his affairs. Instead of ordinary accommodations for writing, each of the persons present was equipped
with a large sheet of drawing-paper and a swan's quill.
It was mournfully ridiculous enough. Skirving made
an admirable likeness of Walker; not a single scar or
mark of the small-pox, which seamed his countenance, but
the too accurate brother of the brush had faithfully laid
it down in longitude and latitude. Poor Walker destroyed it (being in crayons) rather than let the caricature of his ugliness appear at the sale of his effects. I
did learn myself to take some vile views from nature.
When Will Clerk and I lived very much together, I used
sometimes to make them under his instruction. He to
whom, as to all his family, art is a familiar attribute,
wondered at me as a Newfoundland dog would at a grey-
hound which showed fear of the water." [1]

[1] [See *Journal*, vol. i. pp 137–139.]

Notwithstanding all that Scott says about the total failure of his attempts in the art of the pencil, I presume few will doubt that they proved very useful to him afterwards; from them it is natural to suppose he caught the habit of analyzing, with some approach at least to accuracy, the scenes over which his eye might have continued to wander with the vague sense of delight. I may add that a longer and more successful practice of the crayon might, I cannot but think, have proved the reverse of serviceable to him as a future painter with the pen. He might have contracted the habit of copying from pictures rather than from nature itself; and we should thus have lost that which constitutes the very highest charm in his delineations of scenery, namely, that the effect is produced by the selection of a few striking features, arranged with a light, unconscious grace, neither too much nor too little — equally remote from the barren generalizations of a former age, and the dull, servile fidelity with which so many inferior writers of our time fill in both background and foreground, having no more notion of the perspective of genius than Chinese paper-stainers have of that of the atmosphere, and producing in fact not descriptions but inventories.

The illness which he alludes to in his Memoir, as interrupting for a considerable period his attendance on the Latin and Greek classes in Edinburgh College, is spoken of more largely in one of his prefaces.[1] It arose from the bursting of a blood-vessel in the lower bowels; and I have heard him say that his uncle, Dr. Rutherford, considered his recovery from it as little less than miraculous. His sweet temper and calm courage were no doubt important elements of safety. He submitted without a murmur to the severe discipline prescribed by his affectionate physician, and found consolation in poetry, romance, and the enthusiasm of young friendship. Day after day John Irving relieved his mother and sister in

[1] See Preface to *Waverley*, 1829.

then attendance upon him. The bed on which he lay was piled with a constant succession of works of imagination, and sad realities were forgotten amidst the brilliant day-dreams of genius drinking unwearied from the eternal fountains of Spenser and Shakespeare. Chess was recommended as a relief to these unintermitted, though desultory studies; and he engaged eagerly in the game which had found favor with so many of his Paladins. Mr. Irving remembers playing it with him hour after hour, in very cold weather, when, the windows being kept open as a part of the medical treatment, nothing but youthful nerves and spirit could have persevered. But Scott did not pursue the science of chess after his boyhood. He used to say that it was a shame to throw away upon mastering a mere game, however ingenious, the time which would suffice for the acquisition of a new language. "Surely," he said, "chess-playing is a sad waste of brains."

His recovery was completed by another visit to Roxburghshire. Captain Robert Scott, who had been so kind to the sickly infant at Bath, finally retired about this time from his profession, and purchased the elegant villa of Rosebank, on the Tweed, a little below Kelso. Here Walter now took up his quarters, and here, during all the rest of his youth, he found, whenever he chose, a second home, in many respects more agreeable than his own. His uncle, as letters to be subsequently quoted will show, had nothing of his father's coldness for polite letters, but entered into all his favorite pursuits with keen sympathy, and was consulted, from this time forth, upon all his juvenile essays, both in prose and verse.

He does not seem to have resumed attendance at College during the session of 1785-86; so that the Latin and Greek classes, with that of Logic, were the only ones he had passed through previous to the signing of his indentures as an apprentice to his father. The Memoir mentions the ethical course of Dugald Stewart, as if he had gone immediately from the logical professor (Mr. Bruce) to that eminent lecturer; but he, in fact, attended Mr. Stewart four years afterwards, when beginning to consider himself as finally destined for the Bar.

I shall only add to what he sets down on the subject of his early academical studies, that in this, as in almost every case, he appears to have underrated his own attainments. He had, indeed, no pretensions to the name of an extensive, far less of an accurate, Latin scholar; but he could read, I believe, any Latin author, of any age, so as to catch without difficulty his meaning; and although his favorite Latin poet, as well as historian, in later days, was Buchanan, he had preserved, or subsequently acquired, a strong relish for some others of more ancient date. I may mention, in particular, Lucan and Claudian. Of Greek, he does not exaggerate in saying that he had forgotten even the alphabet; for he was puzzled with the words ἀοιδός and ποιητής, which he had occasion to introduce, from some authority on his table, into his Introduction to Popular Poetry, written in April, 1830; and happening to be in the house with him at the time, he sent for me to insert them for him in his MS. Mr. Irving has informed us of the early period at which he enjoyed the real Tasso and Ariosto. I presume he had at least as soon as this enabled himself to read Gil Blas in the original; and, in all probability, we may refer to the same time of his life, or one not much later, his acquisition of as much Spanish as served for the Guerras Civiles de Granada, Lazarillo de Tormes, and, above all, Don Quixote. He read all these languages in after-life with about the same facility. I never but once heard him attempt to speak any of them, and that was when some of the courtiers of Charles X. came to Abbotsford, soon after that unfortunate prince took up his residence for the second time at Holyrood-house. Finding that one or two of these gentlemen could speak no English at all, he made some efforts to amuse them in their own lan-

guage after the champagne had been passing briskly
round the table; and I was amused next morning with
the expression of one of the party, who, alluding to the
sort of reading in which Sir Walter seemed to have
chiefly occupied himself, said, "Mon Dieu! comme il
estropiait, entre deux vins, le Français du bon sire de
Joinville!" Of all these tongues, as of German somewhat later, he acquired as much as was needful for his
own purposes, of which a critical study of any foreign
language made at no time any part. In them he sought
for incidents, and he found images; but for the treasures
of diction he was content to dig on British soil. He had
all he wanted in the old wells of "English undefiled,"
and the still living, though fast shrinking, waters of that
sister idiom which had not always, as he flattered himself, deserved the name of a dialect.

As may be said, I believe, with perfect truth of every
really great man, Scott was self-educated in every branch
of knowledge which he ever turned to account in the
works of his genius — and he has himself told us that his
real studies were those lonely and desultory ones of which
he has given a copy in the third chapter of Waverley,
where the hero is represented as "driving through the
sea of books, like a vessel without pilot or rudder;" that
is to say, obeying nothing but the strong breath of native
inclination: — "He had read, and stored in a memory of
uncommon tenacity, much curious, though ill-arranged and
miscellaneous information. In English literature, he
was master of Shakespeare and Milton, of our earlier dramatic authors, of many picturesque and interesting passages from our old historical chronicles, and was particularly well acquainted with Spenser, Drayton, and other
poets, who have exercised themselves on romantic fiction,
— *of all themes the most fascinating to a youthful imagination, before the passions have roused themselves, and
demand poetry of a more sentimental description.*" I
need not repeat his enumeration of other favorites, Pulci,

the Decameron, Froissart, Brantôme, Delanoue, and the chivalrous and romantic lore of Spain. I have quoted a passage so well known, only for the sake of the striking circumstance by which it marks the very early date of these multifarious studies.

CHAPTER V

1786–1790

In the Minute-books of the Society of Writers to the
Signet appears the following entry: "Edinburgh, 15th
May, 1786. Compeared Walter Scott, and presented
an indenture, dated 31st March last, entered into between
him and Walter Scott, his son, for five years from the
date thereof, under a mutual penalty of £40 sterling."

An inauspicious step this might at first sight appear in
the early history of one so strongly predisposed for pursuits wide as the antipodes asunder from the dry technicalities of conveyancing; but he himself, I believe, was
never heard, in his mature age, to express any regret that
it should have been taken; and I am convinced for my
part that it was a fortunate one. It prevented him,
indeed, from passing with the usual regularity through a
long course of Scotch metaphysics; but I extremely doubt
whether any discipline could ever have led him to derive
either pleasure or profit from studies of that order. His
apprenticeship left him time enough, as we shall find, for
continuing his application to the stores of poetry and
romance, and those old chroniclers, who to the end were
his darling historians. Indeed, if he had wanted any
new stimulus, the necessity of devoting certain hours of
every day to a routine of drudgery, however it might
have operated on a spirit more prone to earth, must have

tended to quicken his appetite for "the sweet bread eaten in secret." But the duties which he had now to fulfil were, in various ways, directly and positively beneficial to the development both of his genius and his character. It was in the discharge of his functions as a Writer's Apprentice that he first penetrated into the Highlands, and formed those friendships among the surviving heroes of 1745, which laid the foundation for one great class of his works. Even the less attractive parts of his new vocation were calculated to give him a more complete insight into the smaller workings of poor human nature than can ever perhaps be gathered from the experience of the legal profession in its higher walk; — the etiquette of the bar in Scotland, as in England, being averse to personal intercourse between the advocate and his client. But finally, and I will say chiefly, it was to this prosaic discipline that he owed those habits of steady, sober diligence, which few imaginative authors had ever before exemplified — and which, unless thus beaten into his composition at a ductile stage, even he, in all probability, could never have carried into the almost professional exercise of some of the highest and most delicate faculties of the human mind. He speaks, in not the least remarkable passage of the preceding Memoir, as if constitutional indolence had been his portion in common with all the members of his father's family. When Gifford, in a dispute with Jacob Bryant, quoted Doctor Johnson's own confession that he knew little Greek, Bryant answered, "Yes, young man; but how shall we know what Johnson would have called much Greek?" and Gifford has recorded the deep impression which this hint left on his own mind. What Scott would have called constitutional diligence, I know not; but surely, if indolence of any kind had been inherent in his nature, even the triumph of Socrates was not more signal than his.

It will be, by some of my friends, considered as trivial to remark on such a circumstance — but the reader who

is unacquainted with the professional habits of the Scotch
lawyers may as well be told that the Writer's Apprentice receives a certain allowance in money for every page
he transcribes; and that, as in those days the greater
part of the business, even of the supreme courts, was
carried on by means of written papers, a ready penman,
in a well-employed chamber, could earn in this way
enough, at all events, to make a handsome addition to
the pocket-money which was likely to be thought suitable
for a youth of fifteen by such a man as the elder Scott.
The allowance being, I believe, threepence for every page
containing a certain fixed number of words, when Walter
had finished, as he tells us he occasionally did, 120 pages
within twenty-four hours, his fee would amount to thirty
shillings; and in his early letters I find him more than
once congratulating himself on having been, by some such
exertion, enabled to purchase a book, or a coin, otherwise
beyond his reach.   A schoolfellow, who was now, like
himself, a Writer's Apprentice, recollects the eagerness
with which he thus made himself master of Evans's Ballads, shortly after their publication; and another of them,
already often referred to, remembers, in particular, his
rapture with Mickle's Cumnor Hall, which first appeared
in that collection.   "After the labors of the day were
over," says Mr. Irving, "we often walked in *the Meadows*" — (a large field intersected by formal alleys of old
trees, adjoining George's Square) — "especially in the
moonlight nights; and he seemed never weary of repeat-
ing the first stanza —

> 'The dews of summer night did fall —
> The Moon, sweet regent of the sky,
> Silvered the walls of Cumnor Hall,
> And many an oak that grew thereby.'"

I have thought it worth while to preserve these reminiscences of his companions at the time, though he has
himself stated the circumstance in his Preface to Kenil-
worth.   "There is a period in youth," he there says,

"when the mere power of numbers has a more strong effect on ear and imagination than in after-life. At this season of immature taste, the author was greatly delighted with the poems of Mickle and Langhorne. The first stanza of Cumnor Hall especially had a peculiar enchantment for his youthful ear — the force of which is not yet (1829) entirely spent." Thus that favorite elegy, after having dwelt on his memory and imagination for forty years, suggested the subject of one of his noblest romances.

It is affirmed by a preceding biographer, on the authority of one of these brother-apprentices, that about this period Scott showed him a MS. poem on the Conquest of Granada, in four books, each amounting to about 400 lines, which, soon after it was finished, he committed to the flames.[1] As he states in his Essay on the Imitation of Popular Poetry, that, for ten years previous to 1796, when his first translation from the German was executed, he had written no verses "except an occasional sonnet to his mistress's eyebrow," I presume this Conquest of Granada, the fruit of his study of the Guerras Civiles, must be assigned to the summer of 1786 — or, making allowance for trivial inaccuracy, to the next year at latest. It was probably composed in imitation of Mickle's Lusiad: — at all events, we have a very distinct statement, that he made no attempts in the manner of the old minstrels, early as his admiration for them had been, until the period of his acquaintance with Bürger. Thus with him, as with most others, genius had hazarded many a random effort ere it discovered the true keynote. Long had

> " Amid the strings his fingers stray'd,
> And an uncertain warbling made,"

before "the measure wild " was caught, and

> " In varying cadence, soft or strong,
> He swept the sounding chords along."

[1] *Life of Scott*, by Mr. Allan, p. 53.

His youthful admiration of Langhorne has been rendered memorable by his own record of his first and only interview with his great predecessor, Robert Burns. Although the letter in which he narrates this incident, addressed to myself in 1827, when I was writing a short biography of that poet, has been often reprinted, it is too important for my present purpose to be omitted here.

"As for Burns," he writes, "I may truly say, *Virgilium vidi tantum*. I was a lad of fifteen in 1786–87, when he came first to Edinburgh, but had sense and feeling enough to be much interested in his poetry, and would have given the world to know him; but I had very little acquaintance with any literary people, and still less with the gentry of the west country, the two sets that he most frequented. Mr. Thomas Grierson was at that time a clerk of my father's. He knew Burns, and promised to ask him to his lodgings to dinner, but had no opportunity to keep his word, otherwise I might have seen more of this distinguished man. As it was, I saw him one day at the late venerable Professor Ferguson's, where there were several gentlemen of literary reputation, among whom I remember the celebrated Mr. Dugald Stewart. Of course we youngsters sat silent, looked, and listened. The only thing I remember which was remarkable in Burns's manner was the effect produced upon him by a print of Bunbury's, representing a soldier lying dead on the snow, his dog sitting in misery on the one side, on the other his widow, with a child in her arms. These lines were written beneath, —

> ' Cold on Canadian hills, or Minden's plain,
> Perhaps that parent wept her soldier slain ;
> Bent o'er her babe, her eye dissolved in dew,
> The big drops, mingling with the milk he drew,
> Gave the sad presage of his future years,
> The child of misery baptized in tears.'

Burns seemed much affected by the print, or rather the ideas which it suggested to his mind. He actually shed tears. He asked whose the lines were, and it chanced that nobody but myself remembered that they occur in a half-forgotten poem of Langhorne's, called by the unpromising title of The Justice of the Peace. I whispered my information to a friend present, who mentioned it to Burns, who rewarded me with a look and a word, which, though of mere civility, I then received, and still recollect, with very great pleasure.

"His person was strong and robust: his manners rustic, not clownish; a sort of dignified plainness and simplicity, which received part of its effect perhaps from one's knowledge of his extraordinary talents. His features are represented in Mr. Nasmyth's picture, but to me it conveys the idea that they are diminished as if seen in perspective. I think his countenance was more massive than it looks in any of the portraits. I would have taken the poet, had I not known what he was, for a very sagacious country farmer of the old Scotch school — *i. e.*, none of your modern agriculturists, who keep laborers for their drudgery, but the *douce gudeman* who held his own plough. There was a strong expression of sense and shrewdness in all his lineaments; the eye alone, I think, indicated the poetical character and temperament. It was large, and of a dark cast, and glowed (I say literally *glowed*) when he spoke with feeling or interest. I never saw such another eye in a human head, though I have seen the most distinguished men in my time. His conversation expressed perfect self-confidence, without the slightest presumption. Among the men who were the most learned of their time and country he expressed himself with perfect firmness, but without the least intrusive forwardness; and when he differed in opinion, he did not hesitate to express it firmly, yet at the same time with modesty. I do not remember any part of his conversation distinctly enough to be quoted, nor did I ever see him again, except in the street, where he did not recognize me, as I could not expect he should. He was much caressed in Edinburgh, but (considering what literary emoluments have been since his day) the efforts made for his relief were extremely trifling.

"I remember on this occasion I mention, I thought Burns's acquaintance with English poetry was rather limited, and also, that having twenty times the abilities of Allan Ramsay and of Fergusson, he talked of them with too much humility as his models; there was doubtless national predilection in his estimate."

I need not remark on the extent of knowledge and justness of taste exemplified in this early measurement of Burns, both as a student of English literature and as a Scottish poet. The print, over which Scott saw Burns shed tears, is still in the possession of Dr. Ferguson's family, and I had often heard him tell the story, in the room where the precious relic hangs, before I requested him to set it down in writing — how little anticipating the use to which I should ultimately apply it![1]

His intimacy with Adam (now Sir Adam) Ferguson was thus his first means of introduction to the higher literary society of Edinburgh; and it was very probably to that connection that he owed, among the rest, his acquaintance with the blind poet Blacklock, whom Johnson, twelve years earlier, "beheld with reverence." We have seen, however, that the venerable author of Douglas was a friend of his own parents, and had noticed him even in his infancy at Bath. John Home now inhabited a villa at no great distance from Edinburgh, and there, all through his young days, Scott was a frequent guest. Nor must it be forgotten that his uncle, Dr. Rutherford, inherited much of the general accomplishments, as well as the professional reputation of his father — and that it was beneath that roof he saw, several years before this, Dr. Cartwright, then in the enjoyment of some fame as a poet. In this family, indeed, he had more than one

[1] ["Long life to thy fame and peace to thy soul, Rob Burns! When I want to express a sentiment which I feel strongly, I find the phrase in Shakespeare — or thee." — *Journal*, December 11, 1826.]

kind and strenuous encourager of his early literary tastes, as will be shown abundantly when we reach certain relics of his correspondence with his mother's sister. Dr. Rutherford's good-natured remonstrances with him, as a boy, for reading at breakfast, are well remembered, and will remind my reader of a similar trait in the juvenile manners both of Burns and Byron; nor was this habit entirely laid aside even in Scott's advanced age.

If he is quite accurate in referring his first acquaintance with the Highlands to his fifteenth year, this incident also belongs to the first season of his apprenticeship. His father had, among a rather numerous list of Highland clients, Alexander Stewart of Invernahyle, an enthusiastic Jacobite, who had survived to recount, in secure and vigorous old age, his active experiences in the insurrections both of 1715 and 1745. He had, it appears, attracted Walter's attention and admiration at a very early date; for he speaks of having "seen him in arms" and heard him "exult in the prospect of drawing his claymore once more before he died," when Paul Jones threatened a descent on Edinburgh; which transaction occurred in September, 1779. Invernahyle, as Scott adds, was the only person who seemed to have retained possession of his cool senses at the period of that disgraceful alarm, and offered the magistrates to collect as many Highlanders as would suffice for cutting off any part of the pirate's crew that might venture, in quest of plunder, into a city full of high houses and narrow lanes, and every way well calculated for defence. The eager delight with which the young apprentice now listened to the tales of this fine old man's early days produced an invitation to his residence among the mountains; and to this excursion he probably devoted the few weeks of an autumnal vacation — whether in 1786 or 1787 it is of no great consequence to ascertain.

In the Introduction to one of his Novels he has preserved a vivid picture of his sensations when the vale of

Perth first burst on his view, in the course of his progress
to Invernahyle, and the description has made classical
ground of the *Wicks of Baiglie*, the spot from which
that beautiful landscape was surveyed. "Childish wonder, indeed," he says, "was an ingredient in my delight,
for I was not above fifteen years old, and as this had
been the first excursion which I was permitted to make
on a pony of my own, I also experienced the glow of independence, mingled with that degree of anxiety which
the most conceited boy feels when he is first abandoned
to his own undirected counsels. I recollect pulling up
the reins without meaning to do so, and gazing on the
scene before me as if I had been afraid it would shift,
like those in a theatre, before I could distinctly observe
its different parts, or convince myself that what I saw
was real. Since that hour the recollection of that inimitable landscape has possessed the strongest influence over
my mind, and retained its place as a memorable thing,
while much that was influential on my own fortunes has
fled from my recollection." So speaks the poet; and
who will not recognize his habitual modesty in thus
undervaluing, as uninfluential in comparison with some
affair of worldly business, the ineffaceable impression
thus stamped on the glowing imagination of his boyhood?

I need not quote the numerous passages scattered over
his writings, both early and late, in which he dwells with
fond affection on the chivalrous character of Invernahyle
— the delight with which he heard the veteran describe
his broadsword duel with Rob Roy — his campaigns with
Mar and Charles Edward — and his long seclusion (as
pictured in the story of Bradwardine) within a rocky cave
situated not far from his own house, while it was garri-
soned by a party of English soldiers, after the battle of
Culloden. Here, too, still survived the trusty henchman
who had attended the chieftain in many a bloody field
and perilous escape, the same "grim-looking old High-
lander" who was in the act of cutting down Colonel

Whitefoord with his Lochaber axe at Prestonpans when his master arrested the blow — an incident to which Invernahyle owed his life, and we are indebted for another of the most striking pages in Waverley.

I have often heard Scott mention some curious particulars of his first visit to the remote fastness of one of these Highland friends; but whether he told the story of Invernahyle, or of one of his own relations of the Clan Campbell, I do not recollect; I rather think the latter was the case. On reaching the brow of a bleak eminence overhanging the primitive tower and its tiny patch of cultivated ground, he found his host and three sons, and perhaps half-a-dozen attendant *gillies*, all stretched half asleep in their tartans upon the heath, with guns and dogs, and a profusion of game about them; while in the courtyard, far below, appeared a company of women actively engaged in loading a cart with manure. The stranger was not a little astonished when he discovered, on descending from the height, that among these industrious females were the laird's own lady, and two or three of her daughters; but they seemed quite unconscious of having been detected in an occupation unsuitable to their rank — retired presently to their "bowers," and when they reappeared in other dresses, retained no traces of their morning's work, except complexions glowing with a radiant freshness, for one evening of which many a high-bred beauty would have bartered half her diamonds. He found the young ladies not ill informed, and exceedingly agreeable; and the song and the dance seemed to form the invariable termination of their busy days. I must not forget his admiration at the principal article of this laird's first course; namely, a gigantic *haggis*, borne into the hall in a wicker basket by two half-naked Celts, while the piper strutted fiercely behind them, blowing a tempest of dissonance.

These Highland visits were repeated almost every summer for several successive years, and perhaps even

the first of them was in some degree connected with his
professional business. At all events, it was to his allotted task of enforcing the execution of a legal instrument
against some Maclarens, refractory tenants of Stewart
of Appin, brother-in-law to Invernahyle, that Scott owed
his introduction to the scenery of The Lady of the Lake.
"An escort of a sergeant and six men," he says, "was
obtained from a Highland regiment lying in Stirling,
and the author, then a Writer's Apprentice, equivalent to
the honorable situation of an attorney's clerk, was invested with the superintendence of the expedition, with
directions to see that the messenger discharged his duty
fully, and that the gallant sergeant did not exceed his
part by committing violence or plunder. And thus it
happened, oddly enough, that the author first entered
the romantic scenery of Loch Katrine, of which he may
perhaps say he has somewhat extended the reputation,
riding in all the dignity of danger, with a front and rear
guard, and loaded arms. The sergeant was absolutely a
Highland Sergeant Kite, full of stories of Rob Roy and
of himself, and a very good companion. We experienced
no interruption whatever, and when we came to Invernenty,
found the house deserted. We took up our quarters for
the night, and used some of the victuals which we found
there. The Maclarens, who probably had never thought
of any serious opposition, went to America, where, having had some slight share in removing them from their
paupera regna, I sincerely hope they prospered." [1]

That he entered with ready zeal into such professional
business as inferred Highland expeditions with comrades
who had known Rob Roy, no one will think strange; but
more than one of his biographers allege that in the ordinary indoor fagging of the chamber in George's Square,
he was always an unwilling, and rarely an efficient assistant. Their addition, that he often played chess with
one of his companions in the office, and had to conceal

[1] Introduction to *Rob Roy*.

the board with precipitation when the old gentleman's footsteps were heard on the staircase, is, I do not doubt, true; and we may remember along with it his own in-sinuation that his father was sometimes poring in his secret nook over Spottiswoode or Wodrow, when his ap-prentices supposed him to be deep in Dirleton's Doubts, or Stair's decisions. But the Memoir of 1808, so can-did — indeed more than candid — as to many juvenile irregularities, contains no confession that supports the broad assertion to which I have alluded; nor can I easily believe, that with his affection for his father, and that sense of duty which seems to have been inherent in his character, and, lastly, with the evidence of a most severe training in industry which the habits of his after-life presented, it is at all deserving of serious acceptation. His mere handwriting, indeed, continued, during the whole of his prime, to afford most striking and irresistible proof how completely he must have submitted himself for some very considerable period to the mechanical disci-pline of his father's office. It spoke to months after months of this humble toil, as distinctly as the illegible scrawl of Lord Byron did to his self-mastership from the hour that he left Harrow. There are some little techni-cal tricks, such as no gentleman who has not been sub-jected to a similar regimen ever can fall into, which he practised invariably while composing his poetry, which appear not unfrequently on the MSS. of his best novels, and which now and then dropt instinctively from his pen, even in the private letters and diaries of his closing years. I allude particularly to a sort of flourish at the bottom of the page, originally, I presume, adopted in engrossing as a safeguard against the intrusion of a forged line between the legitimate text and the attesting signa-ture. He was quite sensible that this ornament might as well be dispensed with; and his family often heard him mutter, after involuntarily performing it, "There goes the old shop again!"

I dwell on this matter because it was always his favorite tenet, in contradiction to what he called the cant of sonneteers, that there is no necessary connection between genius and an aversion or contempt for any of the common duties of life; he thought, on the contrary, that to spend some fair portion of every day in any matter of fact occupation is good for the higher faculties themselves in the upshot. In a word, from beginning to end, he piqued himself on being *a man of business;* and did — with one sad and memorable ' exception — whatever the ordinary course of things threw in his way, in exactly the businesslike fashion which might have been expected from the son of a thoroughbred old Clerk to the Signet, who had never deserted his father's profession.

In the winter of 1788, however, his apprentice habits were exposed to a new danger; and from that date I believe them to have undergone a considerable change. He was then sent to attend the lectures of the Professor of Civil Law in the University, this course forming part of the usual professional education of Writers to the Signet, as well as of Advocates. For some time his companions, when in Edinburgh, had been chiefly, almost solely, his brother-apprentices and the clerks in his father's office. He had latterly seen comparatively little even of the better of his old High School friends, such as Ferguson and Irving — for though both of these also were writer's apprentices, they had been indentured to other masters, and each had naturally formed new intimacies within his own chamber. The Civil Law class brought him again into daily contact with both Irving and Ferguson, as well as others of his earlier acquaintance of the higher ranks; but it also led him into the society of some young gentlemen previously unknown to him, who had from the outset been destined for the Bar, and whose conversation, tinctured with certain prejudices natural to scions of what he calls in Redgauntlet *the Scottish noblesse de la robe*, soon banished from his mind every thought of ultimately adhering to the secondary branch of the law. He found these future barristers cultivating general literature, without the least apprehension that such elegant pursuits could be regarded by any one as interfering with the proper studies of their professional career; justly believing, on the contrary, that for the higher class of forensic exertion some acquaintance with almost every branch of science and letters is a necessary preparative. He contrasted their liberal aspirations, and the encouragement which these received in their domestic circles, with the narrower views which predominated in his own home; and resolved to gratify his ambition by adopting a most precarious walk in life, instead of adhering to that in which he might have counted with perfect security on the early attainment of pecuniary independence. This resolution appears to have been foreseen by his father, long before it was announced in terms; and the handsome manner in which the old gentleman conducted himself upon the occasion is remembered with dutiful gratitude in the preceding Autobiography.

The most important of these new alliances was the intimate friendship which he now formed with Mr. John Irving's near relation, William Clerk of Eldin, of whose powerful talents and extensive accomplishments we shall hereafter meet with many enthusiastic notices. It was in company with this gentleman that he entered the debating societies described in his Memoir; through him he soon became linked in the closest intimacy with George Cranstoun (now Lord Corehouse), George Abercromby (now Lord Abercromby), John James Edmonstone [1] of Newton (whose mother was sister of Sir Ralph Abercromby), Patrick Murray of Simprim, Sir Patrick Murray of Ochtertyre, and a group of other young men, all high in birth and connection, and all remarkable in early life for the qualities which afterwards led them to emi-

[1] Mr. Edmonstone died 19th April, 1840. — (1848.)

nent station, or adorned it. The introduction to their
several families is alluded to by Scott as having opened
to him abundantly certain advantages, which no one could
have been more qualified to improve, but from which he
had hitherto been in great measure debarred in consequence of the retired habits of his parents.

Mr. Clerk says that he had been struck from the first
day he entered the Civil Law class-room with something
odd and remarkable in Scott's appearance; what this
something was he cannot now recall, but he remembers
telling his companion some time afterwards that he
thought he looked like a *hautboy player*. Scott was
amused with this notion, as he had never touched a musical instrument of any kind; but I fancy his friend had
been watching a certain noticeable but altogether indescribable play of the upper lip when in an abstracted
mood. He rallied Walter, he says, during one of their
first evening walks together, on the slovenliness of his
dress: he wore a pair of corduroy breeches, much glazed
by the rubbing of his staff, which he immediately flourished — and said, "They be good enough for drinking in
— let us go and have some oysters in the Covenant
Close."

Convivial habits were then indulged among the young
men of Edinburgh, whether students of law, solicitors,
or barristers, to an extent now happily unknown; and
this anecdote recalls some striking hints on that subject which occur in Scott's brief Autobiography. That
he partook profusely in the juvenile bacchanalia of that
day, and continued to take a plentiful share in such jol-
lities down to the time of his marriage, are facts worthy
of being distinctly stated; for no man in mature life was
more habitually averse to every sort of intemperance.
He could, when I first knew him, swallow a great quantity of wine without being at all visibly disordered by it;
but nothing short of some very particular occasion could
ever induce him to put this strength of head to a trial;

and I have heard him many times utter words which no one in the days of his youthful temptation can be the worse for remembering: — "Depend upon it, of all vices, drinking is the most incompatible with greatness."

The liveliness of his conversation — the strange variety of his knowledge — and above all, perhaps, the portentous tenacity of his memory — riveted more and more Clerk's attention, and commanded the wonder of all his new allies; but of these extraordinary gifts Scott himself appeared to be little conscious; or at least he impressed them all as attaching infinitely greater consequence — (exactly as had been the case with him in the days of the Cowgate Port and the kittle nine steps) — to feats of personal agility and prowess. William Clerk's brother, James, a midshipman in the navy, happened to come home from a cruise in the Mediterranean shortly after this acquaintance began, and Scott and the sailor became almost at sight "sworn brothers." In order to complete his time under the late Sir Alexander Cochrane, who was then on the Leith station, James Clerk obtained the command of a lugger, and the young friends often made little excursions to sea with him. "The first time Scott dined on board," says William Clerk, "we met before embarking at a tavern in Leith — it was a large party, mostly midshipmen, and strangers to him, and our host introducing his landsmen guests said, ' My brother you know, gentlemen; as for Mr. Scott, mayhap you may take him for a poor lamiter, but he is the first to begin a row, and the last to end it;' which eulogium he confirmed with some of the expletives of Tom Pipes."[1] When, many years afterwards, Clerk read The Pirate, he was startled by the resurrection of a hundred traits of the table-talk of this lugger; but the author has since

---

[1] "Dinna steer him," says Hobbie Elliot; " ye may think Elshie's but a lamiter, but I warrant ye, grippie for grippie, he 'll gar the blue blood spin frae your nails — his hand 's like a smith's vice." — *Black Dwarf*, chap. xvii.

traced some of the most striking passages in that novel
to his recollection of the almost childish period when he
hung on his own brother Robert's stories about Rodney's
battles and the haunted *keys* of the West Indies.

One morning Scott called on Clerk, and, exhibiting
his stick all cut and marked, told him he had been attacked in the streets the night before by three fellows,
against whom he had defended himself for an hour.
"By Shrewsbury clock?" said his friend. "No," said
Scott, smiling, "by the Tron." But thenceforth, adds
Mr. Clerk, and for twenty years after, he called his
walking stick by the name of "Shrewsbury."

With these comrades Scott now resumed, and pushed
to a much greater extent, his early habits of wandering
over the country in quest of castles and other remains of
antiquity, his passion for which derived a new impulse
from the conversation of the celebrated John Clerk of
Eldin,[1] the father of his friend. William Clerk well remembers his father telling a story which was introduced
in due time in The Antiquary. While he was visiting
his grandfather, Sir John Clerk, at Dumcrieff, in Dum-
fries-shire, many years before this time, the old Baronet
carried some English virtuosos to see a supposed Roman
camp; and on his exclaiming at a particular spot, "This
I take to have been the Prætorium," a herdsman who
stood by answered, "Prætorium here Prætorium there,
I made it wi' a flaughter spade."[2] Many traits of the
elder Clerk were, his son has no doubt, embroidered on
the character of George Constable in the composition of
Jonathan Oldbuck. The old gentleman's enthusiasm
for antiquities was often played on by these young
friends, but more effectually by his eldest son, John
Clerk (Lord Eldin), who, having a great genius for art,
used to amuse himself with manufacturing mutilated
heads, which, after being buried for a convenient time in

[1] Author of the famous Essay on dividing the Line in Sea-fights.
[2] Compare *The Antiquary*, chap. iv.

the ground, were accidentally discovered in some fortunate hour, and received by the laird with great honor as
valuable accessions to his museum.[1]

On a fishing excursion to a loch near Howgate, among
the Moorfoot Hills, Scott, Clerk, Irving, and Abercromby spent the night at a little public-house kept by
one Mrs. Margaret Dods. When St. Ronan's Well was
published, Clerk, meeting Scott in the street, observed,
"That's an odd name; surely I have met with it somewhere before." Scott smiled, said, "Don't you remember Howgate?" and passed on. The name alone, however, was taken from the Howgate hostess.

At one of their drinking bouts of those days William
Clerk, Sir P. Murray, Edmonstone, and Abercromby,
being of the party, the sitting was prolonged to a very
late hour, and Scott fell asleep. When he awoke, his
friends succeeded in convincing him that he had sung a
song in the course of the evening, and sung it extremely
well. How must these gentlemen have chuckled when
they read Frank Osbaldistone's account of his revels in
the old hall! "It has even been reported by maligners
that I sung a song while under this vinous influence; but
as I remember nothing of it, and never attempted to
turn a tune in all my life, either before or since, I would
willingly hope there is no actual foundation for the calumny."[2]

On one of his first long walks with Clerk and others
of the same set, their pace, being about four miles an
hour, was found rather too much for Scott, and he offered
to contract for three, which measure was thenceforth
considered as the legal one. At this rate they often continued to wander from five in the morning till eight in

---

[1] The most remarkable of these *antique heads* was so highly appreciated by another distinguished connoisseur, the late Earl of Buchan, that
he carried it off from Mr. Clerk's museum, and presented it to the Scottish Society of Antiquaries — in whose collection, no doubt, it may still be
admired.

[2] *Rob Roy*, chap. xii.

the evening, halting for such refreshment at mid-day as any village alehouse might afford. On many occasions, however, they had stretched so far into the country, that they were obliged to be absent from home all night; and though great was the alarm which the first occurrence of this sort created in George's Square, the family soon got accustomed to such things, and little notice was taken, even though Walter remained away for the better part of a week. I have heard him laugh heartily over the recollections of one protracted excursion, towards the close of which the party found themselves a long day's walk — thirty miles, I think — from Edinburgh, without a single sixpence left among them. "We were put to our shifts," said he; "but we asked every now and then at a cottage door for a drink of water; and one or two of the good-wives, observing our worn-out looks, brought forth milk in place of water — so with that, and hips and haws, we came in little the worse." His father met him with some impatient questions as to what he had been living on so long, for the old man well knew how scantily his pocket was supplied. "Pretty much like the young ravens," answered he; "I only wished I had been as good a player on the flute as poor George Primrose in The Vicar of Wakefield. If I had his art I should like nothing better than to tramp like him from cottage to cottage over the world." — "I doubt," said the grave Clerk to the Signet, "I greatly doubt, sir, you were born for nae better than a *gangrel scrape gut.*" Some allusions to reproaches of this kind occur in the Memoir; and we shall find others in letters subsequent to his admission at the Bar.[1]

The debating club formed among these young friends

---

[1] After the cautious father had had further opportunity of observing his son's proceedings, his wife happened one night to express some anxiety on the protracted absence of Walter and his brother Thomas. "My dear Annie," said the old man, "Tom is with Walter this time; and have you not yet perceived that wherever Walter goes, he is pretty sure to find his bread buttered on both sides?" — *From Mrs. Thomas Scott.* — (1839.)

at this era of their studies was called *The Literary
Society;* and is not to be confounded with the more celebrated Speculative Society, which Scott did not join for
two years later. At *The Literary* he spoke frequently,
and very amusingly and sensibly, but was not at all
numbered among the most brilliant members. He had
a world of knowledge to produce; but he had not acquired the art of arranging it to the best advantage in
a continued address; nor, indeed, did he ever, I think,
except under the influence of strong personal feeling,
even when years and fame had given him full confidence
in himself, exhibit upon any occasion the powers of oral
eloquence. His antiquarian information, however, supplied many an interesting feature in these evenings of
discussion. He had already dabbled in Anglo-Saxon
and the Norse Sagas: in his Essay on Imitations of
Popular Poetry, he alludes to these studies as having
facilitated his acquisition of German: — But he was deep
especially in Fordun and Wyntoun, and all the Scotch
chronicles; and his friends rewarded him by the honorable title of *Duns Scotus.*

A smaller society, formed with less ambitious views,
originated in a ride to Pennycuik, the seat of the head
of Mr. Clerk's family, whose elegant hospitalities are
recorded in the Memoir. This was called, by way of
excellence, *The Club*, and I believe it is continued under
the same name to this day. Here, too, Walter had his
sobriquet; and — his corduroy breeches, I presume, not
being as yet worn out — it was *Colonel Grogg.*[1]

[1] " The members of *The Club* used to meet on Friday evenings in a room
in Carrubber's Close, from which some of them usually adjourned to sup at
an oyster tavern in the same neighborhood. In after-life, those of them
who chanced to be in Edinburgh dined together twice every year, at the
close of the winter and summer sessions of the Law Courts; and during
thirty years, Sir Walter was very rarely absent on these occasions. It
was also a rule, that when any member received an appointment or promotion, he should give a dinner to his old associates ; and they had accordingly two such dinners from him — one when he became Sheriff of Selkirkshire, and another when he was named Clerk of Session. The original

Meantime he had not broken up his connection with
Rosebank; he appears to have spent several weeks in the
autumn, both of 1788 and 1789, under his uncle's roof;
and it was, I think, of his journey thither, in the last
named year, that he used to tell an anecdote, which I
shall here set down — how shorn, alas, of all the acces-
sories that gave it life when he recited it. Calling, before he set out, on one of the ancient spinsters of his
family, to inquire if she had any message for Kelso, she
retired, and presently placed in his hands a packet of
some bulk and weight, which required, she said, very
particular attention. He took it without examining the
address, and carried it in his pocket next day, not at all
to the lightening of a forty miles' ride in August. On
his arrival, it turned out to contain one of the old lady's
pattens, sealed up for a particular cobbler in Kelso, and
accompanied with fourpence to pay for mending it, and
special directions that it might be brought back to her
by the same economical conveyance.

It will be seen from the following letter, the earliest
of Scott's writing that has fallen into my hands, that
professional business had some share in this excursion
to Kelso; but I consider with more interest the brief
allusion to a day at Sandy-Knowe: —

members were, in number, nineteen — viz., *Sir Walter Scott*, Mr. William
Clerk, Sir A. Ferguson, Mr. James Edmonstone, Mr. George Abercromby
(Lord Abercromby), Mr. D. Boyle (now Lord Justice-Clerk), Mr. James
Glassford (Advocate), Mr. James Ferguson (Clerk of Session), Mr. David
Monypenny (Lord Pitmilly), Mr. Robert Davidson (Professor of Law at
Glasgow), Sir William Rae, Bart., Sir Patrick Murray, Bart., *David Dou-
glas* (Lord Reston), Mr. Murray of Simprim, Mr. Monteith of Closeburn,
Mr. Archibald Miller (son of Professor Miller). *Baron Reden*, a Hanove-
rian ; the Honorable *Thomas Douglas*, afterwards Earl of Selkirk, — and
John Irving. Except the five whose names are *underlined*, these original
members are all still alive." — *Letter from Mr. Irving*, dated 29th September, 1836.

(*With a parcel.*)

ROSEBANK, 5th September, 1788.

DEAR MOTHER, — I was favored with your letter, and send you Anne's stockings along with this: I would have sent them last week, but had some expectations of a private opportunity. I have been very happy for this fortnight; we have some plan or other for every day. Last week my uncle, my cousin William,[1] and I, rode to Smailholm, and from thence walked to Sandy-Knowe Craigs, where we spent the whole day, and made a very hearty dinner by the side of the Orderlaw Well, on some cold beef and bread and cheese: we had also a small case-bottle of rum to make grog with, which we drank to the Sandy-Knowe bairns, and all their connections. This jaunt gave me much pleasure, and had I time, I would give you a more full account of it.

The fishing has been hitherto but indifferent, and I fear I shall not be able to accomplish my promise with regard to the wild ducks. I was out on Friday, and only saw three. I may probably, however, send you a hare, as my uncle has got a present of two greyhounds from Sir H. MacDougall, and as he has a license, only waits till the corn is off the ground to commence coursing. Be it known to you, however, I am not altogether employed in amusements, for I have got two or three clients besides my uncle, and am busy drawing tacks and contracts, — not, however, of marriage. I am in a fair way of making money, if I stay here long.

Here I have written a pretty long letter, and nothing in it; but you know writing to one's friends is the next thing to seeing them. My love to my father and the boys, from, Dear Mother, your dutiful and affectionate son, WALTER SCOTT.

[1] The present Laird of Raeburn.

It appears from James Ballantyne's *memoranda*, that having been very early bound apprentice to a solicitor in Kelso, he had no intercourse with Scott during the three or four years that followed their companionship at the school of Lancelot Whale; but Ballantyne was now sent to spend a winter in Edinburgh, for the completion of his professional education, and in the course of his attendance on the Scots Law class, became a member of a young Teviotdale club, where Walter Scott seldom failed to make his appearance. They supped together, it seems, once a month; and here, as in the associations above mentioned, good fellowship was often pushed beyond the limits of modern indulgence. The strict intimacy between Scott and Ballantyne was not at this time renewed, — their avocations prevented it, — but the latter was no uninterested observer of his old comrade's bearing on this new scene. "Upon all these occasions," he says, "one of the principal features of his character was displayed as conspicuously as I believe it ever was at any later period. This was the remarkable ascendency he never failed to exhibit among his young companions, and which appeared to arise from their involuntary and unconscious submission to the same firmness of understanding, and gentle exercise of it, which produced the same effects throughout his after-life. Where there was always a good deal of drinking, there was of course now and then a good deal of quarrelling. But three words from Walter Scott never failed to put all such propensities to quietness."

Mr. Ballantyne's account of his friend's peace-making exertions at this club may seem a little at variance with some preceding details. There is a difference, however, between encouraging quarrels in the bosom of a convivial party, and taking a fair part in a *row* between one's own party and another. But Ballantyne adds, that at *The Teviotdale*, Scott was always remarkable for being the most temperate of the set; and if the club consisted

chiefly of persons, like Ballantyne himself, somewhat inferior to Scott in birth and station, his carefulness both
of sobriety and decorum at their meetings was but another feature of his unchanged and unchangeable character — *qualis ab incepto.*

At one of the many merry suppers of this time Walter
Scott had said something, of which, on recollecting himself next morning, he was sensible that his friend Clerk
might have reason to complain. He sent him accordingly a note apologetical, which has by some accident
been preserved, and which I am sure every reader will
agree with me in considering well worthy of preservation.
In it Scott contrives to make use of *both* his own club
designations, and addresses his friend by another of the
same order, which Clerk had received in consequence of
comparing himself on some forgotten occasion to Sir
John Brute in the play. This characteristic document is
as follows: —

TO WILLIAM CLERK, ESQ.

Dear Baronet, — I am sorry to find that our friend
Colonel Grogg has behaved with a very undue degree
of vehemence in a dispute with you last night, occasioned
by what I am convinced was a gross misconception of
your expressions. As the Colonel, though a military
man, is not too haughty to acknowledge an error, he has
commissioned me to make his apology as a mutual friend,
which I am convinced you will accept from yours ever,

Duns Scotus.

Given at Castle Duns,
    Monday.

I should perhaps have mentioned sooner that when
first *Duns Scotus* became *the Baronet's* daily companion,
this new alliance was observed with considerable jealousy by some of his former inseparables of the writing
office. At the next annual supper of the clerks and ap-
prentices, the *gaudy* of the chamber, this feeling showed

itself in various ways, and when the cloth was drawn,
Walter rose and asked what was meant. "Well," said
one of the lads, "since you will have it out, you are *cutting* your old friends for the sake of Clerk and some
more of these dons that look down on the like of us."
"Gentlemen," answered Scott, "I will never *cut* any
man unless I detect him in scoundrelism; but I know
not what right any of you have to interfere with my
choice of my company. If any one thought I had injured him, he would have done well to ask an explanation
in a more private manner. As it is, I fairly own, that
though I like many of you very much, and have long
done so, I think William Clerk well worth you all put
together." The senior in the chair was wise enough to
laugh, and the evening passed off without further disturbance.

As one effect of his office education, Scott soon began
to preserve in regular files the letters addressed to him;
and from the style and tone of such letters, as Mr.
Southey observes in his Life of Cowper, a man's character may often be gathered even more surely than from
those written by himself. The first series of any considerable extent in his collection includes letters dated as
far back as 1786, and proceeds, with not many interruptions, down beyond the period when his fame had been
established. I regret, that from the delicate nature of the
transactions chiefly dwelt upon in the earlier of these
communications, I dare not make a free use of them; but
I feel it my duty to record the strong impression they
have left on my own mind of high generosity of affection,
coupled with calm judgment, and perseverance in well-
doing, on the part of the stripling Scott. To these
indeed every line in the collection bears pregnant testimony. A young gentleman, born of good family, and
heir to a tolerable fortune, is sent to Edinburgh College,
and is seen partaking, along with Scott, through several
apparently happy and careless years, of the studies and

amusements of which the reader may by this time have formed an adequate notion. By degrees, from the usual license of his equal comrades, he sinks into habits of a looser description — becomes reckless, contracts debts, irritates his own family almost beyond hope of reconciliation, is virtually cast off by them, runs away from Scotland, forms a marriage far below his condition in a remote part of the sister kingdom — and, when the poor girl has made him a father, then first begins to open his eyes to the full consequences of his mad career. He appeals to Scott, by this time in his eighteenth year, "as the truest and noblest of friends," who had given him "the earliest and the strongest warnings," had assisted him "the most generously throughout all his wanderings and distresses," and will not now abandon him in his "penitent lowliness of misery," the result of his seeing "virtue and innocence involved in the punishment of his errors." I find Scott obtaining the slow and reluctant assistance of his own careful father — who had long before observed this youth's wayward disposition, and often cautioned his son against the connection — to intercede with the unfortunate wanderer's family, and procure, if possible, some mitigation of their sentence. The result is that he is furnished with the scanty means of removing himself to a distant colony, where he spends several years in the drudgery of a very humble occupation, but by degrees establishes for himself a new character, which commands the anxious interest of strangers; — and I find these strangers, particularly a benevolent and venerable clergyman, addressing, on his behalf, without his privacy, the young person, as yet unknown to the world, whom the object of their concern had painted to them as "uniting the warm feelings of youth with the sense of years " — whose hair he had, "from the day he left England, worn next his heart." Just at the time when this appeal reached Scott, he hears that his exiled friend's father has died suddenly, and, after all, intestate; he has actually been taking steps to ascertain the truth of the case at the moment when the American despatch is laid on his table. I leave the reader to guess with what pleasure Scott has to communicate the intelligence that his repentant and reformed friend may return to take possession of his inheritance. The letters before me contain touching pictures of their meeting — of Walter's first visit to the ancient hall, where a happy family are now assembled — and of the affectionately respectful sense which his friend retained ever afterwards of all that he had done for him in the season of his struggles. But what a grievous loss is Scott's part of this correspondence! I find the comrade over and over again expressing his admiration of the letters in which Scott described to him his early tours both in the Highlands and the Border dales: I find him prophesying from them, as early as 1789, "one day your pen will make you famous," — and already, in 1790, urging him to concentrate his ambition on a "history of the clans." [1]

This young gentleman appears to have had a decided turn for literature; and, though in his earlier epistles he makes no allusion to Scott as ever dabbling in rhyme, he often inserts verses of his own, some of which are not without merit. There is a long letter in doggerel, dated 1788, descriptive of a ramble from Edinburgh to Carlisle — of which I may quote the opening lines, as a sample of the simple habits of these young people: —

> " At four in the morning, I won't be too sure,
> Yet, if right I remember me, that was the hour,
> When with Ferguson, Ramsay, and Jones, sir, and you,
> From Auld Reekie I southward my route did pursue.
> But two of the dogs (yet God bless them, I said)
> Grew tired, and but set me half way to Lasswade,
> While Jones, you, and I, Wat, went on without flutter,
> And at Symonds's feasted on good bread and butter ;
> Where I, wanting a sixpence, you lugged out a shilling,
> And paid for me too, though I was most unwilling.

[1] All Scott's letters to the friend here alluded to are said to have perished in an accidental fire.

> We parted — be sure I was ready to snivel —
> Jones and you to go home — I to go to the devil."

In a letter of later date, describing the adventurer's captivation with the cottage maiden whom he afterwards married, there are some lines of a very different stamp. This couplet at least seems to me exquisite: —

> " Lowly beauty, dear friend, beams with primitive grace,
> And 't is innocence' self plays the rogue in her face."

I find in another letter of this collection — and it is among the first of the series — the following passage: — "Your Quixotism, dear Walter, was highly characteristic. From the description of the blooming fair, as she appeared when she lowered her *manteau vert*, I am hopeful you have not dropt the acquaintance. At least I am certain some of our more rakish friends would have been glad enough of such an introduction." This hint I cannot help connecting with the first scene of *The Lady Green Mantle* in Redgauntlet; but indeed I could easily trace many more coincidences between these letters and that novel, though at the same time I have no sort of doubt that William Clerk was, in the main, *Darsie Latimer*, while Scott himself unquestionably sat for his own picture in young *Alan Fairford*.

The allusion to "our more rakish friends" is in keeping with the whole strain of this juvenile correspondence. Throughout there occurs no coarse or even jocular suggestion as to the conduct of *Scott* in that particular, as to which most youths of his then age are so apt to lay up stores of self-reproach. In this season of hot and impetuous blood he may not have escaped quite blameless, but I have the concurrent testimony of all the most intimate among his surviving associates, that he was remarkably free from such indiscretions; that while his high sense of honor shielded him from the remotest dream of tampering with female innocence, he had an instinctive delicacy about him which made him recoil with utter disgust from low and vulgar debaucheries.

His friends, I have heard more than one of them confess, used often to rally him on the coldness of his nature. By degrees they discovered that he had, from almost the dawn of the passions, cherished a secret attachment, which continued, through all the most perilous stage of life, to act as a romantic charm in safeguard of virtue. This — (however he may have disguised the story by mixing it up with the Quixotic adventure of the damsel in the Green Mantle) — this was the early and innocent affection to which we owe the tenderest pages, not only of Redgauntlet, but of The Lay of the Last Minstrel, and of Rokeby. In all of these works the heroine has certain distinctive features, drawn from one and the same haunting dream of his manly adolescence.

It was about 1790, according to Mr. William Clerk, that Scott was observed to lay aside that carelessness, not to say slovenliness, as to dress, which used to furnish matter for joking at the beginning of their acquaintance. He now did himself more justice in these little matters, became fond of mixing in general female society, and, as his friend expresses it, "began to set up for a squire of dames."

His personal appearance at this time was not unengaging. A lady of high rank,[1] who well remembers him in the Old Assembly Rooms, says, "Young Walter Scott was a comely creature." He had outgrown the sallowness of early ill health, and had a fresh, brilliant complexion. His eyes were clear, open, and well set, with a changeful radiance, to which teeth of the most perfect regularity and whiteness lent their assistance, while the noble expanse and elevation of the brow gave to the whole aspect a dignity far above the charm of mere features. His smile was always delightful; and I can easily fancy the peculiar intermixture of tenderness and gravity, with playful innocent hilarity and humor in the expression, as being well calculated to fix a fair lady's eye. His

[1] The late Countess-Duchess of Sutherland. — (1848.)

figure, excepting the blemish in one limb, must in those
days have been eminently handsome; tall, much above
the usual standard, it was cast in the very mould of a
young Hercules; the head set on with singular grace,
the throat and chest after the truest model of the antique,
the hands delicately finished; the whole outline that of
extraordinary vigor, without as yet a touch of clumsiness.
When he had acquired a little facility of manner, his
conversation must have been such as could have dispensed
with any exterior advantages, and certainly brought swift
forgiveness for the one unkindness of nature. I have
heard him, in talking of this part of his life, say, with
an arch simplicity of look and tone which those who were
familiar with him can fill in for themselves — "It was
a proud night with me when I first found that a pretty
young woman could think it worth her while to sit and
talk with me, hour after hour, in a corner of the ball-
room, while all the world were capering in our view."

I believe, however, that the "pretty young woman"
here specially alluded to had occupied his attention long
before he ever appeared in the Edinburgh Assembly
Rooms, or any of his friends took note of him as "setting up for a squire of dames." I have been told that
their acquaintance began in the Greyfriars' Churchyard,
where rain beginning to fall one Sunday as the congregation were dispersing, Scott happened to offer his umbrella, and the tender being accepted, so escorted her to
her residence, which proved to be at no great distance
from his own.[1] To return from church together had, it
seems, grown into something like a custom, before they
met in society, Mrs. Scott being of the party. It then
appeared that she and the lady's mother had been companions in their youth, though, both living secludedly,

[1] In one of his latest articles for the *Quarterly Review*, Scott observes,
"There have been instances of love tales being favorably received in
England, when told under an umbrella, and in the middle of a shower." —
Miscellaneous Prose Works, vol. xviii.

they had scarcely seen each other for many years; and the two matrons now renewed their former intercourse. But no acquaintance appears to have existed between the fathers of the young people, until things had advanced in appearance farther than met the approbation of the good Clerk to the Signet.

Being aware that the young lady, who was very highly connected, had prospects of fortune far above his son's, the upright and honorable man conceived it his duty to give her parents warning that he observed a degree of intimacy which, if allowed to go on, might involve the parties in future pain and disappointment. He had heard his son talk of a contemplated excursion to the part of the country in which his neighbor's estates lay, and not doubting that Walter's real object was different from that which he announced, introduced himself with a frank statement that he wished no such affair to proceed without the express sanction of those most interested in the happiness of persons as yet too young to calculate consequences for themselves. The northern Baronet had heard nothing of the young apprentice's intended excursion, and appeared to treat the whole business very lightly. He thanked Mr. Scott for his scrupulous attention — but added that he believed he was mistaken; and this paternal interference, which Walter did not hear of till long afterwards, produced no change in his relations with the object of his growing attachment.

I have neither the power nor the wish to give in detail the sequel of this story. It is sufficient to say, that after he had through several long years nourished the dream of an ultimate union with this lady, his hopes terminated in her being married to a gentleman of the highest character, to whom some affectionate allusions occur in one of the greatest of his works, and who lived to act the part of a most generous friend to his early rival throughout the anxieties and distresses of 1826 and 1827. I have said enough for my purpose — which was only to render intelligible a few allusions in the letters which I shall by and by have to introduce; but I may add that I have no doubt this unfortunate passion, besides one good effect already adverted to, had a powerful influence in nerving Scott's mind for the sedulous diligence with which he pursued his proper legal studies, as described in his Memoir, during the two or three years that preceded his call to the Bar.[1]

---

[1] [The object of the strongest, or perhaps it should be said the single, passion of Scott's life was Williamina, the only child of Sir John Wishart Belsches Stuart of Fettercairn, and his wife, the Lady Jane Leslie, daughter of David, Earl of Leven and Melville. Beside beauty of person, sweetness of disposition, a quick intelligence, and cultivated tastes, Miss Stuart seems to have possessed in large measure that indefinable but potent gift, which is called charm. Through some misapprehension, Lockhart appears to have antedated the beginning of her influence over Scott, as in 1790 she was hardly more than a child, and she was not sixteen when he was called to the Bar, though the meeting in the Greyfriars' Churchyard had probably already taken place. The "three years of dreaming" were ended, as the biographer narrates, in the autumn of 1796. On January 19, 1797, Miss Stuart was married to William Forbes, son and heir of Sir William Forbes of Pitsligo, an eminent banker, and the author of a Life of his friend Beattie. Scott's affectionate allusions to his early rival will be found in the Introduction to the Fourth Canto of *Marmion* : —

> " And one whose name I may not say, —
> For not mimosa's tender tree
> Shrinks sooner from the touch than he," —

an Introduction inscribed to James Skene of Rubislaw, whose marriage to a daughter of Sir William had been speedily followed by the father's death. Mr. Forbes succeeded to the baronetcy in 1806, and his wife, on the death of Sir John Stuart, inherited Fettercairn. She died December 5, 1810, after thirteen years of unclouded happiness. Dean Boyle has recorded that Lockhart once read to him the letter "full of beauty," which Scott wrote to the bereaved husband at this time. Lady Stuart-Forbes left six children, four sons and two daughters. The three sons who survived to maturity all were men of unusual ability.

The story of Williamina Stuart's brief life was told for the first time with any fulness by Miss F. M. F. Skene in the *Century Magazine* for July, 1899. As the daughter of one of Scott's earliest and dearest friends and the niece of Sir William Forbes, she could write with knowledge. She says that from the day of his wife's death, " so far as society and the outer world were concerned, Sir William Forbes may be said to have died with her. He retired into the most complete seclusion, maintaining the heartstricken silence of a grief too deep for words, and scarcely seeing even his own nearest relatives. Only at the call of duty did he ever emerge from his retirement," as when he proved so stanch a friend to Scott in the darkest days of 1826 and 1827.

A charming portrait, after a miniature by Cosway, accompanies Miss Skene's sketch of Lady Stuart-Forbes, — a pleasing contrast to the picture, without merit, either as a work of art or as a likeness, which was engraved for the Memoir of her youngest son, James David Forbes.]

CHAPTER VI

ILLUSTRATIONS CONTINUED. — STUDIES FOR THE BAR. — EXCURSION TO NORTHUMBERLAND. — LETTER ON FLODDEN FIELD. — CALL TO THE BAR

1790–1792

THE two following letters may sufficiently illustrate the writer's every-day existence in the autumn of 1790. The first, addressed to his *fidus Achates*, has not a few indications of the vein of humor from which he afterwards drew so largely in his novels; and indeed, even in his last days, he delighted to tell the story of the Jedburgh bailies' *boots*.

TO WILLIAM CLERK, ESQ., AT JOHN CLERK'S, ESQ., OF ELDIN, PRINCE'S STREET, EDINBURGH.

ROSEBANK, 6th August, 1790.

DEAR WILLIAM, — Here am I, the weather, according to your phrase, most bitchiferous; the Tweed, within twenty yards of the window at which I am writing, swelled from bank to brae, and roaring like thunder. It is paying you but a poor compliment to tell you I waited for such a day to perform my promise of writing, but you must consider that it is the point here to reserve such within-doors employment as we think most agreeable for bad weather, which in the country always wants something to help it away. In fair weather we are far from wanting amusement, which at present is my business; on the contrary, every fair day has some plan of pleasure annexed to it, in so much that I can hardly believe I have been here above two days, so swiftly does the time pass away. You will ask how it is employed? Why, negatively, I read *no* civil law. Heineccius and his fellow-worthies have ample time to gather a venerable coat of dust, which they merit by their dulness. As to my positive amusements, besides riding, fishing, and the other usual sports of the country, I often spend an hour or two in the evening in shooting herons, which are numerous on this part of the river. To do this I have no farther to go than the bottom of our garden, which literally hangs over the river. When you fire at a bird, she always crosses the river, and when again shot at with ball, usually returns to your side, and will cross in this way several times before she takes wing. This furnishes fine sport; nor are they easily shot, as you never can get very near them. The intervals between their appearing are spent very agreeably in eating gooseberries.

Yesterday was St. James's Fair, a day of great business. There was a great show of black cattle — I mean of ministers; the narrowness of their stipends here obliges many of them to enlarge their incomes by taking farms and grazing cattle. This, in my opinion, diminishes their respectability, nor can the farmer be supposed to entertain any great reverence for the ghostly advice of a *pastor* (they literally deserve the epithet) who perhaps the day before overreached him in a bargain. I would not have you to suppose there are no exceptions to this character, but it would serve most of them. I had been fishing with my uncle, Captain Scott, on the Teviot, and returned through the ground where the Fair is kept. The servant was waiting there with our horses, as we were to ride the water. Lucky it was that it was so; for just about that time the magistrates of Jedburgh, who preside there, began their solemn procession through the Fair. For the greater dignity upon this occasion they had a pair of boots among three men — *i. e.*, as they ride three in a rank, the *outer* legs of those personages who formed the outside, as it may be called, of the procession,

were each clothed in a boot. This and several other in-
congruous appearances were thrown in the teeth of those
cavaliers by the Kelso populace, and, by the assistance
of whiskey, parties were soon inflamed to a very tight
battle, one of that kind which, for distinction sake, is
called royal. It was not without great difficulty that we
extricated ourselves from the confusion; and had we been
on foot, we might have been trampled down by these
fierce Jedburghians, who charged like so many troopers.
We were spectators of the combat from an eminence, but
peace was soon after restored, which made the older
warriors regret the effeminacy of the age, as, regularly,
it ought to have lasted till night. Two lives were lost,
I mean of horses; indeed, had you seen them, you would
rather have wondered that they were able to bear their
masters to the scene of action, than that they could not
carry them off.[1]

I am ashamed to read over this sheet of nonsense, so
excuse inaccuracies. Remember me to the lads of the
Literary, those of *the club* in particular. I wrote Irving.
Remember my most respectful compliments to Mr. and
Mrs. Clerk and family, particularly James; when you
write, let me know how he did when you heard of him.
Imitate me in writing a long letter, but not in being long
in writing it. Direct to me at Miss Scott's, Garden,
Kelso. My letters lie there for me, as it saves their
being sent down to Rosebank. The carrier puts up at
the Grassmarket, and goes away on Wednesday forenoon. Yours,   WALTER SCOTT.

[1] Mr. Andrew Shortreed (one of a family often mentioned in these *Memoirs*) says, in a letter of November, 1838 : " The joke of the *one pair* of
boots to *three pair* of legs was so unpalatable to the honest burghers of
Jedburgh, that they have suffered the ancient privilege of ' riding the Fair,'
as it was called (during which ceremony the inhabitants of Kelso were
compelled to shut up their shops as on a holiday), to fall into disuse. Huoy,
the runaway forger, a native of Kelso, availed himself of the calumny in a
clever squib on the subject : —
> ' The outside man had each a boot,
>   The three had but a pair.' "

The next letter is dated from a house at which I have often seen the writer in his latter days. Kippilaw, situated about five or six miles behind Abbotsford, on the high ground between the Tweed and the Water of Ayle, is the seat of an ancient laird of the clan Kerr, but was at this time tenanted by the family of Walter's brother-apprentice, James Ramsay, who afterwards realized a fortune in the civil service of Ceylon.

TO WILLIAM CLERK, ESQ.

KIPPILAW, September 3, 1790.

DEAR CLERK, — I am now writing from the country habitation of our friend Ramsay, where I have been spending a week as pleasantly as ever I spent one in my life. Imagine a commodious old house, pleasantly situated amongst a knot of venerable elms, in a fine sporting, open country, and only two miles from an excellent water for trouts, inhabited by two of the best old ladies (Ramsay's aunts), and three as pleasant young ones (his sisters) as any person could wish to converse with — and you will have some idea of Kippilaw. James and I wander about, fish, or look for hares, the whole day, and at night laugh, chat, and play round games at cards. Such is the fatherland in which I have been living for some days past, and which I leave to-night or to-morrow. This day is very bad; notwithstanding which, James has sallied out to make some calls, as he soon leaves the country. I have a great mind to trouble him with the care of this.

And now for your letter, the receipt of which I have not, I think, yet acknowledged, though I am much obliged to you for it. I dare say you would relish your jaunt to Pennycuik very much, especially considering the solitary desert of Edinburgh, from which it relieved you. By the bye, know, O thou devourer of grapes, who contemnest the vulgar gooseberry, that thou art not singular in thy devouring — *nec tam aversus equos sol*

jungit ab urbe (Kelsonianâ scilicet) — my uncle being
the lawful possessor of a vinery measuring no less than
twenty-four feet by twelve, the contents of which come
often in my way; and, according to the proverb, that
enough is as good as a feast, are equally acceptable as
if they came out of the most extensive vineyard in
France. I cannot, however, equal your boast of breakfasting, dining, and supping on them. As for the civilians [1] — peace be with them, and may the dust lie light
upon their heads — they deserve this prayer in return for
those sweet slumbers which their benign influence infuses
into their readers. I fear I shall too soon be forced to
disturb them, for some of our family being now at Kelso,
I am under the agonies lest I be obliged to escort them
into town. The only pleasure I shall reap by this is that
of asking you how you do, and, perhaps, the solid advantage of completing our studies before the College sits
down. Employ, therefore, your mornings in slumber
while you can, for soon it will be chased from your eyes.
I plume myself on my sagacity with regard to C. J.
Fox.[2] I always foretold you would tire of him — a vile
brute. I have not yet forgot the narrow escape of my
fingers. I rejoice at James's [3] intimacy with Miss Men-
zies. She promised to turn out a fine girl, has a fine
fortune, and could James get her, he might sing, "I 'll
go no more to sea, to sea." Give my love to him when
you write. — " God preserve us, what a scrawl! " says
one of the ladies just now, in admiration at the expedition
with which I scribble. Well — I was never able in my
life to do anything with what is called gravity and deliberation.

I dined two days ago *tête-à-tête* with Lord Buchan.
Heard a history of all his ancestors whom he has hung
round his chimney-piece. From counting of pedigrees,

---

[1] Books on Civil Law.
[2] A tame fox of Mr. Clerk's, which he soon dismissed.
[3] Mr. James Clerk, R. N.

good Lord deliver us! He is thinking of erecting a monument to Thomson. He frequented Dryburgh much in my grandfather's time. It will be a handsome thing. As to your scamp of a boy, I saw nothing of him; but the face is enough to condemn there. I have seen a man flogged for stealing spirits on the sole information of his nose. Remember me respectfully to your family.

Believe me yours affectionately,
WALTER SCOTT.

After his return from the scene of these merry doings, he writes as follows to his kind uncle. The reader will see that, in the course of the preceding year, he had announced his early views of the origin of what is called the feudal system, in a paper read before the *Literary Society*. He, in the succeeding winter, chose the same subject for an essay, submitted to Mr. Dugald Stewart, whose prelections on ethics he was then attending. Some time later he again illustrated the same opinions more at length in a disquisition before the Speculative Society; and, indeed, he always adhered to them. One of the last historical books he read, before leaving Abbotsford for Malta in 1831, was Colonel Tod's interesting account of Rajasthan; and I well remember the delight he expressed on finding his views confirmed, as they certainly are in a very striking manner, by the philosophical soldier's details of the structure of society in that remote region of the East.

TO CAPTAIN ROBERT SCOTT, ROSEBANK, KELSO.

EDINBURGH, September 30, 1790.

DEAR UNCLE, — We arrived here without any accident about five o'clock on Monday evening. The good weather made our journey pleasant. I have been attending to your commissions here, and find that the last volume of Dodsley's Annual Register published is that for 1787, which I was about to send you; but the bookseller

I frequent had not one in boards, though he expects to procure one for me. There is a new work of the same title and size, on the same plan, which, being published every year regularly, has almost cut out Dodsley's, so that this last is expected to stop altogether. You will let me know if you would wish to have the new work, which is a good one, will join very well with those volumes of Dodsley's which you already have, and is published up to the present year. Byron's Narrative is not yet published, but you shall have it whenever it comes out.

Agreeable to your permission, I send you the scroll copy of an essay on the origin of the feudal system, written for the Literary Society last year. As you are kind enough to interest yourself in my style and manner of writing, I thought you might like better to see it in its original state, than one on the polishing of which more time had been bestowed. You will see that the intention and attempt of the essay is principally to controvert two propositions laid down by the writers on the subject: — 1st, That the system was invented by the Lombards; and, 2dly, that its foundation depended on the king's being acknowledged the sole lord of all the lands in the country, which he afterwards distributed to be held by military tenures. I have endeavored to assign it a more general origin, and to prove that it proceeds upon principles common to all nations when placed in a certain situation. I am afraid the matter will but poorly reward the trouble you will find in reading some parts. I hope, however, you will make out enough to enable you to favor me with your sentiments upon its faults. There is none whose advice I prize so high, for there is none in whose judgment I can so much confide, or who has shown me so much kindness.

I also send, as amusement for an idle half hour, a copy of the regulations of our Society, some of which will, I think, be favored with your approbation.

My mother and sister join in compliments to aunt and you, and also in thanks for the attentions and hospitality which they experienced at Rosebank. And I am ever your affectionate nephew,

WALTER SCOTT.

P. S. — If you continue to want a mastiff, I think I can procure you one of a good breed, and send him by the carrier.

While attending Mr. Dugald Stewart's class, in the winter of 1790–91, Scott produced, in compliance with the usual custom of ethical students, several essays besides that to which I have already made an allusion, and which was, I believe, entitled, On the Manners and Customs of the Northern Nations. But this essay it was that first attracted, in any particular manner, his Professor's attention. Mr. Robert Ainslie,[1] well known as the friend and fellow-traveller of Burns, happened to attend Stewart the same session, and remembers his saying, *ex cathedra*, "The author of this paper shows much knowledge of his subject, and a great taste for such researches." Scott became, before the close of the session, a frequent visitor in Mr. Stewart's family, and an affectionate intercourse was maintained between them through their after-lives.

Let me here set down a little story which most of his friends must have heard him tell of the same period. While attending Dugald Stewart's lectures on moral philosophy, Scott happened to sit frequently beside a modest and diligent youth, considerably his senior, and obviously of very humble condition. Their acquaintance soon became rather intimate, and he occasionally made this new friend the companion of his country walks, but as to his parentage and place of residence he always preserved total silence. One day towards the end of the session, as Scott was returning to Edinburgh from a soli-

[1] Mr. Ainslie died at Edinburgh, 11th April, 1838, in his 73d year.

tary ramble, his eye was arrested by a singularly venerable *Bluegown*, a beggar of the Edie Ochiltree order,
who stood propped on his stick, with his hat in his hand,
but silent and motionless, at one of the outskirts of the
city. Scott gave the old man what trifle he had in his
pocket, and passed on his way. Two or three times
afterwards the same thing happened, and he had begun
to consider the Bluegown as one who had established a
claim on his bounty: when one day he fell in with him
as he was walking with his humble student. Observing
some confusion in his companion's manner as he saluted
his pensioner, and bestowed the usual benefaction, he
could not help saying, after they had proceeded a few
yards further, "Do you know anything to the old man's
discredit?" Upon which the youth burst into tears, and
cried, "Oh no, sir, God forbid! — but I am a poor wretch
to be ashamed to speak to him — he is my own father.
He has enough laid by to serve for his own old days, but
he stands bleaching his head in the wind, that he may
get the means of paying for my education." Compas-
sionating the young man's situation, Scott soothed his
weakness, and kept his secret, but by no means broke off
the acquaintance. Some months had elapsed before he
again met the Bluegown — it was in a retired place, and
the old man begged to speak a word with him. "I find,
sir," he said, "that you have been very kind to my Willie. He had often spoke of it before I saw you together.
Will you pardon such a liberty, and give me the honor
and pleasure of seeing you under my poor roof? To-
morrow is Saturday; will you come at two o'clock?
Willie has not been very well, and it would do him
meikle good to see your face." His curiosity, besides
better feelings, was touched, and he accepted this strange
invitation. The appointed hour found him within sight
of a sequestered little cottage, near St. Leonard's — the
hamlet where he has placed the residence of his David
Deans. His fellow-student, pale and emaciated from

recent sickness, was seated on a stone bench by the door, looking out for his coming, and introduced him into a not untidy cabin, where the old man, divested of his professional garb, was directing the last vibrations of a leg of mutton that hung by a hempen cord before the fire. The mutton was excellent — so were the potatoes and whiskey; and Scott returned home from an entertaining conversation, in which, besides telling many queer stories of his own life — and he had seen service in his youth — the old man more than once used an expression, which was long afterwards put into the mouth of Dominie Sampson's mother: — "Please God, I may live to see my bairn wag his head in a pulpit yet."

Walter could not help telling all this the same night to his mother, and added, that he would fain see his poor friend obtain a tutor's place in some gentleman's family. "Dinna speak to your father about it," said the good lady; "if it had been *a shoulder* he might have thought less, but he will say *the jigot* was a sin. I 'll see what I can do." Mrs. Scott made her inquiries in her own way among the Professors, and having satisfied herself as to the young man's character, applied to her favorite minister, Dr. Erskine, whose influence soon procured such a situation as had been suggested for him, in the north of Scotland. "And thenceforth," said Sir Walter, "I lost sight of my friend — but let us hope he made out his *curriculum* at Aberdeen, and is now wagging his head where the fine old carle wished to see him." [1]

On the 4th January, 1791, Scott was admitted a member of *The Speculative Society*, where it had, long before, been the custom of those about to be called to the

[1] The reader will find a story not unlike this in the Introduction to *The Antiquary*, 1830. When I first read that note, I asked him why he had altered so many circumstances from the usual oral edition of his anecdote. " Nay," said he, " both stories may be true, and why should I be always lugging in myself, when what happened to another of our class would serve equally well for the purpose I had in view ? " I regretted the *leg of mutton.*

Bar, and those who after assuming the gown were left in possession of leisure by the solicitors, to train or exercise themselves in the arts of elocution and debate. From time to time each member produces an essay, and his treatment of his subject is then discussed by the conclave. Scott's essays were, for November, 1791, On the Origin of the Feudal System; for the 14th February, 1792, On the Authenticity of Ossian's Poems; and on the 11th December of the same year, he read one, On the Origin of the Scandinavian Mythology. The selection of these subjects shows the course of his private studies and predilections; but he appears, from the minutes, to have taken his fair share in the ordinary debates of the Society, — and spoke, in the spring of 1791, on these questions, which all belong to the established text-book for juvenile speculation in Edinburgh: — "Ought any permanent support to be provided for the poor?" "Ought there to be an established religion?" "Is attainder and corruption of blood ever a proper punishment?" "Ought the public expenses to be defrayed by levying the amount directly upon the people, or is it expedient to contract national debt for that purpose?" "Was the execution of Charles I. justifiable?" "Should the slave-trade be abolished?" In the next session, previous to his call to the Bar, he spoke in the debates of which these were the theses: — "Has the belief in a future state been of advantage to mankind, or is it ever likely to be so?" "Is it for the interest of Britain to maintain what is called the balance of Europe?" and again on the eternal question as to the fate of King Charles I., which, by the way, was thus set up for re-discussion on a motion by Walter Scott.

He took, for several winters, an ardent interest in this society. Very soon after his admission (18th January, 1791), he was elected their librarian; and in the November following he became also their secretary and treasurer; all which appointments indicate the reliance placed

on his careful habits of business, the fruit of his chamber
education. The minutes kept in his handwriting attest
the strict regularity of his attention to the small affairs,
literary and financial, of the club; but they show also,
as do all his early letters, a strange carelessness in spelling. His constant good temper softened the asperities
of debate; while his multifarious lore, and the quaint
humor with which he enlivened its display, made him
more a favorite as a speaker than some whose powers of
rhetoric were far above his.

Lord Jeffrey remembers being struck, the first night
he spent at the Speculative, with the singular appearance
of the secretary, who sat gravely at the bottom of the
table in a huge woollen nightcap; and when the president took the chair, pleaded a bad toothache as his apology for coming into that worshipful assembly in such a
"portentous machine." He read that night an essay on
ballads, which so much interested the new member that
he requested to be introduced to him. Mr. Jeffrey called
on him next evening, and found him "in a small den, on
the sunk floor of his father's house in George's Square,
surrounded with dingy books," from which they adjourned to a tavern, and supped together. Such was the
commencement of an acquaintance, which by degrees
ripened into friendship, between the two most distinguished men of letters whom Edinburgh produced in their
time. I may add here the description of that early *den*,
with which I am favored by a lady of Scott's family: —
"Walter had soon begun to collect out-of-the-way things
of all sorts. He had more books than shelves; a small
painted cabinet, with Scotch and Roman coins in it, and
so forth. A claymore and Lochaber axe, given him by
old Invernahyle, mounted guard on a little print of
Prince Charlie; and *Broughton's Saucer* was hooked up
against the wall below it." Such was the germ of the
magnificent library and museum of Abbotsford; and such
were the "new realms" in which he, on taking posses-

sion, had arranged his little paraphernalia about him "with all the feelings of novelty and liberty." Since those days, the habits of life in Edinburgh, as elsewhere, have undergone many changes: and the "convenient parlor," in which Scott first showed Jeffrey his collections of minstrelsy, is now, in all probability, thought hardly good enough for a menial's sleeping-room.

But I have forgotten to explain *Broughton's Saucer.* We read of Mr. Saunders Fairford, that though "an elder of the kirk, and of course zealous for King George and the Government," yet, having "many clients and connections of business among families of opposite political tenets, he was particularly cautious to use all the conventional phrases which the civility of the time had devised as an admissible mode of language betwixt the two parties: Thus he spoke sometimes of the Chevalier, but never either of the *Prince*, which would have been sacrificing his own principles, or of *the Pretender*, which would have been offensive to those of others: Again, he usually designated the Rebellion as the *affair* of 1745, and spoke of any one engaged in it as a person who had been *out* at a certain period — so that, on the whole, he was much liked and respected on all sides."[1] All this was true of Mr. Walter Scott, W. S.; but I have often heard his son tell an anecdote of him, which he dwelt on with particular satisfaction, as illustrative of the man, and of the difficult time through which he had lived.

Mrs. Scott's curiosity was strongly excited one autumn by the regular appearance, at a certain hour every evening, of a sedan chair, to deposit a person carefully muffled up in a mantle, who was immediately ushered into her husband's private room, and commonly remained with him there until long after the usual bedtime of this orderly family. Mr. Scott answered her repeated inquiries with a vagueness which irritated the lady's feelings more and more; until, at last, she could bear the

[1] *Redgauntlet*, chap. i.

thing no longer; but one evening, just as she heard the bell ring as for the stranger's chair to carry him off, she made her appearance within the forbidden parlor with a salver in her hand, observing that she thought the gentlemen had sat so long, they would be the better of a dish of tea, and had ventured accordingly to bring some for their acceptance. The stranger, a person of distinguished appearance, and richly dressed, bowed to the lady, and accepted a cup; but her husband knit his brows, and refused very coldly to partake the refreshment. A moment afterwards the visitor withdrew — and Mr. Scott, lifting up the window-sash, took the cup which he had left empty on the table, and tossed it out upon the pavement. The lady exclaimed for her china, but was put to silence by her husband's saying, "I can forgive your little curiosity, madam, but you must pay the penalty. I may admit into my house, on a piece of business, persons wholly unworthy to be treated as guests by my wife. Neither lip of me nor of mine comes after Mr. Murray of Broughton's."

This was the unhappy man who, after attending Prince Charles Stuart as his secretary throughout the greater part of his expedition, condescended to redeem his own life and fortune by bearing evidence against the noblest of his late master's adherents, when

> "Pitied by gentle hearts Kilmarnock died —
> The brave, Balmerino, were on thy side."

When confronted with Sir John Douglas of Kelhead (ancestor of the Marquess of Queensberry), before the Privy Council in St. James's, the prisoner was asked, "Do you know this witness?" "Not I," answered Douglas; "I once knew a person who bore the designation of Murray of Broughton — but that was a gentleman and a man of honor, and one that could hold up his head!"

The saucer belonging to Broughton's teacup had been preserved; and Walter, at a very early period, made

prize of it. One can fancy young Alan Fairford pointing significantly to the relic, when Mr. Saunders was
vouchsafing him one of his customary lectures about listening with unseemly sympathy to "the blawing, bleezing
stories which the Hieland gentlemen told of those trou-
blous times." [1]

The following letter is the only one of the autumn of
1791 that has reached my hands. It must be read with
particular interest for its account of Scott's first visit to
Flodden field, destined to be celebrated seventeen years
afterwards in the very noblest specimen of his numbers: —

TO WILLIAM CLERK, ESQ., PRINCE'S STREET, EDINBURGH.

NORTHUMBERLAND, 26th August, 1791.

DEAR CLERK, — Behold a letter from the mountains;
for I am very snugly settled here, in a farmer's house,
about six miles from Wooler, in the very centre of the
Cheviot hills, in one of the wildest and most romantic
situations which your imagination, fertile upon the subject of cottages, ever suggested. And what the deuce
are you about there? methinks I hear you say. Why,
sir, of all things in the world — drinking goat's whey —
not that I stand in the least need of it, but my uncle
having a slight cold, and being a little tired of home,
asked me last Sunday evening if I would like to go with
him to Wooler, and I answering in the affirmative, next
morning's sun beheld us on our journey, through a pass
in the Cheviots, upon the back of two special nags, and
man Thomas behind with a portmanteau, and two fishing-
rods fastened across his back, much in the style of St.
Andrew's Cross. Upon reaching Wooler we found the
accommodations so bad that we were forced to use some
interest to get lodgings here, where we are most delightfully appointed indeed. To add to my satisfaction, we
are amidst places renowned by the feats of former days;

[1] *Redgauntlet*, letter ix.

each hill is crowned with a tower, or camp, or cairn, and in no situation can you be near more fields of battle: Flodden, Otterburn, Chevy Chase, Ford Castle, Chillingham Castle, Copland Castle, and many another scene of blood, are within the compass of a forenoon's ride. Out of the brooks, with which these hills are intersected, we pull trouts of half a yard in length, as fast as we did the perches from the pond at Pennycuik, and we are in the very country of muirfowl.

Often as I have wished for your company, I never did it more earnestly than when I rode over Flodden Edge. I know your taste for these things, and could have undertaken to demonstrate that never was an affair more completely bungled than that day's work was. Suppose one army posted upon the face of a hill, and secured by high grounds projecting on each flank, with the river Till in front, a deep and still river, winding through a very extensive valley called Milfield Plain, and the only passage over it by a narrow bridge, which the Scots artillery, from the hill, could in a moment have demolished. Add, that the English must have hazarded a battle while their troops, which were tumultuously levied, remained together; and that the Scots, behind whom the country was open to Scotland, had nothing to do but to wait for the attack as they were posted. Yet did two thirds of the army, actuated by the *perfervidum ingenium Scotorum*, rush down and give an opportunity to Stanley to occupy the ground they had quitted, by coming over the shoulder of the hill, while the other third, under Lord Home, kept their ground, and having seen their king and about 10,000 of their countrymen cut to pieces, retired into Scotland without loss. For the reason of the bridge not being destroyed while the English passed, I refer you to Pitscottie, who narrates at large, and to whom I give credit for a most accurate and clear description, agreeing perfectly with the ground.

My uncle drinks the whey here, as I do ever since I

understood it was brought to his bedside every morning at six, by a very pretty dairy-maid. So much for my residence : all the day we shoot, fish, walk, and ride; dine and sup upon fish struggling from the stream, and the most delicious heath-fed mutton, barn-door fowls, poys,[1] milk-cheese, etc., all in perfection; and so much simplicity resides among these hills, that a pen, which could write at least, was not to be found about the house, though belonging to a considerable farmer, till I shot the crow with whose quill I write this epistle. I wrote to Irving before leaving Kelso. Poor fellow, I am sure his sister's death must have hurt him much; though he makes no noise about feelings, yet still streams always run deepest. I sent a message by him to Edie,[2] poor devil, adding my mite of consolation to him in his afflic-tion. I pity poor * * * * * *, who is more deserving of compassion, being his first offence. Write soon, and as long as the last; you will have Perthshire news, I sup-pose, soon. Jamie's adventure diverted me much. I read it to my uncle, who being long in the India service, was affronted. Remember me to James when you write, and to all your family, and friends in general. I send this to Kelso — you may address as usual; my letters will be forwarded — adieu — au revoir,

WALTER SCOTT.

With the exception of this little excursion, Scott ap-pears to have been nailed to Edinburgh during this au-tumn, by that course of legal study, in company with Clerk, on which he dwells in his Memoir with more satisfaction than on any other passage in his early life. He copied out *twice*, as the fragment tells us, his notes of those lectures of the eminent Scots Law professor (Mr. Hume), which he speaks of in such a high strain of eulogy; and Mr. Irving adds that the second copy, being fairly finished and bound into volumes, was pre-

---

[1] Pies.

[2] Sir A. Ferguson.

sented to his father. The old gentleman was highly
gratified with this performance, not only as a satisfactory
proof of his son's assiduous attention to the law professor, but inasmuch as the lectures afforded himself "very
pleasant reading for leisure hours."

Mr. Clerk assures me that nothing could be more
exact (excepting as to a few petty circumstances introduced for obvious reasons) than the resemblance of the
Mr. Saunders Fairford of Redgauntlet to his friend's
father: — "He was a man of business of the old school,
moderate in his charges, economical, and even niggardly
in his expenditure; strictly honest in conducting his
own affairs and those of his clients; but taught by long
experience to be wary and suspicious in observing the
motions of others. Punctual as the clock of St. Giles
tolled nine" (the hour at which the Court of Session
meets), "the dapper form of the hale old gentleman was
seen at the threshold of the court hall, or, at farthest, at
the head of the Back Stairs " (the most convenient access
to the Parliament House from George's Square), "trimly
dressed in a complete suit of snuff-colored brown, with
stockings of silk or woollen, as suited the weather; a bob
wig and a small cocked hat; shoes blacked as Warren
would have blacked them; silver shoe-buckles, and a gold
stock-buckle. His manners corresponded with his attire,
for they were scrupulously civil, and not a little formal.
. . . On the whole, he was a man much liked and respected, though his friends would not have been sorry if
he had given a dinner more frequently, as his little cellar
contained some choice old wine, of which, on such rare
occasions, he was no niggard. · The whole pleasure of
this good old-fashioned man of method, besides that
which he really felt in the discharge of his own daily
business, was the hope to see his son attain what in the
father's eyes was the proudest of all distinctions — the
rank and fame of a well-employed lawyer. Every profession has its peculiar honors, and his mind was con-

structed upon so limited and exclusive a plan, that he valued nothing save the objects of ambition which his own presented. He would have shuddered at his son's acquiring the renown of a hero, and laughed with scorn at the equally barren laurels of literature; it was by the path of the law alone that he was desirous to see him rise to eminence; and the probabilities of success or disappointment were the thoughts of his father by day, and his dream by night." [1]

It is easy to imagine the original of this portrait, writing to one of his friends, about the end of June, 1792 — "I have the pleasure to tell you that my son has passed his private Scots Law examinations with good approbation — a great relief to my mind, especially as worthy Mr. Pest [2] told me in my ear, there was no fear of the 'callant,' as he familiarly called him, which gives me great heart. His public trials, which are nothing in comparison, save a mere form, are to take place, by order of the Honorable Dean of Faculty, [3] on Wednesday first, and on Friday he puts on the gown, and gives a bit chack of dinner to his friends and acquaintances, as is the custom. Your company will be wished for there by more than him. — *P. S.* His thesis is on the title, *De periculo et commodo rei venditæ,* and is a very pretty piece of Latinity." [4]

And all things passed in due order, even as they are figured. The real *Darsie* was present at the real Alan Fairford's "bit chack of dinner," and the old Clerk of the Signet was very joyous on the occasion. Scott's *thesis* was, in fact, on the Title of the Pandects, *Concerning the disposal of the dead bodies of Criminals.* It

[1] *Redgauntlet,* chap. i.

[2] It has been suggested that *Pest* is a misprint for *Peat.* There was an elderly practitioner of the latter name, with whom Mr. Fairford must have been well acquainted. — (1839)

[3] The situation of Dean of Faculty was filled in 1792 by the Honorable Henry Erskine, of witty and benevolent memory.

[4] *Redgauntlet,* letter ix.

was dedicated, I doubt not by the careful father's advice, to his friend and neighbor in George's Square, the coarsely humorous, but acute and able, and still well-remembered, Macqueen of Braxfield, then Lord Justice-Clerk (or President of the Supreme Criminal Court) of Scotland.[1]

I have often heard both *Alan* and *Darsie* laugh over their reminiscences of the important day when they "put on the gown." After the ceremony was completed, and they had mingled for some time with the crowd of barristers in the Outer Court, Scott said to his comrade, mimicking the air and tone of a Highland lass waiting at the Cross of Edinburgh to be hired for the harvest work — "We 've stood here an hour by the Tron, hinny, and de'il a ane has speered our price." Some friendly solicitor, however, gave him a guinea fee before the Court rose; and as they walked down the High Street together, he said to Mr. Clerk, in passing a hosier's shop — "This is a sort of a wedding-day, Willie; I think I must go in and buy me a new nightcap." He did so accordingly; perhaps this was Lord Jeffrey's "portentous machine." His first fee of any consequence, however, was expended on a silver taper-stand for his mother, which the old lady used to point to with great satisfaction, as it stood on her chimney-piece five-and-twenty years afterwards.

[1] An eminent annotator observes on this passage : — "The praise of Lord Braxfield's capacity and acquirement is perhaps rather too slight. He was a very good lawyer, and a man of extraordinary sagacity, and in quickness and sureness of apprehension resembled Lord Kenyon, as well as in his ready use of his profound knowledge of law." — (1839.)

CHAPTER VII

FIRST EXPEDITION INTO LIDDESDALE. — STUDY OF GER-
MAN. — POLITICAL TRIALS, ETC. — SPECIMEN OF LAW
PAPERS. — BÜRGER'S LENORE TRANSLATED. — DISAP-
POINTMENT IN LOVE

1792–1796

SCOTT was called to the Bar only the day before the
closing of the session, and he appears to have almost
immediately escaped to the country. On the 2d of August I find his father writing, — "I have sent the copies
of your *thesis* as desired;" and on the 15th he addressed
to him at Rosebank a letter, in which there is this paragraph, an undoubted autograph of Mr. Saunders Fairford, *anno ætatis* sixty-three: —

"DEAR WALTER, — . . . I am glad that your expedition to
the west proved agreeable. You do well to warn your mother
against Ashestiel. Although I said little, yet I never thought
that road could be agreeable ; besides, it is taking too wide a
circle. Lord Justice-Clerk is in town attending the Bills.[1] He
called here yesterday, and inquired very particularly for you.
I told him where you was, and he expects to see you at Jedburgh upon the 21st. He is to be at Mellerstain[2] on the 20th,
and will be there all night. His Lordship said, in a very pleasant manner, that something might cast up at Jedburgh to give
you an opportunity of appearing, and that he would insist upon

[1] The Judges then attended in Edinburgh in rotation during the intervals of term, to take care of various sorts of business which could not
brook delay, bills of injunction, etc.

[2] The beautiful seat of the Baillies of Jerviswood, in Berwickshire, a
few miles below Dryburgh.

it, and that in future he meant to give you a share of the criminal business in this Court, — all which is very kind. I told his Lordship that I had dissuaded you from appearing at Jedburgh, but he said I was wrong in doing so, and I therefore leave the matter to you and him. *I think it is probable he will breakfast with Sir H. H. MacDougall on the 21st, on his way to Jedburgh.*" . . .

This last quiet hint, that the young lawyer might as well be at Makerstoun (the seat of a relation) when *His Lordship* breakfasted there, and of course swell the train of His Lordship's little procession into the county town, seems delightfully characteristic. I think I hear Sir Walter himself lecturing *me*, when in the same sort of situation, thirty years afterwards. He declined, as one of the following letters will show, the opportunity of making his first appearance on this occasion at Jedburgh. He was present, indeed, at the Court during the assizes, but "durst not venture." His accounts to William Clerk of his vacation amusements, and more particularly of his second excursion to Northumberland, will, I am sure, interest every reader: —

TO WILLIAM CLERK, ESQ., ADVOCATE, PRINCE'S STREET, EDINBURGH.

ROSEBANK, 10th September, 1792.

DEAR WILLIAM, — Taking the advantage of a very indifferent day, which is likely to float away a good deal of corn, and of my father's leaving this place, who will take charge of this scroll, I sit down to answer your favor. I find you have been, like myself, taking advantage of the good weather to look around you a little, and congratulate you upon the pleasure you must have received from your jaunt with Mr. Russell.[1] I apprehend, though you are silent on the subject, that your conversation was enlivened by many curious disquisitions of the

[1] Mr. Russell, surgeon, afterwards Professor of Clinical Surgery at Edinburgh.

nature of *undulating exhalations*. I should have bowed
before the venerable grove of oaks at Hamilton with as
much respect as if I had been a Druid about to gather
the sacred mistletoe. I should hardly have suspected
your host Sir William [1] of having been the occasion of
the scandal brought upon the library and Mr. Gibb [2] by
the introduction of the Cabinet des Fées, of which I have
a volume or two here. I am happy to think there is an
admirer of *snug things* in the administration of the
library. Poor Linton's [3] misfortune, though I cannot
say it surprises, yet heartily grieves me. I have no
doubt he will have many advisers and animadverters
upon the naughtiness of his ways, whose admonitions will
be forgot upon the next opportunity.

I am lounging about the country here, to speak sincerely, as idle as the day is long. Two old companions
of mine, brothers of Mr. Walker of Wooden, having
come to this country, we have renewed a great intimacy.
As they live directly upon the opposite bank of the river,
we have signals agreed upon by which we concert a plan
of operations for the day. They are both officers, and
very intelligent young fellows, and what is of some consequence, have a brace of fine greyhounds. Yesterday
forenoon we killed seven hares, so you may see how
plenty the game is with us. I have turned a keen duck-
shooter, though my success is not very great; and when
wading through the mosses upon this errand, accoutred
with the long gun, a jacket, mosquito trousers, and a
rough cap, I might well pass for one of my redoubted

---

[1] Sir William Miller (Lord Glenlee).

[2] Mr. Gibb was the Librarian of the Faculty of Advocates.

[3] Clerk, Abercromby, Scott, Ferguson, and others, had occasional boat-
ing excursions from Leith to Inchcolm, Inchkeith, etc. On one of these
their boat was neared by a Newhaven one — Ferguson, at the moment,
was standing up talking; one of the Newhaven fishermen, taking him for
a brother of his own craft, bawled out, "Linton, you lang bitch, is that
you?" From that day Adam Ferguson's cognomen among his friends of
The Club was Linton.

moss-trooper progenitors, Walter Fire-the-Braes,[1] or rather Willie wi' the Bolt-Foot.

For about-doors' amusement, I have constructed a seat in a large tree which spreads its branches horizontally over the Tweed. This is a favorite situation of mine for reading, especially in a day like this, when the west wind rocks the branches on which I am perched, and the river rolls its waves below me of a turbid blood color. I have, moreover, cut an embrasure, through which I can fire upon the gulls, herons, and cormorants, as they fly screaming past my nest. To crown the whole, I have carved an inscription upon it in the ancient Roman taste. I believe I shall hardly return into town, barring accidents, sooner than the middle of next month, perhaps not till November. Next week, weather permitting, is destined for a Northumberland expedition, in which I shall visit some parts of that country which I have not yet seen, particularly about Hexham. Some days ago I had nearly met with a worse accident than the tramp I took at Moorfoot;[2] for having bewildered myself among the Cheviot hills, it was nearly nightfall before I got to the village of Hownam, and the passes with which I was acquainted. You do not speak of being in Perthshire this season, though I suppose you intend it. I suppose we, that is, *nous autres*,[3] are at present completely dispersed.

Compliments to all who are in town, and best respects to your own family, both in Prince's Street and at Eldin. — Believe me ever most sincerely yours,

WALTER SCOTT.

[1] Walter Scott of Synton (elder brother of *Bolt-Foot*, the first Baron of Harden) was thus designated. He greatly distinguished himself in the battle of Melrose, A. D. 1526.

[2] This alludes to being lost in a fishing excursion.

[3] The companions of *The Club*.

ROSEBANK, 30th September, 1792.

DEAR WILLIAM, — I suppose this will find you flourishing like a green bay-tree on the mountains of Perthshire, and in full enjoyment of all the pleasures of the country. All that I envy you is the *noctes cœnæque deum*, which, I take it for granted, you three merry men will be spending together, while I am poring over Bartholine in the long evenings, solitary enough; for, as for the lobsters, as you call them, I am separated from them by the Tweed, which precludes evening meetings, unless in fine weather and full moons. I have had an expedition through Hexham and the higher parts of Northumberland, which would have delighted the very cockles of your heart, not so much on account of the beautiful romantic appearance of the country, though that would have charmed you also, as because you would have seen more Roman inscriptions built into gate-posts, barns, etc., than perhaps are to be found in any other part of Britain. These have been all dug up from the neighboring Roman wall, which is still in many places very entire, and gives a stupendous idea of the perseverance of its founders, who carried such an erection from sea to sea, over rocks, mountains, rivers, and morasses. There are several lakes among the mountains above Hexham, well worth going many miles to see, though their fame is eclipsed by their neighborhood to those of Cumberland. They are surrounded by old towers and castles, in situations the most savagely romantic; what would I have given to have been able to take effect-pieces from some of them! Upon the Tyne, about Hexham, the country has a different aspect, presenting much of the beautiful, though less of the sublime. I was particularly charmed with the situation of Beaufront, a house belonging to a mad sort of genius, whom, I am sure, I have told you some stories about. He used to call himself the Noble

Errington, but of late has assumed the title of Duke of Hexham. Hard by the town is the field of battle where the forces of Queen Margaret were defeated by those of the House of York, a blow which the Red Rose never recovered during the civil wars. The spot where the Duke of Somerset and the northern nobility of the Lancastrian faction were executed after the battle is still called Dukesfield. The inhabitants of this country speak an odd dialect of the Saxon, approaching nearly that of Chaucer, and have retained some customs peculiar to themselves. They are the descendants of the ancient Danes, chased into the fastnesses of Northumberland by the severity of William the Conqueror. Their ignorance is surprising to a Scotchman. It is common for the traders in cattle, which business is carried on to a great extent, to carry all letters received in course of trade to the parish church, where the clerk reads them aloud after service, and answers them according to circumstances.

We intended to visit the lakes in Cumberland, but our jaunt was cut short by the bad weather. I went to the circuit at Jedburgh, to make my bow to Lord J. Clerk, and might have had employment, but durst not venture. Nine of the Dunse rioters were condemned to banishment, but the ferment continues violent in the Merse. Kelso races afforded little sport — Wishaw[1] lost a horse which cost him £500, and foundered irrecoverably on the course. At another time I shall quote George Buchanan's adage of "a fool and his money," but at present labor under a similar misfortune; my Galloway having yesterday thought proper (N. B., without a rider) to leap over a gate, and being lamed for the present. This is not his first *faux-pas*, for he jumped into a water with me on his back when in Northumberland, to the imminent danger of my life. He is, therefore, to be sold (when recovered), and another purchased. This accident has

---

[1] William Hamilton of Wishaw, — who afterwards established his claim to the peerage of Belhaven.

occasioned you the trouble of reading so long an epistle, the day being Sunday, and my uncle, the captain, busily engaged with your father's naval tactics, is too seriously employed to be an agreeable companion. Apropos (des bottes) — I am sincerely sorry to hear that James is still unemployed, but have no doubt a time will come round when his talents will have an opportunity of being displayed to his advantage. I have no prospect of seeing my *chère adorable* till winter, if then. As for you, I pity you not, seeing as how you have so good a succedaneum in M. G.; and, on the contrary, hope, not only that Edmonstone may *roast* you, but that Cupid may again (as erst) *fry* you on the gridiron of jealousy for your infidelity. Compliments to our right trusty and well-beloved Linton and Jean Jacques.[1] If you write, which, by the way, I hardly have the conscience to expect, direct to my father's care, who will forward your letter. I have quite given up duck-shooting for the season, the birds being too old, and the mosses too deep and cold. I have no reason to boast of my experience or success in the sport, and for my own part, should fire at any distance under eighty or even ninety paces, though above forty-five I would reckon it a *coup désespéré*, and as the bird is beyond measure shy, you may be sure I was not very bloody. Believe me, deferring, *as usual*, our dispute till another opportunity, always sincerely yours,

WALTER SCOTT.

P. S. — I believe, if my pony does not soon recover, that misfortune, with the bad weather, may send me soon to town.

It was within a few days after Scott's return from his excursion to Hexham, that, while attending the Michaelmas head-court, as an annual county-meeting is called, at Jedburgh, he was introduced, by an old companion, Charles Kerr of Abbotrule, to Mr. Robert Shortreed,

---

[1] John James Edmonstone.

that gentleman's near relation, who spent the greater
part of his life in the enjoyment of much respect as Sheriff-substitute of Roxburghshire. Scott had been expressing his wish to visit the then wild and inaccessible district of Liddesdale, particularly with a view to examine
the ruins of the famous castle of Hermitage, and to pick
up some of the ancient *riding ballads*, said to be still
preserved among the descendants of the moss-troopers,
who had followed the banner of the Douglases, when
lords of that grim and remote fastness. Mr. Shortreed
had many connections in Liddesdale, and knew its passes
well, and he was pointed out as the very guide the young
advocate wanted. They started, accordingly, in a day
or two afterwards, from Abbotrule; and the laird meant
to have been of the party; but "it was well for him,"
said Shortreed, "that he changed his mind — for he
could never have done as we did." [1]

During seven successive years Scott made a *raid*, as
he called it, into Liddesdale, with Mr. Shortreed for his
guide; exploring every rivulet to its source, and every
ruined *peel* from foundation to battlement. At this time
no wheeled carriage had ever been seen in the district —
the first, indeed, that ever appeared there was a gig,
driven by Scott himself for a part of his way, when on
the last of these seven excursions. There was no inn or
public-house of any kind in the whole valley; the travellers passed from the shepherd's hut to the minister's
manse, and again from the cheerful hospitality of the
manse to the rough and jolly welcome of the homestead;
gathering, wherever they went, songs and tunes, and
occasionally more tangible relics of antiquity — even such

[1] I am obliged to Mr. John Elliot Shortreed, a son of Scott's early
friend, for some *memoranda* of his father's conversations on this subject.
These notes were written in 1824; and I shall make several quotations
from them. I had, however, many opportunities of hearing Mr. Shortreed's stories from his own lips, having often been under his hospitable
roof in company with Sir Walter, who to the last always was his old
friend's guest when business took him to Jedburgh.

"a rowth of auld nicknackets" as Burns ascribes to Captain Grose. To these rambles Scott owed much of the materials of his Minstrelsy of the Scottish Border; and not less of that intimate acquaintance with the living manners of these unsophisticated regions, which constitutes the chief charm of one of the most charming of his prose works. But how soon he had any definite object before him in his researches seems very doubtful. "He was *makin' himsel'* a' the time," said Mr. Shortreed; "but he didna ken maybe what he was about till years had passed: at first he thought o' little, I dare say, but the queerness and the fun."

"In those days," says the Memorandum before me, "advocates were not so plenty — at least about Liddesdale;" and the worthy Sheriff-substitute goes on to describe the sort of bustle, not unmixed with alarm, produced at the first farmhouse they visited (Willie Elliot's at Millburnholm), when the honest man was informed of the quality of one of his guests. When they dismounted, accordingly, he received Mr. Scott with great ceremony, and insisted upon himself leading his horse to the stable. Shortreed accompanied Willie, however, and the latter, after taking a deliberate peep at Scott, "out-by the edge of the door-cheek," whispered, "Weel, Robin, I say, de'il hae me if I's be a bit feared for him now; he's just a chield like ourselves, I think." Half-a-dozen dogs of all degrees had already gathered round "the advocate," and his way of returning their compliments had set Willie Elliot at once at his ease.

According to Mr. Shortreed, this goodman of Millburnholm was the great original of Dandie Dinmont. As he seems to have been the first of these upland sheep-farmers that Scott ever visited, there can be little doubt that he sat for some parts of that inimitable portraiture; and it is certain that the James Davidson, who carried the name of Dandie to his grave with him, and whose thoroughbred deathbed scene is told in the Notes to Guy

Mannering, was first pointed out to Scott by Mr. Shortreed himself, several years after the novel had established
the man's celebrity all over the Border; some accidental
report about his terriers, and their odd names, having
alone been turned to account in the original composition
of the tale.   But I have the best reason to believe that
the kind and manly character of Dandie, the gentle and
delicious one of his wife, and some at least of the most
picturesque peculiarities of the *ménage* at Charlieshope,
were filled up from Scott's observation, years after this
period, of a family, with one of whose members he had,
through the best part of his life, a close and affectionate
connection.   To those who were familiar with him, I
have perhaps already sufficiently indicated the early home
of his dear friend, William Laidlaw, among "the braes
of Yarrow."

They dined at Millburnholm, and after having lingered
over Willie Elliot's punch-bowl, until, in Mr. Shortreed's phrase, they were "half-glowrin," mounted their
steeds again, and proceeded to Dr. Elliot's at Cleughhead,
where ("for," says my Memorandum, "folk were na very
nice in those days") the two travellers slept in one and
the same bed — as, indeed, seems to have been the case
with them throughout most of their excursions in this
primitive district.   This Dr. Elliot had already a large
MS. collection of the ballads Scott was in quest of; and
finding how much his guest admired his acquisitions,
thenceforth exerted himself, for several years, with redoubled diligence, in seeking out the living depositaries
of such lore among the darker recesses of the mountains.
"The Doctor," says Mr. Shortreed, "would have gane
through fire and water for Sir Walter, when he ance
kenned him."

Next morning they seem to have ridden a long way,
for the express purpose of visiting one "auld Thomas o'
Twizzlehope," another Elliot, I suppose, who was celebrated for his skill on the Border pipe, and in particular

for being in possession of the real *lilt* of *Dick o' the Cow*. Before starting, that is, at six o'clock, the ballad-hunters had, "just to lay the stomach, a devilled duck or twae, and some *London* porter." Auld Thomas found them, nevertheless, well disposed for "breakfast" on their arrival at Twizzlehope; and this being over, he delighted them with one of the most hideous and unearthly of all the specimens of "riding music," and, moreover, with considerable libations of whiskey-punch, manufactured in a certain wooden vessel, resembling a very small milk-pail, which he called "Wisdom," because it "made" only a few spoonfuls of spirits — though he had the art of replenishing it so adroitly, that it had been celebrated for fifty years as more fatal to sobriety than any bowl in the parish. Having done due honor to "Wisdom," they again mounted, and proceeded over moss and moor to some other equally hospitable master of the pipe. "Eh me," says Shortreed, "sic an endless fund o' humor and drollery as he then had wi' him! Never ten yards but we were either laughing or roaring and singing. Wherever we stopped, how brawlie he suited himsel' to everybody! He aye did as the lave did; never made himsel' the great man, or took ony airs in the company. I've seen him in a' moods in these jaunts, grave and gay, daft and serious, sober and drunk — (this, however, even in our wildest rambles, was but rare) — but, drunk or sober, he was aye the gentleman. He looked excessively heavy and stupid when he was *fou*, but he was never out o' gude-humor."

On reaching, one evening, some *Charlieshope* or other (I forget the name) among those wildernesses, they found a kindly reception as usual; but to their agreeable surprise, after some days of hard living, a measured and orderly hospitality as respected liquor. Soon after supper, at which a bottle of elderberry wine alone had been produced, a young student of divinity, who happened to be in the house, was called upon to take the "big ha'

Bible," in the good old fashion of Burns's Saturday
Night; and some progress had been already made in the
service, when the goodman of the farm, whose "tendency," as Mr. Mitchell says, "was soporific," scandalized
his wife and the dominie by starting suddenly from his
knees, and rubbing his eyes, with a stentorian exclamation of "By ——, here's the keg at last!" and in tum-
bled, as he spake the word, a couple of sturdy herdsmen,
whom, on hearing a day before of the advocate's approaching visit, he had despatched to a certain smuggler's
haunt, at some considerable distance, in quest of a supply
of *run* brandy from the Solway Frith. The pious "exercise" of the household was hopelessly interrupted.
With a thousand apologies for his hitherto shabby entertainment, this jolly Elliot, or Armstrong, had the welcome *keg* mounted on the table without a moment's delay,
and gentle and simple, not forgetting the dominie, continued carousing about it until daylight streamed in upon
the party. Sir Walter Scott seldom failed, when I saw
him in company with his Liddesdale companion, to mimic
with infinite humor the sudden outburst of his old host,
on hearing the clatter of horses' feet, which he knew
to indicate the arrival of the keg — the consternation of
the dame — and the rueful despair with which the young
clergyman closed the book.

" It was in that same season, I think," says Mr. Shortreed,
" that Sir Walter got from Dr. Elliot the large old border war-
horn, which ye may still see hanging in the armory at Abbotsford.   How *great* he was when he was made master o' *that* !
I believe it had been found in Hermitage Castle — and one of
the Doctor's servants had used it many a day as a grease-horn
for his scythe, before they discovered its history.   When cleaned
out, it was never a hair the worse — the original chain, hoop,
and mouth-piece of steel, were all entire, just as you now see
them.   Sir Walter carried it home all the way from Liddesdale
to Jedburgh, slung about his neck like Johnny Gilpin's bottle,
while I was entrusted with an ancient bridle-bit, which we had
likewise picked up.

' The feint o' pride — na pride had he . . .
    A lang kail-gully hung down by his side,
    And a great meikle nowt-horn to rout on had he,'

and meikle and sair we routed on 't, and ' hotched and blew,
wi' micht and main.' O what pleasant days ! And then a' the
nonsense we had cost us naething. We never put hand in
pocket for a week on end. Toll-bars there were none — and
indeed I think our haill charges were a feed o' corn to our
horses in the gangin' and comin' at Riccartoun mill."

It is a pity that we have no letters of Scott's describing this first *raid* into Liddesdale; but as he must have
left Kelso for Edinburgh very soon after its conclusion,
he probably chose to be the bearer of his own tidings.
At any rate, the wonder perhaps is, not that we should
have so few letters of this period, as that any have been
recovered. "I ascribe the preservation of my little hand-
ful," says Mr. Clerk, "to a sort of instinctive prophetic
sense of his future greatness."

I have found, however, two note-books, inscribed
"Walter Scott, 1792," containing a variety of scraps
and hints which may help us to fill up our notion of his
private studies during that year. He appears to have
used them indiscriminately. We have now an extract
from the author he happened to be reading; now a memorandum of something that had struck him in conversation; a fragment of an essay; transcripts of favorite
poems; remarks on curious cases in the old records of
the Justiciary Court; in short, a most miscellaneous collection, in which there is whatever might have been
looked for, with perhaps the single exception of original
verse. One of the books opens with: " *Vegtam's
Kvitha*, or The Descent of Odin, with the Latin of
Thomas Bartholine, and the English poetical version of
Mr. Gray; with some account of the death of Balder,
both as narrated in the Edda, and as handed down to us
by the Northern historians — *Auctore Gualtero Scott*."
The Norse original and the two versions are then tran-

scribed; and the historical account appended, extending
to seven closely written quarto pages, was, I doubt not,
read before one or other of his debating societies. Next
comes a page, headed "Pecuniary Distress of Charles
the First," and containing a transcript of a receipt for
some plate lent to the King in 1643. He then copies
Langhorne's Owen of Carron; the verses of Canute, on
passing Ely; the lines to a cuckoo, given by Warton as
the oldest specimen of English verse; a translation "by
a gentleman in Devonshire," of the death-song of Regner
Lodbrog; and the beautiful quatrain omitted in Gray's
Elegy, —

> " There scattered oft, the earliest of the year," etc.

After this we have an Italian canzonet, on the praises of
blue eyes (which were much in favor at this time); several pages of etymologies from Ducange; some more of
notes on the Morte Arthur; extracts from the books of
Adjournal, about Dame Janet Beaton, the Lady of Branksome of The Lay of the Last Minstrel, and her husband,
"Sir Walter Scott of Buccleuch, called *Wicked Wat;*"
other extracts about witches and fairies; various couplets
from Hall's Satires; a passage from Albania; notes on
the Second Sight, with extracts from Aubrey and Glan-
ville; a "List of Ballads to be discovered or recovered;"
extracts from Guerin de Montglave; and after many more
similar entries, a table of the Mæso-Gothic, Anglo-Saxon
and Runic alphabets — with a fourth section, headed *German*, but left blank. But enough perhaps of this record.

In November, 1792, Scott and Clerk began their regular attendance at the Parliament House, and Scott, to
use Mr. Clerk's words, "by and by crept into a tolerable
share of such business as may be expected from a writer's
connection." By this we are to understand that he was
employed from time to time by his father, and probably
a few other solicitors, in that dreary every-day task-
work, chiefly of long written *informations*, and other

papers for the Court, on which young counsellors of the Scotch Bar were then expected to bestow a great deal of trouble for very scanty pecuniary remuneration, and with scarcely a chance of finding reserved for their hands any matter that could elicit the display of superior knowledge of understanding. He had also his part in the cases of persons suing *in forma pauperis;* but how little important those that came to his share were, and how slender was the impression they had left on his mind, we may gather from a note on Redgauntlet, wherein he signifies his doubts whether he really had ever been engaged in what he has certainly made the *cause célèbre* of *Poor Peter Peebles.*

But he soon became as famous for his powers of story-telling among the lawyers of the Outer-House, as he had been among the companions of his High School days. The place where these idlers mostly congregated was called, it seems, by a name which sufficiently marks the date — it was *the Mountain.* Here, as Roger North says of the Court of King's Bench in his early day, "there was more news than law;" — here hour after hour passed away, week after week, month after month, and year after year, in the interchange of light-hearted merriment among a circle of young men, more than one of whom, in after-times, attained the highest honors of the profession. Among the most intimate of Scott's daily associates from this time, and during all his subsequent attendance at the Bar, were, besides various since-eminent persons that have been already named, the first legal antiquary of our time in Scotland, Mr. Thomas Thomson, and William Erskine, afterwards Lord Kinnedder. Mr. Clerk remembers complaining one morning on finding the group convulsed with laughter, that *Duns Scotus* had been forestalling him in a good story, which he had communicated privately the day before — adding, moreover, that his friend had not only stolen, but disguised it. "Why," answered he, skilfully waiving the main charge,

"this is always the way with *the Baronet*. He is continually saying that I change his stories, whereas in fact I
only put a cocked hat on their heads, and stick a cane
into their hands — to make them fit for going into company."

The German class, of which we have an account in one
of the Prefaces of 1830, was formed before the Christmas
of 1792, and it included almost all these loungers of *the
Mountain*. In the essay now referred to Scott traces
the interest excited in Scotland on the subject of German
literature to a paper read before the Royal Society of
Edinburgh, on the 21st of April, 1788, by the author of
The Man of Feeling. "The literary persons of Edinburgh," he says, "were then first made aware of the existence of works of genius in a language cognate with the
English, and possessed of the same manly force of expression; they learned at the same time that the taste
which dictated the German compositions was of a kind as
nearly allied to the English as their language: those who
were from their youth accustomed to admire Shakespeare
and Milton, became acquainted for the first time with a
race of poets, who had the same lofty ambition to spurn
the flaming boundaries of the universe, and investigate
the realms of Chaos and Old Night; and of dramatists,
who, disclaiming the pedantry of the unities, sought, at
the expense of occasional improbabilities and extrava-
gance, to present life on the stage in its scenes of wildest
contrast, and in all its boundless variety of character.
. . . Their fictitious narratives, their ballad poetry, and
other branches of their literature, which are particularly
apt to bear the stamp of the extravagant and the supernatural, began also to occupy the attention of the British
literati. In Edinburgh, where the remarkable coinci-
dence between the German language and the Lowland
Scottish encouraged young men to approach this newly
discovered spring of literature, a class was formed of six
or seven intimate friends, who proposed to make them-

selves acquainted with the German language. They were in the habit of being much together, and the time they spent in this new study was felt as a period of great amusement. One source of this diversion was the laziness of one of their number, the present author, who, averse to the necessary toil of grammar, and the rules, was in the practice of fighting his way to the knowledge of the German by his acquaintance with the Scottish and Anglo-Saxon dialects, and of course frequently committed blunders which were not lost on his more accurate and more studious companions." The teacher, Dr. Willich, a medical man, is then described as striving with little success to make his pupils sympathize in his own passion for the "sickly monotony" and "affected ecstasies" of Gessner's Death of Abel; and the young students, having at length acquired enough of the language for their respective purposes, as selecting for their private pursuits, some the philosophical treatises of Kant, others the dramas of Schiller and Goethe. The chief, if not the only *Kantist* of the party, was, I believe, John Macfarlan of Kirkton; among those who turned zealously to the popular belles-lettres of Germany were, with Scott, his most intimate friends of the period, William Clerk, William Erskine, and Thomas Thomson.

These studies were much encouraged by the example, and assisted by the advice, of an accomplished person, considerably Scott's superior in standing, Alexander Fraser Tytler, afterwards a Judge of the Court of Session by the title of Lord Woodhouselee. His version of Schiller's Robbers was one of the earliest from the German theatre, and no doubt stimulated his young friend to his first experiments in the same walk.

The contemporary familiars of those days almost all survive; but one, and afterwards the most intimate of them all, went before him; and I may therefore hazard in this place a few words on the influence which he exercised at this critical period on Scott's literary tastes and

studies. William Erskine was the son of an Episcopalian clergyman in Perthshire, of a good family, but far
from wealthy. He had received his early education at
Glasgow, where, while attending the college lectures, he
was boarded under the roof of Andrew Macdonald, the
author of Vimonda, who then officiated as minister to
a small congregation of Episcopalian nonconformists.
From this unfortunate but very ingenious man, Erskine
had derived, in boyhood, a strong passion for old English
literature, more especially the Elizabethan dramatists;
which, however, he combined with a far livelier relish
for the classics of antiquity than either Scott or his master
ever possessed. From the beginning, accordingly, Scott
had in Erskine a monitor who — entering most warmly
into his taste for national lore — the life of the past —
and the bold and picturesque style of the original English
school — was constantly urging the advantages to be derived from combining with its varied and masculine
breadth of delineation such attention to the minor graces
of arrangement and diction as might conciliate the fas-
tidiousness of modern taste. Deferring what I may have
to say as to Erskine's general character and manners,
until I shall have approached the period when I myself
had the pleasure of sharing his acquaintance, I introduce
the general bearing of his literary opinions thus early,
because I conceive there is no doubt that his companionship was, even in those days, highly serviceable to Scott
as a student of the German drama and romance. Directed, as he mainly was in the ultimate determination of
his literary ambition, by the example of their great
founders, he appears to have run at first no trivial hazard
of adopting the extravagances, both of thought and language, which he found blended in their works with such
a captivating display of genius, and genius employed on
subjects so much in unison with the deepest of his own
juvenile predilections. His friendly critic was just, as well
as delicate; and unmerciful severity as to the mingled

absurdities and vulgarities of German detail commanded deliberate attention from one who admired not less enthusiastically than himself the genuine sublimity and pathos of his new favorites. I could, I believe, name one other at least among Scott's fellow-students of the same time, whose influence was combined in this matter with Erskine's; but his was that which continued to be exerted the longest, and always in the same direction. That it was not accompanied with entire success, the readers of The Doom of Devorgoil, to say nothing of minor blemishes in far better works, must acknowledge.

These German studies divided Scott's attention with the business of the courts of law, on which he was at least a regular attendant during the winter of 1792-93.

In March, when the Court rose, he proceeded into Galloway, where he had not before been, in order to make himself acquainted with the persons and localities mixed up with the case of a certain Rev. Mr. M'Naught, minister of Girthon, whose trial, on charges of habitual drunkenness, singing of lewd and profane songs, dancing and toying at a penny-wedding with a "sweetie wife" (that is, an itinerant vender of gingerbread, etc.), and moreover of promoting irregular marriages as a justice of the peace, was about to take place before the General Assembly of the Kirk.

As his "Case for M'Naught," dated May, 1793, is the first of his legal papers that I have discovered, and contains several characteristic enough turns, I make no apology for introducing a few extracts: —

At the head of the first class of offences stands the extraordinary assertion, that, being a Minister of the Gospel, the respondent had illegally undertaken the office of a justice of peace. It is, the respondent believes, the first time that ever the undertaking an office of such extensive utility was stated as a crime; for he humbly apprehends, that by conferring the office of a justice of the peace upon clergymen, their influence may, in the general case, be rendered more extensive among their parishioners, and many trifling causes be settled by them, which might lead the litigants to enormous expenses, and become the subject of much contention before other courts. The duty being only occasional, and not daily, cannot be said to interfere with those of their function; and their education, and presumed character, render them most proper for the office. It is indeed alleged that the Act 1584, chap. 133, excludes clergymen from acting under a commission of the peace. This Act, however, was passed at a time when it was of the highest importance to the Crown to wrench from the hands of the clergy the power of administering justice in civil cases, which had, from the ignorance of the laity, been enjoyed by them almost exclusively. During the whole reign of James VI., as is well known to the Reverend Court, such a jealousy subsisted betwixt the Church and the State, that those who were at the head of the latter endeavored, by every means in their power, to diminish the influence of the former. At present, when these dissensions happily no longer subsist, the law, as far as regards the office of justice of the peace, appears to have fallen into disuse, and the respondent conceives that any minister is capable of acting in that, or any other judicial capacity, provided it is of such a nature as not to withdraw much of his time from what the statute calls the comfort and edification of the flock committed to him. Further, the Act 1584 is virtually repealed by the statute 6th Anne, c. 6, sect. 2, which makes the Scots Law on the subject of justices of the peace the same with that of England, where the office is publicly exercised by the clergy of all descriptions.

. . . Another branch of the accusation against the defender as a justice of peace, is the ratification of irregular marriages. The defender must here also call the attention of his reverend brethren and judges to the expediency of his conduct. The girls were usually with child at the time the application was made to the defender. In this situation, the children born out of matrimony, though begot under promise of marriage, must have been thrown upon the parish, or perhaps murdered in infancy, had not the men been persuaded to consent to a solemn declaration of betrothment, or private marriage, emitted before the defender as a justice of peace. The defender himself, commiserating the situation of such women, often endeavored to persuade their seducers to do them justice; and men frequently acquiesced in this sort of marriage, when they could by no means have been prevailed upon to go through the ceremonies of proclamation of banns, or the expense and trouble of a public wedding. The declaration of a previous marriage was sometimes literally true ; sometimes a fiction voluntarily emitted by the parties themselves, under the belief that it was the most safe way of constituting a private marriage *de presenti*. The defender had been induced, from the practice of other justices, to consider the receiving these declarations, whether true or false, as a part of his duty, which he could not decline, even had he been willing to do so. Finally, the defender must remind the Venerable Assembly that he acted upon these occasions as a justice of peace, which brings him back to the point from which he set out, namely, that the Reverend Court are utterly incompetent to take cognizance of his conduct in that character, which no sentence that they can pronounce could give or take away.

The second grand division of the libel against the defender refers to his conduct as a clergyman and a Christian. He was charged in the libel with the most gross and vulgar behavior, with drunkenness, blasphemy, and impiety ; yet all the evidence which the appellants have been able to bring forward tends only to convict him of three acts of drunkenness during the course of fourteen years : for even the Presbytery, severe as they have been, acquit him *quoad ultra*. But the attention of the Reverend Court is earnestly entreated to the situation of the defender at the time, the circumstances which conduced to his imprudence, and the share which some of those had in occasioning his guilt, who have since been most active in persecuting and distressing him on account of it.

The defender must premise, by observing, that the crime of drunkenness consists not in a man's having been in that situation twice or thrice in his life, but in the constant and habitual practice of the vice ; the distinction between *ebrius* and *ebriosus* being founded in common sense, and recognized by law. A thousand cases may be supposed, in which a man, without being aware of what he is about, may be insensibly led on to intoxication, especially in a country where the vice is unfortunately so common, that upon some occasions a man may go to excess from a false sense of modesty, or a fear of disobliging his

entertainer. The defender will not deny, that after losing his
senses upon the occasions, and in the manner to be afterwards
stated, he may have committed improprieties which fill him
with sorrow and regret : but he hopes, that in case he shall be
able to show circumstances which abridge and palliate the guilt
of his imprudent excess, the Venerable Court will consider these
improprieties as the effects of that excess only, and not as arising from any radical vice in his temper or disposition. When
a man is bereft of his judgment by the influence of wine, and
commits any crime, he can only be said to be morally culpable,
in proportion to the impropriety of the excess he has committed,
and not in proportion to the magnitude of its evil consequences.
In a legal view, indeed, a man must be held as answerable and
punishable for such a crime, precisely as if he had been in a
state of sobriety ; but his crime is, in a moral light, comprised
in the *origo mali*, the drunkenness only. His senses being once
gone, he is no more than a human machine, as insensible of
misconduct, in speech and action, as a parrot or an automaton.
This is more particularly the case with respect to indecorums,
such as the defender is accused of ; for a man can no more be
held a common swearer, or a habitual talker of obscenity, because he has been guilty of using such expressions when intoxicated, than he can be termed an idiot, because, when intoxicated,
he has spoken nonsense. If, therefore, the defender can exten-
uate the guilt of his intoxication, he hopes that its consequences
will be numbered rather among his misfortunes than faults ;
and that his Reverend Brethren will consider him, while in that
state, as acting from a mechanical impulse, and as incapable of
distinguishing between right and wrong. For the scandal which
his behavior may have occasioned, he feels the most heartfelt
sorrow, and will submit with penitence and contrition to the
severe rebuke which the Presbytery have decreed against him.
But he cannot think that his unfortunate misdemeanor, cir-
cumstanced as he was, merits a severer punishment. He can
show that pains were at these times taken to lead him on, when
bereft of his senses, to subjects which were likely to call forth
improper or indecent expressions. The defender must further
urge, that not being originally educated for the church, he may,
before he assumed the sacred character, have occasionally permitted himself freedoms of expression which are reckoned less

culpable among the laity. Thus he may, during that time, have learned the songs which he is accused of singing, though rather inconsistent with his clerical character. What, then, was more natural, than that, when thrown off his guard by the assumed conviviality and artful solicitations of those about him, former improper habits, though renounced during his thinking moments, might assume the reins of his imagination, when his situation rendered him utterly insensible of their impropriety?

. . . The Venerable Court will now consider how far three instances of ebriety, and their consequences, should ruin at once the character and the peace of mind of the unfortunate defender, and reduce him, at his advanced time of life, about sixty years, together with his aged parent, to a state of beggary. He hopes his severe sufferings may be considered as some atonement for the improprieties of which he may have been guilty ; and that the Venerable Court will, in their judgment, remember mercy.

In respect whereof, etc.

WALTER SCOTT.

This argument (for which he received five guineas) was sustained by Scott in a speech of considerable length at the Bar of the Assembly. It was far the most important business in which any solicitor had as yet employed him, and *The Club* mustered strong in the gallery. He began in a low voice, but by degrees gathered more confidence; and when it became necessary for him to analyze the evidence touching a certain penny-wedding, repeated some very coarse specimens of his client's alleged conversation, in a tone so bold and free, that he was called to order with great austerity by one of the leading members of the Venerable Court. This seemed to confuse him not a little; so when, by and by, he had to recite a stanza of one of M'Naught's convivial ditties, he breathed it out in a faint and hesitating style; whereupon, thinking he needed encouragement, the allies in the gallery astounded the Assembly by cordial shouts of *hear! hear! — encore! encore!* They were immediately turned out, and Scott got through the rest of his harangue very little to his own satisfaction.

He believed, in a word, that he had made a complete failure, and issued from the Court in a melancholy mood. At the door he found Adam Ferguson waiting to inform him that the brethren so unceremoniously extruded from the gallery had sought shelter in a neighboring tavern, where they hoped he would join them. He complied with the invitation, but seemed for a long while incapable of enjoying the merriment of his friends. "Come, *Duns*," cried *the Baronet*, — "cheer up, man, and fill another tumbler; here's * * * * * * going to give us *The Tailor*." — "Ah!" he answered, with a groan, "the tailor was a better man than me, sirs; for he didna venture *ben* until he *kenned the way*." A certain comical old song, which had, perhaps, been a favorite with the minister of Girthon —

> " The tailor he came here to sew,
> And weel he kenn'd the way o't," etc.

was, however, sung and chorused; and the evening ended in the full jollity of *High Jinks*.

Mr. M'Naught was deposed from the ministry, and his young advocate has written out at the end of the printed papers on the case two of the *songs* which had been alleged in the evidence. They are both grossly indecent. It is to be observed, that the research he had made with a view to pleading this man's cause carried him, for the first, and I believe for the last time, into the scenery of his Guy Mannering; and I may add that several of the names of the minor characters of the novel (that of *M'Guffog*, for example) appear in the list of witnesses for and against his client.

If the preceding autumn forms a remarkable point in Scott's history, as first introducing him to the manners of the wilder Border country, the summer which followed left traces of equal importance. He gave the greater part of it to an excursion which much extended his knowledge of Highland scenery and character; and in particular furnished him with the richest stores, which he after-

wards turned to account in one of the most beautiful of
his great poems, and in several, including the first, of
his prose romances.

Accompanied by Adam Ferguson, he visited on this
occasion some of the finest districts of Stirlingshire and
Perthshire; and not in the percursory manner of his more
boyish expeditions, but taking up his residence for a
week or ten days in succession at the family residences of
several of his young allies of *the Mountain*, and from
thence familiarizing himself at leisure with the country
and the people round about. In this way he lingered
some time at Tullibody, the seat of the father of Sir
Ralph Abercromby, and grandfather of his friend Mr.
George Abercromby (now Lord Abercromby); and heard
from the old gentleman's own lips his narrative of a
journey which he had been obliged to make, shortly after
he first settled in Stirlingshire, to the wild retreat of Rob
Roy. The venerable laird told how he was received by
the cateran "with much courtesy," in a cavern exactly
such as that of *Bean Lean ;* dined on collops cut from
some of his own cattle, which he recognized hanging by
their heels from the rocky roof beyond; and returned in
all safety, after concluding a bargain of *blackmail* — in
virtue of which annual payment Rob Roy guaranteed the
future security of his herds against, not his own followers
merely, but all freebooters whatever. Scott next visited
his friend Edmonstone, at Newton, a beautiful seat close
to the ruins of the once magnificent Castle of Doune,
and heard another aged gentleman's vivid recollections
of all that happened there when John Home, the author
of Douglas, and other Hanoverian prisoners, escaped
from the Highland garrison in 1745.[1] Proceeding towards the sources of the Teith, he was received for the
first time under a roof which, in subsequent years, he
regularly revisited, that of another of his associates, Buchanan, the young Laird of Cambusmore. It was thus

[1] *Waverley*, chap. xxxviii. note.

that the scenery of Loch Katrine came to be so associated with "the recollection of many a dear friend and merry expedition of former days," that to compose The Lady of the Lake was "a labor of love, and no less so to recall the manners and incidents introduced."[1] It was starting from the same house, when the poem itself had made some progress, that he put to the test the practicability of riding from the banks of Loch Vennachar to the Castle of Stirling within the brief space which he had assigned to Fitz-James's Grey Bayard, after the duel with Roderick Dhu; and the principal landmarks in the description of that fiery progress are so many hospitable mansions, all familiar to him at the same period — Blairdrummond, the residence of Lord Kaimes; Ochtertyre, that of John Ramsay, the scholar and antiquary (now best remembered for his kind and sagacious advice to Burns); and "the lofty brow of ancient Kier," the splendid seat of the chief family of the name of Stirling; from which, to say nothing of remoter objects, the prospect has, on one hand, the rock of "Snowdon," and in front the field of Bannockburn.

Another resting-place was Craighall, in Perthshire, the seat of the Rattrays, a family related to Mr. Clerk, who accompanied him. From the position of this striking place, as Mr. Clerk at once perceived, and as the author afterwards confessed to him, that of the *Tully-Veolan* was very faithfully copied; though in the description of the house itself, and its gardens, many features were adopted from Bruntsfield and Ravelston.[2] Mr. Clerk has told me that he went through the first chapters of Waverley without more than a vague suspicion of the new novelist; but that when he read the arrival at Tully-Veolan, his suspicion was at once converted into certainty, and he handed the book to a common friend of his and the author's, saying, "This is Scott's — and I 'll

---

[1] Introduction to *The Lady of the Lake*, 1830.
[2] *Waverley*, chap. viii.

lay a bet you'll find such and such things in the next chapter." I hope Mr. Clerk will forgive me for mentioning *the* particular circumstance that first flashed the conviction on his mind. In the course of a ride from Craighall they had both become considerably fagged and heated, and Clerk, seeing the smoke of a *clachan* a little way before them, ejaculated — "How agreeable if we should here fall in with one of those signposts where a red lion predominates over a punch-bowl!" The phrase happened to tickle Scott's fancy — he often introduced it on similar occasions afterwards — and at the distance of twenty years Mr. Clerk was at no loss to recognize an old acquaintance in the "huge bear" which "predominates" over the stone basin in the courtyard of Baron Bradwardine.

I believe the longest stay he made this autumn was at Meigle in Forfarshire, the seat of Patrick Murray of Simprim, a gentleman whose enthusiastic passion for antiquities, and especially military antiquities, had peculiarly endeared him both to Scott and Clerk. Here Adam Ferguson, too, was of the party; and I have often heard them each and all dwell on the thousand scenes of adventure and merriment which diversified that visit. In the village churchyard, close beneath Mr. Murray's gardens, tradition still points out the tomb of Queen Guenever; and the whole district abounds in objects of historical interest. Amidst them they spent their wandering days, while their evenings passed in the joyous festivity of a wealthy young bachelor's establishment, or sometimes under the roofs of neighbors less refined than their host, the *Balmawhapples* of the Braes of Angus. From Meigle they made a trip to Dunnottar Castle, the ruins of the huge old fortress of the Earls Marischall, and it was in the churchyard of that place that Scott then saw for the first and last time Robert Paterson, the living *Old Mortality*. He and Mr. Walker, the minister of the parish, found the poor man refreshing the epitaphs on the tombs of certain Cameronians who had fallen under the oppressions of James the Second's brief insanity. Being invited into the manse after dinner to take a glass of whiskey-punch, "to which he was supposed to have no objections," he joined the minister's party accordingly; but "he was in bad humor," says Scott, "and, to use his own phrase, had no freedom for conversation. His spirit had been sorely vexed by hearing, in a certain Aberdonian kirk, the psalmody directed by a pitch-pipe or some similar instrument, which was to Old Mortality the abomination of abominations."

It was also while he had his headquarters at Meigle at this time that Scott visited for the first time *Glammis*, the residence of the Earls of Strathmore, by far the noblest specimen of the real feudal castle, entire and perfect, that had as yet come under his inspection. What its aspect was when he first saw it, and how grievously he lamented the change it had undergone when he revisited it some years afterwards, he has recorded in one of the most striking passages that I think ever came from his pen. Commenting, in his Essay on Landscape Gardening (1828), on the proper domestic ornaments of the Castle *Pleasaunce*, he has this beautiful burst of lamentation over the barbarous innovations of *the Capability men* : — "Down went many a trophy of old magnificence, courtyard, ornamented enclosure, fosse, avenue, barbican, and every external muniment of battled wall and flanking tower, out of the midst of which the ancient dome, rising high above all its characteristic accompaniments, and seemingly girt round by its appropriate defences, which again circled each other in their different gradations, looked, as it should, the queen and mistress of the surrounding country. It was thus that the huge old tower of Glammis, ' whose birth tradition notes not,' once showed its lordly head above seven circles (if I remember aright) of defensive boundaries, through which the friendly guest was admitted, and at each of which a suspicious person was unquestionably put to his answer. A disciple of Kent had the cruelty to render this splendid old mansion (the more modern part of which was the work of Inigo Jones) more *parkish*, as he was pleased to call it; to raze all those exterior defences, and bring his mean and paltry gravel-walk up to the very door from which, deluded by the name, one might have imagined Lady Macbeth (with the form and features of Siddons) issuing forth to receive King Duncan. It is thirty years and upwards since I have seen Glammis, but I have not yet forgotten or forgiven the atrocity which, under pretence of improvement, deprived that lordly place of its appropriate accompaniments,

> ' Leaving an ancient dome and towers like these
> Beggar'd and outraged.' " [1]

The night he spent at the yet unprofaned Glammis in 1793 was, as he elsewhere says, one of the "*two* periods distant from each other" at which he could recollect experiencing " that degree of superstitious awe which his countrymen call *eerie*."

" The heavy pile," he writes, "contains much in its appearance, and in the traditions connected with it, impressive to the imagination. It was the scene of the murder of a Scottish King of great antiquity — not indeed the gracious Duncan, with whom the name naturally associates itself, but Malcolm II. It contains also a curious monument of the peril of feudal times, being a secret chamber, the entrance of which, by the law or custom of the family, must only be known to three persons at once, namely, the Earl of Strathmore, his heir-apparent, and any third person whom they may take into their confidence. The extreme antiquity of the building is vouched by the thickness of the walls, and the wild straggling arrangement of the accommodation within doors. As the late Earl seldom resided at Glammis, it was when I was there but half furnished, and that with movables of great antiquity, which, with the pieces of chivalric armor hanging on the walls, greatly contributed to the general effect of the whole. After a very hospitable reception

---

[1] Wordsworth's Sonnet on Neidpath Castle.

from the late Peter Proctor, seneschal of the castle, I was conducted to my apartment in a distant part of the building. I must own, that when I heard door after door shut, after my conductor had retired, I began to consider myself as too far from the living, and somewhat too near the dead. We had passed through what is called *the King's Room*, a vaulted apartment, garnished with stags' antlers and other trophies of the chase, and said by tradition to be the spot of Malcolm's murder, and I had an idea of the vicinity of the castle chapel. In spite of the truth of history, the whole night scene in Macbeth's Castle rushed at once upon me, and struck my mind more forcibly than even when I have seen its terrors represented by John Kemble and his inimitable sister. In a word, I experienced sensations which, though not remarkable for timidity or superstition, did not fail to affect me to the point of being disagreeable, while they were mingled at the same time with a strange and indescribable sort of pleasure, the recollection of which affords me gratification at this moment." [1]

He alludes here to the hospitable reception which had preceded the mingled sensations of this *eerie* night; but one of his notes on Waverley touches this not unimportant part of the story more distinctly; for we are there informed that the *silver bear* of Tully-Veolan, "the *poculum potatorium* of the valiant baron*," had its prototype at Glammis — a massive beaker of silver, double gilt, moulded into the form of a *lion*, the name and bearing of the Earls of Strathmore, and containing about an English pint of wine. "The author," he says, "ought perhaps to be ashamed of recording that he had the honor of swallowing the contents of *the lion ;* and the recollection of the feat suggested the story of the Bear of Bradwardine."

From this pleasant tour, so rich in its results, Scott returned in time to attend the autumnal assizes at Jedburgh, on which occasion he made his first appearance as counsel in a criminal court; and had the satisfaction of helping a veteran poacher and sheep-stealer to escape through some of the meshes of the law. "You 're a

[1] *Letters on Demonology and Witchcraft*, p. 398.

lucky scoundrel," Scott whispered to his client, when the
verdict was pronounced. "I 'm just o' your mind,"
quoth the desperado, "and I 'll send ye a maukin[1] the
morn, man." I am not sure whether it was at these assizes or the next in the same town, that he had less success in the case of a certain notorious housebreaker. The
man, however, was well aware that no skill could have
baffled the clear evidence against him, and was, after his
fashion, grateful for such exertions as had been made in
his behalf. He requested the young advocate to visit
him once more before he left the place. Scott's curiosity
induced him to accept this invitation, and his friend, as
soon as they were alone together in the *condemned cell*,
said — "I am very sorry, sir, that I have no fee to offer
you — so let me beg your acceptance of two bits of advice
which may be useful perhaps when you come to have a
house of your own. I am done with practice, you see,
and here is my legacy. Never keep a large watchdog
out of doors — we can always silence them cheaply — indeed if it be a *dog*, 't is easier than whistling — but tie
a little tight yelping terrier within; and secondly, put no
trust in nice, clever, gimcrack locks — the only thing
that bothers us is a huge old heavy one, no matter how
simple the construction, — and the ruder and rustier the
key, so much the better for the housekeeper." I remember hearing him tell this story some thirty years after at
a Judges' dinner at Jedburgh, and he summed it up with
a rhyme — "Ay, ay, my lord," (I think he addressed
his friend Lord Meadowbank) —

> " Yelping terrier, rusty key,
> Was Walter Scott's best Jeddart fee."

At these, or perhaps the next assizes, he was also
counsel in an appeal case touching a cow which his client
had sold as sound, but which the court below (the sheriff)
had pronounced to have what is called *the cliers* — a disease analogous to glanders in a horse. In opening his

[1] A hare.

case before Sir David Rae, Lord Eskgrove, Scott stoutly
maintained the healthiness of the cow, who, as he said,
had merely a cough. "Stop there," quoth the judge;
"I have had plenty of healthy kye in my time, but I
never heard of ane of them coughing. A coughin' cow!
— that will never do. Sustain the sheriff's judgment,
and decern."

A day or two after this, Scott and his old companion
were again on their way into Liddesdale, and "just,"
says the Shortreed Memorandum, "as we were passing
by Singdon, we saw a grand herd o' cattle a' feeding by
the roadside, and a fine young bullock, the best in the
whole lot, was in the midst of them, coughing lustily.
' Ah,' said Scott, ' what a pity for my client that old
Eskgrove had not taken Singdon on his way to the town.
That bonny creature would have saved us —

> "A Daniel come to judgment, yea a Daniel ;
> O wise young judge, how I do honor thee ! " ' "

TO PATRICK MURRAY OF SIMPRIM, ESQ., MEIGLE.

ROSEBANK, near Kelso, September 13, 1793.

DEAR MURRAY, — I would have let fly an epistle at
you long ere this, had I not known I should have some
difficulty in hitting so active a traveller, who may in that
respect be likened unto a bird of passage. Were you to
follow the simile throughout, I might soon expect to see
you winging your way to the southern climes, instead of
remaining to wait the approach of winter in the colder
regions of the north. Seriously, I have been in weekly
hopes of hearing of your arrival in the Merse, and have
been qualifying myself by constant excursions to be your
Border *Cicerone*.

As the facetious Linton will no doubt make one of
your party, I have got by heart for his amusement a
reasonable number of Border ballads, most of them a
little longer than Chevy Chase, which I intend to throw
in at intervals, just by way of securing my share in the

conversation. As for *you*, as I know your picturesque turn, I can be in this country at no loss how to cater for your entertainment, especially if you would think of moving before the fall of the leaf. I believe with respect to the real *To Kalon*, few villages can surpass that near which I am now writing; and as to your rivers, it is part of my creed that the Tweed and Teviot yield to none in the world, nor do I fear that even in your eyes, which have been feasted on classic ground, they will greatly sink in comparison with the Tiber or Po. Then for antiquities, it is true we have got no temples or heathenish fanes to show; but if substantial old castles and ruined abbeys will serve in their stead, they are to be found in abundance. So much for Linton and you. As for Mr. Robertson,[1] I don't know quite so well how to bribe him. We had indeed lately a party of strollers here, who might in some degree have entertained him, *i. e.*, in case he felt no compassion for the horrid and tragical murders which they nightly committed, — but now, *Alas, Sir! the players be gone.*

I am at present very uncertain as to my own motions, but I still hope to be northwards again before the commencement of the session, which (d—n it) is beginning to draw nigher than I could wish. I would esteem myself greatly favored by a few lines informing me of your motions when they are settled; since visiting you, should I go north, or attending you if you come this way, are my two grand plans of amusement.

What think you of our politics now? Had I been within reach of you, or any of the chosen, I suspect the taking of Valenciennes would have been sustained as a reason for examining the contents of t'other bottle, which has too often suffered for slighter pretences. I have

---

[1] Dr. Robertson was tutor to the Laird of Simprim, and afterwards minister of Meigle — a man of great worth, and an excellent scholar. In his younger days he was fond of the theatre, and encouraged and directed *Simprim, Grogg, Linton & Co.* in their histrionic diversions. — (1839.)

little doubt, however, that by the time we meet in glory
(terrestrial glory, I mean) Dunkirk will be an equally
good apology. Adieu, my good friend; remember me
kindly to Mr. Robertson, to Linton, and to the Baronet.
I understand both these last intend seeing you soon. I
am very sincerely yours,   WALTER SCOTT.

The winter of 1793–94 appears to have been passed
like the preceding one: the German class resumed their
sittings; Scott spoke in his debating club on the questions of Parliamentary Reform and the Inviolability of
the Person of the First Magistrate, which the circumstances of the time had invested with extraordinary interest, and in both of which he no doubt took the side
adverse to the principles of the English, and the practice
of the French Liberals. His love-affair continued on
exactly the same footing as before; — and for the rest,
like the young heroes in Redgauntlet, he "swept the
boards of the Parliament House with the skirts of his
gown; laughed, and made others laugh; drank claret at
Bayle's, Fortune's, and Walker's, and eat oysters in the
Covenant Close." On his desk "the new novel most in
repute lay snugly intrenched beneath Stair's Institute, or
an open volume of Decisions;" and his dressing-table
was littered with "old play-bills, letters respecting a
meeting of the Faculty, Rules of the Speculative, Syl-
labus of Lectures — all the miscellaneous contents of a
young advocate's pocket, which contains everything but
briefs and bank-notes." His professional occupation was
still very slender; but he took a lively interest in the
proceedings of the criminal court, and more especially in
those arising out of the troubled state of the public feeling as to politics.

In the spring of 1794 I find him writing to his friends
in Roxburghshire with great exultation about the "good
spirit" manifesting itself among the upper classes of the
citizens of Edinburgh, and, above all, the organization of

a regiment of volunteers, in which his brother Thomas, now a fine active young man, equally handsome and high-spirited, was enrolled as a grenadier, while, as he remarks, his own "unfortunate infirmity" condemned him to be "a mere spectator of the drills." In the course of the same year, the plan of a corps of volunteer light horse was started; and, if the recollection of Mr. Skene be accurate, the suggestion originally proceeded from Scott himself, who certainly had a principal share in its subsequent success. He writes to his uncle at Rose-bank, requesting him to be on the lookout for a "strong gelding, such as would suit a stalwart dragoon;" and intimating his intention to part with his collection of Scottish coins, rather than not be mounted to his mind. The corps, however, was not organized for some time; and in the mean while he had an opportunity of display-ing his zeal in a manner which Captain Scott by no means considered as so respectable.

A party of Irish medical students began, towards the end of April, to make themselves remarkable in the Edinburgh Theatre, where they mustered in a particular corner of the pit, and lost no opportunity of insulting the Loyalists of the boxes, by calling for revolutionary tunes, applauding every speech that could bear a seditious meaning, and drowning the national anthem in howls and hootings. The young Tories of the Parliament House resented this license warmly, and after a succession of minor disturbances, the quarrel was put to the issue of a regular trial by combat. Scott was conspicuous among the juvenile advocates and solicitors who on this grand night assembled in front of the pit, armed with stout cudgels, and determined to have God save the King not only played without interruption, but sung in full chorus by both company and audience. The Irishmen were ready at the first note of the anthem. They rose, clapped on their hats, and brandished their shillelahs; a stern battle ensued, and after many a head had been cracked, the Loyalists at length found themselves in possession of the field. In writing to Simprim a few days afterwards, Scott says — "You will be glad to hear that the *affair* of Saturday passed over without any worse consequence to the Loyalists than that five, including your friend and humble servant Colonel Grogg, have been bound over to the peace, and obliged to give bail for their good behavior, which, you may believe, was easily found. The said Colonel had no less than three broken heads laid to his charge by as many of the Democrats." Alluding to Simprim's then recent appointment as Captain in the Perthshire Fencibles (Cavalry), he adds — "Among my own military (I mean mock-military) achievements, let me not fail to congratulate you and the country on the real character you have agreed to accept. Remember, in case of real action, I shall beg the honor of admission to your troop as a volunteer."

One of the theatrical party, Sir Alexander Wood, whose notes lie before me, says — "Walter was certainly our Coryphæus, and signalized himself splendidly in this desperate fray; and nothing used afterwards to afford him more delight than dramatizing its incidents. Some of the most efficient of our allies were persons previously unknown to him, and of several of these whom he had particularly observed, he never lost sight afterwards. There were, I believe, cases in which they owed most valuable assistance in life to his recollection of *the playhouse row*." To this last part of Sir Alexander's testimony I can also add mine; and I am sure my worthy friend, Mr. Donald M'Lean, W. S., will gratefully confirm it. When that gentleman became candidate for some office in the Exchequer, about 1822 or 1823, and Sir Walter's interest was requested on his behalf, — "To be sure!" said he; "did not he sound the charge upon Paddy? Can I ever forget Donald's *Sticks by G—t?*" [1]

[1] According to a friendly critic, one of the Liberals exclaimed, as the *row* was thickening, "No Blows!" — and Donald, suiting the action to the word, responded, "Plows by —— !" — (1829.)

On the 9th May, 1794, Charles Kerr of Abbotrule writes to him — "I was last night at Rosebank, and your uncle told me he had been giving you a very long and very sage lecture upon the occasion of these Edinburgh squabbles; I am happy to hear they are now at an end. They were rather of the serious cast, and though you encountered them with spirit and commendable resolution, I, with your uncle, should wish to see your abilities conspicuous on another theatre." The same gentleman, in his next letter (June 3), congratulates Scott on having "seen *his name in the newspaper*," namely, as counsel for another Roxburghshire laird, by designation *Bedrule*. Such, no doubt, was Abbotrule's "other theatre."

Scott spent the long vacation of this year chiefly in Roxburghshire, but again visited Keir, Cambusmore, and others of his friends in Perthshire, and came to Edinburgh, early in September, to be present at the trials of Watt and Downie, on a charge of high treason. Watt seems to have tendered his services to Government as a spy upon the Society of the Friends of the People in Edinburgh, but ultimately, considering himself as underpaid, to have embraced, to their wildest extent, the schemes he had become acquainted with in the course of this worthy occupation; and he, and one Downie, a mechanic, were now arraigned as having taken a prominent part in the organizing of a plot for a general rising in Edinburgh, to seize the Castle, the Bank, the persons of the Judges, and proclaim a Provisional Republican Government; all which was supposed to have been arranged in concert with the Hardies, Thelwalls, Holcrofts, and so forth, who were a few weeks later brought to trial in London for an alleged conspiracy to "summon delegates to a National Convention, with a view to subvert the Government, and levy war upon the King." The English prisoners were acquitted, but Watt and Downie were not so fortunate. Scott writes as follows to his aunt, Miss Christian Rutherford, then at Ashestiel, in Selkirkshire: —

ADVOCATES' LIBRARY, 5th September, 1794.

My dear Miss Christy will perceive, from the date of this epistle, that I have accomplished my purpose of coming to town to be present at the trial of the Edinburgh traitors. I arrived here on Monday evening from Kelso, and was present at Watt's trial on Wednesday, which displayed to the public the most atrocious and deliberate plan of villainy which has occurred, perhaps, in the annals of Great Britain. I refer you for particulars to the papers, and shall only add, that the equivocations and perjury of the witnesses (most of them being accomplices in what they called the *great plan*) set the abilities of Mr. Anstruther, the King's counsel, in the most striking point of view. The patience and temper with which he tried them on every side, and screwed out of them the evidence they were so anxious to conceal, showed much knowledge of human nature; and the art with which he arranged the information he received, made the trial, upon the whole, the most interesting I ever was present at. Downie's trial is just now going forwards over my head; but as the evidence is just the same as formerly brought against Watt, is not so interesting. You will easily believe that on Wednesday my curiosity was too much excited to retire at an early hour, and, indeed, I sat in the Court from seven in the morning till two the next morning; but as I had provided myself with some cold meat and a bottle of wine, I contrived to support the fatigue pretty well. It strikes me, upon the whole, that the plan of these miscreants might, from its very desperate and improbable nature, have had no small chance of succeeding, at least as far as concerned cutting off the soldiers, and obtaining possession of the banks, besides shedding the blood of the most distinguished inhabitants. There, I think, the evil must have stopped, unless they had further support than has yet appeared. Stooks was the prime mover of the whole, and the person who supplied the money; and our theatrical disturbances are found to have formed one link of the chain. So, I have no doubt, Messrs. Stooks, Burk, etc., would have found out a new way of paying old debts. The *people* are perfectly quiescent upon this grand occasion, and seem to interest themselves very little in the fate of their *soi-disant friends.* The Edinburgh volunteers make a respectable and formidable appearance already. They are exercised four hours almost every day, with all the rigor of military discipline. The grenadier company consists entirely of men above six feet. So much for public news.

As to home intelligence — you know that my mother and Anne had projected a *jaunt* to Inverleithen; fate, however, had destined otherwise. The intended day of departure was ushered in by a most complete deluge, to which, and the consequent disappointment, our proposed travellers did not submit with that Christian meekness which might have beseemed. In short, both within and without doors, it was a *devil* of a day. The second was like unto it. The third day came a post, a killing post,[1] and in the shape of a letter from this fountain of health, informed us no lodgings were to be had there; so, whatever be its virtues, or the grandeur attending a journey to its streams, we might as well have proposed to visit the river Jordan, or the walls of Jericho. Not so our heroic John; he has been arrived here for some time (much the same as when he went away), and has formed the desperate resolution of riding out with me to Kelso to-morrow morning. I have stayed a day longer, waiting for the arrival of a pair of new boots and buckskin etcs., in which the soldier is to be equipt. I ventured to hint the convenience of a roll of diaculum plaister, and a box of the most approved horseman-salve, in which recommendation our doctor[2] warmly joined. His impatience for the journey has been somewhat cooled by some incli-

---

[1] "The third day comes a frost, a killing frost."
                                        King Henry VIII.

[2] Dr. Rutherford.

nation yesterday displayed by his charger (a pony belonging to Anne) to lay his warlike rider in the dust —
a purpose he had nearly effected. He next mounted
Queen Mab, who treated him with little more complai-
sance, and, in carters' phrase, would neither *hap* nor
wynd till she got rid of him. Seriously, however, if
Jack has not returned covered with laurels, a crop which
the Rock[1] no longer produces, he has brought back all
his own good-nature, and a manner considerably improved, so that he is at times very agreeable company.
Best love to Miss R., Jean, and Anne (I hope they are
improved at the battledore), and the boys, not forgetting
my friend Archy, though least not last in my remembrance. Best compliments to the Colonel.[2] I shall
remember with pleasure Ashestiel hospitality, and not
without a desire to put it to the proof next year. Adieu,
ma chère amie. When you write, direct to Rosebank,
and I shall be a good boy, and write you another sheet
of nonsense soon. All friends here well. Ever yours
affectionately,   WALTER SCOTT.

The letter, of which the following is an extract, must
have been written in October or November — Scott having been in Liddesdale, and again in Perthshire, during
the interval. It is worth quoting for the little domestic
allusions with which it concludes, and which every one
who has witnessed the discipline of a Presbyterian family
of the old school, at the time of preparation for *the Com-
munion,* will perfectly understand. Scott's father, though
on particular occasions he could permit himself, like
Saunders Fairford, to play the part of a good Amphi-
tryon, was habitually ascetic in his habits. I have heard
his son tell, that it was common with him, if any one
observed that the soup was good, to taste it again, and

[1] Captain John Scott had been for some time with his regiment at
Gibraltar.
[2] Colonel Russell of Ashestiel, married to a sister of Scott's mother.

say, — "Yes, it is too good, bairns," and dash a tumbler of cold water into his plate. It is easy, therefore, to imagine with what rigidity he must have enforced the ultra-Catholic severities which marked, in those days, the yearly or half-yearly *retreat* of the descendants of John Knox.

TO MISS CHRISTIAN RUTHERFORD, ASHESTIEL.

Previous to my ramble, I stayed a single day in town, to witness the exit of the *ci-devant* Jacobin, Mr. Watt. It was a very solemn scene, but the pusillanimity of the unfortunate victim was astonishing, considering the boldness of his nefarious plans. It is matter of general regret that his associate Downie should have received a reprieve, which, I understand, is now prolonged for a second month, I suppose to wait the issue of the London trials. Our volunteers are now completely embodied, and, notwithstanding the heaviness of their dress, have a martial and striking appearance. Their accuracy in firing and manœuvring excites the surprise of military gentlemen, who are the best judges of their merit in that way. Tom is very proud of the grenadier company, to which he belongs, which has indisputably carried off the palm upon all public occasions. And now, give me leave to ask you whether the approaching *winter* does not remind you of your snug parlor in George's Street? Do you not feel a little uncomfortable when you see

> " how bleak and bare
> He wanders o'er the heights of *Yair ?* "

Amidst all this regard for your accommodation, don't suppose I am devoid of a little self-interest when I press your speedy return to Auld Reekie, for I am really tiring excessively to see the said parlor again inhabited. Besides that, I want the assistance of your eloquence to convince my honored father that Nature did not mean me either for a vagabond or *travelling merchant*, when she

honored me with the wandering propensity lately so conspicuously displayed. I saw D.ʳ yesterday, who is well.
I did not choose to intrude upon the little lady, this being
sermon week; for the same reason we are looking very
religious and very sour at home. However, it is with
some folk selon les règles, that in proportion as they are
pure themselves, they are entitled to render uncomfortable those whom they consider as less perfect. Best love
to Miss R., cousins and friends in general, and believe
me ever most sincerely yours,   WALTER SCOTT.

In July, 1795, a young lad, James Niven by name,
who had served for some time with excellent character on
board a ship of war, and been discharged in consequence
of a wound which disabled one of his hands, had the misfortune, in firing off a toy cannon in one of the narrow
wynds of Edinburgh, to kill on the spot David Knox,
one of the attendants of the Court of Session; a button,
or some other hard substance, having been accidentally
inserted with his cartridge. Scott was one of his counsel
when he was arraigned for murder, and had occasion to
draw up a written argument or *information* for the prisoner, from which I shall make a short quotation. Considered as a whole, the production seems both crude and
clumsy, but the following passages have, I think, several
traces of the style of thought and language which he
afterwards made familiar to the world: —

" Murder," he writes, " or the premeditated slaughter of a
citizen, is a crime of so deep and scarlet a dye, that there is
scarce a nation to be found in which it has not, from the earliest
period, been deemed worthy of a capital punishment. ' He
who sheddeth man's blood, by man shall his blood be shed,' is
a general maxim which has received the assent of all times and
countries. But it is equally certain that even the rude legisla-
tors of former days soon perceived that the death of one man
may be occasioned by another, without the slayer himself being
the proper object of the *lex talionis*. Such an accident may

happen either by the carelessness of the killer, or through that excess and vehemence of passion to which humanity is incident. In either case, though blamable, he ought not to be confounded with the cool and deliberate assassin, and the species of criminality attaching itself to those acts has been distinguished by the term *dolus*, in opposition to the milder term *culpa*. Again, there may be a third species of homicide, in which the perpetrator being the innocent and unfortunate cause of casual misfortune, becomes rather an object of compassion than punishment.

"Admitting there may have been a certain degree of culpability in the panel's conduct, still there is one circumstance which pleads strongly in his favor, so as to preclude all presumption of *dole*. This is the frequent practice, whether proper or improper, of using this amusement in the streets. It is a matter of public notoriety, that boys of all ages and descriptions are, or at least till the late very proper proclamation of the magistrates were, to be seen every evening in almost every corner of this city, amusing themselves with fire-arms and small cannons, and that without being checked or interfered with. When the panel, a poor ignorant raw lad, lately discharged from a ship of war — certainly not the most proper school to learn a prudent aversion to unlucky or mischievous practices — observed the sons of gentlemen of the first respectability engaged in such amusements, unchecked by their parents or by the magistrates, surely it can hardly be expected that he should discover that in imitating them in so common a practice, he was constituting himself *hostis humani generis*, a wretch the pest and scourge of mankind.

"There is, no doubt, attached to every even the most innocent of casual slaughter, a certain degree of blame, inasmuch as almost everything of the kind might have been avoided had the slayer exhibited the strictest degree of diligence. A well-known and authentic story will illustrate the proposition. A young gentleman, just married to a young lady of whom he was passionately fond, in affectionate trifling presented at her a pistol, of which he had drawn the charge some days before. The lady, entering into the joke, desired him to fire: he did so, and shot her dead; the pistol having been again charged by his servant without his knowledge. Can any one read this story, and feel any emotion but that of sympathy towards the unhappy husband? Can they ever connect the case with an idea of punishment? Yet, divesting it of these interesting circumstances which act upon the imagination, it is precisely that of the panel at your Lordships' Bar; and though no one will pretend to say that such a homicide is other than casual, yet there is not the slightest question but it might have been avoided had the killer taken the precaution of examining his piece. But this is not the degree of *culpa* which can raise a misfortune to the pitch of a crime. It is only an instance that no accident can take place without its afterwards being discovered that the chief actor might have avoided committing it, had he been gifted with the spirit of prophecy, or with such an extreme degree of prudence as is almost equally rare.

"In the instance of shooting at butts, or at a bird, the person killed must have been somewhat in the line previous to the discharge of the shot, otherways it could never have come near him. The shooter must therefore have been guilty *culpæ levis seu levissimæ* in firing while the deceased was in such a situation. In like manner, it is difficult to conceive how death should happen in consequence of a boxing or wrestling match, without some excess upon the part of the killer. Nay, in the exercise of the martial amusements of our forefathers, even by royal commission, should a champion be slain in running his barriers, or performing his tournament, it could scarcely happen without some *culpa seu levis seu levissima* on the part of his antagonist. Yet all these are enumerated in the English lawbooks as instances of casual homicide only; and we may therefore safely conclude, that by the law of the sister country a slight degree of blame will not subject the slayer *per infortunium* to the penalties of culpable homicide.

"Guilt, as an object of punishment, has its origin in the mind and intention of the actor; and therefore, where that is wanting, there is no proper object of chastisement. A madman, for example, can no more properly be said to be guilty of murder than the sword with which he commits it, both being equally incapable of intending injury. In the present case, in like manner, although it ought no doubt to be matter of deep sorrow and contrition to the panel that his folly should have occasioned the loss of life to a fellow-creature; yet as that folly can nei-

ther be termed malice, nor yet doth amount to a gross negligence, he ought rather to be pitied than condemned. The fact
done can never be recalled, and it rests with your Lordships to
consider the case of this unfortunate young man, who has served
his country in an humble though useful station, — deserved
such a character as is given him in the letter of his officers, —
and been disabled in that service. You will best judge how
(considering he has suffered a confinement of six months) he
can in humanity be the object of further or severer punishment,
for a deed of which his mind at least, if not his hand, is guilt-
less. When a case is attended with some nicety, your Lordships will allow mercy to incline the balance of justice, well
considering with the legislator of the East, ' It is better ten
guilty should escape than that one innocent man should perish
in his innocence.' "

The young sailor was acquitted.

To return for a moment to Scott's love-affair. I find
him writing as follows, in March, 1795, to his cousin,
William Scott, now Laird of Raeburn, who was then in
the East Indies : — "The lady you allude to has been in
town all this winter, and going a good deal into public, which has not in the least altered the meekness
of her manners. Matters, you see, stand just as they
did."

To another friend he writes thus, from Rosebank, on
the 23d of August, 1795 : —

It gave me the highest satisfaction to find, by the
receipt of your letter of the 14th current, that you have
formed precisely the same opinion with me, both with
regard to the interpretation of [Miss Stuart's] letter as
highly flattering and favorable, and to the mode of conduct I ought to pursue — for, after all, what she has
pointed out is the most prudent line of conduct for us
both, at least till better days, which, I think myself now
entitled to suppose, she, as well as I myself, will look
forward to with pleasure. If you were surprised at read-

ing the important billet, you may guess how agreeably I
was so at receiving it; for I had, to anticipate disappointment, struggled to suppress every rising gleam of hope;
and it would be very difficult to describe the mixed feelings her letter occasioned, which, *entre nous*, terminated
in a very hearty fit of crying. I read over her epistle
about ten times a day, and always with new admiration
of her generosity and candor — and as often take shame
to myself for the mean suspicions, which, after knowing
her so long, I could listen to, while endeavoring to guess
how she would conduct herself. To tell you the truth,
I cannot but confess that my *amour propre*, which one
would expect should have been exalted, has suffered not
a little upon this occasion, through a sense of my own
unworthiness, pretty similar to that which afflicted Linton upon sitting down at Keir's table. I ought perhaps
to tell you, what indeed you will perceive from her letter,
that I was always attentive, while consulting with you
upon the subject of my declaration, rather to under- than
over-rate the extent of our intimacy. By the way, I
must not omit mentioning the respect in which I hold
your knowledge of the fair sex, and your capacity of
advising in these matters, since it certainly is to your
encouragement that I owe the present situation of my
affairs. I wish to God, that, since you have acted as so
useful an auxiliary during my attack, which has succeeded in bringing the enemy to terms, you would next
sit down before some fortress yourself, and were it as
impregnable as the rock of Gibraltar, I should, notwithstanding, have the highest expectations of your final success. Not a line from poor Jack — What can he be
doing? Moping, I suppose, about some watering-place,
and deluging his guts with specifics of every kind — or
lowering and snorting in one corner of a post-chaise, with
Kennedy, as upright and cold as a poker, stuck into the
other. As for Linton, and Crab, I anticipate with pleasure their marvellous adventures, in the course of which

Dr. Black's *self-denying ordinance* will run a shrewd chance of being neglected.[1] They will be a source of fun for the winter evening conversations. Methinks I see the pair upon the mountains of Tipperary — John with a beard of three inches, united and blended with his shaggy black locks, an ellwand-looking cane with a gilt head in his hand, and a bundle in a handkerchief over his shoulder, exciting the cupidity of every Irish raparee who passes him, by his resemblance to a Jew pedlar who has sent forward his pack — Linton, tired of trailing his long legs, exalted in state upon an Irish garron, without stirrups, and a halter on its head, tempting every one to ask —

> " Who is that upon the pony,
> So long, so lean, so raw, so bony ? " [2]

— calculating, as he moves along, the expenses of the salt horse — and grinning a ghastly smile, when the hollow voice of his fellow-traveller observes — "God! Adam, if ye gang on at this rate, the eight shillings and sevenpence halfpenny will never carry us forward to my uncle's at Lisburn." Enough of a thorough Irish expedition.

We have a great marriage towards here — Scott of Harden, and a daughter of Count Brühl, the famous chess-player, a lady of sixteen quarters, half-sister to the Wyndhams. I wish they may come down soon, as we shall have fine racketing, of which I will, probably, get my share. I think of being in town some time next month, but whether for good and all, or only for a visit,

---

[1] *Crab* was the nickname of a friend who had accompanied Ferguson this summer on an Irish tour. Dr. Black, celebrated for his discoveries in chemistry, was Adam Ferguson's uncle; and had, it seems, given the young travellers a strong admonition touching the dangers of Irish hospitality.

[2] These lines are part of a song on *Little-tony* — i. e., the Parliamentary orator Littleton. They are quoted in Boswell's *Life of Johnson*, originally published in 1791.

I am not certain. Oh, for November! Our meeting will
be a little embarrassing one. How will she look, etc.,
etc., etc., are the important subjects of my present conjectures — how different from what they were three weeks
ago! I give you leave to laugh when I tell you seriously,
I had begun to "dwindle, peak, and pine," upon the
subject — but now, after the charge I have received, it
were a shame to resemble Pharaoh's lean kine. If good
living and plenty of exercise can avert that calamity, I
am in little danger of disobedience, and so, to conclude
classically,

Dicite Io pœan, et Io bis dicite pœan! —

Jubeo te bene valere,

GUALTERUS SCOTT.

I have had much hesitation about inserting the preceding letter, but could not make up my mind to omit what
seems to me a most exquisite revelation of the whole character of Scott at this critical period of his history, both
literary and personal; — more especially of his habitual
effort to suppress, as far as words were concerned, the
more tender feelings, which were in no heart deeper than
in his.

It must, I think, have been, while he was indulging
his *vagabond* vein, during the autumn of 1795, that Mrs.
Barbauld paid her visit to Edinburgh, and entertained a
party at Mr. Dugald Stewart's, by reading Mr. William
Taylor's then unpublished version of Bürger's Lenore.
In the essay on Imitation of Popular Poetry, the reader
has a full account of the interest with which Scott heard,
some weeks afterwards, a friend's imperfect recollections
of this performance; the anxiety with which he sought
after a copy of the original German; the delight with
which he at length perused it; and how, having just been
reading the specimens of ballad poetry introduced into
Lewis's romance of The Monk, he called to mind the
early facility of versification which had lain so long in

abeyance, and ventured to promise his friend a rhymed
translation of Lenore from his own pen. The friend in
question was Miss Cranstoun, afterwards Countess of
Purgstall, the sister of his friend George Cranstoun, now
Lord Corehouse. He began the task, he tells us, after
supper, and did not retire to bed until he had finished it,
having by that time worked himself into a state of excitement which set sleep at defiance.

Next morning, before breakfast, he carried his MS.
to Miss Cranstoun, who was not only delighted but astonished at it; for I have seen a letter of hers to a common
friend in the country, in which she says — "Upon my
word, Walter Scott is going to turn out a poet — something of a cross, I think, between Burns and Gray." The
same day he read it also to his friend Sir Alexander
Wood, who retains a vivid recollection of the high strain
of enthusiasm into which he had been exalted by dwelling on the wild unearthly imagery of the German bard.
"He read it over to me," says Sir Alexander, "in a very
slow and solemn tone, and after we had said a few words
about its merits, continued to look at the fire silent and
musing for some minutes, until he at length burst out
with 'I wish to Heaven I could get a skull and two cross-
bones.'" Wood said that if Scott would accompany
him to the house of John Bell, the celebrated surgeon,
he had no doubt this wish might be easily gratified.
They went thither accordingly on the instant; — Mr.
Bell smiled on hearing the object of their visit, and pointing to a closet, at the corner of his library, bade Walter
enter and choose. From a well-furnished museum of
mortality, he selected forthwith what seemed to him the
handsomest skull and pair of cross-bones it contained,
and wrapping them in his handkerchief, carried the formidable bundle home to George's Square. The trophies
were immediately mounted on the top of his little book-
case; and when Wood visited him, after many years of
absence from this country, he found them in possession

of a similar position in his dressing-room at Abbots-ford.[1]

All this occurred in the beginning of April, 1796. A few days afterwards, Scott went to pay a visit at a country house, where he expected to meet the "lady of his love." Jane Anne Cranstoun was in the secret of his attachment, and knew, that however doubtful might be Miss [Stuart's] feeling on that subject, she had a high admiration of Scott's abilities, and often corresponded with him on literary matters; so, after he had left Edinburgh, it occurred to her that she might perhaps forward his views in this quarter, by presenting him in the character of a printed author. William Erskine being called into her councils, a few copies of the ballad were forthwith thrown off in the most elegant style, and one, richly bound and blazoned, followed Scott in the course of a few days to the country. The verses were read and approved of, and Miss Cranstoun at least flattered herself that he had not made his first appearance in types to no purpose.[2]

I ought to have mentioned before, that in June, 1795, he was appointed one of the curators of the Advocates' Library, an office always reserved for those members of the Faculty who have the reputation of superior zeal in literary affairs. He had for colleagues David Hume, the Professor of Scots Law, and Malcolm Laing, the historian; and his discharge of his functions must have given satisfaction, for I find him further nominated, in March, 1796, together with Mr. Robert Hodgson Cay — an accomplished gentleman, afterwards Judge of the Admiralty Court in Scotland — to "put the Faculty's cabinet of medals in proper arrangement."

---

[1] Sir A. Wood was himself the son of a distinguished surgeon in Edinburgh. He married one of the daughters of Sir William Forbes — rose in the diplomatic service — and died in 1846. — (1848.)

[2] This story was told by the Countess of Purgstall on her deathbed to Captain Basil Hall. See his *Schloss Hainfeld*, p. 333.

On the 4th of June, 1796 (the birthday of George III.), there seems to have been a formidable riot in Edinburgh, and Scott is found again in the front. On the 5th, he writes as follows to his aunt, Christian Rutherford, who was then in the north of Scotland, and had meant to visit, among other places, the residence of the "chère adorable."

EDINBURGH, 5th June, 1796.

MY CHÈRE AMIE, — Nothing doubting that your curiosity will be upon the tenters to hear the wonderful events of the long-expected 4th of June, I take the pen to inform you that not one worth mentioning has taken place. Were I inclined to prolixity, I might, indeed, narrate at length *how* near a thousand gentlemen (myself among the number) offered their services to the magistrates to act as *constables* for the preservation of the peace — how their services were accepted — what fine speeches were made upon the occasion — *how* they were furnished with pretty painted brown *batons* — *how* they were assembled in the aisle of the New Church, and treated with claret and sweetmeats — *how* Sir John Whiteford was chased by the mob, and *how* Tom, Sandy Wood, and I rescued him, and dispersed his tormentors *à beaux coups de batons* — *how* the Justice-Clerk's windows were broke by a few boys, and *how* a large body of constables and a press-gang of near two hundred men arrived, and were much disappointed at finding the coast entirely clear; with many other matters of equal importance, but of which you must be contented to remain in ignorance till you return to your castle. Seriously, everything, with the exception of the very trifling circumstances above mentioned, was perfectly quiet — much more so than during any King's birthday I can recollect. That very stillness, however, shows that something is brewing among our friends the Democrats, which they will take their own time of bringing forward. By the wise precautions of the magistrates, or rather of the pro-

vost, and the spirited conduct of the gentlemen, I hope
their designs will be frustrated. Our association meets
to-night, when we are to be divided into districts according to the place of our abode, places of rendezvous and
captains named; so that, upon the hoisting of a flag on
the Tron-steeple, and ringing out all the large bells, we
can be on duty in less than five minutes. I am sorry to
say that the complexion of the town seems to justify all
precautions of this kind. I hope we shall demean ourselves as *quiet* and *peaceable* magistrates; and intend,
for the purpose of learning the duties of my new office,
to con diligently the instructions delivered to the watch
by our brother Dogberry, of facetious memory. So much
for information. By way of inquiry, pray let me know
— that is, when you find a very idle hour — how you accomplished the perilous passage of her Majestie's Ferry
without the assistance and escort of your preux-chevalier,
and whether you will receive them on your return — how
Miss R. and you are spending your time, whether station-
ary or otherwise — above all, whether you have been at
[Invermay] and all the etcs., etcs., which the question in-
volves. Having made out a pretty long scratch, which,
as Win Jenkins says, will take you some time to de-
cipher, I shall only inform you farther, that I shall tire
excessively till you return to your shop. I beg to be
remembered to Miss Kerr, and in particular to La Belle
Jeanne. Best love to Miss Rutherford; and believe me
ever, my dear Miss Christy, sincerely and affectionately
your	WALTER SCOTT.

During the autumn of 1796 he visited again his favorite haunts in Perthshire and Forfarshire. It was in
the course of this tour that he spent a day or two at
Montrose with his old tutor Mitchell, and astonished and
grieved that worthy Presbyterian by his zeal about
witches and fairies.[1] The only letter of his, written dur-

[1] See *ante*, p. 97.

ing this expedition, that I have recovered, was addressed to another of his clerical friends — one by no means of Mitchell's stamp — Mr. Walker, the minister of Dunnottar, and it is chiefly occupied with an account of his researches at a vitrified fort, in Kincardineshire, commonly called Lady Fenella's Castle, and, according to tradition, the scene of the murder of Kenneth III. While in the north, he visited also the residence of the lady who had now for so many years been the object of his attachment; and that his reception was not adequate to his expectations, may be gathered pretty clearly from some expressions in a letter addressed to him when at Montrose by his friend and confidante, Miss Cranstoun: —

TO WALTER SCOTT, ESQ., POST-OFFICE, MONTROSE.

DEAR SCOTT, — Far be it from me to affirm that there are no diviners in the land. The voice of the people and the voice of God are loud in their testimony. Two years ago, when I was in the neighborhood of Montrose, we had recourse for amusement one evening to chiromancy, or, as the vulgar say, having our fortunes read ; and read mine were in such a sort, that either my letters must have been inspected, or the devil was by in his own proper person. I never mentioned the circumstance since, for obvious reasons ; but now that you are on the spot, I feel it my bounden duty to conjure you not to put your shoes rashly from off your feet, for you are not standing on holy ground.

I bless the gods for conducting your poor dear soul safely to Perth. When I consider the wilds, the forests, the lakes, the rocks — and the spirits in which you must have whispered to their startled echoes, it amazeth me how you escaped. Had you but dismissed your little squire and Earwig,[1] and spent a few days as Orlando would have done, all posterity might have profited by it ; but to trot quietly away, without so much as one stanza to despair — never talk to me of love again — never, never, never ! I am dying for your collection of exploits.

[1] A servant-boy and pony.

When will you return? In the mean time, Heaven speed you! Be sober, and hope to the end.

William Taylor's translation of your ballad is published, and so inferior, that I wonder we could tolerate it. Dugald Stewart read yours to * * * * the other day. When he came to the fetter dance,[1] he looked up, and poor * * * * * was sitting with his hands nailed to his knees, and the big tears rolling down his innocent nose in so piteous a manner, that Mr. Stewart could not help bursting out a-laughing. An angry man was * * * * *. I have seen another edition, too, but it is below contempt. So many copies make the ballad famous, so that every day adds to your renown.

This here place is very, very dull. Erskine is in London; my dear Thomson at Daily; Macfarlan hatching Kant — and George [2] Fountainhall.[3] I have nothing more to tell you, but that I am most affectionately yours. Many an anxious thought I have about you. Farewell. — J. A. C.

[1] "'Dost fear? dost fear? — The moon shines clear; —
    Dost fear to ride with me?
   Hurrah! hurrah! the dead can ride!' —
    'Oh, William, let them be!'

"'See there! see there! What yonder swings
    And creaks 'mid whistling rain?' —
   Gibbet and steel, the accursed wheel,
    A murderer in his chain.

"'Hollo! thou felon, follow here,
    To bridal bed we ride;
   And thou shalt prance a fetter dance
    Before me and my bride.'

"And hurry, hurry! clash, clash, clash!
    The wasted form descends;
   And fleet as wind, through hazel bush,
    The wild career attends.

"Tramp, tramp! along the land they rode;
    Splash, splash! along the sea;
   The scourge is red, the spur drops blood.
    The flashing pebbles flee."

[2] George Cranstoun, Lord Corehouse.
[3] Decisions by Lord Fountainhall.

The affair in which this romantic creature took so lively an interest was now approaching its end. It was known, before this autumn closed, that the lady of his vows had finally promised her hand to his amiable rival; and, when the fact was announced, some of those who knew Scott the best appear to have entertained very serious apprehensions as to the effect which the disappointment might have upon his feelings. For example, one of those brothers of *the Mountain* wrote as follows to another of them, on the 12th October, 1796: "Mr. [Forbes] marries Miss [Stuart]. This is not good news. I always dreaded there was some self-deception on the part of our romantic friend, and I now shudder at the violence of his most irritable and ungovernable mind. Who is it that says, 'Men have died, and worms have eaten them, but not for LOVE'? I hope sincerely it may be verified on this occasion."

Scott had, however, in all likelihood, digested his agony during the solitary ride in the Highlands to which Miss Cranstoun's last letter alludes.

Talking of this story with Lord Kinnedder, I once asked him whether Scott never made it the subject of verses at the period. His own confession, that, even during the time when he had laid aside the habit of versification, he did sometimes commit "a sonnet on a mistress's eyebrow," had not then appeared. Lord Kinnedder answered, "Oh yes, he made many little stanzas about the lady, and he sometimes showed them to Cranstoun, Clerk, and myself — but we really thought them in general very poor. Two things of the kind, however, have been preserved — and one of them was done just after the conclusion of the business." He then took down a volume of the English Minstrelsy, and pointed out to me some lines On a Violet, which had not at that time been included in Scott's collected works. Lord Kinnedder read them over in his usual impressive, though not quite unaffected, manner, and said, "I remember well, that when I first

saw these, I told him they were his best, but he had
touched them up afterwards."

> " The violet in her greenwood bower,
>   Where birchen boughs with hazels mingle,
> May boast itself the fairest flower
>   In glen or copse or forest dingle.

> " Though fair her gems of azure hue
>   Beneath the dewdrop's weight reclining,
> I 've seen an eye of lovelier blue
>   More sweet through watery lustre shining.

> " The summer sun that dew shall dry,
>   Ere yet the sun be past its morrow,
> Nor longer in my false love's eye
>   Remained the tear of parting sorrow ! "

In turning over a volume of MS. papers, I have found
a copy of verses, which, from the hand, Scott had evidently written down within the last ten years of his life.
They are headed "To Time — by a Lady;" but certain *initials* on the back satisfy me that the authoress
was no other than the object of his first passion.[1] I
think I must be pardoned for transcribing the lines which
had dwelt so long on his memory — leaving it to the
reader's fancy to picture the mood of mind in which the
fingers of a gray-haired man may have traced such a
relic of his youthful dreams: —

> " Friend of the wretch oppress'd with grief,
>   Whose lenient hand, though slow, supplies
> The balm that lends to care relief,
>   That wipes her tears — that checks her sighs !

> " 'T is thine the wounded soul to heal
>   That hopeless bleeds from sorrow's smart,
> From stern misfortune's shaft to steal
>   The barb that rankles in the heart.

---

[1] A very intimate friend both of Scott and of the lady tells me that
these verses were great favorites of hers — she gave himself a copy of
them, and no doubt her recitation had made them known to Scott — but
that he believes them to have been composed by Mrs. Hunter of Norwich.
— (1839.)

" What though with thee the roses fly,
    And jocund youth's gay reign is o'er ;
Though dimm'd the lustre of the eye,
    And hope's vain dreams enchant no more ?

" Yet in thy train come dove-eyed peace,
    Indifference with her heart of snow ;
At her cold couch, lo ! sorrows cease,
    No thorns beneath her roses grow.

" O haste to grant thy suppliant's prayer,
    To me thy torpid calm impart ;
Rend from my brow youth's garland fair,
    But take the thorn that 's in my heart.

" Ah ! why do fabling poets tell
    That thy fleet wings outstrip the wind ?
Why feign thy course of joy the knell,
    And call thy slowest pace unkind ?

" To me thy tedious feeble pace
    Comes laden with the weight of years ;
With sighs I view morn's blushing face,
    And hail mild evening with my tears."

I venture to recall here to the reader's memory the
opening of the twelfth chapter of Peveril of the Peak,
written twenty-six years after the date of this youthful
disappointment.

" Ah me ! for aught that ever I could read,
    Could ever hear by tale or history,
The course of true love never did run smooth ! "
                  Midsummer Night's Dream.

"The celebrated passage which we have prefixed to
this chapter has, like most observations of the same
author, its foundation in real experience. The period
at which love is formed for the first time, and felt most
strongly, is seldom that at which there is much prospect
of its being brought to a happy issue. The state of artificial society opposes many complicated obstructions to
early marriages; and the chance is very great, that such
obstacles prove insurmountable. In fine, there are few
men who do not look back in secret to some period of

their youth, at which a sincere and early affection was repulsed or betrayed, or became abortive from opposing circumstances. It is these little passages of secret history, which leave a tinge of romance in every bosom, scarce permitting us, even in the most busy or the most advanced period of life, to listen with total indifference to a tale of true love."

CHAPTER VIII

1796–1797

REBELLING, as usual, against circumstances, Scott
seems to have turned with renewed ardor to his literary
pursuits; and in that same October, 1796, he was "prevailed on," as he playfully expresses it, "by the *request
of friends*, to indulge his own vanity, by publishing the
translation of Lenore, with that of The Wild Huntsman,
also from Bürger, in a thin quarto." The little volume,
which has no author's name on the title-page, was printed
for Manners and Miller of Edinburgh. The first named
of these respectable publishers had been a fellow-student
in the German class of Dr. Willich; and this circumstance probably suggested the negotiation. It was conducted by William Erskine, as appears from his post-
script to a letter addressed to Scott by his sister, who,
before it reached its destination, had become the wife of
Mr. Campbell Colquhoun of Clathick and Killermont —
in after-days Lord Advocate of Scotland. This was
another of Scott's dearest female friends. The humble
home which she shared with her brother during his early
struggles at the Bar had been the scene of many of his
happiest hours; and her letter affords such a pleasing
idea of the warm affectionateness of the little circle that
I cannot forbear inserting it: —

Monday evening.

If it were not that etiquette and I were constantly at war,
I should think myself very blamable in thus trespassing against
one of its laws ; but as it is long since I forswore its dominion,
I have acquired a prescriptive right to act as I will — and I
shall accordingly anticipate the station of a *matron* in addressing
a young man.

I can express but a very, very little of what I feel, and
shall ever feel, for your unintermitting friendship and attention.
I have ever considered you as a brother, and shall *now* think
myself entitled to make even larger claims on your confidence.
Well do I remember the *dark* conference we lately held together ! The intention of unfolding *my own* future fate was
often at my lips.

I cannot tell you my distress at leaving this house, wherein
I have enjoyed so much real happiness, and giving up the service of so gentle a master, whose yoke was indeed easy. I will
therefore only commend him to your care as the last bequest of
Mary Anne Erskine, and conjure you to continue to each other
through all your pilgrimage as you have commenced it. May
every happiness attend you ! Adieu !

Your most sincere friend and sister,

M. A. E.

Mr. Erskine writes on the other page, "The poems
are gorgeous, but I have made no bargain with any bookseller. I have told M. and M. that I won't be satisfied
with indemnity, but an offer must be made. They will
be out before the end of the week." On what terms the
publication really took place, I know not.

It has already been mentioned that Scott owed his
copy of Bürger's works to the young lady of Harden,
whose marriage occurred in the autumn of 1795. She
was daughter of Count Brühl of Martkirchen, long
Saxon ambassador at the Court of St. James's, by his
wife Almeria, Countess-Dowager of Egremont. The
young kinsman was introduced to her soon after her

arrival at Mertoun, and his attachment to German studies excited her attention and interest. Mrs. Scott supplied him with many standard German books, besides
Bürger; and the gift of an Adelung's dictionary from
his old ally, George Constable (Jonathan Oldbuck), enabled him to master their contents sufficiently for the purposes of translation. The ballad of The Wild Huntsman
appears to have been executed during the month that
preceded his first publication; and he was thenceforth
engaged in a succession of versions from the dramas of
Meier and Iffland, several of which are still extant in his
MS., marked 1796 and 1797. These are all in prose
like their originals; but he also versified at the same
time some lyrical fragments of Goethe, as, for example,
the Morlachian Ballad,

"What yonder glimmers so white on the mountain,"

and the song from Claudina von Villa Bella. He consulted his friend at Mertoun on all these essays; and I
have often heard him say, that, among those many "obligations of a distant date which remained impressed on
his memory, after a life spent in a constant interchange of
friendship and kindness," he counted not as the least, the
lady's frankness in correcting his Scotticisms, and more
especially his Scottish *rhymes.*

His obligations to this lady were indeed various; but
I doubt, after all, whether these were the most important. He used to say that she was the first *woman of
real fashion* that *took him* up; that she used the privi-
leges of her sex and station in the truest spirit of kindness; set him right as to a thousand little trifles, which
no one else would have ventured to notice; and, in short,
did for him what no one but an elegant woman can do
for a young man, whose early days have been spent in
narrow and provincial circles. "When I first saw Sir
Walter," she writes to me, "he was about four- or five-
and-twenty, but looked much younger. He seemed bash-

ful and awkward; but there were from the first such
gleams of superior sense and spirit in his conversation,
that I was hardly surprised when, after our acquaintance
had ripened a little, I felt myself to be talking with a
man of genius. He was most modest about himself, and
showed his little pieces apparently without any consciousness that they could possess any claim on particular attention. Nothing so easy and good-humored as the way
in which he received any hints I might offer, when he
seemed to be tampering with the King's English. I remember particularly how he laughed at himself, when I
made him take notice that ' the little two dogs,' in some
of his lines, did not please an English ear accustomed to
' the two little dogs.' "

Nor was this the only person at Mertoun who took a
lively interest in his pursuits. Harden entered into all
the feelings of his beautiful bride on this subject; and
his mother, the Lady Diana Scott, daughter of the last
Earl of Marchmont, did so no less. She had conversed,
in her early days, with the brightest ornaments of the
cycle of Queen Anne, and preserved rich stores of anecdote, well calculated to gratify the curiosity and excite
the ambition of a young enthusiast in literature. Lady
Diana soon appreciated the minstrel of the clan; and,
surviving to a remarkable age, she had the satisfaction
of seeing him at the height of his eminence — the solitary
person who could give the author of Marmion personal
reminiscences of Pope.[1]

On turning to James Ballantyne's Memorandum (already quoted), I find an account of Scott's journey from
Rosebank to Edinburgh, in the November after the Ballads from Bürger were published, which gives an interesting notion of his literary zeal and opening ambition at
this remarkable epoch of his life. Mr. Ballantyne had

---

[1] Mr. Scott of Harden's right to the peerage of Polwarth, as representing, through his mother, the line of Marchmont, was allowed by the
House of Lords in 1835.

settled in Kelso as a solicitor in 1795; but, not immediately obtaining much professional practice, time hung
heavy on his hands, and he willingly listened, in the
summer of 1796, to a proposal of some of the neighboring nobility and gentry respecting the establishment of
a weekly newspaper,[1] in opposition to one of a democratic
tendency, then widely circulated in Roxburghshire and
the other Border counties. He undertook the printing
and editing of this new journal, and proceeded to London, in order to engage correspondents and make other
necessary preparations. While thus for the first time in
the metropolis, he happened to meet with two authors,
whose reputations were then in full bloom, — namely,
Thomas Holcroft and William Godwin, — the former, a
popular dramatist and novelist; the latter, a novelist of
far greater merit, but "still more importantly distinguished," says the Memorandum before me, "by those
moral, legal, political, and religious heterodoxies, which
his talents enabled him to present to the world in a very
captivating manner. His Caleb Williams had then just
come out, and occupied as much public attention as any
work has done before or since." "Both these eminent
persons," Ballantyne continues, "I saw pretty frequently;
and being anxious to hear whatever I could tell about
the literary men in Scotland, they both treated me with
remarkable freedom of communication. They were both
distinguished by the clearness of their elocution, and very
full of triumphant confidence in the truth of their sys-
tems. They were as willing to speak, therefore, as I
could be to hear; and as I put my questions with all the
fearlessness of a very young man, the result was, that I
carried away copious and interesting stores of thought
and information: that the greater part of what I heard
was full of error, never entered into my contemplation.
Holcroft at this time was a fine-looking, lively man, of
green old age, somewhere about sixty. Godwin, some

[1] *The Kelso Mail.*

twenty years younger, was more shy and reserved. As to me, my delight and enthusiasm were boundless."

After returning home, Ballantyne made another journey to Glasgow for the purchase of types; and on entering the Kelso coach for this purpose, "It would not be easy," says he, "to express my joy on finding that Mr. Scott was to be one of my partners in the carriage, the only other passenger being a fine, stout, muscular, old Quaker. A very few miles reëstablished us on our ancient footing. Travelling not being half so speedy then as it is now, there was plenty of leisure for talk, and Mr. Scott was exactly what is called *the old man*. He abounded, as in the days of boyhood, in legendary lore, and had now added to the stock, as his recitations showed, many of those fine ballads which afterwards composed the Minstrelsy. Indeed, I was more delighted with him than ever; and, by way of reprisal, I opened on him my London budget, collected from Holcroft and Godwin. I doubt if Boswell ever showed himself a more skilful *Reporter* than I did on this occasion. Hour after hour passed away, and found my borrowed eloquence still flowing, and my companion still hanging on my lips with unwearied interest. It was customary in those days to break the journey (only forty miles) by dining on the road, the consequence of which was, that we both became rather oblivious; and after we had reëntered the coach, the worthy Quaker felt quite vexed and disconcerted with the silence which had succeeded so much conversation. ' I wish,' said he, ' my young friends, that you would cheer up, and go on with your pleasant songs and tales as before: they entertained me much.' And so," says Ballantyne, "it went on again until the evening found us in Edinburgh; and from that day, until within a very short time of his death — a period of not less than five-and-thirty years — I may venture to say that our intercourse never flagged."

The reception of the two ballads had, in the mean

time, been favorable, in his own circle at least. The
many inaccuracies and awkwardnesses of rhyme and diction, to which he alludes in republishing them towards
the close of his life, did not prevent real lovers of poetry
from seeing that no one but a poet could have transfused
the daring imagery of the German in a style so free,
bold, masculine, and full of life; but, wearied as all such
readers had been with that succession of feeble, flimsy,
lackadaisical trash which followed the appearance of the
Reliques by Bishop Percy, the opening of such a new vein
of popular poetry as these verses revealed would have
been enough to produce lenient critics for far inferior
translations. Many, as we have seen, sent forth copies
of the Lenore about the same time; and some of these
might be thought better than Scott's in particular passages; but, on the whole, it seems to have been felt and
acknowledged by those best entitled to judge, that he
deserved the palm. Meantime, we must not forget that
Scotland had lost that very year the great poet Burns,
— her glory and her shame. It is at least to be hoped
that a general sentiment of self-reproach, as well as of
sorrow, had been excited by the premature extinction of
such a light; and, at all events, it is agreeable to know
that they who had watched his career with the most affectionate concern were among the first to hail the promise
of a more fortunate successor. Scott found on his table,
when he reached Edinburgh, the following letters from
two of Burns's kindest and wisest friends: —

TO WALTER SCOTT, ESQ., ADVOCATE, GEORGE'S SQUARE.

MY DEAR SIR, — I beg you will accept of my best thanks
for the favor you have done me by sending me four copies of
your beautiful translations. I shall retain two of them, as Mrs.
Stewart and I both set a high value on them as gifts from the
author. The other two I shall take the earliest opportunity of
transmitting to a friend in England, who, I hope, may be in-
strumental in making their merits more generally known at the

time of their first appearance. In a few weeks, I am fully persuaded they will engage public attention to the utmost extent of your wishes, without the aid of any recommendation whatever. I ever am, Dear Sir, yours most truly,

DUGALD STEWART.

CANONGATE, Wednesday evening.

TO THE SAME.

DEAR SIR, — On my return from Cardross, where I had been for a week, I found yours of the 14th, which had surely loitered by the way. I thank you most cordially for your present. I meet with little poetry nowadays that touches my heart; but your translations excite mingled emotions of pity and terror, insomuch, that I would not wish any person of weaker nerves to read William and Helen before going to bed. Great must be the original, if it equals the translation in energy and pathos. One would almost suspect you have used as much liberty with Bürger as Macpherson was suspected of doing with Ossian. It is, however, easier to *backspeir* you. Sober reason rejects the machinery as unnatural ; it reminds me, however, of the magic of Shakespeare. Nothing has a finer effect than the repetition of certain words, that are echoes to the sense, as much as the celebrated lines in Homer about the rolling up and falling down of the stone : *Tramp, tramp ! splash, splash !* is to me perfectly new ; and much of the imagery is nature. I should consider this muse of yours (if you carry the intrigue far) more likely to steal your heart from the law than even a wife. I am, Dear Sir, your most obedient, humble servant,

JO. RAMSAY.

OCHTERTYRE, 30th November, 1796.

Among other literary persons at a distance, I may mention George Chalmers, the celebrated antiquary, with whom he had been in correspondence from the beginning of this year, supplying him with Border ballads for the illustration of his researches into Scotch history. This gentleman had been made acquainted with Scott's large collections in that way by a common friend, Dr. Somerville, minister of Jedburgh, author of the History of

Queen Anne;[1] and the numerous MS. copies communicated to him in consequence were recalled in the course
of 1799, when the plan of the Minstrelsy began to take
shape. Chalmers writes in great transports about Scott's
versions; but weightier encouragement came from Mr.
Taylor of Norwich, himself the first translator of the
Lenore.

I need not tell you, sir [he writes], with how much eagerness I opened your volume — with how much glow I followed
The Chase — or with how much alarm I came to William and
Helen. Of the latter I will say nothing ; praise might seem
hypocrisy — criticism envy. The ghost nowhere makes his appearance so well as with you, or his exit so well as with Mr.
Spenser. I like very much the recurrence of

> " The scourge is red, the spur drops blood,
>   The flashing pebbles flee ; "

but of William and Helen I had resolved to say nothing. Let
me return to The Chase, of which the metric stanza style pleases
me entirely ; yet I think a few passages written in too elevated
a strain for the general spirit of the poem. This age leans too
much to the Darwin style. Mr. Percy's Lenore owes its coldness to the adoption of this ; and it seems peculiarly incongru-
ous in the ballad — where habit has taught us to expect simplicity. Among the passages too stately and pompous, I should
reckon —

> " The mountain echoes startling wake —
>   And for devotion's choral swell
>   Exchange the rude discordant noise —
>   Fell Famine marks the maddening throng
>   With cold Despair's averted eye," —

and perhaps one or two more. In the twenty-first stanza, I

---

[1] Some extracts from this venerable person's unpublished Memoirs of
his own Life have been kindly sent to me by his son, the well-known physician of Chelsea College ; from which it appears that the reverend doctor, and, more particularly still, his wife, a lady of remarkable talent and
humor, had formed a high notion of Scott's future eminence at a very
early period of his life. Dr. S. survived to a great old age, preserving his
faculties quite entire, and I have spent many pleasant hours under his hospitable roof in company with Sir Walter Scott. We heard him preach an
excellent circuit sermon when he was upwards of eighty-two, and at the
Judges' dinner afterwards he was among the gayest of the company.

prefer Bürger's *trampling the corn into chaff and dust*, to your more metaphorical, and therefore less picturesque, "destructive sweep the field along." In the thirtieth, "On whirlwind's pinions swiftly borne," to me seems less striking than the still disapparition of the tumult and bustle — the earth has opened, and he is sinking with his evil genius to the nether world — as he approaches, *dumpf rauscht es wie ein fernes Meer* — it should be rendered, therefore, not by "Save what a distant torrent gave," but by some sounds which shall necessarily excite the idea of being *hell-sprung* — the sound of simmering seas of fire — pinings of goblins damned — or some analogous noise. The forty-seventh stanza is a very great improvement of the original. The profanest blasphemous speeches need not have been softened down, as, in proportion to the impiety of the provocation, increases the poetical probability of the final punishment. I should not have ventured upon these criticisms, if I did not think it required a microscopic eye to make any, and if I did not on the whole consider The Chase as a most spirited and beautiful translation. I remain (to borrow in another sense a concluding phrase from the Spectator), your constant admirer,

W. TAYLOR, JUN.

NORWICH, 14th December, 1796.

The anticipations of these gentlemen, that Scott's versions would attract general attention in the south, were not fulfilled. He himself attributes this to the contemporaneous appearance of so many other translations from Lenore. "In a word," he says, "my adventure, where so many pushed off to sea, proved a dead loss, and a great part of the edition was condemned to the service of the trunkmaker. This failure did not operate in any unpleasant degree either on my feelings or spirits. I was coldly received by strangers, but my reputation began rather to increase among my own friends, and on the whole I was more bent to show the world that it had neglected something worth notice, than to be affronted by its indifference; or rather, to speak candidly, I found pleasure in the literary labors in which I had almost by accident become engaged, and labored less in the hope of

pleasing others, though certainly without despair of doing
so, than in a pursuit of a new and agreeable amusement
to myself." [1]

On the 12th of December Scott had the curiosity to
witness the trial of one James Mackean, a shoemaker,
for the murder of Buchanan, a carrier, employed to
convey money weekly from the Glasgow bank to a manufacturing establishment at Lanark. Mackean invited
the carrier to spend the evening in his house; conducted
family worship in a style of much seeming fervor; and
then, while his friend was occupied, came behind him,
and almost severed his head from his body by one stroke
of a razor. I have heard Scott describe the sanctimo-
nious air which the murderer maintained during his trial
— preserving throughout the aspect of a devout person,
who believed himself to have been hurried into his accumulation of crime by an uncontrollable exertion of diabolical influence; and on his copy of the "Life of James
Mackean, executed 25th January, 1797," I find the following marginal note: —

"I went to see this wretched man when under sentence
of death, along with my friend, Mr. William Clerk, advocate. His great anxiety was to convince us that his
diabolical murder was committed from a sudden impulse
of revengeful and violent passion, not from deliberate
design of plunder. But the contrary was manifest from
the accurate preparation of the deadly instrument — a
razor strongly lashed to an iron bolt — and also from the
evidence on the trial, from which it seems he had invited
his victim to drink tea with him on the day he perpetrated the murder, and that this was a reiterated invitation. Mackean was a good-looking elderly man, having
a thin face and clear gray eye; such a man as may be
ordinarily seen beside a collection-plate at a seceding
meeting-house, a post which the said Mackean had occupied in his day. All Mackean's account of the murder

[1] *Remarks on Popular Poetry.* 1830.

is apocryphal. Buchanan was a powerful man, and
Mackean slender. It appeared that the latter had engaged Buchanan in writing, then suddenly clapped one
hand on his eyes, and struck the fatal blow with the
other. The throat of the deceased was cut through his
handkerchief to the back bone of the neck, against which
the razor was hacked in several places."

In his pursuit of his German studies, Scott acquired,
about this time, a very important assistant in Mr. Skene
of Rubislaw, in Aberdeenshire — a gentleman considerably his junior,[1] who had just returned to Scotland from
a residence of several years in Saxony, where he had
obtained a thorough knowledge of the language, and accumulated a better collection of German books than any
to which Scott had, as yet, found access. Shortly after
Mr. Skene's arrival in Edinburgh, Scott requested to be
introduced to him by a mutual friend, Mr. Edmonstone
of Newton; and their fondness for the same literature,
with Scott's eagerness to profit by his new acquaintance's
superior attainment in it, thus opened an intercourse
which general similarity of tastes, and I venture to add,
in many of the most important features of character, soon
ripened into the familiarity of a tender friendship — "An
intimacy," Mr. Skene says, in a paper before me, "of
which I shall ever think with so much pride — a friendship so pure and cordial as to have been able to with-
stand all the vicissitudes of nearly forty years, without
ever having sustained even a casual chill from unkind
thought or word." Mr. Skene adds, "During the whole
progress of his varied life, to that eminent station which
he could not but feel he at length held in the estimation,
not of his countrymen alone, but of the whole world, I
never could perceive the slightest shade of variance from
that simplicity of character with which he impressed me
on the first hour of our meeting."[2]

[1] [James Skene, son of George Skene of Rubislaw, was born in 1775.]

[2] [Beside the memoranda placed by Mr. Skene in Lockhart's hands and

Among the common tastes which served to knit these friends together was their love of horsemanship, in which, as in all other manly exercises, Skene highly excelled; and the fears of a French invasion becoming every day more serious, their thoughts were turned with corresponding zeal to the project of organizing a force of mounted volunteers in Scotland. "The London Light Horse had set the example," says Mr. Skene; "but in truth it was to Scott's ardor that this force in the North owed its origin. Unable, by reason of his lameness, to serve amongst his friends on foot, he had nothing for it but to rouse the spirit of the moss-trooper, with which he readily inspired all who possessed the means of substituting the sabre for the musket."

On the 14th February, 1797, these friends and many more met and drew up an offer to serve as a body of volunteer cavalry in Scotland; which offer being transmitted through the Duke of Buccleuch, Lord-Lieutenant of Mid-Lothian, was accepted by Government. The organization of the corps proceeded rapidly; they extended their offer to serve in any part of the island in case of invasion; and this also being accepted, the whole arrangement was shortly completed; when Charles Maitland of Rankeillor was elected Major-Commandant; (Sir) William Rae of St. Catharine's, Captain; James Gordon of Craig, and George Robinson of Clermiston, Lieutenants; (Sir) William Forbes of Pitsligo, and James Skene of Rubislaw, Cornets; Walter Scott, Paymaster, Quartermaster, and Secretary; John Adams, Adjutant. But the treble duties thus devolved on Scott were found to interfere too severely with his other avocations, and Colin Mackenzie of Portmore relieved him soon afterwards from those of paymaster.

used by him in various portions of the *Life*, the friend's unpublished *Reminiscences*, from which Mr. Douglas has fortunately been enabled to draw largely in annotating the *Journal*, contain recollections of peculiar interest.]

"The part of quartermaster," says Mr. Skene, "was purposely selected for him, that he might be spared the rough usage of the ranks; but, notwithstanding his infirmity, he had a remarkably firm seat on horseback, and in all situations a fearless one: no fatigue ever seemed too much for him, and his zeal and animation served to sustain the enthusiasm of the whole corps, while his ready ' mot à rire ' kept up, in all, a degree of good-humor and relish for the service, without which the toil and privations of long *daily* drills would not easily have been submitted to by such a body of gentlemen. At every interval of exercise, the order, *sit at ease*, was the signal for the quartermaster to lead the squadron to merriment; every eye was intuitively turned on ' Earl Walter,' as he was familiarly called by his associates of that date, and his ready joke seldom failed to raise the ready laugh. He took his full share in all the labors and duties of the corps, had the highest pride in its progress and proficiency, and was such a trooper himself as only a very powerful frame of body and the warmest zeal in the cause could have enabled any one to be. But his habitual good-humor was the great charm, and at the daily mess (for we all dined together when in quarters) that reigned supreme."

Earl Walter's first charger, by the way, was a tall and powerful animal, named Lenore. These daily drills appear to have been persisted in during the spring and summer of 1797; the corps spending moreover some weeks in quarters at Musselburgh. The majority of the troop having professional duties to attend to, the ordinary hour for drill was five in the morning; and when we reflect, that after some hours of hard work in this way, Scott had to produce himself regularly in the Parliament House with gown and wig, for the space of four or five hours at least, while his chamber practice, though still humble, was on the increase — and that he had found a plentiful source of new social engagements in his troop connections — it certainly could have excited no surprise had his literary studies been found suffering total intermission during this busy period. That such was not the case, however, his correspondence and note-books afford ample evidence.

He had no turn, at this time of his life, for early rising; so that the regular attendance at the morning drills was of itself a strong evidence of his military zeal; but he must have, in spite of them, and of all other circumstances, persisted in what was the usual custom of all his earlier life, namely, the devotion of the best hours of the night to solitary study. In general, both as a young man, and in more advanced age, his constitution required a good allowance of sleep, and he, on principle, indulged in it, saying, "He was but half a man if he had not full seven hours of utter unconsciousness;" but his whole mind and temperament were, at this period, in a state of most fervent exaltation, and spirit triumphed over matter. His translation of Steinberg's Otho of Wittelsbach is marked "1796-7;" from which, I conclude, it was finished in the latter year. The volume containing that of Meier's Wolfred of Dromberg, a drama of Chivalry, is dated 1797; and, I think, the reader will presently see cause to suspect, that though not alluded to in his imperfect note-book, these tasks must have been accomplished in the very season of the daily drills.

The letters addressed to him in March, April, and June, by Kerr of Abbotrule, George Chalmers, and his uncle at Rosebank, indicate his unabated interest in the collection of coins and ballads; and I shall now make a few extracts from his private note-book, some of which will at all events amuse the survivors of the Edinburgh Light Horse: —

"*March* 15, 1797. — Read Stanfield's trial, and the conviction appears very doubtful indeed. Surely no one could seriously believe, in 1688, that the body of the

murdered bleeds at the touch of the murderer, and I see
little else that directly touches Philip Stanfield. He was
a very bad character, however; and tradition says, that
having insulted Welsh, the wild preacher, one day in
his early life, the saint called from the pulpit that God
had revealed to him that this blasphemous youth would
die in the sight of as many as were then assembled. It
was believed at the time that Lady Stanfield had a hand
in the assassination, or was at least privy to her son's
plans; but I see nothing inconsistent with the old gentleman's having committed suicide.[1] The ordeal of touching
the corpse was observed in Germany. They call it *bar-
recht*.

"*March 27.* —

> ' The friers of Fail
> Gat never owre hard eggs, or owre thin kale ;
> For they made their eggs thin wi' butter,
> And their kale thick wi' bread.
> And the friers of Fail they made gude kale
> On Fridays when they fasted ;
> They never wanted gear enough
> As lang as their neighbours' lasted.'

"Fairy-rings. — *N. B.* Delrius says the same appearance occurs wherever the witches have held their Sabbath.

"For the ballad of ' Willie's lady,' compare Apuleius,
lib. i. p. 33. . . .

"*April* 20. — The portmanteau to contain the following articles: 2 shirts; 1 black handkerchief; 1 nightcap, woollen; 1 pair pantaloons, blue; 1 flannel shirt
with sleeves; 1 pair flannel drawers; 1 waistcoat; 1 pair
worsted stockings or socks.

"In the slip, in cover of portmanteau, a case with
shaving-things, combs, and a knife, fork, and spoon; a
German pipe and tobacco-bag, flint, and steel; pipe-clay

---

[1] See particulars of Stanfield's case in Lord Fountainhall's *Chronological
Notes of Scottish Affairs*, 1680-1701, edited by Sir Walter Scott. 4to,
Edinburgh, 1822. Pp. 233-236.

and oil, with brush for laying it on; a shoe-brush; a pair of shoes or hussar-boots; a horse-picker, and other loose articles.

"Belt with the flap and portmanteau, currycomb, brush, and mane-comb, with sponge.

"Over the portmanteau, the blue overalls, and a spare jacket for stable; a small horse-sheet, to cover the horse's back with, and a spare girth or two.

"In the cartouche-box, screw-driver and picker for pistol, with three or four spare flints.

"The horse-sheet may be conveniently folded below the saddle, and will save the back in a long march or bad weather. Beside the holster, two forefeet shoes.[1]

"*May* 22. — Apuleius, lib. ii. . . . Anthony-a-Wood. . . . Mr. Jenkinson's name (now Lord Liverpool) being proposed as a difficult one to rhyme to, a lady present hit off this verse extempore. — *N. B.* Both father and son (Lord Hawkesbury) have a peculiarity of vision: —

> ' Happy Mr. Jenkinson,
> Happy Mr. Jenkinson,
> I 'm sure to you
> Your lady 's true,
> For you have got a winking son.'

"23. — Delrius. . . .

"24. — ' I, John Bell of Brackenbrig, lies under this stane ;

---

[1] Some of Scott's most intimate friends at the Bar, partly, no doubt, from entertaining political opinions of another caste, were by no means disposed to sympathize with the demonstrations of his military enthusiasm at this period. For example, one of these gentlemen thus writes to another in April, 1797 : " By the way, Scott is become the merest trooper that ever was begotten by a drunken dragoon on his trull in a hay-loft. Not an idea crosses his mind, or a word his lips, that has not an allusion to some d——d instrument or evolution of the Cavalry — ' Draw your swords — by single files to the right of front — to the left wheel — charge ! ' After all, he knows little more about wheels and charges than I do about the wheels of Ezekiel, or the King of Pelew about charges of horning on six days' date. I saw them charge on Leith Walk a few days ago, and I can assure you it was by no means orderly proceeded. Clerk and I are continually obliged to open a six-pounder upon him in self-defence, but in spite of a temporary confusion, he soon rallies and returns to the attack."

Four of my sons laid it on my wame.
I was man of my meat, and master of my wife,
And lived in mine ain house without meikle strife.
Gif thou be'st a better man in thy time than I was in mine,
Tak this stane off my wame, and lay it upon thine.'
" 25. — Meric Casaubon on Spirits. . . .
" 26. — ' There saw we learned Maroe's golden tombe ;
        The way he cut an English mile in length
        Thorow a rock of stone in one night's space.'

"Christopher Marlowe's Tragicall History of Dr.
Faustus — a very remarkable thing.   Grand subject —
end grand. . . . Copied Prophecy of Merlin from Mr.
Clerk's MS.
"27. — Read Everybody's Business is Nobody's Business, by Andrew Moreton.   This was one of Defoe's
many *aliases* — like his pen, in parts. . . .

' To Cuthbert, Car, and Collingwood, to Shafto and to Hall ;
  To every gallant generous heart that for King James did fall.'

"28. — . . . Anthony-a-Wood. . . . Plain Proof of
the True Father and Mother of the Pretended Prince
of Wales, by W. Fuller.   This fellow was pilloried for
a forgery some years later. . . . Began *Nathan der
Weise*.
"*June* 29. — Read Introduction to a Compendium on
Brief Examination, by W. S. — viz., William Stafford
— though it was for a time given to no less a W. S. than
William Shakespeare.   A curious treatise — the Political
Economy of the Elizabethan Day — worth reprinting. . . .
"*July* 1. — Read Discourse of Military Discipline, by
Captain Barry — a very curious account of the famous
Low Countries armies — full of military hints worth note.
. . . *Anthony Wood* again.
"3. — *Nathan der Weise*. . . . *Delrius*. . . .
"5. — Geutenberg's *Braut* begun.
"6. — The Bride again.   *Delrius*."

The note-book from which I have been copying is
chiefly filled with extracts from Apuleius and Anthony-a-

Wood — most of them bearing, in some way, on the subject of popular superstitions. It is a pity that many leaves have been torn out; for if unmutilated, the record would probably have enabled one to guess whether he had already planned his Essay on Fairies.

I have mentioned his business at the Bar as increasing at the same time. His *fee-book* is now before me, and it shows that he made by his first year's practice £24 3s.; by the second, £57 15s.; by the third, £84 4s.; by the fourth, £90; and in his fifth year at the Bar — that is, from November, 1796 to July, 1797 — £144 10s.; of which £50 were fees from his father's chamber.

His friend, Charles Kerr of Abbotrule, had been residing a good deal about this time in Cumberland: indeed, he was so enraptured with the scenery of the lakes, as to take a house in Keswick with the intention of spending half of all future years there. His letters to Scott (March, April, 1797) abound in expressions of wonder that he should continue to devote so much of his vacations to the Highlands of Scotland, "with every crag and precipice of which," says he, "I should imagine you would be familiar by this time; nay, that the goats themselves might almost claim you for an acquaintance;" while another district lay so near him, at least as well qualified "to give a swell to the fancy."

After the rising of the Court of Session in July, Scott accordingly set out on a tour to the English lakes, accompanied by his brother John, and Adam Ferguson. Their first stage was Halyards in Tweeddale, then inhabited by his friend's father, the philosopher and historian; and they stayed there for a day or two, in the course of which Scott had his first and only interview with David Ritchie, the original of his Black Dwarf.[1] Proceeding southwards, the tourists visited Carlisle, Penrith, — the vale of the Eamont, including Mayburgh and Brougham Castle, — Ullswater and Windermere; and at length

[1] See the Introduction to this novel in the edition of 1830.

fixed their headquarters at the then peaceful and sequestered little watering-place of Gilsland, making excursions from thence to the various scenes of romantic interest which are commemorated in The Bridal of Triermain,
and otherwise leading very much the sort of life depicted
among the loungers of St. Ronan's Well. Scott was, on
his first arrival in Gilsland, not a little engaged with the
beauty of one of the young ladies lodged under the same
roof with him; and it was on occasion of a visit in her
company to some part of the Roman Wall that he indited
his lines —

> "Take these flowers, which, purple waving,
>   On the ruined rampart grew," etc.[1]

But this was only a passing glimpse of flirtation. A
week or so afterwards commenced a more serious affair.

Riding one day with Ferguson, they met, some miles
from Gilsland, a young lady taking the air on horseback,
whom neither of them had previously remarked, and
whose appearance instantly struck both so much that
they kept her in view until they had satisfied themselves
that she also was one of the party at Gilsland. The
same evening there was a ball, at which Captain Scott
produced himself in his regimentals, and Ferguson also
thought proper to be equipped in the uniform of the
Edinburgh Volunteers. There was no little rivalry
among the young travellers as to who should first get
presented to the unknown beauty of the morning's ride;
but though both the gentlemen in scarlet had the advantage of being dancing partners, their friend succeeded in
handing the fair stranger to supper — and such was his
first introduction to Charlotte Margaret Carpenter.

Without the features of a regular beauty, she was rich
in personal attractions; "a form that was fashioned as
light as a fay's;" a complexion of the clearest and light-

---

[1] I owe this circumstance to the recollection of Mr. Claud Russell,
accountant in Edinburgh, who was one of the party. Previously I had
always supposed these verses to have been inspired by Miss Carpenter.

est olive; eyes large, deep-set and dazzling, of the finest
Italian brown; and a profusion of silken tresses, black
as the raven's wing; her address hovering between the
reserve of a pretty young Englishwoman who has not
mingled largely in general society, and a certain natural
archness and gayety that suited well with the accompani-
ment of a French accent. A lovelier vision, as all who
remember her in the bloom of her days have assured me,
could hardly have been imagined; and from that hour
the fate of the young poet was fixed.[1]

She was the daughter of Jean Charpentier, of Lyons,
a devoted royalist, who held an office under Government,[2]
and Charlotte Volere, his wife. She and her only brother, Charles Charpentier, had been educated in the
Protestant religion of their mother; and when their father
died, which occurred in the beginning of the Revolution,
Madame Charpentier made her escape with her children,
first to Paris, and then to England, where they found
a warm friend and protector in the late Marquis of
Downshire, who had, in the course of his travels in
France, formed an intimate acquaintance with the family,
and, indeed, spent some time under their roof. M.
Charpentier had, in his first alarm as to the coming Revolution, invested £4000 in English securities — part in
a mortgage upon Lord Downshire's estates. On the
mother's death, which occurred soon after her arrival in
London, this nobleman took on himself the character of
sole guardian to her children; and Charles Charpentier
received in due time, through his interest, an appoint-

---

[1] [" You may perhaps have remarked Miss Carpenter at a Carlisle ball,
but more likely not, as her figure is not very *frappant*. A smart-looking
little girl with dark brown hair would probably be her portrait if drawn
by an indifferent hand. But I, you may believe, should make a piece of
work of my sketch, as little like the original as Hercules to me." — Scott
to P. Murray, December, 1797. — *Familiar Letters*, vol. i. p. 10.]

[2] In several deeds which I have seen, M. Charpentier is designed
" Ecuyer du Roi ; " one of those purchasable ranks peculiar to the latter
stages of the old French Monarchy. What the post he held was, I never
heard.

ment in the service of the East India Company, in which he had by this time risen to the lucrative situation of Commercial Resident at Salem. His sister was now making a little excursion, under the care of the lady who had superintended her education, Miss Jane Nicolson, a daughter of Dr. Nicolson, Dean of Exeter, and grand-daughter of William Nicolson, Bishop of Carlisle, well known as the editor of The English Historical Library. To some connections which the learned prelate's family had ever since his time kept up in the diocese of Carlisle, Miss Carpenter owed the direction of her summer tour.

Scott's father was now in a very feeble state of health, which accounts for his first announcement of this affair being made in a letter to his mother; it is undated; — but by this time the young lady had left Gilsland for Carlisle, where she remained until her destiny was set-tled.

TO MRS. SCOTT, GEORGE'S SQUARE, EDINBURGH.

My dear Mother, — I should very ill deserve the care and affection with which you have ever regarded me, were I to neglect my duty so far as to omit consult-ing my father and you in the most important step which I can possibly take in life, and upon the success of which my future happiness must depend. It is with pleasure I think that I can avail myself of your advice and instruc-tions in an affair of so great importance as that which I have at present on my hands. You will probably guess from this preamble that I am engaged in a matrimonial plan, which is really the case. Though my acquaintance with the young lady has not been of long standing, this circumstance is in some degree counterbalanced by the intimacy in which we have lived, and by the opportuni-ties which that intimacy has afforded me of remarking her conduct and sentiments on many different occasions, some of which were rather of a delicate nature, so that in fact I have seen more of her during the few weeks we

have been together than I could have done after a much
longer acquaintance, shackled by the common forms of
ordinary life. You will not expect from me a description of her person — for which I refer you to my brother,
as also for a fuller account of all the circumstances attending the business than can be comprised in the compass of a letter. Without flying into raptures, for I
must assure you that my judgment as well as my affections are consulted upon this occasion — without flying
into raptures, then, I may safely assure you that her
temper is sweet and cheerful, her understanding good,
and, what I know will give you pleasure, her principles
of religion very serious. I have been very explicit with
her upon the nature of my expectations, and she thinks
she can accommodate herself to the situation which I
should wish her to hold in society as my wife, which,
you will easily comprehend, I mean should neither be
extravagant nor degrading. Her fortune, though partly
dependent upon her brother, who is high in office at
Madras, is very considerable — at present £500 a year.
This, however, we must, in some degree, regard as precarious — I mean to the full extent; and indeed, when
you know her, you will not be surprised that I regard
this circumstance chiefly because it removes those pru-
dential considerations which would otherwise render our
union impossible for the present. Betwixt her income
and my own professional exertions, I have little doubt
we will be enabled to hold the rank in society which my
family and situation entitle me to fill.

My dear mother, I cannot express to you the anxiety
I have that you will not think me flighty nor inconsider-
ate in this business. Believe me, that experience, in
one instance — you cannot fail to know to what I allude
— is too recent to permit my being so hasty in my conclusions as the warmth of my temper might have otherwise prompted. I am also most anxious that you should
be prepared to show her kindness, which I know the

goodness of your own heart will prompt, more especially when I tell you that she is an orphan, without relations, and almost without friends. Her guardian is — I should say *was*, for she is of age — Lord Downshire, to whom I must write for his consent, — a piece of respect to which he is entitled for his care of her, — and there the matter rests at present. I think I need not tell you that if I assume the new character which I threaten, I shall be happy to find that in that capacity I may make myself more useful to my brothers, and especially to Anne, than I could in any other. On the other hand, I shall certainly expect that my friends will endeavor to show every attention in their power to a woman who forsakes for me prospects much more splendid than what I can offer, and who comes into Scotland without a single friend but myself. I find I could write a great deal more upon this subject, but as it is late, and as I must write to my father, I shall restrain myself. I think (but you are best judge) that in the circumstances in which I stand, you should write to her, Miss Carpenter, under cover to me at Carlisle.

Write to me very fully upon this important subject — send me your opinion, your advice, and, above all, your blessing; you will see the necessity of not delaying a minute in doing so, and in keeping this business *strictly private*, till you hear farther from me, since you are not ignorant that even at this advanced period an objection on the part of Lord Downshire, or many other accidents, may intervene; in which case, I should little wish my disappointment to be public.

Believe me, my dear Mother,

Ever your dutiful and affectionate son,

WALTER SCOTT.

Scott remained in Cumberland until the Jedburgh assizes recalled him to his legal duties. On arriving in that town, he immediately sent for his friend Shortreed, whose *memorandum* records that the evening of the 30th September, 1797, was one of the most joyous he ever spent. "Scott," he says, "was *sair* beside himself about Miss Carpenter; — we toasted her twenty times over — and sat together, he raving about her, until it was one in the morning." He soon returned to Cumberland; and the following letters will throw light on the character and conduct of the parties, and on the nature of the difficulties which were presented by the prudence and prejudices of the young advocate's family connections. It appears, that at one stage of the business, Scott had seriously contemplated leaving the Bar at Edinburgh, and establishing himself with his bride (I know not in what capacity) in one of the colonies.

TO WALTER SCOTT, ESQ., ADVOCATE, EDINBURGH.

CARLISLE, October 4, 1797.

It is only an hour since I received Lord Downshire's letter. You will say, I hope, that I am indeed very good to write so soon, but I almost fear that all my goodness can never carry me through all this plaguy writing. Lord Downshire will be happy to hear from you. He is the very best man on earth — his letter is kind and affectionate, and full of advice, much in the style of *your last*. I am to consult *most carefully my heart*. Do you believe I did not do it when I gave you my consent? It is true, I don't like to reflect on that subject. I am afraid. It is very awful to think it is for life. How can I ever laugh after such tremendous thoughts? I believe never more. I am hurt to find that your friends don't think the match a prudent one. If it is not agreeable to them all, you must then forget me, for I have too much pride to think of connecting myself in a family were I not equal to them. Pray, my dear sir, write to Lord D. immediately — explain yourself to him as you would to me, and he will, I am sure, do all he can to serve us. If

you really love me, you must love him, and write to him
as you would to a friend.

Adieu, — au plaisir de vous revoir bientôt.

C. C.

TO ROBERT SHORTREED, ESQ., SHERIFF-SUBSTITUTE, JEDBURGH.

SELKIRK, 8th October, 1797.

DEAR BOB, — This day a long train of anxieties was
put an end to by a letter from Lord Downshire, couched
in the most flattering terms, giving his consent to my
marriage with his ward. I am thus far on my way to
Carlisle — only for a visit — because, betwixt her reluctance to an immediate marriage and the imminent approach of the session, I am afraid I shall be thrown back
to the Christmas holidays. I shall be home in about
eight days.

Ever yours sincerely,

W. SCOTT.

TO MISS CHRISTIAN RUTHERFORD, ASHESTIEL, BY SELKIRK.

Has it never happened to you, my dear Miss Christy,
in the course of your domestic economy, to meet with a
drawer stuffed so very, so *extremely* full, that it was very
difficult to pull it open, however desirous you might be
to exhibit its contents? In case this miraculous event
has ever taken place, you may somewhat conceive from
thence the cause of my silence, which has really proceeded
from my having a very great deal to communicate; so
much so, that I really hardly know how to begin. As
for my affection and friendship for you, believe me sincerely, they neither slumber nor sleep, and it is only your
suspicions of their drowsiness which incline me to write
at this period of a business highly interesting to me,
rather than when I could have done so with something
like certainty — Hem! Hem! It must come out at once
— I am in a very fair way of being married to a very

amiable young woman, with whom I formed an attachment in the course of my tour. She was born in France
— her parents were of English extraction — the name
Carpenter. She was left an orphan early in life, and educated in England, and is at present under the care of a
Miss Nicolson, a daughter of the late Dean of Exeter,
who was on a visit to her relations in Cumberland. Miss
Carpenter is of age, but as she lies under great obligations to the Marquis of Downshire, who was her guardian, she cannot take a step of such importance without
his consent — and I daily expect his final answer upon
the subject. Her fortune is dependent, in a great measure, upon an only and very affectionate brother. He is
Commercial Resident at Salem in India, and has settled
upon her an annuity of £500. Of her personal accomplishments I shall only say that she possesses very good
sense, with uncommon good temper, which I have seen
put to most severe trials. I must bespeak your kindness
and friendship for her. You may easily believe I shall
rest very much both upon Miss R. and you for giving
her the *carte de pays*, when she comes to Edinburgh. I
may give you a hint that there is no *romance* in her composition — and that, though born in France, she has the
sentiments and manners of an Englishwoman, and does
not like to be thought otherwise. A very slight tinge in
her pronunciation is all which marks the foreigner. She
is at present at Carlisle, where I shall join her as soon
as our arrangements are finally made. Some difficulties
have occurred in settling matters with my father, owing
to certain prepossessions which you can easily conceive
his adopting. One main article was the uncertainty of
her provision, which has been in part removed by the
safe arrival of her remittances for this year, with assurances of their being regular and even larger in future,
her brother's situation being extremely lucrative. Another objection was her birth: "Can any good thing
come out of Nazareth?" but as it was *birth merely and*

solely, this has been abandoned. *You* will be more interested about other points regarding her, and I can only say that — though our acquaintance was shorter than ever I could have thought of forming such a connection upon — it was exceedingly close, and gave me full opportunities for observation — and if I had parted with her, it must have been forever, which both parties began to think would be a disagreeable thing. She has conducted herself through the whole business with so much propriety as to make a strong impression in her favor upon the minds of my father and mother, prejudiced as they were against her, from the circumstances I have mentioned. We shall be your neighbors in the New Town, and intend to live very quietly; Charlotte will need many lessons from Miss R. in housewifery. Pray show this letter to Miss R. with my very best compliments. Nothing can now stand in the way except Lord Downshire, who may not think the match a prudent one for Miss C.; but he will surely think her entitled to judge for herself at her age, in what she would wish to place her happiness. She is not a beauty, by any means, but her person and face are very engaging. She is a brunette; her manners are lively, but when necessary she can be very serious. She was baptized and educated a Protestant of the Church of England. I think I have now said enough upon this subject. Do not write till you hear from me again, which will be when all is settled. I wish this important event may hasten your return to town. I send a goblin story, with best compliments to the misses, and ever am, yours affectionately,   WALTER SCOTT.

THE ERL-KING.[1]

(The Erl-King is a goblin that haunts the Black Forest in Thuringia. —
To be read by a candle particularly long in the snuff.)

O, who rides by night thro' the woodland so wild ?
It is the fond father embracing his child ;

[1] From the German of Goethe.

And close the boy nestles within his loved arm,
To hold himself fast, and to keep himself warm.

" O father, see yonder ! see yonder ! " he says.
" My boy, upon what doest thou fearfully gaze ? " —
" O, 't is the Erl-King with his crown and his shroud." —
" No, my son, it is but a dark wreath of the cloud."

(*The Erl-King speaks.*)
" O, come and go with me, thou loveliest child ;
By many a gay sport shall thy time be beguiled ;
My mother keeps for thee full many a fair toy,
And many a fine flower shall she pluck for my boy."

" O father, my father, and did you not hear
The Erl-King whisper so low in my ear ? "
" Be still, my heart's darling — my child, be at ease ;
It was but the wild blast as it sung thro' the trees."

Erl-King.
" O wilt thou go with me, thou loveliest boy ?
My daughter shall tend thee with care and with joy ;
She shall bear thee so lightly thro' wet and thro' wild,
And press thee, and kiss thee, and sing to my child."

" O father, my father, and saw you not plain
The Erl-King's pale daughter glide past thro' the rain ? " —
" O yes, my loved treasure, I knew it full soon ;
It was the gray willow that danced to the moon."

Erl-King.
" O, come and go with me, no longer delay,
Or else, silly child, I will drag thee away. " —
" O father ! O father ! now, now keep your hold,
The Erl-King has seized me — his grasp is so cold ! "

Sore trembled the father ; he spurr'd thro' the wild,
Clasping close to his bosom his shuddering child ;
He reaches his dwelling in doubt and in dread,
But, clasp'd to his bosom, the infant was *dead !*

You see I have not altogether lost the faculty of rhyming. I assure you, there is no small impudence in attempting a version of that ballad, as it has been translated by *Lewis.* — All good things be with you.   W. S.

LONDON, October 15, 1797.

SIR, — I received your letter with pleasure, instead of considering it as an intrusion. One thing more being fully stated would have made it perfectly satisfactory, — namely, the sort of income you immediately possess, and the sort of maintenance Miss Carpenter, in case of your demise, might reasonably expect. Though she is of an age to judge for herself in the choice of an object that she would like to run the race of life with, she has referred the subject to me. As her friend and guardian, I in duty must try to secure her happiness, by endeavoring to keep her comfortable immediately, and to prevent her being left destitute, in case of any unhappy contingency. Her good sense and good education are her chief fortune; therefore, in the worldly way of talking, she is not entitled to much. Her brother, who was also left under my care at an early period, is excessively fond of her; he has no person to think of but her as yet; and will certainly be enabled to make her very handsome presents, as he is doing very well in India, where I sent him some years ago, and where he bears a very high character, I am happy to say. I do not throw out this to induce you to make any proposal beyond what prudence and discretion recommend; but I hope I shall hear from you by return of post, as I may be shortly called out of town to some distance. As children are in general the consequence of an happy union, I should wish to know what may be your thoughts or wishes upon that subject. I trust you will not think me too particular; indeed I am sure you will not, when you consider that I am endeavoring to secure the happiness and welfare of an estimable young woman whom you admire and profess to be partial and attached to, and for whom I have the highest regard, esteem, and respect.

I am, Sir, your obedient humble servant,

DOWNSHIRE.

TO THE SAME.

CARLISLE, October 22.

Your last letter, my dear sir, contains a very fine train of *perhaps*, and of so many pretty conjectures, that it is not flattering you to say you excel in the art of tormenting yourself. As it happens, you are quite wrong in all your suppositions. I have been waiting for Lord D.'s answer to your letter, to give a full answer to your very proper inquiries about my family. Miss Nicolson says, that when she did offer to give you some information, you refused it — and advises me *now* to wait for Lord D.'s letter. Don't believe I have been idle; I have been writing very long letters to him, and all about you. How can you think that I will give an answer about the house until I hear from London? — that is quite impossible; and I believe you are a little out of your senses to imagine I can be in Edinburgh before the twelfth of next month. O, my dear sir, no — you must not think of it this *great while*. I am much flattered by your mother's remembrance; present my respectful compliments to her. You don't mention your father in your last *anxious* letter — I hope he is better. I am expecting every day to hear from my brother. You may tell your uncle he is Commercial Resident at Salem. He will find the name of Charles C. in his India list. My compliments to Captain Scott. *Sans adieu,*

C. C.

TO THE SAME.

CARLISLE, October 25.

Indeed, Mr. Scott, I am by no means pleased with all this writing. I have told you how much I dislike it, and yet you still persist in asking me to write, and that by return of post. O, you really are quite out of your senses. I should not have indulged you in that whim of yours, had you not given me that hint that my silence gives an air of mystery. I have no reason that can

detain me in acquainting you that my father and mother
were French, of the name of Charpentier; he had a place
under government; their residence was at Lyons, where
you would find on inquiries that they lived in good repute and in *very good style*. I had the misfortune of
losing my father before I could know the value of such
a parent. At his death we were left to the care of Lord
D., who was his very great friend; and very soon after
I had the affliction of losing my mother. Our taking the
name of Carpenter was on my brother's going to India,
to prevent any little difficulties that might have occurred.
I hope now you are pleased. Lord D. could have given
you every information, as he has been acquainted with
all my family. You say you almost love *him ;* but until
your *almost* comes to a *quite*, I cannot love *you*. Before
I conclude this famous epistle, I will give you a little
hint — that is, not to put so many *musts* in your letters —
it is beginning *rather too soon ;* and another thing is,
that I take the liberty not to mind them much, but I
expect you mind me. You *must* take care of yourself;
you *must* think of me, and believe me yours sincerely,

C. C.

TO THE SAME.

CARLISLE, October 26.

I have only a minute before the post goes, to assure
you, my dear sir, of the welcome reception of the
stranger.[1] The very great likeness to a friend of mine
will endear him to me; he shall be my constant companion, but I wish he could give me an answer to a thousand
questions I have to make — one in particular, what reason have you for so many fears you express? Have your
friends changed? Pray let me know the truth — they
perhaps don't like me *being French*. Do write immediately — let it be in better spirits. Et croyez-moi toujours votre sincere

C. C.

---

[1] A miniature of Scott.

October 31.

. . . All your apprehensions about your friends make me very uneasy. At your father's age, prejudices are not easily overcome — old people have, you know, so much more wisdom and experience, that we must be guided by them. If he has an objection on my being *French*, I excuse him with all my heart, as I don't love them myself. O how all these things plague me! — when will it end? And to complete the matter, you talk of going to the West Indies. I am certain your father and uncle say you are a hot *heady* young man, quite mad, and I assure you I join with them; and I must believe, that when you have such an idea, you have then determined to think no more of me. I begin to repent of having accepted your picture. I will send it *back again*, if you ever think again about the West Indies. Your family then would *love me* very much — to forsake them for a *stranger*, a person who does not possess half the charms and good qualities that you *imagine*. I think I hear your uncle calling you a hot heady young man. I am certain of it, and I am *generally right* in my conjectures. What does your sister say about it? I suspect that she thinks on the matter as I should do, with fears and anxieties for the happiness of her brother. If it be proper, and you think it would be *acceptable*, present my best compliments to your mother; and to my old acquaintance Captain Scott I beg to be remembered. This evening is the first ball — don't you wish to be of our party? I guess your answer — it would give me infinite pleasure. En attendant le plaisir de vous revoir, je suis toujours votre constante   CHARLOTTE.

THE CASTLE, HARTFORD, October 29, 1797.

SIR, — I received the favor of your letter. It was so manly, honorable, candid, and so full of good sense, that

I think Miss Carpenter's friends cannot in any way object to the union you propose. Its taking place, when or where, will depend upon herself, as I shall write to her by this night's post. Any provision that may be given to her by her brother, you will have settled upon her and her children; and I hope, with all my heart, that every earthly happiness may attend you both. I shall be always happy to hear it, and to subscribe myself your faithful friend and obedient humble servant,

DOWNSHIRE.

(ON THE SAME SHEET.)

CARLISLE, November 4.

Last night I received the enclosed for you from Lord Downshire. If it has your approbation, I shall be very glad to see you as soon as will be convenient. I have a thousand things to tell you; but let me beg of you not to think for some time of a house. I am sure I can convince you of the propriety and prudence of waiting until your father will settle things more to your satisfaction, and until I have heard from my brother. You *must* be of my way of thinking. — Adieu.   C. C.

Scott obeyed this summons, and I suppose remained in Carlisle until the Court of Session met, which is always on the 12th of November.

TO W. SCOTT, ESQ., ADVOCATE, EDINBURGH.

CARLISLE, November 14.

Your letter never could have come in a more favorable moment. Anything you could have said would have been well received. You surprise me much at the regret you express you had of leaving Carlisle. Indeed, I can't believe it was on my account, I was so uncommonly stupid. I don't know what could be the matter with me, I was so very low, and felt really ill: it was even a trouble to speak. The settling of our little plans — all looked so much in earnest — that I began reflecting more seriously than I generally do, or *approve of*. I don't think that very thoughtful people ever can be happy. As this is my maxim, adieu to all thoughts. I have made a determination of being pleased with everything, and with everybody in Edinburgh; a wise system for happiness, is it not? I enclose the lock. I have had almost all my hair cut off. Miss Nicolson has taken some, which she sends to London to be made to something, but this you are not to know of, as she intends to present it to you. . . . I am happy to hear of your father's being better pleased as to money matters ; it will come at last; don't let that trifle disturb you. Adieu, Monsieur. J'ai l'honneur d'être votre très humble et très   Obéissante   C. C.

CARLISLE, November 27.

You have made me very *triste* all day. Pray never more complain of being poor. Are you not ten times richer than I am? Depend on yourself and your profession. I have no doubt you will rise very high, and be a *great rich man*, but we should look down to be contented with our lot, and banish all disagreeable thoughts. We shall do very well. I am very sorry to hear you have such a *bad head*. I hope I shall nurse away all your aches. I think you write too much. When I am *mistress* I shall not allow it. How very angry I should be with you if you were to part with Lenore. Do you really believe I should think it an *unnecessary expense* where your health and pleasure can be concerned? I have a better opinion of you, and I am very glad you don't give up the cavalry, as I love anything that is *stylish*. Don't forget to find a stand for the old carriage, as I shall like to keep it, in case we should have to go any journey; it is so much more convenient than the post-chaises, and will do very well till we can keep *our carriage*. What an idea of yours was that to men-

tion where you wish to have your *bones laid!* [1] If you
were married, I should think you were tired of me. A
very pretty compliment *before marriage.* I hope sincerely that I shall not live to see that day. If you always
have those cheerful thoughts, how very pleasant and gay
you must be.

Adieu, my dearest friend. Take care of yourself if
you love me, as I have *no wish* that you should *visit* that
beautiful and *romantic* scene, the burying-place. Adieu,
once more, and believe that you are loved very sincerely
by   C. C.

December 10.

If I could but really believe that my letter gave you
only half the pleasure you express, I should almost think,
my dearest Scott, that I should get very fond of writing
merely for the pleasure to *indulge* you — that is saying
a great deal. I hope you are sensible of the compliment
I pay you, and don't expect I shall *always* be so pretty
behaved. You may depend on me, my dearest friend,
for fixing as *early* a day as I possibly can; and if it
happens to be not quite so soon as you wish, you must
not be angry with me. It is very unlucky you are such
a bad housekeeper — as I am no better. I shall try. I
hope to have very soon the pleasure of seeing you, and
to tell you how much I love you; but I wish the first
fortnight was over. With all my love, and those sort
of pretty things — adieu.   CHARLOTTE.

---

[1] ["I had a visit from Mr. Haliburton to-day, and asked him all about
your brother, who was two years in his house. My father is Mr. Haliburton's relation and chief, as he represents a very old family of that name.
When you go to the south of Scotland with me, you will see their burying-place, now all that remains with my father of a very handsome
property. It is one of the most beautiful and romantic scenes you ever
saw, among the ruins of an old abbey. When I die, Charlotte, you must
cause my bones to be laid there; but we shall have many happy days before that, I hope." — Scott to Miss Carpenter, November 22, 1797. — *Familiar Letters*, vol. i. p. 8.]

P. S. — Etudiez votre Français. Remember you are to teach me Italian in return, but I shall be but a stupid scholar. *Aimez Charlotte.*

CARLISLE, December 14.

. . . I heard last night from my friends in London, and I shall certainly have the deed this week. I will send it to you directly; but not to lose so much time, as you have been reckoning, I will prevent any little delay that might happen by the post, by fixing already next Wednesday for your coming here, and on Thursday the 21st — Oh, my dear Scott, on that day I shall be yours forever.   C. C.

P. S. — Arrange it so that we shall see none of your family the night of our arrival. I shall be so tired, and such a fright, I should not be seen to advantage.

To these extracts I may add the following from the first leaf of an old black-letter Bible at Abbotsford : —

" *Secundum morem majorum hæc de familiâ Gualteri Scott, Jurisconsulti Edinensis, in librum hunc sacrum manu suâ conscripta sunt.*

" *Gualterus Scott, filius Gualteri Scott et Annæ Rutherford, natus erat apud Edinam 15mo die Augusti,* A. D. 1771.

" *Socius Facultatis Juridicæ Edinensis receptus erat 11mo die Julii,* A. D. 1792.

" *In ecclesiam Sanctæ Mariæ apud Carlisle, uxorem duxit Margaretam Charlottam Carpenter, filiam quondam Joannis Charpentier et Charlottæ Volere, Lugdunensem, 24to die Decembris, 1797."* [1]

---

[1] The account in the text of Miss Carpenter's origin has been, I am aware, both spoken and written of as an uncandid one : it had been expected that even in 1837 I would not pass in silence a rumor of early prevalence, which represented her and her brother as children of Lord Downshire by Madame Charpentier. I did not think it necessary to allude to this story while any of Sir Walter's own children were living ;

and I presume it will be sufficient for me to say now, that neither I, nor, I firmly believe, any one of them, ever heard either from Sir Walter, or from his wife, or from Miss Nicolson (who survived them both) the slightest hint as to the rumor in question. There is not an expression in the preserved correspondence between Scott, the young lady, and the Marquis, that gives it a shadow of countenance. Lastly, Lady Scott always kept hanging by her bedside, and repeatedly kissed in her dying moments, a miniature of her father which is now in my hands; and it is the well-painted likeness of a handsome gentleman — but I am assured the features have no resemblance to Lord Downshire or any of the Hill family. — (1848.)

CHAPTER IX

1798-1799

SCOTT carried his bride to a lodging in George Street,
Edinburgh; a house which he had taken in South Castle
Street not being quite prepared for her reception. The
first fortnight, to which she had looked with such anxiety,
was, I believe, more than sufficient to convince her husband's family that, however rashly he had formed the
connection, she had the sterling qualities of a good wife.
Notwithstanding the little leaning to the pomps and vani-
ties of the world, which her letters have not concealed,
she had made up her mind to find her happiness in better
things; and so long as their circumstances continued
narrow, no woman could have conformed herself to them
with more of good feeling and good sense. Some habits,
new in the quiet domestic circles of Edinburgh citizens,
did not escape criticism; and in particular, I have heard
herself, in her most prosperous days, laugh heartily at
the remonstrances of her George Street landlady, when
it was discovered that the *southron* lodger chose to sit
usually, and not on high occasions merely, in her draw-

ing-room, — on which subject the mother-in-law was disposed to take the thrifty old-fashioned dame's side.

I cannot fancy that Lady Scott's manners or ideas could ever have amalgamated very well with those of her husband's parents; but the feeble state of the old gentleman's health prevented her from seeing them constantly; and without any affectation of strict intimacy, they soon were, and always continued to be, very good friends. Anne Scott, the delicate sister to whom the Ashestiel Memoir alludes so tenderly, speedily formed a warm and sincere attachment for the stranger; but death, in a short time, carried off that interesting creature, who seems to have had much of her brother's imaginative and romantic temperament, without his power of controlling it.

Mrs. Scott's arrival was welcomed with unmingled delight by the brothers of *the Mountain*. The two ladies, who had formerly given life and grace to their society, were both recently married. We have seen Miss Erskine's letter of farewell; and I have before me another not less affectionate, written when Miss Cranstoun gave her hand (a few months later) to Godfrey Wenceslaus, Count of Purgstall, a nobleman of large possessions in Styria, who had been spending some time in Edinburgh. Scott's house in South Castle Street (soon after exchanged for one of the same sort in North Castle Street, which he purchased, and inhabited down to 1826) became now to *the Mountain* what Cranstoun's and Erskine's had been while their accomplished sisters remained with them. The officers of the Light Horse, too, established a club among themselves, supping once a week at each other's houses in rotation. The young lady thus found two somewhat different, but both highly agreeable circles ready to receive her with cordial kindness; and the evening hours passed in a round of innocent gayety, all the arrangements being conducted in a simple and inexpensive fashion, suitable to young people whose days were mostly laborious, and very few of their purses heavy. Scott

and Erskine had always been fond of the theatre; the
pretty bride was passionately so — and I doubt if they
ever spent a week in Edinburgh without indulging themselves in this amusement. But regular dinners and
crowded assemblies were in those years quite unthought
of. Perhaps nowhere could have been found a society
on so small a scale including more of vigorous intellect,
varied information, elegant tastes, and real virtue, affection, and mutual confidence. How often have I heard
its members, in the midst of the wealth and honors which
most of them in due season attained, sigh over the recollection of those humbler days, when love and ambition
were young and buoyant — and no difference of opinion
was able to bring even a momentary chill over the warmth
of friendship.

You will imagine [writes the Countess Purgstall to Scott,
from one of her Styrian castles], how my heart burnt within
me, my dear, dear friend, while I read your thrice-welcome
letter. Had all the gods and goddesses, from Saturn to La
Liberté, laid their heads together, they could not have presented
me with anything that so accorded with my fondest wishes.
To have a conviction that those I love are happy, and don't
forget me — I have no way to express my feelings — they come
in a flood and destroy me. Could my George but light on another Charlotte, there would be but one crook left in my lot[1] —
to wit, that Reggersburg does not serve as a vista for the Parliament Square.[2] Would some earthquake engulf the vile tract
between, or the spirit of our rock introduce me to Jack the
Giant-Queller's shoemaker; Lord, Lord, how delightful! Could
I choose, I should just for the present patronize the shoemaker,

---

[1] A long-popular manual of Presbyterian Theology is entitled *The
Crook in the Lot:* the author's name, Thomas Boston, Minister of Ettrick.

[2] The ancient castle of Reggersburg (if engravings may be trusted, one
of the most magnificent in Germany) was the chief seat of the Purgstalls.
In situation and extent it seems to resemble the castle of Stirling. The
Countess writes thus, about the same time, to another of *the Mountain:*
" As for Scott and his sweet little wife, I consider them as a sort of papa
and mamma to you all, and am happy the gods have ordered it so."

and then the moment I got you all snug in this old hall, steal the shoes, and lock them away till the indignation of the Lord passes by poor Old England! Earl Walter would play the devil with me, but his Charlotte's smiles would speak thanks ineffable, and the angry clouds pass as before the sun in his strength. How divinely your spectre scenes would come in here! Surely there is no vanity in saying that earth has no mountains like ours. O, how delightful to see the lady that is blessed with Earl Walter's love, and that had mind enough to discover the blessing. Some kind post, I hope, will soon tell me that your happiness is enlarged, in the only way it can be enlarged, for you have no chance now I think of taking Buonaparte prisoner. What sort of a genius will he be, is a very anxious speculation indeed; whether the philosopher, the lawyer, the antiquary, the poet, or the hero will prevail — the spirit whispers unto me a happy *mélange* of the two last — he will lisp in numbers, and kick at *la Nourrice*. On his arrival, present my fondest wishes to his honor, and don't, pray, give him a name out of your list of round-table knights, but some simple Christian appellation from the House of Harden. And is it then true, my God, that Earl Walter is a Benedick, and that I am in Styria? Well, bless us all, prays the separated from her brethren,   J. A. P.

HAINFELD, July 20, 1798.

Another extract from the Family Bible may close this letter — "*M. C. Scott puerum edidit 14to die Octobris, 1798, qui postero die obiit apud Edinburgum.*"

In the summer of this year Scott had hired a pretty cottage at Lasswade, on the Esk, about six miles from Edinburgh, and there, as the back of Madame de P.'s letter shows, he received it from the hands of Professor Stewart. It is a small house, but with one room of good dimensions, which Mrs. Scott's taste set off to advantage at very humble cost — a paddock or two — and a garden (commanding a most beautiful view) in which Scott delighted to train his flowers and creepers. Never, I have heard him say, was he prouder of his handiwork than

when he had completed the fashioning of a rustic arch-
way, now overgrown with hoary ivy, by way of ornament
to the entrance from the Edinburgh road. In this retreat
they spent some happy summers, receiving the visits of
their few chosen friends from the neighboring city, and
wandering at will amidst some of the most romantic scenery that Scotland can boast — Scott's dearest haunt in
the days of his boyish ramblings. They had neighbors,
too, who were not slow to cultivate their acquaintance.
With the Clerks of Pennycuik, with Mackenzie the
Man of Feeling, who then occupied the charming villa
of Auchendinny, and with Lord Woodhouselee, Scott
had from an earlier date been familiar; and it was while
at Lasswade that he formed intimacies, even more important in their results, with the noble families of Melville
and Buccleuch, both of whom have castles in the same
valley.

> "Sweet are the paths, O passing sweet,
>   By Esk's fair streams that run,
> O'er airy steep, thro' copsewood deep
>   Impervious to the sun;

> "From that fair dome where suit is paid
>   By blast of bugle free,[1]
> To Auchendinny's hazel shade,
>   And haunted Woodhouselee.

> "Who knows not Melville's beechy grove,
>   And Roslin's rocky glen;
> Dalkeith, which all the virtues love,
>   And classic Hawthornden?"[2]

Another verse reminds us that

> "There the rapt poet's step may rove;" —

and it was amidst these delicious solitudes that he did
produce the pieces which laid the imperishable founda-
tions of all his fame. It was here, that when his warm
heart was beating with young and happy love, and his

---

[1] Pennycuik.
[2] [See *Poetical Works*, Cambridge Edition, p. 18.]

whole mind and spirit were nerved by new motives for exertion — it was here, that in the ripened glow of manhood he seems to have first felt something of his real strength, and poured himself out in those splendid original ballads which were at once to fix his name.

I must, however, approach these more leisurely. When William Erskine was in London in the spring of this year, he happened to meet in society with Matthew Gregory Lewis, M. P. for Hindon, whose romance of The Monk, with the ballads which it included, had made for him, in those barren days, a brilliant reputation. This good-natured fopling, the pet and plaything of certain fashionable circles, was then busy with that miscellany which at length came out in 1801, under the name of Tales of Wonder, and was beating up in all quarters for contributions. Erskine showed Lewis Scott's versions of Lenore and The Wild Huntsman; and when he mentioned that his friend had other specimens of the German *diablerie* in his portfolio, the collector anxiously requested that Scott might be enlisted in his cause. The brushwood splendor of "The Monk's" fame,

> "The false and foolish fire that's whiskt about
> By popular air, and glares, and then goes out," [1]

had a dazzling influence among the unknown aspirants of Edinburgh; and Scott, who was perhaps at all times rather disposed to hold popular favor as the surest test of literary merit, and who certainly continued through life to over-estimate all talents except his own, considered this invitation as a very flattering compliment. He immediately wrote to Lewis, placing whatever pieces he had translated and imitated from the German *Volkslieder* at his disposal. The following is the first of Lewis's letters to him that has been preserved — it is without date, but marked by Scott "1798."

[1] Oldham.

TO WALTER SCOTT, ESQ., ADVOCATE, EDINBURGH.

SIR, — I cannot delay expressing to you how much I feel obliged to you, both for the permission to publish the ballads I requested, and for the handsome manner in which that permission was granted. The plan I have proposed to myself is to collect all the *marvellous* ballads which I can lay hands upon. Ancient as well as modern will be comprised in my design; and I shall even allow a place to Sir Gawaine's Foul Ladye, and the Ghost that came to Margaret's door and tirled at the pin. But as a ghost or a witch is a *sine-qua-non* ingredient in all the dishes of which I mean to compose my hobgoblin repast, I am afraid the Lied von Treue does not come within the plan. With regard to the romance in Claudina von Villa Bella, if I am not mistaken, it is only a fragment in the original; but, should you have finished it, you will oblige me much by letting me have a copy of it, as well as of the other *marvellous* traditionary ballads you were so good as to offer me.

Should you be in Edinburgh when I arrive there, I shall request Erskine to contrive an opportunity for my returning my personal thanks. Meanwhile, I beg you to believe me your most obedient and obliged   M. G. LEWIS.

When Lewis reached Edinburgh, he met Scott accordingly, and the latter told Allan Cunningham, thirty years afterwards, that he thought he had never felt such elation as when the "Monk" invited him to dine with him for the first time at his hotel. Since he gazed on Burns in his seventeenth year, he had seen no one enjoying, by general consent, the fame of a poet; and Lewis, whatever Scott might, on maturer consideration, think of his title to such fame, had certainly done him no small service; for the ballads of Alonzo the Brave and the Fair Imogine, and Durandarte, had rekindled effectually in his breast the spark of poetical ambition. Lady Charlotte Campbell (now Bury), always distinguished by her passion for elegant letters, was ready, "in pride of rank, in beauty's bloom," to do the honors of Scotland to the

"Lion of Mayfair;" and I believe Scott's first introduction to Lewis took place at one of her Ladyship's parties. But they met frequently, and, among other places, at Dalkeith — as witness one of Scott's marginal notes, written in 1825, on Lord Byron's Diary: "Poor fellow," says Byron, "he died a martyr to his new riches — of a second visit to Jamaica.

> ' I'd give the lands of Deloraine
> Dark Musgrave were alive again ; '

that is,

> ' I would give many a sugar-cane
> Monk Lewis were alive again.' "

To which Scott adds: "I would pay my share! how few friends one has whose faults are only ridiculous. His visit was one of humanity to ameliorate the condition of his slaves. He did much good by stealth, and was a most generous creature. . . . Lewis was fonder of great people than he ought to have been, either as a man of talent or as a man of fashion. He had always dukes and duchesses in his mouth, and was pathetically fond of any one that had a title. You would have sworn he had been a *parvenu* of yesterday, yet he had lived all his life in good society. . . . Mat had queerish eyes — they projected like those of some insects, and were flattish on the orbit. His person was extremely small and boyish — he was indeed the least man I ever saw, to be strictly well and neatly made. I remember a picture of him by Saunders being handed round at Dalkeith House. The artist had ingeniously flung a dark folding-mantle around the form, under which was half hid a dagger, a dark lantern, or some such cut-throat appurtenance; with all this the features were preserved and ennobled. It passed from hand to hand into that of Henry, Duke of Buccleuch, who, hearing the general voice affirm that it was very like, said aloud, ' Like Mat Lewis! Why, that picture's like a MAN!' He looked, and lo, Mat Lewis's head was at his elbow. This boyishness went through life with him. He was a child, and a spoiled child, but a child of high imagination; and so he wasted himself on ghost stories and German romances. He had the finest ear for rhythm I ever met with — finer than Byron's."

During Lewis's stay in Scotland this year, he spent a day or two with Scott at Musselburgh, where the yeomanry corps were in quarters. Scott received him in his lodgings, under the roof of an ancient dame, who afforded him much amusement by her daily colloquies with the fishwomen — the *Mucklebackets* of the place. His delight in studying the dialect of these people is well remembered by the survivors of the cavalry, and must have astonished the stranger dandy. While walking about before dinner on one of these days, Mr. Skene's recitation of the German *Kriegslied*, "Der Abschied's Tag ist da" (the day of departure is come), delighted both Lewis and the Quartermaster; and the latter produced next morning that spirited little piece in the same measure, which, embodying the volunteer ardor of the time, was forthwith adopted as the troop-song of the Edinburgh Light Horse.[1]

In January, 1799, Mr. Lewis appears negotiating with a bookseller, named Bell, for the publication of Scott's version of Goethe's tragedy, Goetz von Berlichingen of the Iron Hand. Bell seems finally to have purchased the copyright for twenty-five guineas, and twenty-five more to be paid in case of a second edition — which was never called for until long after the copyright had expired. Lewis writes, "I have made him distinctly understand, that, if you accept so small a sum, it will be only because this is your first publication." The edition of Lenore and the Yäger, in 1796, had been completely forgotten; and Lewis thought of those ballads exactly as if they had been MS. contributions to his own Tales of Wonder, still lingering on the threshold of the press. The Goetz appeared accordingly, with Scott's name on the title-page, in the following February.

[1] See *Poetical Works,* vol. iv. p. 230 [Cambridge Edition, p. 9].

In March, 1799, he carried his wife to London, this being the first time that he had seen the metropolis since the days of his infancy. The acquaintance of Lewis served to introduce him to some literary and fashionable society, with which he was much amused; but his great anxiety was to examine the antiquities of the Tower and Westminster Abbey, and to make some researches among the MSS. of the British Museum. He found his Goetz spoken of favorably, on the whole, by the critics of the time; but it does not appear to have attracted general attention. The truth is, that, to have given Goethe anything like a fair chance with the English public, his first drama ought to have been translated at least ten years before. The imitators had been more fortunate than the master, and this work, which constitutes one of the most important landmarks in the history of German literature, had not come even into Scott's hands, until he had familiarized himself with the ideas which it first opened, in the feeble and puny mimicries of writers already forgotten. He readily discovered the vast gulf which separated Goethe from the German dramatists on whom he had heretofore been employing himself; but the public in general drew no such distinctions, and the English Goetz was soon afterwards condemned to oblivion, through the unsparing ridicule showered on whatever bore the name of *German play*, by the inimitable caricature of The Rovers.

The tragedy of Goethe, however, has in truth nothing in common with the wild absurdities against which Canning and Ellis levelled the arrows of their wit. It is a broad, bold, free, and most picturesque delineation of real characters, manners, and events; the first-fruits, in a word, of that passionate admiration for Shakespeare, to which all that is excellent in the recent imaginative literature of Germany must be traced. With what delight must Scott have found the scope and manner of our Elizabethan drama revived on a foreign stage at the call

of a real master! with what double delight must he
have seen Goethe seizing for the noblest purposes of art,
men and modes of life, scenes, incidents, and transactions, all claiming near kindred with those that had from
boyhood formed the chosen theme of his own sympathy
and reflection! In the baronial robbers of the Rhine,
stern, bloody, and rapacious, but frank, generous, and,
after their fashion, courteous — in their forays upon each
other's domains, the besieged castles, the plundered
herds, the captive knights, the browbeaten bishop, and
the baffled liege-lord, who vainly strove to quell all these
turbulences — Scott had before him a vivid image of the
life of his own and the rival Border clans, familiarized
to him by a hundred nameless minstrels. If it be doubtful whether, but for Percy's Reliques, he would ever have
thought of editing their Ballads, I think it not less so,
whether, but for the Iron Handed Goetz, it would ever
have flashed upon his mind, that in the wild traditions
which these recorded, he had been unconsciously assembling materials for more works of high art than the longest life could serve him to elaborate.

As the version of the Goetz has at length been included
in Scott's poetical works, I need not make it the subject
of more detailed observation here. The reader who
turns to it for the first time will be no less struck than I
was under similar circumstances a dozen years ago, with
the many points of resemblance between the tone and
spirit of Goethe's delineation, and that afterwards adopted
by the translator in some of the most remarkable of his
original works. One example, however, may be forgiven: —

A loud alarm, with shouts and firing — SELBISS *is borne in,
wounded, by two Troopers.*

Selbiss. Leave me here, and hasten to Goetz.

1st Trooper. Let us stay — you need our aid.

Sel. Get one of you on the watch-tower, and tell me how it
goes.

1st Troop. How shall I get up?

2d Troop. Get upon my shoulder; you can then reach the ruined part.

1st Troop. (*On the tower.*) Alas! Alas!

Sel. What seest thou?

Troop. Your cavaliers fly to the hill.

Sel. Hellish cowards! I would that they stood, and that I had a ball through my head! Ride one of you at full speed — Curse and thunder them back to the field! Seest thou Goetz?

Troop. I see the three black feathers in the midst of the tumult.

Sel. Swim, brave swimmer — I lie here.

Troop. A white plume! Whose is that?

Sel. The Captain.

Troop. Goetz gallops upon him — Crash — down he goes.

Sel. The Captain?

Troop. Yes.

Sel. Bravo! — bravo!

Troop. Alas! Alas! I see Goetz no more.

Sel. Then die, Selbiss!

Troop. A dreadful tumult where he stood. George's blue plume vanishes too.

Sel. Climb higher! — Seest thou Lerse?

Troop. No — everything is in confusion.

Sel. No further — come down — tell me no more.

Troop. I cannot — Bravo! I see Goetz.

Sel. On horseback?

Troop. Ay, ay — high on horseback — victory! — they fly!

Sel. The Imperialists?

Troop. Standard and all — Goetz behind them — he has it — he has it!

The first hint of this (as of what not in poetry?) may be found in the Iliad — where Helen points out the persons of the Greek heroes to old Priam seated on the walls of Troy; and Shakespeare makes some use of the same idea in his Julius Cæsar. But who does not recognize in Goethe's drama the true original of the death scene of Marmion, and the storm in Ivanhoe?

Scott executed about the same time his House of

Aspen, rather a *rifacimento* than a translation from one of the minor dramatists that had crowded to partake the popularity of Goetz of the Iron Hand. It also was sent to Lewis in London, where having first been read and much recommended by the celebrated actress, Mrs. Esten, it was taken up by Kemble, and I believe actually put in rehearsal for the stage. If so, the trial did not encourage further preparation, and the notion was abandoned. Discovering the play thirty years after among his papers, Scott sent it to one of the literary almanacs (the Keepsake of 1829). In the advertisement he says, "he had lately chanced to look over these scenes with feelings very different from those of the adventurous period of his literary life during which they were written, and yet with such, perhaps, as a reformed libertine might regard the illegitimate production of an early amour." He adds, "There is something to be ashamed of, certainly; but after all, paternal vanity whispers that the child has some resemblance to the father." This piece being also now included in the general edition of his works, I shall not dwell upon it here. It owes its most effective scenes to the Secret Tribunal, which fountain of terror had first been disclosed by Goethe, and had by this time lost much of its effect through the "clumsy alacrity" of a hundred followers. Scott's scenes are interspersed with some lyrics, the numbers of which, at least, are worthy of attention. One has the metre — and not a little of the spirit, of the boat-song of Roderick Dhu and Clan Alpine: —

> " Joy to the victors, the sons of old Aspen,
> Joy to the race of the battle and scar !
> Glory's proud garland triumphantly grasping,
> Generous in peace, and victorious in war.
> Honor acquiring,
> Valor inspiring,
> Bursting resistless through foemen they go,
> War axes wielding,
> Broken ranks yielding,
> Till from the battle proud Roderick retiring,
> Yields in wild rout the fair palm to his foe."

Another is the first draft of The Maid of Toro;[1] and perhaps he had forgotten the more perfect copy of that song, when he sent the original to the Keepsake.

I incline to believe that the House of Aspen was written after Scott's return from London; but it has been mentioned in the same page with the Goetz, to avoid any recurrence to either the German or the Germanized dramas. His return was accelerated by the domestic calamity which forms the subject of the following letter: —

TO MRS. SCOTT, GEORGE'S SQUARE, EDINBURGH.

LONDON, 19th April, 1799.

MY DEAR MOTHER, — I cannot express the feelings with which I sit down to the discharge of my present melancholy duty, nor how much I regret the accident which has removed me from Edinburgh, at a time, of all others, when I should have wished to administer to your distress all the consolation which sympathy and affection could have afforded. Your own principles of virtue and religion will, however, I well know, be your best support in this heaviest of human afflictions. The removal of my regretted parent from this earthly scene is to him, doubtless, the happiest change, if the firmest integrity and the best spent life can entitle us to judge of the state of our departed friends. When we reflect upon this, we ought almost to suppress the selfish feelings of regret that he was not spared to us a little longer, especially when we consider that it was not the will of Heaven that he should share the most inestimable of its earthly blessings, such a portion of health as might have enabled him to enjoy his family. To my dear father, then, the putting off this mortal mask was happiness, and to us who remain, a lesson so to live that we also may have hope in our latter end; and with you, my dearest Mother, remain many blessings and some duties, a grateful recollection

---

[1] [See *Poetical Works*, Cambridge Edition, p. 10.]

of which will, I am sure, contribute to calm the current of your affliction. The affection and attention which you have a right to expect from your children, and which I consider as the best tribute we can pay to the memory of the parent we have lost, will also, I am sure, contribute its full share to the alleviation of your distress. The situation of Charlotte's health, in its present delicate state, prevented me from setting off directly for Scotland, when I heard that immediate danger was apprehended. I am now glad I did not do so, as I could not with the utmost expedition have reached Edinburgh before the lamented event had taken place. The situation of my affairs must detain me here for a few days more; the instant I can I will set off for Scotland. I need not tell you not even to attempt to answer this letter — such an exertion would be both unnecessary and improper. John or Tom will let me know how my sister and you do. I am, ever, dear Mother, your dutiful and affectionate son, W. S.

P. S. — Permit me, my dear Madam, to add a line to Scott's letter, to express to you how sincerely I feel for your loss, and how much I regret that I am not near you to try by the most tender care to soften the pain that so great a misfortune must inflict on you and on all those who had the happiness of being connected with him. I hope soon to have the pleasure of returning to you, and to convince you of the sincere affection of your daughter, M. C. S.

The death of this worthy man, in his 70th year, after a long series of feeble health and suffering, was an event which could only be regarded as a great deliverance to himself. He had had a succession of paralytic attacks, under which, mind as well as body had by degrees been laid quite prostrate. When the first Chronicles of the Canongate appeared, a near relation of the family said to me: "I had been out of Scotland for some time, and

did not know of my good friend's illness, until I reached
Edinburgh, a few months before his death. Walter
carried me to visit him, and warned me that I should see
a great change. I saw the very scene that is here painted
of the elder Croftangry's sickroom — not a feature different — poor Anne Scott, the gentlest of creatures, was
treated by the fretful patient precisely like this niece."[1]

I have lived to see the curtain rise and fall once more
on a like scene.

Mr. Thomas Scott continued to manage his father's
business. He married early;[2] he was in his circle of
society extremely popular; and his prospects seemed fair
in all things. The property left by the old gentleman
was less than had been expected, but sufficient to make
ample provision for his widow, and a not inconsiderable
addition to the resources of those among whom the remainder was divided.

Scott's mother and sister, both much exhausted with
their attendance on a protracted sickbed, and the latter
already in the first stage of the malady which in two
years more carried her also to her grave, spent the greater
part of the following summer and autumn in his cottage
at Lasswade.

There he was now again laboring assiduously in the
service of Lewis's "hobgoblin repast," and the specimens
of his friend's letters on his contributions, as they were
successively forwarded to London, which were printed by
way of appendix to the Essay on Imitations of the Ancient Ballad, in 1830,[3] may perhaps be sufficient for the
reader's curiosity. The versions from Bürger were, in
consequence of Lewis's remarks, somewhat corrected;
and, indeed, although Scott speaks of himself as having

---

[1] See *Chronicles of the Canongate*, chap. i.

[2] Mrs. Thomas Scott, Miss Macculloch of Ardwell, was one of the best
and wisest and most agreeable women I have ever known. She had a
motherly affection for all Sir Walter's family, and she survived them all.
She died at Canterbury in April, 1848, aged 72. — (1848.)

[3] See *Minstrelsy*, vol. iv. p. 79.

paid no attention "*at the time*," to the lectures of his "martinet in rhymes and numbers" — "lectures which were," he adds, "severe enough, but useful eventually, as forcing on a young and careless versifier criticisms absolutely necessary to his future success" — it is certain that his memory had in some degree deceived him when he used this language, for, of all the false rhymes and Scotticisms which Lewis had pointed out in these "lectures," hardly one appears in the printed copies of the ballads contributed by Scott to the Tales of Wonder.

As to his imperfect *rhymes* of this period, I have no doubt he owed them to his recent zeal about collecting the ballads of the Border. He had, in his familiarity with compositions so remarkable for merits of a higher order, ceased to be offended, as in the days of his devotion to Langhorne and Mickle he would probably have been, with their loose and vague assonances, which are often, in fact, not rhymes at all; a license pardonable enough in real minstrelsy, meant to be chanted to moss-troopers with the accompanying tones of the war-pipe, but certainly not worthy of imitation in verses written for the eye of a polished age. Of this carelessness as to rhyme, we see little or nothing in our few specimens of his boyish verse, and it does not occur, to any extent that has ever been thought worth notice, in his great works.

But Lewis's collection did not engross the leisure of this summer. It produced also what Scott justly calls his "first serious attempts in verse;" and of these, the earliest appears to have been the Glenfinlas. Here the scene is laid in the most favorite district of his favorite Perthshire Highlands; and the Gaelic tradition on which it is founded was far more likely to draw out the secret strength of his genius, as well as to arrest the feelings of his countrymen, than any subject with which the stores of German *diablerie* could have supplied him. It has been alleged, however, that the poet makes a German use of his Scottish materials; that the legend, as briefly told in the simple prose of his preface, is more *affecting* than the lofty and sonorous stanzas themselves; that the vague terror of the original dream loses, instead of gaining, by the expanded elaboration of the detail. There may be something in these objections: but no man can pretend to be an impartial critic of the piece which first awoke his own childish ear to the power of poetry and the melody of verse.

The next of these compositions was, I believe, The Eve of St. John, in which Scott repeoples the tower of Smailholm, the awe-inspiring haunt of his infancy; and here he touches, for the first time, the one superstition which can still be appealed to with full and perfect effect; the only one which lingers in minds long since weaned from all sympathy with the machinery of witches and goblins. And surely this mystery was never touched with more thrilling skill than in that noble ballad. It is the first of his original pieces, too, in which he uses the measure of his own favorite Minstrels; a measure which the monotony of mediocrity had long and successfully been laboring to degrade, but in itself adequate to the expression of the highest thoughts, as well as the gentlest emotions; and capable, in fit hands, of as rich a variety of music as any other of modern times. This was written at Mertoun-house in the autumn of 1799. Some dilapidations had taken place in the tower of Smailholm, and Harden, being informed of the fact, and entreated with needless earnestness by his kinsman to arrest the hand of the spoiler, requested playfully a ballad, of which Smailholm should be the scene, as the price of his assent. The stanza in which the groves of Mertoun are alluded to has been quoted in a preceding page.

Then came The Gray Brother, founded on another superstition, which seems to have been almost as ancient as the belief in ghosts; namely, that the holiest service of the altar cannot go on in the presence of an unclean person — a heinous sinner unconfessed and unabsolved.

The fragmentary form of this poem greatly heightens the
awfulness of its impression; and in construction and
metre, the verses which really belong to the story appear
to me the happiest that have ever been produced ex-
pressly in imitation of the ballad of the Middle Ages. In
the stanzas, previously quoted, on the scenery of the
Esk, however beautiful in themselves, and however interesting now as marking the locality of the composition, he
must be allowed to have lapsed into another strain, and
produced a *pannus purpureus* which interferes with and
mars the general texture.

He wrote at the same period the fine chivalrous ballad
entitled The Fire-King, in which there is more than
enough to make us forgive the machinery.

It was in the course of this autumn that he first visited
Bothwell Castle, the seat of Archibald, Lord Douglas,
who had married the Lady Frances Scott, sister to Henry,
Duke of Buccleuch; a woman whose many amiable virtues were combined with extraordinary strength of mind,
and who had, from the first introduction of the young
poet at Dalkeith, formed high anticipations of his future
career. Lady Douglas was one of his dearest friends
through life; and now, under her roof, he improved an
acquaintance (begun also at Dalkeith) with one whose
abilities and accomplishments not less qualified her to
estimate him, and who still survives to lament the only
event that could have interrupted their cordial confidence
— the Lady Louisa Stuart,[1] daughter of the celebrated

---

[1] [Lady Louisa Stuart inherited a large measure of the talent of her
maternal grandmother, Lady Mary Wortley Montagu, and her letters
form a peculiarly attractive part of the Scott correspondence. A selection from these, to the year 1826, was first published in the *Familiar Letters* (1893), and some later letters, both of Lady Louisa and of Sir Walter,
are included in *Selections from the Manuscripts of Lady Louisa Stuart*
(1899).

Lady Douglas was the kinswoman as well as dear friend of Lady Louisa, one being the granddaughter, the other the grand-niece of John, Duke
of Argyle and Greenwich. Lady Louisa long outlived Scott and all the
other friends of her prime, dying in 1851, at the age of 94.]

John, Earl of Bute. These ladies, who were sisters in
mind, feeling, and affection, he visited among scenes the
noblest and most interesting that all Scotland can show
— alike famous in history and romance; and he was not
unwilling to make Bothwell and Blantyre the subject of
another ballad. His purpose was never completed. I
think, however, the reader will not complain of my introducing the fragment which I have found among his
papers.

> " When fruitful Clydesdale's apple-bowers
>   Are mellowing in the noon ;
> When sighs round Pembroke's ruin'd towers
>   The sultry breath of June ;
>
> " When Clyde, despite his sheltering wood,
>   Must leave his channel dry ;
> And vainly o'er the limpid flood
>   The angler guides his fly ;
>
> " If chance by Bothwell's lovely braes
>   A wanderer thou hast been,
> Or hid thee from the summer's blaze
>   In Blantyre's bowers of green,
>
> " Full where the copsewood opens wild
>   Thy pilgrim step hath stayed,
> Where Bothwell's towers in ruins piled
>   O'erlook the verdant glade ;
>
> " And many a tale of love and fear
>   Hath mingled with the scene —
> Of Bothwell's banks that bloom'd so dear
>   And Bothwell's bonny Jean.
>
> " O, if with rugged minstrel lays
>   Unsated be thy ear,
> And thou of deeds of other days
>   Another tale wilt hear,
>
> " Then all beneath the spreading beech
>   Flung careless on the lea,
> The Gothic muse the tale shall teach
>   Of Bothwell's sisters three.

" Wight Wallace stood on Deckmont head,
    He blew his bugle round,
Till the wild bull in Cadyow wood
    Has started at the sound.

" St. George's cross, o'er Bothwell hung,
    Was waving far and wide,
And from the lofty turret flung
    Its crimson blaze on Clyde;

" And rising at the bugle blast
    That marked the Scottish foe,
Old England's yeomen muster'd fast,
    And bent the Norman bow.

" Tall in the midst Sir Aylmer rose,
    Proud Pembroke's Earl was he —
While " —— . . .

One morning, during his visit to Bothwell, was spent
on an excursion to the ruins of Craignethan Castle, the
seat, in former days, of the great Evandale branch of
the house of Hamilton, but now the property of Lord
Douglas; and the poet expressed such rapture with the
scenery, that his hosts urged him to accept, for his lifetime, the use of a small habitable house, enclosed within
the circuit of the ancient walls. This offer was not at
once declined; but circumstances occurred before the end
of the year which rendered it impossible for him to establish his summer residence in Lanarkshire. The castle
of Craignethan is the original of his "Tillietudlem." [1]

Another imperfect ballad, in which he had meant to
blend together two legends familiar to every reader of
Scottish history and romance, has been found in the same
portfolio, and the handwriting proves it to be of the same
early date. Though long and very unfinished, it contains
so many touches of his best manner that I cannot with-
hold

[1] The name *Tillietudlem* was no doubt taken from that of the ravine
under the old castle of Lanark — which town is near Craignethan. This
ravine is called Gillytudlem.

THE SHEPHERD'S TALE.

. . . .

" And ne'er but once, my son," he says,
    " Was yon sad cavern trod,
In persecution's iron days,
    When the land was left by God.

" From Bewlie bog, with slaughter red,
    A wanderer hither drew,
And oft he stopt and turned his head,
    As by fits the night wind blew;

" For trampling round by Cheviot edge
    Were heard the troopers keen,
And frequent from the Whitelaw ridge
    The death-shot flashed between.

" The moonbeams through the misty shower
    On yon dark cavern fell;
Through the cloudy night the snow gleamed white,
    Which sunbeam ne'er could quell.

" Yon cavern dark is rough and rude,
    And cold its jaws of snow;
But more rough and rude are the men of blood,
    That hunt my life below;

" Yon spell-bound den, as the aged tell,
    Was hewn by demons' hands;
But I had lourd [1] melle with the fiends of hell,
    Than with Clavers and his band."

He heard the deep-mouthed bloodhound bark,
    He heard the horses neigh,
He plunged him in the cavern dark,
    And downward sped his way.

Now faintly down the winding path
    Came the cry of the faulting hound,
And the muttered oath of baulkèd wrath
    Was lost in hollow sound.

He threw him on the flinted floor,
    And held his breath for fear;

---

[1] *Lourd;* i. e., liefer — rather.

He rose and bitter cursed his foes,
    As the sounds died on his ear.

"O bare thine arm, thou battling Lord,
    For Scotland's wandering band;
Dash from the oppressor's grasp the sword,
    And sweep him from the land!

"Forget not thou thy people's groans
    From dark Dunnottar's tower,
Mix'd with the seafowl's shrilly moans,
    And ocean's bursting roar!

"O in fell Clavers' hour of pride,
    Even in his mightiest day,
As bold he strides through conquest's tide,
    O stretch him on the clay!

"His widow and his little ones,
    O may their tower of trust
Remove its strong foundation stones,
    And crush them in the dust!" —

"Sweet prayers to me," a voice replied,
    "Thrice welcome, guest of mine!" —
And glimmering on the cavern side,
    A light was seen to shine.

An aged man, in amice brown,
    Stood by the wanderer's side,
By powerful charm, a dead man's arm
    The torch's light supplied.

From each stiff finger stretched upright,
    Arose a ghastly flame,
That waved not in the blast of night
    Which through the cavern came.

O deadly blue was that taper's hue,
    That flamed the cavern o'er,
But more deadly blue was the ghastly hue
    Of his eyes who the taper bore.

He laid on his head a hand like lead,
    As heavy, pale, and cold: —
"Vengeance be thine, thou guest of mine,
    If thy heart be firm and bold.

" But if faint thy heart, and caitiff fear
  Thy recreant sinews know,
The mountain erne thy heart shall tear,
  Thy nerves the hooded crow."

The wanderer raised him undismay'd :
  " My soul, by dangers steeled,
Is stubborn as my border blade,
  Which never knew to yield.

" And if thy power can speed the hour
  Of vengeance on my foes,
Theirs be the fate, from bridge and gate
  To feed the hooded crows."

The Brownie looked him in the face,
  And his color fled with speed —
" I fear me," quoth he, " uneath it will be
  To match thy word and deed.

" In ancient days when English bands
  Sore ravaged Scotland fair,
The sword and shield of Scottish land
  Was valiant Halbert Kerr.

" A warlock loved the warrior well,
  Sir Michael Scott by name,
And he sought for his sake a spell to make,
  Should the Southern foemen tame :

" ' Look thou,' he said, ' from Cessford head,
  As the July sun sinks low,
And when glimmering white on Cheviot's height
  Thou shalt spy a wreath of snow,
The spell is complete which shall bring to thy feet
  The haughty Saxon foe.'

" For many a year wrought the wizard here,
  In Cheviot's bosom low,
Till the spell was complete, and in July's heat
  Appeared December's snow ;
But Cessford's Halbert never came
  The wondrous cause to know.

" For years before in Bowden aisle
  The warrior's bones had lain,
And after short while, by female guile,
  Sir Michael Scott was slain.

" But me and my brethren in this cell
   His mighty charms retain, —
And he that can quell the powerful spell
   Shall o'er broad Scotland reign."

He led him through an iron door
   And up a winding stair,
And in wild amaze did the wanderer gaze
   On the sight which opened there.

Through the gloomy night flashed ruddy light —
   A thousand torches' glow;
The cave rose high, like the vaulted sky,
   O'er stalls in double row.

In every stall of that endless hall
   Stood a steed in barbing bright;
At the foot of each steed, all armed save the head,
   Lay stretched a stalwart knight.

In each mailed hand was a naked brand;
   As they lay on the black bull's hide,
Each visage stern did upwards turn,
   With eyeballs fixed and wide.

A launcegay strong, full twelve ells long,
   By every warrior hung;
At each pommel there, for battle yare,
   A Jedwood axe was slung.

The casque hung near each cavalier;
   The plumes waved mournfully
At every tread which the wanderer made
   Through the hall of Gramarye;

The ruddy beam of the torches' gleam
   That glared the warriors on,
Reflected light from armor bright,
   In noontide splendor shone.

And onward seen in lustre sheen,
   Still lengthening on the sight,
Through the boundless hall, stood steeds in stall,
   And by each lay a sable knight.

Still as the dead lay each horseman dread,
   And moved nor limb nor tongue;
Each steed stood stiff as an earthfast cliff,
   Nor hoof nor bridle rung.

No sounds through all the spacious hall
    The deadly still divide,
Save where echoes aloof from the vaulted roof
    To the wanderer's step replied.

At length before his wondering eyes,
    On an iron column borne,
Of antique shape, and giant size,
    Appear'd a sword and horn.

" Now choose thee here," quoth his leader,
    " Thy venturous fortune try ;
Thy woe and weal, thy boot and bale,
    In yon brand and bugle lie."

To the fatal brand he mounted his hand,
    But his soul did quiver and quail ;
The life-blood did start to his shuddering heart,
    And left him wan and pale.

The brand he forsook, and the horn he took
    To 'say a gentle sound ;
But so wild a blast from the bugle brast,
    That the Cheviot rock'd around.

From Forth to Tees, from seas to seas,
    The awful bugle rung ;
On Carlisle wall, and Berwick withal,
    To arms the warders sprung.

With clank and clang the cavern rang,
    The steeds did stamp and neigh ;
And loud was the yell as each warrior fell
    Sterte up with hoop and cry.

" Woe, woe," they cried, " thou caitiff coward,
    That ever thou wert born !
Why drew ye not the knightly sword
    Before ye blew the horn ? "

The morning on the mountain shone,
    And on the bloody ground
Hurled from the cave with shiver'd bone,
    The mangled wretch was found.

And still beneath the cavern dread,
    Among the glidders gray,
A shapeless stone with lichens spread
    Marks where the wanderer lay.

.   .   .   .

The reader may be interested by comparing with this ballad the author's prose version of part of its legend, as given in one of the last works of his pen. He says, in the Letters on Demonology and Witchcraft, 1830: "Thomas of Ercildoune, during his retirement, has been supposed, from time to time, to be levying forces to take the field in some crisis of his country's fate. The story has often been told, of a daring horse-jockey having sold a black horse to a man of venerable and antique appearance, who appointed the remarkable hillock upon Eildon hills, called the Lucken-hare, as the place where, at twelve o'clock at night, he should receive the price. He came, his money was paid in ancient coin, and he was invited by his customer to view his residence. The trader in horses followed his guide in the deepest astonishment through several long ranges of stalls, in each of which a horse stood motionless, while an armed warrior lay equally still at the charger's feet. 'All these men,' said the wizard in a whisper, 'will awaken at the battle of Sheriffmuir.' At the extremity of this extraordinary depôt hung a sword and a horn, which the prophet pointed out to the horse-dealer as containing the means of dissolving the spell. The man in confusion took the horn and attempted to wind it. The horses instantly started in their stalls, stamped, and shook their bridles, the men arose and clashed their armor, and the mortal, terrified at the tumult he had excited, dropped the horn from his hand. A voice like that of a giant, louder even than the tumult around, pronounced these words: —

'Woe to the coward that ever he was born,
  That did not draw the sword before he blew the horn.'

A whirlwind expelled the horse-dealer from the cavern, the entrance to which he could never again find. A moral might be perhaps extracted from the legend, namely, that it is best to be armed against danger before bidding it defiance."

One more fragment, in another style, and I shall have

exhausted this budget. I am well aware that the introduction of such things will be considered by many as of
questionable propriety; but, on the whole, it appears to
me the better course to omit nothing by which it is in my
power to throw light on this experimental period.

. . . .

" Go sit old Cheviot's crest below,
   And pensive mark the lingering snow
     In all his scaurs abide,
   And slow dissolving from the hill
   In many a sightless, soundless rill,
     Feed sparkling Bowmont's tide.

" Fair shines the stream by bank and lea,
   As wimpling to the eastern sea
     She seeks Till's sullen bed,
   Indenting deep the fatal plain,
   Where Scotland's noblest, brave in vain,
     Around their monarch bled.

" And westward hills on hills you see,
   Even as old Ocean's mightiest sea
     Heaves high her waves of foam,
   Dark and snow-ridged from Cutsfeld's wold
   To the proud foot of Cheviot roll'd,
     Earth's mountain billows come."

. . . .

Notwithstanding all these varied essays, and the
charms of the distinguished society into which his reputation had already introduced him, Scott's friends do not
appear to have as yet entertained the slightest notion
that literature was to be the main business of his life.
A letter of Kerr of Abbotrule congratulates him on his
having had more to do at the autumnal assizes of Jedburgh this year than on any former occasion, which intelligence he seems himself to have communicated with no
feeble expressions of satisfaction. "I greatly enjoy this,"
says Kerr; "go on; and with your strong sense and
hourly ripening knowledge, that you must rise to the top
of the tree in the Parliament House in due season, I hold
as certain as that Murray died Lord Mansfield. But

don't let many an Ovid,[1] or rather many a Burns (which
is better), be lost in you. I rather think men of business
have produced as good poetry in their by-hours as the
professed regulars; and I don't see any sufficient reason
why a Lord President Scott should not be a famous poet
(in the vacation time), when we have seen a President
Montesquieu step so nobly beyond the trammels in the
Esprit des Loix. I suspect Dryden would have been a
happier man had he had your profession. The reason-
ing talents visible in his verses assure me that he would
have ruled in Westminster Hall as easily as he did at
Button's, and he might have found time enough besides
for everything that one really honors his memory for."
This friend appears to have entertained, in October, 1799,
the very opinion as to the *profession of literature* on
which Scott acted through life.

Having again given a week to Liddesdale, in company
with Mr. Shortreed, he spent a few days at Rosebank,
and was preparing to return to Edinburgh for the winter,
when James Ballantyne called on him one morning, and
begged him to supply a few paragraphs on some legal
question of the day for his newspaper. Scott complied;
and carrying his article himself to the printing-office,
took with him also some of his recent pieces, designed
to appear in Lewis's collection. With these, especially,
as his Memorandum says, the "Morlachian fragment
after Goethe," Ballantyne was charmed, and he expressed his regret that Lewis's book was so long in appearing. Scott talked of Lewis with rapture; and, after
reciting some of his stanzas, said, "I ought to apologize
to you for having troubled you with anything of my own
when I had things like this for your ear." "I felt at
once," says Ballantyne, "that his own verses were far
above what Lewis could ever do, and though, when I said

---

[1] " How sweet an Ovid, Murray was our boast ;
    How many Martials were in Pult'ney lost ! "
                 The Dunciad, b. iv. v. 170.

this, he dissented, yet he seemed pleased with the warmth of my approbation." At parting, Scott threw out a casual observation, that he wondered his old friend did not try to get some little booksellers' work, "to keep his types in play during the rest of the week." Ballantyne answered, that such an idea had not before occurred to him — that he had no acquaintance with the Edinburgh "trade;" but, if he had, his types were good, and he thought he could afford to work more cheaply than town printers. Scott, "with his good-humored smile," said, "You had better try what you can do. You have been praising my little ballads; suppose you print off a dozen copies or so of as many as will make a pamphlet, sufficient to let my Edinburgh acquaintances judge of your skill for themselves." Ballantyne assented; and I believe exactly twelve copies of William and Helen, The Fire-King, The Chase, and a few more of those pieces, were thrown off accordingly, with the title (alluding to the long delay of Lewis's collection) of Apology for Tales of Terror — 1799. This first specimen of a press, afterwards so celebrated, pleased Scott; and he said to Ballantyne, "I have been for years collecting old Border ballads, and I think I could, with little trouble, put together such a selection from them as might make a neat little volume, to sell for four or five shillings. I will talk to some of the booksellers about it when I get to Edinburgh, and if the thing goes on, you shall be the printer." Ballantyne highly relished the proposal; and the result of this little experiment changed wholly the course of his worldly fortunes, as well as of his friend's.

Shortly after the commencement of the Winter Session, the office of Sheriff-depute of Selkirkshire became vacant by the death of an early ally of Scott's, Andrew Plummer of Middlestead, a scholar and antiquary, who had entered with zeal into his ballad researches, and whose name occurs accordingly more than once in the notes to the Border Minstrelsy. Perhaps the commu-

nity of their tastes may have had some part in suggesting
to the Duke of Buccleuch, that Scott might fitly succeed
Mr. Plummer in the magistrature. Be that as it might,
his Grace's influence was used with the late Lord Melville, who, in those days, had the general control of the
Crown patronage in Scotland, and his Lordship was prepared to look favorably on Scott's pretensions to some
office of this description. Though neither the Duke nor
this able Minister were at all addicted to literature, they
had both seen Scott frequently under their own roofs,
and been pleased with his manners and conversation;
and he had by this time come to be on terms of affectionate intimacy with some of the younger members of either
family. The Earl of Dalkeith (afterwards Duke Charles
of Buccleuch), and his brother Lord Montagu,[1] had been
participating, with kindred ardor, in the military patri-
otism of the period, and had been thrown into Scott's
society under circumstances well qualified to ripen acquaintance into confidence. The Honorable Robert
Dundas, eldest son of the statesman whose title he has
inherited, had been one of Scott's companions in the
High School; and he, too, had been of late a lively par-
taker in the business of the yeomanry cavalry; and, last
not least, Scott always remembered with gratitude the
strong intercession on this occasion of Lord Melville's
nephews, Robert Dundas of Arniston, then Lord Advocate, and afterwards Chief Baron of the Exchequer in
Scotland, and the Right Honorable William Dundas,
then Secretary to the Board of Control, and now Lord
Clerk Register.

His appointment to the *Sheriffship* bears date 16th
December, 1799. It secured him an annual salary of
£300; an addition to his resources which at once relieved his mind from whatever degree of anxiety he might

---

[1] [Henry James Scott, the second son of Duke Henry of Buccleuch, succeeded to the Barony of Montagu on the death of his maternal grandfather, the last Duke of Montagu. Lord Montagu died in 1845.]

have felt in considering the prospect of an increasing family, along with the ever precarious chances of a profession, in the daily drudgery of which it is impossible to suppose that he ever could have found much pleasure.[1] The duties of the office were far from heavy; the district, small, peaceful, and pastoral, was in great part the property of the Duke of Buccleuch; and he turned with redoubled zeal to his project of editing the ballads, many of the best of which belonged to this very district of his favorite Border — those "tales," which, as the Dedication of the Minstrelsy expresses it, had "in elder times celebrated the prowess and cheered the halls" of his noble patron's ancestors.

---

[1] "My profession and I came to stand nearly upon the footing which honest Slender consoled himself on having established with Mistress Anne Page: ' There was no great love between us at the beginning, and it pleased heaven to decrease it on farther acquaintance.' " — Introduction to *The Lay of the Last Minstrel*, 1830.

CHAPTER X

1800–1802

JAMES BALLANTYNE, in his Memorandum, after mentioning his ready acceptance of Scott's proposal to print the Minstrelsy, adds, "I do not believe, that even at this time, he seriously contemplated giving himself much to literature." I confess, however, that a letter of his, addressed to Ballantyne in the spring of 1800, inclines me to question the accuracy of this impression. After alluding to an intention which he had entertained, in consequence of the delay of Lewis's collection, to *publish* an edition of the ballads contained in his own little volume, entitled Apology for Tales of Terror, he goes on to detail plans for the future direction of his printer's career, which were, no doubt, primarily suggested by the friendly interest he took in Ballantyne's fortunes; but there are some hints which, considering what afterwards did take place, lead me to suspect, that even thus early the writer contemplated the possibility at least of being himself very intimately connected with the result of these air-drawn schemes. The letter is as follows: —

TO MR. J. BALLANTYNE, KELSO MAIL OFFICE, KELSO.

CASTLE STREET, 22d April, 1800.

DEAR SIR, — I have your favor, since the receipt of which some things have occurred which induce me to postpone my intention of publishing my ballads, particularly a letter from a friend, assuring me that The Tales of Wonder are actually in the printer's hand. In this situation I endeavor to strengthen my small stock of patience, which has been nearly exhausted by the delay of this work, to which (though for that reason alone) I almost regret having promised assistance. I am still resolved to have recourse to your press for the Ballads of the Border, which are in some forwardness.

I have now to request your forgiveness for mentioning a plan which your friend Gillon and I have talked over together with a view as well to the public advantage as to your individual interest. It is nothing short of a migration from Kelso to this place, which I think might be effected upon a prospect of a very flattering nature.

Three branches of printing are quite open in Edinburgh, all of which I am well convinced you have both the ability and inclination to unite in your person. The first is that of an editor of a newspaper, which shall contain something of an uniform historical deduction of events, distinct from the farrago of detached and unconnected plagiarisms from the London paragraphs of The Sun. Perhaps it might be possible (and Gillon has promised to make inquiry about it) to treat with the proprietors of some established paper — suppose the Caledonian Mercury — and we would all struggle to obtain for it some celebrity. To this might be added a Monthly Magazine, and Caledonian Annual Register, if you will; for both of which, with the excellent literary assistance which Edinburgh at present affords, there is a fair opening. The next object would naturally be the execution of Session papers, the best paid work which a printer undertakes, and of which, I dare say, you would soon have a considerable share; for as you make it your business to superintend the proofs yourself, your education and abilities would insure your employers against the gross and provoking blunders which the poor composers are often obliged to submit to. The publication of works, either ancient or modern, opens a third fair field for ambition. The only gentleman who attempts anything in that way is in very bad health; nor can I, at any rate, compliment either the accuracy or the execution of his press. I believe it is well understood that with equal attention an Edinburgh press would have superior advantages even to those of the metropolis; and though I would not advise launching into that line at once, yet it would be easy to feel your way by occupying your press in this manner on vacant days only.

It appears to me that such a plan, judiciously adopted and diligently pursued, opens a fair road to an ample fortune. In the mean while, the Kelso Mail might be so arranged as to be still a source of some advantage to you; and I dare say, if wanted, pecuniary assistance might be procured to assist you at the outset, either upon terms of a share or otherwise; but I refer you for particulars to Joseph, in whose room I am now assuming the pen, for reasons too distressing to be declared, but at which you will readily guess. I hope, at all events, you will impute my interference to anything rather than an impertinent intermeddling with your concerns on the part of, Dear Sir, your obedient servant,

WALTER SCOTT.

The Joseph Gillon here named was a solicitor of some eminence; a man of strong abilities and genuine wit and humor, for whom Scott, as well as Ballantyne, had a warm regard.[1] The intemperate habits alluded to at the close of Scott's letter gradually undermined his business, his health, and his character; and he was glad, on leaving Edinburgh, which became quite necessary some years afterwards, to obtain a humble situation about the House

[1] Calling on him one day in his writing-office, Scott said, "Why, Joseph, this place is as hot as an oven." "Well," quoth Gillon, "and is n't it here that I make my bread?"

of Lords — in which he died.[1] The answer of Ballantyne has not been preserved.

To return to the Minstrelsy. — Scott found able assistants in the completion of his design. Richard Heber (long Member of Parliament for the University of Oxford) happened to spend this winter in Edinburgh, and was welcomed, as his talents and accomplishments entitled him to be, by the cultivated society of the place. With Scott his multifarious learning, particularly his profound knowledge of the literary monuments of the Middle Ages, soon drew him into habits of close alliance; the stores of his library, even then extensive, were freely laid open, and his own oral commentaries were not less valuable. But through him Scott made acquaintance with a person still more qualified to give him effectual aid in this undertaking; a native of the Border — from infancy, like himself, an enthusiastic lover of its legends, and who had already saturated his mind with every species of lore that could throw light upon these relics.

Few who read these pages can be unacquainted with the leading facts in the history of John Leyden. Few can need to be reminded that this extraordinary man, born in a shepherd's cottage in one of the wildest valleys of Roxburghshire, and of course almost entirely self-educated, had, before he attained his nineteenth year, confounded the doctors of Edinburgh by the portentous mass of his acquisitions in almost every department of learning. He had set the extremest penury at utter defiance, or rather he had never been conscious that it could operate as a bar; for bread and water, and access to books and lectures, comprised all within the bound of his wishes; and thus he toiled and battled at the gates of

---

[1] The poet casually meeting Joseph in the street, on one of his visits to London, expressed his regret at having lost his society in Edinburgh; Joseph responded by a quotation from the Scotch Metrical Version of the Psalms —

" rather in
The Lord's house would I keep a door,
Than dwell in tents of sin."

science after science, until his unconquerable perseverance carried everything before it; and yet with this mo-
nastic abstemiousness and iron hardness of will, perplexing those about him by manners and habits in which it
was hard to say whether the moss-trooper or the school-
man of former days most prevailed, he was at heart a
poet.

Archibald Constable, in after-life one of the most
eminent of British publishers, was at this period the
keeper of a small book-shop, into which few, but the poor
students of Leyden's order, had hitherto found their way.
Heber, in the course of his bibliomaniacal prowlings,
discovered that it contained some of

" The small old volumes, dark with tarnished gold,"

which were already the Delilahs of his imagination; and,
moreover, that the young bookseller had himself a strong
taste for such charmers. Frequenting the place accordingly, he observed with some curiosity the barbarous aspect and gestures of another daily visitant, who came
not to purchase, evidently, but to pore over the more
recondite articles of the collection — often balanced for
hours on a ladder with a folio in his hand, like Dominie
Sampson. The English virtuoso was on the lookout for
any books or MSS. that might be of use to the editor of
the projected Minstrelsy, and some casual colloquy led
to the discovery that this unshorn stranger was, amidst
the endless labyrinth of his lore, a master of legend and
tradition — an enthusiastic collector and most skilful
expounder of these very Border ballads in particular.
Scott heard with much interest Heber's account of his
odd acquaintance, and found, when introduced, the person
whose initials, affixed to a series of pieces in verse, chiefly
translations from Greek, Latin, and the northern languages, scattered, during the last three or four years,
over the pages of the Edinburgh Magazine, had often
much excited his curiosity, as various indications pointed

out the Scotch Border to be the native district of this
unknown "J. L."

These new friendships led to a great change in Leyden's position, purposes, and prospects. He was presently received into the best society of Edinburgh, where
his strange, wild uncouthness of demeanor does not seem
to have at all interfered·with the general appreciation of
his genius, his gigantic endowments, and really amiable
virtues. Fixing his ambition on the East, where he
hoped to rival the achievements of Sir William Jones,
he at length, about the beginning of 1802, obtained the
promise of some literary appointment in the East India
Company's service; but when the time drew near, it was
discovered that the patronage of the season had been exhausted, with the exception of one *surgeon-assistant's*
commission — which had been with difficulty secured for
him by Mr. William Dundas; who, moreover, was
obliged to inform him, that if he accepted it, he must
be qualified to pass his medical trials within six months.
This news, which would have crushed any other man's
hopes to the dust, was only a welcome fillip to the ardor
of Leyden. He that same hour grappled with a new
science, in full confidence that whatever ordinary men
could do in three or four years, his energy could accomplish in as many months; took his degree accordingly in
the beginning of 1803, having just before published his
beautiful poem, the Scenes of Infancy; sailed to India;
raised for himself, within seven short years, the reputation of the most marvellous of Orientalists; and died,
in the midst of the proudest hopes, at the same age with
Burns and Byron, in 1811.

But to return: Leyden was enlisted by Scott in the
service of Lewis, and immediately contributed a ballad,
called The Elf-King, to the Tales of Terror. Those
highly spirited pieces, The Cout of Keildar, Lord Soulis,
and The Mermaid, were furnished for the original department of Scott's own collection: and the Dissertation on

Fairies, prefixed to its second volume, "although arranged and digested by the editor, abounds with instances of such curious reading as Leyden only had read, and was originally compiled by him;" but not the least of his labors was in the collection of the old ballads themselves. When he first conversed with Ballantyne on the subject of the proposed work, and the printer signified his belief that a single volume of moderate size would be sufficient for the materials, Leyden exclaimed, "Dash it, does Mr. Scott mean another thin thing like Goetz of Berlichingen? I have more than that in my head myself: we shall turn out three or four such volumes at least." He went to work stoutly in the realization of these wider views. "In this labor," says Scott, "he was equally interested by friendship for the editor, and by his own patriotic zeal for the honor of the Scottish borders; and both may be judged of from the following circumstance. An interesting fragment had been obtained of an ancient historical ballad; but the remainder, to the great disturbance of the editor and his coadjutor, was not to be recovered. Two days afterwards, while the editor was sitting with some company after dinner, a sound was heard at a distance like that of the whistling of a tempest through the torn rigging of the vessel which scuds before it. The sounds increased as they approached more near; and Leyden (to the great astonishment of such of the guests as did not know him) burst into the room, chanting the desiderated ballad with the most enthusiastic gesture, and all the energy of what he used to call the *saw-tones* of his voice. It turned out that he had walked between forty and fifty miles and back again, for the sole purpose of visiting an old person who possessed this precious remnant of antiquity." [1]

Various allusions to the progress of Leyden's fortunes will occur in letters to be quoted hereafter. I may refer the reader, for further particulars, to the biographical

[1] Essay on the Life of Leyden — Scott's *Miscellaneous Prose Works*, vol. iv.

sketch by Scott from which the preceding anecdote is
taken.   Many tributes to his memory are scattered over
his friend's other works, both prose and verse; and,
above all, Scott did not forget him when exploring, three
years after his death, the scenery of his Mermaid: —

> "Scarba's isle, whose tortured shore
> Still rings to Corrievreken's roar,
>   And lonely Colonsay ; —
> Scenes sung by him who sings no more ;
> His bright and brief career is o'er,
>   And mute his tuneful strains ;
> Quench'd is his lamp of varied lore,
> That loved the light of song to pour ;
> A distant and a deadly shore
>   Has Leyden's cold remains ! " [1]

During the years 1800 and 1801, the Minstrelsy
formed its editor's chief occupation — a labor of love
truly, if ever such there was; but neither this nor his
sheriffship interfered with his regular attendance at the
Bar, the abandonment of which was all this while as far
as it ever had been from his imagination, or that of any
of his friends.   He continued to have his summer headquarters at Lasswade; and Mr. (now Sir John) Stoddart,
who visited him there in the course of his Scottish tour,[2]
dwells on "the simple unostentatious elegance of the cottage, and the domestic picture which he there contemplated — a man of native kindness and cultivated talent,
passing the intervals of a learned profession amidst scenes
highly favorable to his poetic inspirations, not in churlish
and rustic solitude, but in the daily exercise of the most
precious sympathies as a husband, a father, and a friend."
His means of hospitality were now much enlarged, and
the cottage, on a Saturday and Sunday at least, was seldom without visitors.

Among other indications of greater ease in his circumstances, which I find in his letter-book, he writes to

---

[1] *Lord of the Isles*, Canto iv. st. 11.
[2] The account of this tour was published in 1801.

Heber, after his return to London in May, 1800, to request his good offices on behalf of Mrs. Scott, who had "set her heart on a phaeton, at once strong, and low, and handsome, and not to cost more than thirty guineas;" which combination of advantages Heber seems to have found by no means easy of attainment. The phaeton was, however, discovered; and its springs must soon have been put to a sufficient trial, for this was "the first wheeled carriage that ever penetrated into Liddesdale" — namely, in August, 1800. The friendship of the Buccleuch family now placed better means of research at his disposal, and Lord Dalkeith had taken special care that there should be a band of pioneers in waiting for his orders when he reached Hermitage.

Though he had not given up Lasswade, his sheriffship now made it necessary for him that he should be frequently in Ettrick Forest. On such occasions he took up his lodgings in the little inn at Clovenford, a favorite fishing station on the road from Edinburgh to Selkirk. From this place he could ride to the county town whenever business required his presence, and he was also within a few miles of the vales of Yarrow and Ettrick, where he obtained large accessions to his store of ballads. It was in one of these excursions that, penetrating beyond St. Mary's Lake, he found a hospitable reception at the farm of Blackhouse, situated on the Douglas-burn, then tenanted by a remarkable family, to which I have already made allusion — that of William Laidlaw. He was then a very young man, but the extent of his acquirements was already as noticeable as the vigor and originality of his mind; and their correspondence, where "Sir" passes, at a few bounds, through "Dear Sir," and "Dear Mr. Laidlaw," to "Dear Willie," shows how speedily this new acquaintance had warmed into a very tender affection. Laidlaw's zeal about the ballads was repaid by Scott's anxious endeavors to get him removed from a sphere for which, he writes, "it is no flattery to say that

you are much too good." It was then, and always continued to be, his opinion, that his friend was particularly
qualified for entering with advantage on the study of the
medical profession; but such designs, if Laidlaw himself
ever took them up seriously, were not ultimately persevered in; and I question whether any worldly success
could, after all, have overbalanced the retrospect of an
honorable life spent happily in the open air of nature,
amidst scenes the most captivating to the eye of genius,
and in the intimate confidence of, perhaps, the greatest
of contemporary minds.

James Hogg spent ten years of his life in the service
of Mr. Laidlaw's father, but he had passed into that of
another sheep farmer in a neighboring valley before Scott
first visited Blackhouse. William Laidlaw and Hogg
were, however, the most intimate of friends, and the
former took care that Scott should see, without delay,
one whose enthusiasm about the minstrelsy of the Forest
was equal to his own, and whose mother, then an aged
woman, though she lived many years afterwards, was
celebrated for having by heart several ballads in a more
perfect form than any other inhabitant of the vale of
Ettrick. The personal history of James Hogg must have
interested Scott even more than any acquisition of that
sort which he owed to this acquaintance with, perhaps,
the most remarkable man that ever wore the *maud* of a
shepherd. But I need not here repeat a tale which his
own language will convey to the latest posterity. Under
the garb, aspect, and bearing of a rude peasant — and
rude enough he was in most of these things, even after
no inconsiderable experience of society — Scott found a
brother poet, a true son of nature and genius, hardly conscious of his powers. He had taught himself to write by
copying the letters of a printed book as he lay watching
his flock on the hillside, and had probably reached the
utmost pitch of his ambition when he first found that his
artless rhymes could touch the heart of the ewe-milker

who partook the shelter of his mantle during the passing
storm. As yet his naturally kind and simple character
had not been exposed to any of the dangerous flatteries
of the world; his heart was pure — his enthusiasm buoyant as that of a happy child; and well as Scott knew
that reflection, sagacity, wit, and wisdom, were scattered
abundantly among the humblest rangers of these pastoral
solitudes, there was here a depth and a brightness that
filled him with wonder, combined with a quaintness of
humor, and a thousand little touches of absurdity, which
afforded him more entertainment, as I have often heard
him say, than the best comedy that ever set the pit in
a roar.

Scott opened in the same year a correspondence with
the venerable Bishop of Dromore, who seems, however,
to have done little more than express a warm interest in
an undertaking so nearly resembling that which will ever
keep his own name in remembrance. He had more success in his applications to a more unpromising quarter —
namely, with Joseph Ritson, the ancient and virulent
assailant of Bishop Percy's editorial character. This
narrow-minded, sour, and dogmatical little word-catcher
had hated the very name of a Scotsman, and was utterly
incapable of sympathizing with any of the higher views
of his new correspondent. Yet the bland courtesy of
Scott disarmed even this half-crazy pedant; and he communicated the stores of his really valuable learning in a
manner that seems to have greatly surprised all who had
hitherto held any intercourse with him on antiquarian
topics. It astonished, above all, the late amiable and
elegant George Ellis, whose acquaintance was about the
same time opened to Scott through their common friend
Heber. Mr. Ellis was now busily engaged in collecting
the materials for his charming works, entitled Specimens
of Ancient English Poetry, and Specimens of Ancient
English Romance. The correspondence between him and
Scott soon came to be constant. They met personally,

not long after the correspondence had commenced, conceived for each other a cordial respect and affection, and continued on a footing of almost brotherly intimacy ever after. To this valuable alliance Scott owed, among other advantages, his early and ready admission to the acquaintance and familiarity of Ellis's bosom friend, his coadjutor in the Anti-Jacobin, and the confidant of all his literary schemes, the late illustrious statesman, Mr. Canning.

The first letter of Scott to Ellis is dated March 27, 1801, and begins thus: "Sir, as I feel myself highly flattered by your inquiries, I lose no time in answering them to the best of my ability. Your eminence in the literary world, and the warm praises of our mutual friend Heber, had made me long wish for an opportunity of being known to you. I enclose the first sheet of Sir Tristrem, that you may not so much rely upon my opinion as upon that which a specimen of the style and versification may enable your better judgment to form for itself. . . . These pages are transcribed by Leyden, an excellent young man, of uncommon talents, patronized by Heber, and who is of the utmost assistance to my literary undertakings."

As Scott's edition of Sir Tristrem did not appear until May, 1804, and he and Leyden were busy with the Border Minstrelsy when his correspondence with Ellis commenced, this early indication of his labors on the former work may require explanation. The truth is, that both Scott and Leyden, having eagerly arrived at the belief, from which neither of them ever permitted himself to falter, that the Sir Tristrem of the Auchinleck MS. was virtually, if not literally, the production of Thomas the Rhymer, laird of Ercildoune in Berwickshire, who flourished at the close of the thirteenth century — the original intention had been to give it, not only a place, but a very prominent one, in the Minstrelsy of the Scottish Border. The doubts and difficulties which Ellis suggested, however, though they did not shake Scott in his opinion as to the parentage of the romance, induced researches which occupied so much time, and gave birth to notes so bulky, that he eventually found it expedient first to pass it over in the two volumes of the Minstrelsy which appeared in 1802, and then even in the third, which followed a year later; thus reserving Tristrem for a separate publication, which did not take place until after Leyden had sailed for India.

I must not swell these pages by transcribing the entire correspondence of Scott and Ellis, the greater part of which consists of minute antiquarian discussion which could hardly interest the general reader; but I shall give such extracts as seem to throw light on Scott's personal history during this period.

TO GEORGE ELLIS, ESQ.

LASSWADE COTTAGE, 20th April, 1801.

MY DEAR SIR, — I should long ago have acknowledged your instructive letter, but I have been wandering about in the wilds of Liddesdale and Ettrick Forest, in search of additional materials for the Border Minstrelsy. I cannot, however, boast much of my success. One of our best reciters has turned religious in his later days, and finds out that old songs are unlawful. If so, then, as Falstaff says, is many an acquaintance of mine damned. I now send you an accurate analysis of Sir Tristrem. Philo-Tomas, whoever he was, must surely have been an Englishman; when his hero joins battle with Moraunt, he exclaims —

> " God help Tristrem the Knight,
> *He fought for Ingland.*"

This strain of national attachment would hardly have proceeded from a Scottish author, even though he had laid his scene in the sister country. In other respects the language appears to be Scottish, and certainly contains the essence of Tomas's work. . . . You shall have

Sir Otuel in a week or two, and I shall be happy to compare your Romance of Merlin with our Arthur and Merlin, which is a very good poem, and may supply you with some valuable additions. . . . I would very fain lend your elephant [1] *a lift*, but I fear I can be of little use to you. I have been rather an observer of detached facts respecting antiquities, than a regular student. At the same time, I may mention one or two circumstances, were it but to place your elephant upon a tortoise. From Selkirkshire to Cumberland, we have a ditch and bulwark of great strength, called the Catrail, running north and south, and obviously calculated to defend the western side of the island against the inhabitants of the eastern half. Within this bulwark, at Drummelzier, near Peebles, we find the grave of Merlin, the account of whose madness and death you will find in Fordun. The

---

[1] This phrase will be best explained by an extract from a letter addressed by Sir Walter Scott, on the 12th February, 1830, to William Brockedon, Esq., acknowledging that gentleman's courtesy in sending him a copy of the beautiful work entitled *Passes of the Alps :* —

"My friend the late George Ellis, one of the most accomplished scholars, and delightful companions whom I have ever known, himself a great geographer on the most extended and liberal plan, used to tell me an anecdote of the eminent antiquary General Melville, who was crossing the Alps, with Livy and other historical accounts in his post-chaise, determined to follow the route of Hannibal. He met Ellis, I forget where at this moment, on the western side of that tremendous ridge, and pushed onwards on his journey after a day spent with his brother antiquary. After journeying more slowly than his friend, Ellis was astonished to meet General Melville coming back. 'What is the matter, my dear friend ? how come you back on the journey you had so much at heart ?' — 'Alas !' said Melville, very dejectedly, 'I would have got on myself well enough, but I could not get my *elephants* over the pass.' He had, in idea, Hannibal with his train of elephants in his party. It became a sort of by-word between Ellis and me ; and in assisting each other during a close correspondence of some years, we talked of a lift to the elephants.

"You, Sir, have put this theoretical difficulty at an end, and show how, without bodily labor, the antiquary may traverse the Alps with his elephants, without the necessity of a retrograde movement. In giving a distinct picture of so interesting a country as Switzerland, so peculiar in its habits and its history, you have added a valuable chapter to the history of Europe, in which the Alpine regions make so distinguished a figure. Accept my best congratulations on achieving so interesting a task."

same author says he was seized with his madness during a dreadful battle on the Liddle, which divides Cumberland from Scotland. All this seems to favor your ingenious hypothesis, that the sway of the British Champion [Arthur] extended over Cumberland and Strathcluyd, as well as Wales. Ercildoune is hardly five miles from the Catrail. . . .

Leyden has taken up a most absurd resolution to go to Africa on a journey of discovery. Will you have the goodness to beg Heber to write to him seriously on so ridiculous a plan, which can promise nothing either pleasant or profitable. I am certain he would get a church in Scotland with a little patience and prudence, and it gives me great pain to see a valuable young man of uncommon genius and acquirements fairly throw himself away. Yours truly,   W. SCOTT.

TO THE SAME.

" MUSSELBURGH, 11th May, 1801.

. . . " I congratulate you upon the health of your elephants — as an additional mouthful of provender for them, pray observe that the tale of Sir Gawain's Foul Ladie, in Percy's Reliques, is originally Scaldic, as you will see in the history of Hrolfe Kraka, edited by Torfæus from the ancient Sagas regarding that prince. I think I could give you some more crumbs of information were I at home; but I am at present discharging the duties of quartermaster to a regiment of volunteer cavalry — an office altogether inconsistent with romance; for where do you read that Sir Tristrem weighed out hay and corn; that Sir Lancelot du Lac distributed billets; or that any Knight of the Round Table condescended to higgle about a truss of straw? Such things were left for our degenerate days, when no warder sounds his horn from the barbican as the *preux chevalier* approaches to claim hospitality. Bugles indeed we have; but it is only to scream us out of bed at five in the morning — hospitality such as the seneschals of Don Quixote's castles were wont to offer him — and all to troopers, to whom, for valor eke and courtesy, Major Sturgeon [1] himself might yield the palm. In the midst of this scene of motley confusion, I long, like the hart for water-brooks, for the arrival of your *grande opus*. The nature of your researches animates me to proceed in mine (though of a much more limited and local nature), even as iron sharpeneth iron. I am in utter despair about some of the hunting terms in Sir Tristrem. There is no copy of Lady Juliana Berners's work [2] in Scotland, and I would move heaven and earth to get a sight of it. But as I fear this is utterly impossible, I must have recourse to your friendly assistance, and communicate a set of doubts and queries, which, if any man in England can satisfy, I am well assured it must be you. You may therefore expect, in a few days, another epistle. Meantime I must invoke the spirit of Nimrod."

"Edinburgh, 10th June, 1801.

"My dear Sir, — A heavy family misfortune, the loss of an only sister in the prime of life, has prevented, for some time, my proposed communication regarding the hunting terms of Sir Tristrem. I now enclose the passage, accurately copied, with such explanations as occur to myself, subject always to your correction and better judgment. . . . I have as yet had only a glance of The Specimens. Thomson, to whom Heber entrusted them, had left them to follow him from London in a certain trunk, which has never yet arrived. I should have quarrelled with him excessively for making so little allowance for my impatience, had it not been that a violent epidemic fever, to which I owe the loss already mentioned, has threatened also to deprive me, in his person, of one of

[1] See Foote's farce of *The Mayor of Garrat*.
[2] *The Boke of St. Albans* — first printed in 1486 — reprinted by Mr. Haslewood in 1810.

my dearest friends, and the Scottish literary world of one
of its most promising members.

"Some prospect seems to open for getting Leyden out
to India, under the patronage of Mackintosh, who goes
as chief of the intended academical establishment at Calcutta. That he is highly qualified for acting a distinguished part in any literary undertaking will be readily
granted; nor do I think Mr. Mackintosh will meet with
many half so likely to be useful in the proposed institution. The extent and versatility of his talents would
soon raise him to his level, even although he were at first
to go out in a subordinate department. If it be in your
power to second his application, I rely upon Heber's interest with you to induce you to do so."

"EDINBURGH, 13th July, 1801.

. . "I am infinitely obliged to you, indeed, for your
interference in behalf of our Leyden, who, I am sure,
will do credit to your patronage, and may be of essential
service to the proposed mission. What a difference from
broiling himself, or getting himself literally broiled, in
Africa. ' Que diable vouloit-il faire dans cette galère?'
. . . His brother is a fine lad, and is likely to enjoy
some advantages which he wanted — I mean by being
more early introduced into society. I have intermitted
his transcript of Merlin, and set him to work on Otuel,
of which I send a specimen." . . .

"EDINBURGH, 7th December, 1801.

. . . "My literary amusements have of late been much
retarded and interrupted, partly by professional avocations, and partly by removing to a house newly furnished,
where it will be some time before I can get my few
books put into order, or clear the premises of painters
and workmen; not to mention that these worthies do not
nowadays proceed upon the plan of Solomon's archi-
tects, whose saws and hammers were not heard, but

rather upon the more ancient system of the builders of
Babel. To augment this confusion, my wife has fixed
upon this time as proper to present me with a fine chop-
ping boy, whose pipe, being of the shrillest, is heard
amid the storm, like a boatswain's whistle in a gale of
wind. These various causes of confusion have also interrupted the labors of young Leyden on your behalf; but
he has again resumed the task of transcribing Arthour,
of which I once again transmit a part. I have to acknowledge, with the deepest sense of gratitude, the beautiful analysis of Mr. Douce's Fragments, which throws
great light upon the romance of Sir Tristrem. In arranging that, I have anticipated your judicious hint, by
dividing it into three parts, where the story seems naturally to pause, and prefixing an accurate argument, referring to the stanzas as numbered.

"I am glad that Mrs. Ellis and you have derived any
amusement from the House of Aspen. It is a very hurried dramatic sketch; and the fifth act, as you remark,
would require a total revisal previous to representation
or publication. At one time I certainly thought, with my
friends, that it might have ranked well enough by the
side of the Castle Spectre, Bluebeard, and the other drum
and trumpet exhibitions of the day; but the Plays on
the Passions[1] have put me entirely out of conceit with
my Germanized brat; and should I ever again attempt
dramatic composition, I would endeavor after the genuine old English model. . . . The publication of The
Complaynt[2] is delayed. It is a work of multifarious
lore. I am truly anxious about Leyden's Indian journey, which seems to hang fire. Mr. William Dundas
was so good as to promise me his interest to get him

---

[1] The first volume of Joanna Baillie's *Plays on the Passions* appeared in
1798. Volume II. followed in 1802.

[2] *The Complaynt of Scotland, written in 1548; with a Preliminary Dissertation and Glossary, by John Leyden,* was published by Constable in January, 1802.

appointed Secretary to the Institution;[1] but whether he has succeeded or not, I have not yet learned. The various kinds of distress under which literary men, I mean such as have no other profession than letters, must labor, in a commercial country, is a great disgrace to society. I own to you I always tremble for the fate of genius when left to its own exertions, which, however powerful, are usually, by some bizarre dispensation of nature, useful to every one but themselves. If Heber could learn by Mackintosh, whether anything could be done to fix Leyden's situation, and what sort of interest would be most likely to succeed, his friends here might unite every exertion in his favor. . . . Direct Castle Street, as usual; my new house being in the same street with my old dwelling."

"EDINBURGH, 8th January, 1802.

. . . "Your favor arrived just as I was sitting down to write to you, with a sheet or two of King Arthur. I fear, from a letter which I have received from Mr. William Dundas, that the Indian Establishment is tottering, and will probably fall. Leyden has therefore been induced to turn his mind to some other mode of making his way to the East; and proposes taking his degree as a physician and surgeon, with the hope of getting an appointment in the Company's Service as surgeon. If the Institution goes forward, his having secured this step will not prevent his being attached to it; at the same time that it will afford him a provision independent of what seems to be a very precarious establishment. Mr. Dundas has promised to exert himself. . . . I have just returned from the hospitable halls of Hamilton, where I have spent the Christmas." . . .

"14th February, 1802.

"I have been silent, but not idle. The transcript of King Arthur is at length finished, being a fragment of

---

[1] A proposed Institution for purposes of Education at Calcutta.

about 7000 lines. Let me know how I shall transmit a parcel containing it, with The Complaynt and the Border Ballads, of which I expect every day to receive some copies. I think you will be disappointed in the Ballads. I have as yet touched very little on the more remote antiquities of the Border, which, indeed, my songs, all comparatively modern, did not lead me to discuss. Some scattered herbage, however, the elephants may perhaps find. By the way, you will not forget to notice the mountain called *Arthur's Seat*, which overhangs this city. When I was at school, the tradition ran that King Arthur occupied as his throne a huge rock upon its summit, and that he beheld from thence some naval engagement upon the Frith of Forth. I am pleasantly interrupted by the post; he brings me a letter from William Dundas, fixing Leyden's appointment as an assistant-surgeon to one of the India settlements — which, is not yet determined; and another from my printer, a very ingenious young man, telling me, that he means to escort the Minstrelsy up to London in person. I shall, therefore, direct him to transmit my parcel to Mr. Nicol." . . .

"2d March, 1802.

"I *hope* that long ere this you have received the Ballads, and that they have afforded you some amusement. I hope, also, that the *threatened* third volume will be more interesting to Mrs. Ellis than the dry antiquarian detail of the two first could prove. I hope, moreover, that I shall have the pleasure of seeing you soon, as some circumstances seem not so much to call me to London, as to furnish me with a decent apology for coming up some time this spring; and I long particularly to say that I know my friend Mr. Ellis *by sight* as well as *intimately*. I am glad you have seen the Marquess of Lorn, whom I have met frequently at the house of his charming sister, Lady Charlotte Campbell, whom, I am sure, if you are acquainted with her, you must admire as much as I do.

Her Grace of Gordon, a great admirer of yours, spent some days here lately, and, like Lord Lorn, was highly entertained with an account of our friendship *à la distance*. I do not, nor did I ever, intend to fob you off with twenty or thirty lines of the second part of Sir Guy. Young Leyden has been much engaged with his studies, otherwise you would have long since received what I now send, namely, the combat between Guy and Colbronde, which I take to be the cream of the romance. . . . If I do not come to London this spring, I will find a safe opportunity of returning Lady Juliana Berners, with my very best thanks for the use of her reverence's work."

The preceding extracts are picked out of letters, mostly very long ones, in which Scott discusses questions of antiquarian interest, suggested sometimes by Ellis, and sometimes by the course of his own researches among the MSS. of the Advocates' Library. The passages which I have transcribed appear sufficient to give the reader a distinct notion of the tenor of Scott's life while his first considerable work was in progress through the press. In fact, they place before us in a vivid light the chief features of a character which, by this time, was completely formed and settled — which had passed unmoved through the first blandishments of worldly applause, and which no subsequent trials of that sort could ever shake from its early balance: His calm delight in his own pursuits — the patriotic enthusiasm which mingled with all the best of his literary efforts; his modesty as to his own general merits, combined with a certain dogged resolution to maintain his own first view of a subject, however assailed; his readiness to interrupt his own tasks by any drudgery by which he could assist those of a friend; his steady and determined watchfulness over the struggling fortunes of young genius and worth.

The reader has seen that he spent the Christmas of 1801 at Hamilton Palace, in Lanarkshire. To Lady

Anne Hamilton he had been introduced by her friend,
Lady Charlotte Campbell, and both the late and the
present Dukes of Hamilton appear to have partaken of
Lady Anne's admiration for Glenfinlas and The Eve of
St. John. A morning's ramble to the majestic ruins
of the old baronial castle on the precipitous banks of the
Evan, and among the adjoining remains of the primeval
Caledonian forest, suggested to him a ballad, not inferior
in execution to any that he had hitherto produced, and
especially interesting as the first in which he grapples
with the world of picturesque incident unfolded in the
authentic annals of Scotland. With the magnificent
localities before him, he skilfully interwove the daring
assassination of the Regent Murray by one of the clans-
men of "the princely Hamilton." Had the subject been
taken up in after-years, we might have had another
Marmion or Heart of Mid-Lothian; for in Cadyow Castle we have the materials and outline of more than one
of the noblest of ballads.

About two years before this piece began to be handed
about in Edinburgh, Thomas Campbell had made his
appearance there, and at once seized a high place in the
literary world by his Pleasures of Hope. Among the
most eager to welcome him had been Scott; and I find
the brother-bard thus expressing himself concerning the
MS. of Cadyow: —

"The verses of Cadyow Castle are perpetually ringing
in my imagination —

> ' Where, mightiest of the beasts of chase
>   That roam in woody Caledon,
>   Crashing the forest in his race,
>   The mountain bull comes thundering on — '

and the arrival of Hamilton, when

> ' Reeking from the recent deed,
>   He dashed his carbine on the ground.'

I have repeated these lines so often on the North Bridge

that the whole fraternity of coachmen know me by tongue as I pass. To be sure, to a mind in sober, serious street-walking humor, it must bear an appearance of lunacy when one stamps with the hurried pace and fervent shake of the head, which strong, pithy poetry excites."

Scott finished Cadyow Castle before the last sheets of the second volume of his Minstrelsy had passed through the press; but "the two volumes," as Ballantyne says, "were already full to overflowing;" so it was reserved for the "threatened third." The two volumes appeared in the course of January, 1802, from the respectable house of Cadell and Davies, in the Strand; and, owing to the cold reception of Lewis's Tales of Wonder, which had come forth a year earlier, these may be said to have first introduced Scott as an original writer to the English public.

In his Remarks on the Imitation of Popular Poetry, he says: "Owing to the failure of the vehicle I had chosen, my first efforts to present myself before the public as an original writer proved as vain as those by which I had previously endeavored to distinguish myself as a translator. Like Lord Home, however, at the battle of Flodden, I did so far well, that I was able to stand and save myself; and amidst the general depreciation of the Tales of Wonder, my small share of the obnoxious publication was dismissed without censure, and in some cases obtained praise from the critics. The consequences of my escape made me naturally more daring, and I attempted in my own name, a collection of ballads of various kinds, both ancient and modern, to be connected by the common tie of relation to the Border districts in which I had collected them. The edition was curious, as being the first example of a work printed by my friend and schoolfellow, Mr. James Ballantyne, who at that period was editor of a provincial paper. When the book came out, the imprint, Kelso, was read with wonder by amateurs of typography, who had never heard of such a place, and were astonished at the example of handsome printing which so obscure a town had produced. As for the editorial part of the task, my attempt to imitate the plan and style of Bishop Percy, observing only more strict fidelity concerning my originals, was favorably received by the public."

The first edition of Volumes I. and II. of the Minstrelsy consisted of eight hundred copies, fifty of which were on large paper. One of the embellishments was a view of Hermitage Castle, the history of which is rather curious. Scott executed a rough sketch of it during the last of his "Liddesdale raids" with Shortreed, standing for that purpose for an hour or more up to his middle in the snow. Nothing can be ruder than the performance, which I have now before me; but his friend William Clerk made a better drawing from it; and from his, a third and further improved copy was done by Hugh Williams, the elegant artist, afterwards known as "Greek Williams."[1] Scott used to say, the oddest thing of all was, that the engraving, founded on the labors of three draughtsmen, one of whom could not draw a straight line, and the two others had never seen the place meant to be represented, was nevertheless pronounced by the natives of Liddesdale to give a very fair notion of the ruins of Hermitage.

The edition was exhausted in the course of the year, and the terms of publication having been that Scott should have half the clear profits, his share was exactly £78 10s. — a sum which certainly could not have repaid him for the actual expenditure incurred in the collection of his materials. Messrs. Cadell and Davies, however, complained, and probably with good reason, that a premature advertisement of a "second and improved edition" had rendered some copies of the first unsalable.

I shall transcribe the letter in which Mr. George Ellis acknowledges the receipt of his copy of the book: —

[1] Mr. Williams's Travels in Italy and Greece were published in 1820.

TO WALTER SCOTT, ESQ., ADVOCATE, CASTLE STREET, EDINBURGH.

SUNNING HILL, March 5, 1802.

MY DEAR SIR, — The volumes are arrived, and I have been devouring them, not as a pig does a parcel of grains (by which simile you will judge that I must be brewing, as indeed I am), putting in its snout, shutting its eyes, and swallowing as fast as it can without consideration — but as a schoolboy does a piece of gingerbread; nibbling a little bit here, and a little bit there, smacking his lips, surveying the number of square inches which still remain for his gratification, endeavoring to look it into larger dimensions, and making at every mouthful a tacit vow to protract his enjoyment by restraining his appetite. Now, therefore — but no! I must first assure you on the part of Mrs. E., that if you cannot, or will not come to England soon, she must gratify her curiosity and gratitude, by setting off for Scotland, though at the risk of being tempted to pull caps with Mrs. Scott when she arrives at the end of her journey. Next, I must request you to convey to Mr. Leyden my very sincere acknowledgment for his part of the precious parcel. How truly vexatious that such a man should embark, not for the "fines Atticæ," but for those of Asia; that the genius of Scotland, instead of a poor *Complaint*, and an address in the style of "Navis, quæ tibi creditum debes Virgilium — reddas incolumem, precor," should not interfere to prevent his loss. I wish to hope that we should, as Sterne says, "manage these matters better" in England; but now, as regret is unavailing, to the main point of my letter.

You will not, of course, expect that I should as yet give you anything like an opinion, *as a critic*, of your volumes; first, because you have thrown into my throat a cate of such magnitude that Cerberus, who had three throats, could not have swallowed a third part of it without shutting his eyes; and secondly, because, although I have gone a little farther than George Nicol the bookseller, who cannot cease exclaiming, "What a beautiful book!" and is distracted with jealousy of your Kelso Bulmer, yet, as I said before, I have not been able yet to *digest* a great deal of your Border Minstrelsy. I have, however, taken such a survey as satisfies me that your plan is neither too comprehensive

nor too contracted ; that the parts are properly distinct; and
that they are (to preserve the painter's metaphor) *made out*
just as they ought to be. Your introductory chapter is, I think,
particularly good ; and I was much pleased, although a little
surprised, at finding that it was made to serve as a *recueil des
pièces justificatives* to your view of the state of manners among
your Borderers, which I venture to say will be more thumbed
than any part of the volume.

You will easily believe that I cast many an anxious look
for the annunciation of Sir Tristrem, and will not be surprised
that I was at first rather disappointed at not finding anything
like a solemn engagement to produce him to the world within
some fixed and limited period. Upon reflection, however, I
really think you have judged wisely, and that you have best
promoted the interests of literature, by sending, as the *harbinger*
of the Knight of Leonais, a collection which must form a par-
lor-window book in every house in Britain which contains a
parlor and a window. I am happy to find my *old favorites* in
their natural situation — indeed in the only situation which can
enable a Southern reader to estimate their merits. You remember what somebody said of the Prince de Condé's army
during the wars of the Fronde, namely, — " that it would be a
very fine army whenever it came of age." Of the Murrays and
Armstrongs of your Border Ballads, it might be said that they
might grow, when the age of good taste should arrive, to a
Glenfinlas or an Eve of St. John. Leyden's additional poems
are also very beautiful. I meant, at setting out, a few simple
words of thanks, and behold I have written a letter ; but no
matter — I shall return to the charge after a more attentive
perusal. Ever yours very faithfully,   G. ELLIS.

I might fill many pages by transcribing similar letters
from persons of acknowledged discernment in this branch
of literature; John, Duke of Roxburghe, is among the
number, and he conveys also a complimentary message
from the late Earl Spencer; Pinkerton issues his decree
of approbation as *ex cathedrâ ;* Chalmers overflows with
heartier praise; and even Joseph Ritson extols his presentation copy as "the most valuable literary treasure in

his possession." There follows enough of female admiration to have been dangerous for another man; a score
of fine ladies contend who shall be the most extravagant
in encomium — and as many professed blue stockings
come after; among or rather above the rest, Anna Seward, "the Swan of Lichfield," who laments that her
"bright luminary," Darwin, does not survive to partake
her raptures; — observes, that "in the Border Ballads
the first strong rays of the Delphic orb illuminate Jellon
Graeme;" and concludes with a fact indisputable, but
strangely expressed, namely, that "the Lady Anne Bothwell's Lament, Cowdenknowes, etc., etc., *climatically*
preceded the treasures of Burns, and the consummate
Glenfinlas and Eve of St. John." Scott felt as acutely
as any malevolent critic the pedantic affectations of Miss
Seward's epistolary style, but in her case sound sense as
well as vigorous ability had unfortunately condescended
to an absurd disguise; he looked below it, and was far
from confounding her honest praise with the flat superla-
tives either of wordy parrots or weak enthusiasts.

CHAPTER XI

1802-1803

THE approbation with which the first two volumes of
the Minstrelsy were received stimulated Scott to fresh
diligence in the preparation of a third; while Sir Tristrem — it being now settled that this romance should
form a separate volume — was transmitted, without delay, to the printer at Kelso. As early as March 30,
1802, Ballantyne, who had just returned from London,
writes thus: —

TO WALTER SCOTT, ESQ., CASTLE STREET, EDINBURGH.

DEAR SIR, — By to-morrow's Fly I shall send the remaining
materials for Minstrelsy, together with three sheets of Sir
Tristrem. . . . I shall ever think the printing the Scottish
Minstrelsy one of the most fortunate circumstances of my life.
I have gained, not lost by it, in a pecuniary light; and the
prospects it has been the means of opening to me may advantageously influence my future destiny. I can never be sufficiently grateful for the interest you unceasingly take in my welfare. Your query respecting *Edinburgh*, I am *yet* at a loss
to answer. To say truth, the expenses I have incurred in my

resolution to acquire a character for elegant printing, whatever
might be the result, cramp considerably my present exertions.
A short time, I trust, will make me easier, and I shall then
contemplate the road before me with a steady eye. One thing
alone is clear — that Kelso cannot be my abiding place for aye;
sooner or later, emigrate I must and will; but, at all events, I
must wait till my plumes are grown. I am, Dear Sir, your
faithful and obliged   J. B.

On learning that a third volume of the Minstrelsy was
in progress, Miss Seward forwarded to the editor Rich
Auld Willie's Farewell, a Scotch ballad of her own man-
ufacture, meaning, no doubt, to place it at his disposal,
for the section of Imitations. His answer (dated Edinburgh, June 29, 1802), after many compliments to the
Auld Willie, of which he made the use that had been
intended, proceeds as follows: —

"I have some thoughts of attempting a Border ballad
in the comic manner; but I almost despair of bringing it
well out. A certain Sir William Scott, from whom I
am descended, was ill-advised enough to plunder the estate
of Sir Gideon Murray of Elibank, ancestor to the present
Lord Elibank. The marauder was defeated, seized, and
brought in fetters to the castle of Elibank, upon the
Tweed. The Lady Murray (agreeably to the custom of
all ladies in ancient tales) was seated on the battlements,
and descried the return of her husband with his prisoner.
She immediately inquired what he meant to do with the
young Knight of Harden, which was the *petit titre* of
Sir William Scott. 'Hang the robber, assuredly,' was
the answer of Sir Gideon. 'What!' answered the lady,
'hang the handsome young knight of Harden, when I
have three ill-favored daughters unmarried! No, no, Sir
Gideon, we'll force him to marry our Meg.' Now tradition says that Meg Murray was the ugliest woman in
the four counties, and that she was called, in the homely
dialect of the time, *meikle-mouthed Meg*. (I will not

affront you by an explanation.) [1] Sir Gideon, like a good husband and tender father, entered into his wife's sentiments, and proffered to Sir William the alternative of becoming his son-in-law, or decorating with his carcase the *kindly* gallows of Elibank. The lady was so very ugly, that Sir William, the handsomest man of his time, positively refused the honor of her hand. Three days were allowed him to make up his mind; and it was not until he found one end of a rope made fast to his neck, and the other knitted to a sturdy oak bough, that his resolution gave way, and he preferred an ugly wife to the literal noose. It is said they were afterwards a very happy couple. She had a curious hand at pickling the beef which he stole; and, marauder as he was, he had little reason to dread being twitted by the pawky gowk. This, either by its being perpetually told to me when young, or by a perverted taste for such anecdotes, has always struck me as a good subject for a comic ballad, and how happy should I be were Miss Seward to agree in opinion with me.

"This little tale may serve for an introduction to some observations I have to offer upon our popular poetry. It will at least so far disclose your correspondent's weak side, as to induce you to make allowance for my mode of arguing. Much of its peculiar charm is indeed, I believe, to be attributed solely to its *locality*. A very commonplace and obvious epithet, when applied to a scene which we have been accustomed to view with pleasure, recalls to us not merely the local scenery, but a thousand little nameless associations, which we are unable to separate or to define. In some verses of that eccentric but admirable poet, Coleridge, he talks of

> ' An old rude tale that suited well
> The ruins wild and hoary.'

[1] It is commonly said that all Meg's descendants have inherited something of her characteristic feature. The Poet certainly was no exception to the rule.

I think there are few who have not been in some degree touched with this local sympathy. Tell a peasant an ordinary tale of robbery and murder, and perhaps you may fail to interest him; but to excite his terrors, you assure him it happened on the very heath he usually crosses, or to a man whose family he has known, and you rarely meet such a mere image of Humanity as remains entirely unmoved. I suspect it is pretty much the same with myself, and many of my countrymen, who are charmed by the effect of local description, and sometimes impute that effect to the poet, which is produced by the recollections and associations which his verses excite. Why else did Sir Philip Sidney feel that the tale of Percy and Douglas moved him like the sound of a trumpet? or why is it that a Swiss sickens at hearing the famous Ranz des Vaches, to which the native of any other country would have listened for a hundred days, without any other sensation than ennui? I fear our poetical taste is in general much more linked with our prejudices of birth, of education, and of habitual thinking, than our vanity will allow us to suppose; and that, let the point of the poet's dart be as sharp as that of Cupid, it is the wings lent it by the fancy and prepossessions of the gentle reader which carry it to the mark. It may appear like great egotism to pretend to illustrate my position from the reception which the productions of so mere a ballad-monger as myself have met with from the public; but I cannot help observing that all Scotchmen prefer The Eve of St. John to Glenfinlas, and most of my English friends entertain precisely an opposite opinion. . . . I have been writing this letter by a paragraph at a time for about a month, this being the season when we are most devoted to the

> ' Drowsy bench and babbling hall.'

"I have the honor," etc., etc. . . .

Miss Seward, in her next letter, offers an apology for

not having sooner begged Scott to place her name among the *subscribers* to his third volume. His answer is in these words:—

"LASSWADE, July, 1802.

"I am very sorry to have left you under a mistake about my third volume. The truth is, that highly as I should feel myself flattered by the encouragement of Miss Seward's name, I cannot, in the present instance, avail myself of it, as the Ballads are not published by subscription. Providence having, I suppose, foreseen that my literary qualifications, like those of many more distinguished persons, might not, *par hazard*, support me exactly as I would like, allotted me a small patrimony, which, joined to my professional income, and my appointments in the characteristic office of Sheriff of Ettrick Forest, serves to render my literary pursuits more a matter of amusement than an object of emolument. With this explanation, I hope you will honor me by accepting the third volume as soon as published, which will be in the beginning of next year, and I also hope, that under the circumstances, you will hold me acquitted of the silly vanity of wishing to be thought a *gentleman*-author.

"The ballad of The Reiver's Wedding is not yet written, but I have finished one of a tragic cast, founded upon the death of Regent Murray, who was shot in Linlithgow, by James Hamilton of Bothwellhaugh. The following verses contain the catastrophe, as told by Hamilton himself to his chief and his kinsmen:—

' With hackbut bent,' etc., etc.

. . . .
. . . . . .

"This Bothwellhaugh has occupied such an unwarrantable proportion of my letter, that I have hardly time to tell you how much I join in your admiration of Tam o' Shanter, which I verily believe to be inimitable, both in the serious and ludicrous parts, as well as the singularly happy combination of both. I request Miss Seward to believe," etc.

The Reiver's Wedding never was completed, but I have found two copies of its commencement, and I shall make no apologies for inserting here what seems to have been the second one. It will be seen that he had meant to mingle with Sir William's capture, Auld Wat's Foray of the Bassened Bull, and the Feast of Spurs; and that, I know not for what reason, Lochwood, the ancient fortress of the Johnstones in Annandale, has been substituted for the real locality of his ancestor's drum-head Wedding Contract: —

THE REIVER'S WEDDING.

O will ye hear a mirthful bourd ?
    Or will ye hear of courtesie ?
Or will ye hear how a gallant lord
    Was wedded to a gay ladye ?

"Ca' out the kye," quo the village herd,
    As he stood on the knowe,
"Ca' this ane's nine and that ane's ten,
    And bauld Lord William's cow."

"Ah! by my sooth," quoth William then,
    "And stands it that way now,
When knave and churl have nine and ten,
    That the Lord has but his cow ?

"I swear by the light of the Michaelmas moon
    And the might of Mary high,
And by the edge of my braidsword brown,
    They shall soon say Harden's kye."

He took a bugle frae his side,
    With names carved o'er and o'er —
Full many a chief of meikle pride,
    That Border bugle bore — [1]

He blew a note baith sharp and hie,
    Till rock and water rang around —

[1] This celebrated horn is still in the possession of Lord Polwarth.

Three-score of moss-troopers and three
 Have mounted at that bugle sound.

The Michaelmas moon had entered then,
 And ere she wan the full,
Ye might see by her light in Harden glen
 A bow o' kye and a bassened bull.

And loud and loud in Harden tower
 The quaigh gaed round wi' meikle glee,
For the English beef was brought in bower,
 And the English ale flowed merrilie.

And mony a guest from Teviotside
 And Yarrow's Braes were there;
Was never a lord in Scotland wide
 That made more dainty fare.

They ate, they laugh'd, they sang and quaff'd,
 Till nought on board was seen,
When knight and squire were boune to dine,
 But a spur of silver sheen.

Lord William has ta'en his berry brown steed —
 A sore shent man was he;
" Wait ye, my guests, a little speed —
 Weel feasted ye shall be."

He rode him down by Falsehope burn,
 His cousin dear to see,
With him to take a riding turn —
 Wat-draw-the-sword was he.

And when he came to Falsehope glen,
 Beneath the trysting tree,
On the smooth green was carvèd plain,[1]
 " To Lochwood bound are we."

" O if they be gane to dark Lochwood
 To drive the Warden's gear,
Betwixt our names, I ween, there 's feud;
 I 'll go and have my share:

[1] " At Linton, in Roxburghshire, there is a circle of stones surrounding a smooth plot of turf, called the *Tryst*, or place of appointment, which tradition avers to have been the rendezvous of the neighboring warriors. The name of the leader was cut in the turf, and the arrangement of the letters announced to his followers the course which he had taken." — Introduction to the *Minstrelsy*, p. 185.

" For little reck I for Johnstone's feud,
  The Warden though he be."
So Lord William is away to dark Lochwood,
  With riders barely three.

The Warden's daughters in Lochwood sate,
  Were all both fair and gay,
All save the Lady Margaret,
  And she was wan and wae.

The sister, Jean, had a full fair skin,
  And Grace was bauld and braw ;
But the leal-fast heart her breast within
  It weel was worth them a'.

Her father 's pranked her sisters twa
  With meikle joy and pride ;
But Margaret maun seek Dundrennan's wa' —
  She ne'er can be a bride.

On spear and casque by gallants gent
  Her sisters' scarfs were borne,
But never at tilt or tournament
  Were Margaret's colors worn.

Her sisters rode to Thirlstane bower,
  But she was left at hame
To wander round the gloomy tower,
  And sigh young Harden's name.

" Of all the knights, the knights most fair,
  From Yarrow to the Tyne,"
Soft sighed the maid, " is Harden's heir,
  But ne'er can he be mine ;

" Of all the maids, the foulest maid
  From Teviot to the Dee,
Ah ! " sighing sad, that lady said,
  " Can ne'er young Harden's be." —

She looked up the briery glen,
  And up the mossy brae,
And she saw a score of her father's men
  Yclad in the Johnstone grey.

O fast and fast they downwards sped
  The moss and briers among,

And in the midst the troopers led
A shackled knight along.

．　．　．　．　．　．　．

As soon as the autumn vacation set Scott at liberty,
he proceeded to the Borders with Leyden. "We have
just concluded," he tells Ellis on his return to Edinburgh,
"an excursion of two or three weeks through my jurisdiction of Selkirkshire, where, in defiance of mountains,
rivers, and bogs damp and dry, we have penetrated the
very recesses of Ettrick Forest, to which district if I ever
have the happiness of welcoming you, you will be convinced that I am truly the sheriff of the ' cairn and the
scaur.' In the course of our grand tour, besides the risks
of swamping and breaking our necks, we encountered
the formidable hardships of sleeping upon peat-stacks,
and eating mutton slain by no common butcher, but
deprived of life by the judgment of God, as a coroner's
inquest would express themselves. I have, however, not
only escaped safe ' per varios casus, per tot discrimina
rerum,' but returned *loaded* with the treasures of oral
tradition. The principal result of our inquiries has been
a complete and perfect copy of ' Maitland with his Auld
Berd Graie,' referred to by Douglas in his Palice of Hon-
our, along with John the Reef and other popular characters, and celebrated also in the poems from the Maitland MS. You may guess the surprise of Leyden and
myself when this was presented to us, copied down from
the recitation of an old shepherd, by a country farmer,
and with no greater corruptions than might be supposed
to be introduced by the lapse of time, and the ignorance
of reciters. I don't suppose it was originally composed
later than the days of Blind Harry. Many of the old
words are retained, which neither the reciter nor the cop-
ier understood. Such are the military engines *sowies*,
springwalls (springalds), and many others. Though the
poetical merit of this curiosity is not striking, yet it has
an odd energy and dramatic effect."

A few weeks later, he thus answers Ellis's inquiries as to the progress of the Sir Tristrem: "The worthy knight is still in embryo, though the whole poetry is printed. The fact is, that a second edition of the Minstrelsy has been demanded more suddenly than I expected, and has occupied my immediate attention. I have also my third volume to compile and arrange; for the Minstrelsy is now to be completed altogether independent of the *preux chevalier*, who might hang heavy upon its skirts. I assure you my *Continuation* is mere doggerel, not poetry — it is *argued in the same division* with Thomas's own production, and therefore not worth sending. However, you may depend on having the whole long before publication. I have derived much information from Turner: he combines the knowledge of the Welsh and northern authorities, and, in despite of a most detestable *Gibbonism*, his book is interesting.[1] I intend to study the Welsh triads before I finally commit myself on the subject of Border poetry. . . . As for Mr. Ritson, he and I still continue on decent terms; and, in truth, he makes *patte de velours ;* but I dread I shall see ' a whisker first and then a claw ' stretched out against my unfortunate lucubrations. Ballantyne, the Kelso printer, who has a book of his in hand, groans in spirit over the peculiarities of his orthography, which, sooth to say, hath seldom been equalled since the days of Elphinstone, the ingenious author of the mode of spelling according to the pronunciation, which he aptly termed ' Propriety ascertained in her Picture.' I fear the remark of Festus to St. Paul might be more justly applied to this curious investigator of antiquity, and it is a pity such research should be rendered useless by the infirmities of his temper. I have lately had from him *a copie* of Ye litel wee Mon, of which I think I can make some use. In return, I have sent him a sight of Auld Mait-

---

[1] The first part of Mr. Sharon Turner's *History of the Anglo-Saxons* was published in 1799 ; the second in 1801.

land, the original MS. If you are curious, I dare say you may easily see it. Indeed, I might easily send you a transcribed copy, — but I wish him to see it *in puris naturalibus*."

Ritson had visited Lasswade in the course of this autumn, and his conduct had been such as to render the precaution here alluded to very proper in the case of one who, like Scott, was resolved to steer clear of the feuds and heartburnings that gave rise to such scandalous scenes among the other antiquaries of the day. Leyden met Ritson at the cottage, and, far from imitating his host's forbearance, took a pleasure of tormenting the half-mad pedant by every means in his power. Among other circumstances, Scott delighted to detail the scene that occurred when his two uncouth allies first met at dinner. Well knowing Ritson's holy horror of all animal food, Leyden complained that the joint on the table was overdone. "Indeed, for that matter," cried he, "meat can never be too little done, and raw is best of all." He sent to the kitchen accordingly for a plate of literally raw beef, and manfully ate it up, with no sauce but the exquisite ruefulness of the Pythagorean's glances.

Mr. Robert Pearse Gillies, a gentleman of the Scotch Bar, well known, among other things, for some excellent translations from the German, was present at the cottage another day, when Ritson was in Scotland. He has described the whole scene in the second section of his Recollections of Sir Walter Scott, — a set of papers in which many inaccurate statements occur, but which convey, on the whole, a lively impression of the persons introduced.[1] "In approaching the cottage," he says, "I was struck with the exceeding air of neatness that prevailed around. The hand of tasteful cultivation had been there, and all methods employed to convert an ordi-

[1] These papers appeared in *Fraser's Magazine* for September, November, and December, 1835, and January, 1836. [They were reissued in an enlarged form in a little volume in 1837.]

nary thatched cottage into a handsome and comfortable abode. The doorway was in an angle formed by the original old cabin and the additional rooms which had been built to it. In a moment I had passed through the lobby, and found myself in the presence of Mr. and Mrs. Scott, and Mr. William Erskine. At this early period, Scott was more like the portrait, by Saxon, engraved for the first edition of The Lady of the Lake, than to any subsequent picture. He retained in features and form an impress of that elasticity and youthful vivacity, which he used to complain wore off after he was forty, and by *his own* account was exchanged for the plodding heaviness of an operose student. He had now, indeed, somewhat of a boyish gayety of look, and in person was tall, slim, and extremely active. On my entrance, he was seated at a table near the window, and occupied in transcribing from an old MS. volume into his commonplace book. As to costume, he was carelessly attired in a widely made shooting-dress, with a colored handkerchief round his neck; the very antithesis of style usually adopted either by student or barrister. ' Hah!' he exclaimed, 'welcome, thrice welcome! for we are just proposing to have lunch, and then a long, long walk through wood and wold, in which I am sure you will join us. But no man can thoroughly appreciate the pleasure of such a life who has not known what it is to rise spiritless in a morning, and *daidle* out half the day in the Parliament House, where we must all *compear* within another fortnight; then to spend the rest of one's time in applying proofs to *condescendences*, and hauling out papers to bamboozle judges, most of whom are *daized* enough already. What say you, Counsellor Erskine? Come — *alla guerra* — rouse, and say whether you are for a walk to-day.' — ' Certainly, in such fine weather I don't see what we can propose better. It is the last I shall see of the country this vacation.' — 'Nay, say not so, man; we shall all be merry twice and once yet before the evil days arrive.' — ' I 'll tell you what I have thought of this half-hour: it is a plan of mine to rent a cottage and a cabbage-garden — not here, but somewhere farther out of town, and never again, after this one session, to enter the Parliament House.' — 'And you 'll ask Ritson, perhaps,' said Scott, ' to stay with you, and help to consume the cabbages. Rest assured we shall both sit on the bench one day; but, heigho! we shall both have become very old and philosophical by that time.' — ' Did you not expect Lewis here this morning?' — 'Lewis, I venture to say, is not up yet, for he dined at Dalkeith yesterday, and of course found the wine very good. Besides, you know, I have entrusted him with Finella till his own steed gets well of a sprain, and he could not join our walking excursion. — I see you are admiring that broken sword,' he added, addressing me, ' and your interest would increase if you knew how much labor was required to bring it into my possession. In order to grasp that mouldering weapon, I was obliged to drain the well at the Castle of Dunnottar. But it is time to set out; and here is one friend ' (addressing himself to a large dog) ' who is very impatient to be in the field. He tells me he knows where to find a hare in the woods of Mavisbank. And here is another ' (caressing a terrier), ' who longs to have a battle with the weasels and water-rats, and the foumart that *wons* near the caves of Gorthy: so let us be off.' "

Mr. Gillies tells us that in the course of their walk to Rosslyn, Scott's foot slipped, as he was scrambling towards a cave on the edge of a precipitous bank, and that, "had there been no trees in the way, he must have been killed, but midway he was stopped by a large root of hazel, when, instead of struggling, which would have made matters greatly worse, he seemed perfectly resigned to his fate, and slipped through the tangled thicket till he lay flat on the river's brink. He rose in an instant from his recumbent attitude, and with a hearty laugh

called out, ' Now, let me see who else will do the like.'
He scrambled up the cliff with alacrity, and entered the
cave, where we had a long dialogue."

Even after he was an old and hoary man, he continually encountered such risks with the same recklessness.
The extraordinary strength of his hands and arms was
his great reliance in all such difficulties, and if he could
see anything to lay hold of, he was afraid of no leap, or
rather hop, that came in his way. Mr. Gillies says that
when they drew near the famous chapel of Rosslyn, Erskine expressed a hope that they might, as habitual visitors, escape hearing the usual endless story of the silly
old woman that showed the ruins; but Scott answered,
"There is a pleasure in the song which none but the
songstress knows, and by telling her we know it all already, we should make the poor devil unhappy."

On their return to the cottage, Scott inquired for *the
learned cabbage-eater*, meaning Ritson, who had been
expected to dinner. "Indeed," answered his wife, "you
may be happy he is not here, he is so very disagreeable.
Mr. Leyden, I believe, frightened him away." It turned
out that it was even so. When Ritson appeared, a
round of cold beef was on the luncheon-table, and Mrs.
Scott, forgetting his peculiar creed, offered him a slice.
"The antiquary, in his indignation, expressed himself in
such outrageous terms to the lady, that Leyden first tried
to correct him by ridicule, and then, on the madman
growing more violent, became angry in his turn, till at
last he threatened, that if he were not silent, he would
thraw his neck. Scott shook his head at this recital,
which Leyden observing, grew vehement in his own jus-
tification. Scott said not a word in reply, but took up a
large bunch of feathers fastened to a stick, denominated
a duster, and shook it about the student's ears till he
laughed — then changed the subject."

All this is very characteristic of the parties. Scott's
playful aversion to dispute was a trait in his mind and

manners that could alone have enabled him to make use
at one and the same time, and for the same purpose, of
two such persons as Ritson and Leyden.

To return to Ellis. In answer to Scott's letter last
quoted, he urged him to make Sir Tristrem *volume fourth*
of the Minstrelsy. "As to his hanging heavy on hand,"
says he, "I admit, that as a separate publication he may
do so, but the Minstrelsy is now established as a library
book, and in this bibliomaniac age no one would think
it perfect without the *preux chevalier*, if you avow the
said chevalier as your adopted son. Let him, at least,
be printed in the same size and paper, and then I am
persuaded our booksellers will do the rest fast enough,
upon the credit of your reputation." Scott replies (November) that it is now too late to alter the fate of Sir
Tristrem. "Longman, of Paternoster Row, has been
down here in summer, and purchased the copyright of
the Minstrelsy. Sir Tristrem is a separate property, but
will be on the same scale in point of size."

The next letter introduces to Ellis's personal acquaintance Leyden, who had by this time completed his medical
studies, and taken his degree as a physician. In it Scott
says, "At length I write to you per favor of John Leyden. I presume Heber has made you sufficiently acquainted with this original (for he is a true one), and
therefore I will trust to your own kindness, should an
opportunity occur of doing him any service in furthering
his Indian plans. You will readily judge, from convers-
ing with him, that with a very uncommon stock of acquired knowledge, he wants a good deal of another sort
of knowledge — which is only to be gleaned from an
early intercourse with polished society. But he dances
his bear with a good confidence, and the bear itself is a
very good-natured and well-conditioned animal. All his
friends are much interested about him, as the qualities
both of his heart and head are very uncommon." He
adds, "My third volume will appear as soon after the

others as the despatch of the printers will admit. Some
parts will, I think, interest you; particularly the preservation of the entire Auld Maitland by oral tradition,
probably from the reign of Edward II. or III. As I
have never met with such an instance, I must request you
to inquire all about it of Leyden, who was with me when
I received my first copy. In the third volume I intend
to publish Cadyow Castle, a historical sort of a ballad
upon the death of the Regent Murray, and besides this,
a long poem of my own. It will be a kind of romance
of Border chivalry, in a light-horseman sort of stanza."

He appears to have sent a copy of Cadyow Castle by
Leyden, whose reception at Mr. Ellis's villa, near Windsor, is thus described in the next letter of the correspondence: "Let me thank you," says Ellis, "for your poem,
which Mrs. E. has *not* received, and which, indeed, I
could not help feeling glad, in the first instance (though
we now begin to grow very impatient for it), that she
did not receive. Leyden would not have been your
Leyden if he had arrived like a careful citizen, with all
his packages carefully docketed in his portmanteau. If
on the point of leaving for many years, perhaps forever, his country and the friends of his youth, he had
not deferred to the last, and till it was too late, all that
could be easily done, and that stupid people find time to
do — if he had not arrived with all his ideas perfectly
bewildered — and tired to death, and sick — and without
any settled plans for futurity, or any accurate recollection of the past — we should have felt much more disappointed than we were by the non-arrival of your
poem, which he assured us he remembered to have left
somewhere or other, and therefore felt very confident of
recovering. In short, his whole air and countenance
told us, ' I am come to be one of your friends,' and we
immediately took him at his word."

By the "romance of Border chivalry," which was designed to form part of the third volume of the Minstrelsy,

the reader is to understand the first draft of The Lay
of the Last Minstrel; and the author's description of it
as being "in a light-horseman sort of stanza," was probably suggested by the circumstances under which the
greater part of that original draft was composed. He
has told us, in his Introduction of 1830, that the poem
originated in a request of the young and lovely Countess
of Dalkeith, that he would write a ballad on the legend
of Gilpin Horner: that he began it at Lasswade, and
read the opening stanzas, as soon as they were written,
to his friends, Erskine and Cranstoun: that their reception of these was apparently so cold as to discourage him,
and disgust him with what he had done; but that finding,
a few days afterwards, that the stanzas had nevertheless
excited their curiosity, and haunted their memory, he
was encouraged to resume the undertaking. The scene
and date of this resumption I owe to the recollection of
the then Cornet of the Edinburgh Light Horse. While
the troop were on permanent duty at Musselburgh, in
the autumnal recess of 1802, the Quartermaster, during
a charge on Portobello sands, received a kick of a horse,
which confined him for three days to his lodgings. Mr.
Skene found him busy with his pen; and he produced
before these three days expired the first canto of the Lay,
very nearly, if his friend's memory may be trusted, in
the state in which it was ultimately published. That the
whole poem was sketched and filled in with extraordinary
rapidity, there can be no difficulty in believing. He
himself says (in the Introduction of 1830), that after he
had once got fairly into the vein, it proceeded at the rate
of about a canto in a week. The Lay, however, like
the Tristrem, soon outgrew the dimensions which he had
originally contemplated; the design of including it in the
third volume of the Minstrelsy was of course abandoned;
and it did not appear until nearly three years after that
fortunate mishap on the beach of Portobello.

To return to Scott's correspondence: it shows that

Ellis had, although involved at the time in serious family afflictions, exerted himself strenuously and effectively in behalf of Leyden; a service which Scott acknowledges most warmly. His friend writes, too, at great length, about the completion of the Minstrelsy, urging, in particular, the propriety of prefixing to it a good map of the Scottish Border — "for, in truth," he says, "I have never been able to find even *Ercildoune* on any map in my possession." The poet answers (January 30, 1803), "The idea of a map pleases me much, but there are two strong objections to its being prefixed to this edition. *First*, we shall be out in a month, within which time it would be difficult, I apprehend, for Mr. Arrowsmith, laboring under the disadvantages which I am about to mention, to complete the map. *Secondly*, you are to know that I am an utter stranger to geometry, surveying, and all such *inflammatory* branches of study, as Mrs. Malaprop calls them. My education was unfortunately interrupted by a long indisposition, which occasioned my residing for about two years in the country with a good maiden aunt, who permitted and encouraged me to run about the fields, as wild as any buck that ever fled from the face of man. Hence my geographical knowledge is merely practical, and though I think that in the *South country*, 'I could be a guide worth ony twa that may in Liddesdale be found,' yet I believe Hobby Noble, or Kinmont Willie, would beat me at laying down a map. I have, however, sense enough to see that our mode of executing maps in general is anything but perfect. The country is most inaccurately defined, and had your General (Wade) marched through Scotland by the assistance of Ainslie's map, his flying artillery would soon have stuck fast among our morasses, and his horse broke their knees among our cairns. Your system of a bird's-eye view is certainly the true principle." He goes on to mention some better maps than Ellis seemed to have consulted, and to inform him where he may discover Ercildoune, under its modern form of Earlston, upon the river Leader; and concludes, "the map then must be deferred until the *third* edition, about which, I suppose, Longman thinks courageously." He then adds, "I am almost glad Cadyow Castle is miscarried, as I have rather lost conceit of it at present, being engaged on what I think will be a more generally interesting legend. I have called it The Lay of the Last Minstrel, and put it in the mouth of an old bard, who is supposed to have survived all his brethren, and to have lived down to 1690. The thing itself will be very long, but I would willingly have sent you the *Introduction*, had you been still in possession of your senatorial privilege; — but double postage would be a strange innovation on the established price of ballads, which have always sold at the easy rate of one half-penny."

I must now give part of a letter in which Leyden recurs to the kindness, and sketches the person and manners of George Ellis, in a highly characteristic fashion. He says to Scott (January 25, 1803), "You were, no doubt, surprised, my dear sir, that I gave you so little information about my movements; but it is only this day I have been able to speak of them with any precision. Such is the tardiness in everything connected with the India House, that a person who is present in the character of spectator is quite amazed; but if we consider it as the centre of a vast commercial concern, in comparison of which Tyre and Sidon, and the Great Carthage itself, must inevitably dwindle into huckster shops, we are induced to think of them with more patience. Even yet I cannot answer you exactly — being very uncertain whether I am to sail on the 18th of next month, or the 28th.

1.

"Now shal i telen to ye, i wis,
Of that kind Squeyere Ellis,
That wonnen in this cité;

Courtess he is, by God almizt !
That he nis nought ymaked knizt
    It is the more pitie.

2.

" He konnen better eche glewe
Than I konnen to ye shewe,
    Baith maist and least.
So wel he wirketh in eche thewe
That where he commen, I tell ye trewe,
    He is ane welcome guest.

3.

" His eyen graye as glas ben,
And his looks ben alto kene,
    Loveliche to paramour.
Brown as acorn ben his faxe,
His face is thin as bettel axe
    That dealeth dintis doure.

4.

" His wit ben both keene and sharpe,
To knizt or dame that carll can carpe
    Either in hall or bower;
And had I not this squeyere yfonde,
I had been at the se-gronde,
    Which had been great doloure.

5.

" In him Ich finden non other euil,
Save that his nostril so doth snivel,
    It is not myche my choice.
But than his wit ben so perquire,
That thai who can his carpynge here
    Thai thynke not of his voice.

6.

" To speake not of his gentel dame
Ich wis it war bothe sin and shame,
    Lede is not to layne :
She is a ladye of sich pryce,
To leven in that dame's service
    Meni wer ful fain.

7.

" Hir wit is ful kene and queynt,
And hir stature smale and gent,
    Semeleche to be seene ;

Armes, hondes, and fingres smale,
Of pearl beth eche fingre nale ;
    She mizt be ferys Quene.

8.

" That lady she wil giv a scarf
To him that wold ykillen a dwarf
    Churle of Paynim kinde ;
That dwarf he is so fell of mode
Tho ye shold drynk his hert blode,
    Gode wold ze never finde.

9.

" That dwarf he ben beardless and bare
And weaselblowen ben al his hair,
    Like an ympe or elfe ;
And in this world beth al and hale
Ben nothynge that he loveth an dele
    Safe his owen selfe." . . .

The fourth of these verses refers to the loss of the
Hindostan, in which ship Leyden, but for Mr. Ellis's
interference, must have sailed, and which foundered in
the Channel.   The dwarf is, of course, Ritson.

After various letters of the same kind, I find one,
dated Isle of Wight, April the 1st (1803), the morning
before Leyden finally sailed.   "I have been two days on
board," he writes, "and you may conceive what an excellent change I made from the politest society of London
to the brutish skippers of Portsmouth.   Our crew consists of a very motley party; but there are some of them
very ingenious, and Robert Smith, Sydney's brother, is
himself a host.   He is almost the most powerful man I
have met with.   My money concerns I shall consider
you as trustee of; and all remittances, as well as divi-
dends from Longman, will be to your direction.   These,
I hope, we shall soon be able to adjust very accurately.
Money may be paid, but kindness never.   Assure your
excellent Charlotte, whom I shall ever recollect with
affection and esteem, how much I regret that I did not
see her before my departure, and say a thousand pretty
things, for which my mind is too much agitated, being

in the situation of Coleridge's devil and his grannam,
' expecting and hoping the trumpet to blow.'[1] And now,
my dear Scott, adieu. Think of me with indulgence,
and be certain, that wherever, and in whatever situation,
John Leyden is, his heart is unchanged by place, and
his soul by time."

This letter was received by Scott, not in Edinburgh,
but in London. He had hurried up to town as soon as
the Court of Session rose for the spring vacation, in
hopes of seeing his friend once more before he left England; but he came too late. He had, however, done his
part: he had sent Leyden £50, through Messrs. Longman,
a week before; and on the back of that bill there is the
following memorandum: "Dr. Leyden's total debt to me
£150; he also owes £50 to my uncle."

He thus writes to Ballantyne, on the 21st April, 1803:
"I have to thank you for the accuracy with which the
Minstrelsy is thrown off. Longman and Rees are delighted with the printing. Be so good as to disperse the
following presentation copies, with ' From the Editor '
on each: —

James Hogg, Ettrick House, care of **Mr. Oliver,**
Hawick — by the carrier — a complete set.

Thomas Scott (my brother), ditto.

Colin Mackenzie, Esq., Prince's Street, **third volume**
only.

Mrs. Scott, George Street, ditto.

Dr. Rutherford, York Place, ditto.

Captain Scott, Rosebank, ditto.

I mean all these to be ordinary paper. Send one set
fine paper to Dalkeith House, addressed to the Duchess;
another, by the Inverary carrier, to Lady Charlotte
Campbell; the remaining *ten*, fine paper, with any of
Vol. III. which may be on fine paper, to be sent **to me**

[1] This is a line of Coleridge's *jeu d'esprit* on Mackintosh.

by sea. I think they will give you some *éclat* here, where printing is so much valued. I have settled about printing an edition of the Lay, 8vo, with vignettes, provided I can get a draughtsman whom I think well of. We may throw off a few superb in quarto. To the Minstrelsy I mean this note to be added, by way of advertisement: ' In the press, and will speedily be published, The Lay of the Last Minstrel, by Walter Scott, Esq., Editor of the Minstrelsy of the Scottish Border. Also, Sir Tristrem, a Metrical Romance, by Thomas of Ercildoune, called the Rhymer, edited from an ancient MS., with an Introduction and Notes, by Walter Scott, Esq.' Will you cause such a thing to be appended in your own way and fashion ? "

This letter is dated "No. 15, Piccadilly West," — he and Mrs. Scott being there domesticated under the roof of the late M. Charles Dumergue, a man of very superior abilities and of excellent education, well known as surgeon-dentist to the royal family — who had been intimately acquainted with the Charpentiers in his own early life in France, and had warmly befriended Mrs. Scott's mother on her first arrival in England. M. Dumergue's house was, throughout the whole period of the emigration, liberally opened to the exiles of his native country; nor did some of the noblest of those unfortunate refugees scruple to make a free use of his purse, as well as of his hospitality. Here Scott met much highly interesting French society, and until a child of his own was established in London, he never thought of taking up his abode anywhere else, as often as he had occasion to be in town.

The letter is addressed to "Mr. James Ballantyne, printer, Abbey-hill, Edinburgh;" which shows, that before the third volume of the Minstrelsy passed through the press, the migration recommended two years earlier had at length taken place. "It was about the end of 1802," says Ballantyne in his Memorandum, "that I closed with a plan so congenial to my wishes. I removed, bag and baggage, to Edinburgh, finding accommodation for two presses, and a proof one, in the precincts of Holyrood-house, then deriving new lustre and interest from the recent arrival of the royal exiles of France. In these obscure premises some of the most beautiful productions of what we called *The Border Press* were printed." The Memorandum states that Scott having renewed his hint as to pecuniary assistance, so soon as the printer found his finances straitened, "a liberal loan was advanced accordingly." Of course Scott's interest was constantly exerted in procuring employment, both legal and literary, for his friend's types.

Heber, and Mackintosh, then at the height of his reputation as a conversationist, and daily advancing also at the Bar, had been ready to welcome Scott in town as old friends; and Rogers, William Stewart Rose, and several other men of literary eminence, were at the same time added to the list of his acquaintance. His principal object, however, — having missed Leyden, — was to peruse and make extracts from some MSS. in the library of John, Duke of Roxburghe, for the illustration of the Tristrem; and he derived no small assistance in other researches of the like kind from the collections which the indefatigable and obliging Douce placed at his disposal. Having completed these labors, he and Mrs. Scott went, with Heber and Douce, to Sunning Hill, where they spent a happy week, and Mr. and Mrs. Ellis heard the first two or three cantos of The Lay of the Last Minstrel read under an old oak in Windsor Forest.

I should not omit to say that Scott was attended on this trip by a very large and fine bull-terrier, by name Camp, and that Camp's master and mistress too were delighted by finding that the Ellises cordially sympathized in their fondness for this animal, and indeed for all his race. At parting, Scott promised to send one of Camp's progeny, in the course of the season, to Sunning Hill.

From thence they proceeded to Oxford, accompanied by Heber; and it was on this occasion, as I believe, that Scott first saw his friend's brother, Reginald, in after-days the apostolic Bishop of Calcutta. He had just been declared the successful competitor for that year's poetical prize, and read to Scott at breakfast, in Brasenose College, the MS. of his Palestine. Scott observed that, in the verses on Solomon's Temple, one striking circumstance had escaped him, namely, that no tools were used in its erection. Reginald retired for a few minutes to the corner of the room, and returned with the beautiful lines, —

> " No hammer fell, no ponderous axes rung,
> Like some tall palm the mystic fabric sprung.
> Majestic silence," etc. [1]

After inspecting the University and Blenheim, under the guidance of the Hebers, Scott returned to London, as appears from the following letter to Miss Seward, who had been writing to him on the subject of her projected biography of Dr. Darwin. The conclusion and date are lost: —

"I have been for about a fortnight in this huge and bustling metropolis, when I am agreeably surprised by a packet from Edinburgh, containing Miss Seward's letter. I am truly happy at the information it communicates respecting the life of Dr. Darwin, who could not have wished his fame and character entrusted to a pen more capable of doing them ample, and, above all, discriminating justice. Biography, the most interesting perhaps of every species of composition, loses all its interest with me, when the shades and lights of the principal character are not accurately and faithfully detailed; nor have I much patience with such exaggerated daubing as Mr. Hayley has bestowed upon poor Cowper. I can no more sympathize with a mere eulogist, than I can with a ranting hero upon the stage; and it unfortunately hap-

[1] See *Life of Bishop Heber*, by his widow, edition 1830, vol. i. p. 30.

pens that some of our disrespect is apt, rather unjustly,
to be transferred to the subject of the panegyric in the
one case, and to poor Cato in the other. Unapprehen-
sive that even friendship can bias Miss Seward's duty
to the public, I shall wait most anxiously for the volume
her kindness has promised me.

"As for my third volume, it was very nearly printed
when I left Edinburgh, and must, I think, be ready for
publication in about a fortnight, when it will have the
honor of travelling to Lichfield. I doubt you will find
but little amusement in it, as there are a good many old
ballads, particularly those of 'the Covenanters,' which,
in point of composition, are mere drivelling trash. They
are, however, curious in an historical point of view, and
have enabled me to slide in a number of notes about that
dark and bloody period of Scottish history. There is a
vast convenience to an editor in a tale upon which, without the formality of adapting the notes very precisely to
the shape and form of the ballad, he may hang on a set
like a herald's coat without sleeves, saving himself the
trouble of taking measure, and sending forth the tale of
ancient time, ready equipped from the Monmouth Street
warehouse of a commonplace book. Cadyow Castle is to
appear in volume third.

"—— I proceeded thus far about three weeks ago, and,
shame to tell, have left my epistle unfinished ever since;
yet I have not been wholly idle, about a fortnight of that
period having been employed as much to my satisfaction
as any similar space of time during my life. I was, the
first week of that fortnight, with my invaluable friend
George Ellis, and spent the second week at Oxford,
which I visited for the first time. I was peculiarly fortunate in having for my patron at Oxford, Mr. Heber,
a particular friend of mine, who is intimately acquainted
with all, both animate and inanimate, that is worth knowing at Oxford. The time, though as much as I could
possibly spare, has, I find, been too short to convey to

me separate and distinct ideas of all the variety of wonders which I saw. My memory only at present furnishes a grand but indistinct picture of towers, and chapels, and oriels, and vaulted halls, and libraries, and paintings. I hope, in a little time, my ideas will develop themselves a little more distinctly, otherwise I shall have profited little by my tour. I was much flattered by the kind reception and notice I met with from some of the most distinguished inhabitants of the halls of Isis, which was more than such a truant to the classic page as myself was entitled to expect at the source of classic learning.

"On my return, I find an apologetic letter from my printer, saying the third volume will be despatched in a day or two. There has been, it seems, a meeting among the printers' devils; also among the paper-makers. I never heard of authors *striking work*, as the mechanics call it, until their masters the booksellers should increase their pay; but if such a combination could take place, the revolt would now be general in all branches of literary labor. How much sincere satisfaction would it give me could I conclude this letter (as I once hoped), by saying I should visit Lichfield, and pay my personal respects to my invaluable correspondent in my way northwards; but as circumstances render this impossible, I shall depute the poetry of the olden time in the editor's stead. My ' Romance ' is not yet finished. I prefer it much to anything I have done of the kind." . . .

He was in Edinburgh by the middle of May; and thus returns to his view of Oxford in a letter to his friend at Sunning Hill:—

TO GEORGE ELLIS, ESQ., ETC., ETC.

EDINBURGH, 25th May, 1803.

MY DEAR ELLIS, — . . . I was equally delighted with that venerable seat of learning, and flattered by the polite attention of Heber's friends. I should have been enchanted to have spent a couple of months among the curious libraries. What stores must be reserved for some painful student to bring forward to the public! Under the guidance and patronage of our good Heber, I saw many of the literary men of his Alma Mater, and found matters infinitely more active in every department than I had the least previous idea of. Since I returned home, my time has been chiefly occupied in professional labors; my truant days spent in London having thrown me a little behind; but now, I hope, I shall find spare moments to resume Sir Tristrem — and the Lay, which has acquired additional value in my estimation from its pleasing you. How often do Charlotte and I think of the little paradise at Sunning Hill and its kind inhabitants; and how do we regret, like Dives, the gulf which is placed betwixt us and friends, with whom it would give us such pleasure to spend much of our time. It is one of the vilest attributes of the best of all possible worlds, that it contrives to split and separate and subdivide everything like congenial pursuits and habits, for the paltry purpose, one would think, of diversifying every little spot with a share of its various productions. I don't know why the human and vegetable departments should differ so excessively. Oaks and beeches, and ashes and elms, not to mention cabbages and turnips, are usually arrayed *en masse ;* but where do we meet a town of antiquaries, a village of poets, or a hamlet of philosophers? But, instead of fruitless lamentations, we sincerely hope Mrs. Ellis and you will unrivet yourselves from your forest, and see how the hardy blasts of our mountains will suit you for a change of climate. . . . The new edition of Minstrelsy is published here, but not in London as yet, owing to the embargo on our shipping. An invasion is expected from Flushing, and no measures of any kind taken to prevent or repel it. Yours ever faithfully W. SCOTT.

This letter enclosed a sheet of extracts from Fordun,

in Scott's handwriting; the subject being the traditional marriage of one of the old Counts of Anjou with a female demon, by which the Scotch chronicler accounts for all the crimes and misfortunes of the English Plantagenets.

Messrs. Longman's new edition of the first two volumes of the Minstrelsy consisted of 1000 copies — of volume third there were 1500. A complete edition of 1250 copies followed in 1806; a fourth, also of 1250, in 1810; a fifth, of 1500, in 1812; a sixth, of 500, in 1820; and since then it has been incorporated in various successive editions of Scott's Collected Poetry — to the extent of at least 15,000 copies more. Of the Continental and American editions I can say nothing, except that they have been very numerous. The book was soon translated into German, Danish, and Swedish; and, the structure of those languages being very favorable to the undertaking, the Minstrelsy of the Scottish Border has thus become widely naturalized among nations themselves rich in similar treasures of legendary lore. Of the extraordinary accuracy and felicity of the German version of Schubart, Scott has given some specimens in the last edition which he himself superintended — that of 1830.

He speaks, in the Essay to which I have referred, as if the first reception of the Minstrelsy on the south of the Tweed had been cold. "The curiosity of the English," he says, "was not much awakened by poems in the rude garb of antiquity, accompanied with notes referring to the obscure feuds of barbarous clans, of whose very names civilized history was ignorant." In writing those beautiful Introductions of 1830, however, Scott, as I have already had occasion to hint, trusted entirely to his recollection of days long since gone by, and he has accordingly let fall many statements, which we must take with some allowance. His impressions as to the reception of the Minstrelsy were different, when, writing to his brother-in-law, Charles Carpenter, on the 3d March, 1803, for the purpose of introducing Leyden, he said:

"I have contrived to turn a very slender portion of literary talents to some account, by a publication of the poetical antiquities of the Border, where the old people had preserved many ballads descriptive of the manners of the country during the wars with England. This trifling collection was so well received by a *discerning public*, that, after receiving about £100 profit for the first edition, which my vanity cannot omit informing you went off in six months, I have sold the copyright for £500 more." This is not the language of disappointment; and though the edition of 1803 did not move off quite so rapidly as the first, and the work did not perhaps attract much notice beyond the more cultivated students of literature, until the Editor's own genius blazed out in full splendor in the Lay, and thus lent general interest to whatever was connected with his name, I suspect there never was much ground for accusing the English public of regarding the Minstrelsy with more coldness than the Scotch — the population of the Border districts themselves being, of course, excepted. Had the sale of the original edition been chiefly Scotch, I doubt whether Messrs. Longman would have so readily offered £500, in those days of the trade a large sum, for the second. Scott had become habituated, long before 1830, to a scale of bookselling transactions, measured by which the largest editions and copy-monies of his own early days appeared insignificant; but the evidence seems complete that he was well contented at the time.

He certainly had every reason to be so as to the impression which the Minstrelsy made on the minds of those entitled to think for themselves upon such a subject. The ancient ballads in his collection, which had never been printed at all before, were in number forty-three; and of the others — most of which were in fact all but new to the modern reader — it is little to say that his editions were superior in all respects to those that had preceded them. He had, I firmly believe, interpolated

hardly a line or even an epithet of his own; but his diligent zeal had put him in possession of a variety of copies
in different stages of preservation; and to the task of
selecting a standard text among such a diversity of materials, he brought a knowledge of old manners and phraseology, and a manly simplicity of taste, such as had never
before been united in the person of a poetical antiquary.
From among a hundred corruptions he seized, with instinctive tact, the primitive diction and imagery; and
produced strains in which the unbroken energy of half-
civilized ages, their stern and deep passions, their daring
adventures and cruel tragedies, and even their rude wild
humor, are reflected with almost the brightness of a
Homeric mirror, interrupted by hardly a blot of what
deserves to be called vulgarity, and totally free from any
admixture of artificial sentimentalism. As a picture of
manners, the Scottish Minstrelsy is not surpassed, if
equalled, by any similar body of poetry preserved in any
other country; and it unquestionably owes its superiority
in this respect over Percy's Reliques, to the Editor's
conscientious fidelity, on the one hand, which prevented
the introduction of anything new — to his pure taste, on
the other, in the balancing of discordant recitations.
His introductory essays and notes teemed with curious
knowledge, not hastily grasped for the occasion, but
gradually gleaned and sifted by the patient labor of
years, and presented with an easy, unaffected propriety
and elegance of arrangement and expression, which it
may be doubted if he ever materially surpassed in the
happiest of his imaginative narrations. I well remember, when Waverley was a new book, and all the world
were puzzling themselves about its authorship, to have
heard the Poet of the Isle of Palms exclaim impa-
tiently, "I wonder what all these people are perplexing
themselves with: have they forgotten the *prose* of the
Minstrelsy?" Even had the Editor inserted none of his
own verse, the work would have contained enough, and

more than enough, to found a lasting and graceful reputation.

It is not to be denied, however, that the Minstrelsy of the Scottish Border has derived a very large accession of interest from the subsequent career of its Editor. One of the critics of that day said that the book contained "the elements of a hundred historical romances;" — and this critic was a prophetic one. No person who has not gone through its volumes for the express purpose of comparing their contents with his great original works, can have formed a conception of the endless variety of incidents and images now expanded and emblazoned by his mature art, of which the first hints may be found either in the text of those primitive ballads, or in the notes, which the happy rambles of his youth had gathered together for their illustration. In the edition of the Minstrelsy published since his death, not a few such instances are pointed out; but the list might have been extended far beyond the limits which such an addition allowed. The taste and fancy of Scott appear to have been formed as early as his moral character; and he had, before he passed the threshold of authorship, assembled about him, in the uncalculating delight of native enthusiasm, almost all the materials on which his genius was destined to be employed for the gratification and instruction of the world.

CHAPTER XII

1803–1804

SHORTLY after the complete Minstrelsy issued from
the press, Scott made his first appearance as a reviewer.
The Edinburgh Review had been commenced in October,
1802, under the superintendence of the Rev. Sydney
Smith, with whom, during his short residence in Scotland, he had lived on terms of great kindness and familiarity. Mr. Smith soon resigned the editorship to Mr.
Jeffrey, who had by this time been for several years
among the most valued of Scott's friends and companions
at the Bar; and, the new journal being far from committing itself to violent politics at the outset, he appreciated
the brilliant talents regularly engaged in it far too highly,
not to be well pleased with the opportunity of occasionally exercising his pen in its service. His first contribution was an article on Southey's Amadis of Gaul, included in the number for October, 1803. Another, on
Sibbald's Chronicle of Scottish Poetry, appeared in the
same number; — a third, on Godwin's Life of Chaucer;
a fourth, on Ellis's Specimens of Ancient English Poetry;
and a fifth, on the Life and Works of Chatterton, followed in the course of 1804.[1]

---

[1] Scott's contributions to our periodical literature have been, with some
trivial exceptions, included in the recent collection of his *Miscellaneous
Prose Writings.*

During the summer of 1803, however, his chief literary labor was still on the Tristrem; and I shall presently give some further extracts from his letters to Ellis, which will amply illustrate the spirit in which he continued his researches about the Seer of Ercildoune, and the interruptions which these owed to the prevalent alarm of French invasion. Both as Quartermaster of the Edinburgh Light Horse, and as Sheriff of The Forest, he had a full share of responsibility in the warlike arrangements to which the authorities of Scotland had at length been roused; nor were the duties of his two offices considered as strictly compatible by Francis, Lord Napier, then Lord-Lieutenant of Selkirkshire; for I find several letters in which his Lordship complains that the incessant drills and musters of Musselburgh and Portobello prevented the Sheriff from attending county meetings held at Selkirk in the course of this summer and autumn, for the purpose of organizing the trained bands of the Forest, on a scale hitherto unattempted. Lord Napier strongly urges the propriety of his resigning his connection with the Edinburgh troop, and fixing his summer residence somewhere within the limits of his proper jurisdiction; nay, he goes so far as to hint, that if these suggestions should be neglected, it must be his duty to state the case to the Government. Scott could not be induced (least of all by a threat), while the fears of invasion still prevailed, to resign his place among his old companions of "the voluntary band;" but he seems to have presently acquiesced in the propriety of the Lord-Lieutenant's advice respecting a removal from Lasswade to Ettrick Forest.

The following extract is from a letter written at Musselburgh during this summer or autumn: —

"Miss Seward's acceptable favor reaches me in a place, and at a time, of great bustle, as the corps of voluntary cavalry to which I belong is quartered for a short time in this village, for the sake of drilling and discipline. Nevertheless, had your letter announced the name of the

gentleman who took the trouble of forwarding it, I would
have made it my business to find him out, and to prevail
on him, if possible, to spend a day or two with us in
quarters. We are here assuming a very military appearance. Three regiments of militia, with a formidable
park of artillery, are encamped just by us. The Edinburgh troop, to which I have the honor to be quartermaster, consists entirely of young gentlemen of family,
and is, of course, admirably well mounted and armed.
There are other four troops in the regiment, consisting
of yeomanry, whose iron faces and muscular forms an-
nounce the hardness of the climate against which they
wrestle, and the powers which nature has given them to
contend with and subdue it. These corps have been
easily raised in Scotland, the farmers being in general a
high-spirited race of men, fond of active exercises, and
patient of hardship and fatigue. For myself, I must
own that to one who has, like myself, *la tête un peu
exaltée*, the ' pomp and circumstance of war ' gives, for a
time, a very poignant and pleasing sensation. The imposing appearance of cavalry, in particular, and the rush
which marks their onset, appear to me to partake highly
of the sublime. Perhaps I am the more attached to this
sort of sport of swords, because my health requires much
active exercise, and a lameness contracted in childhood
renders it inconvenient for me to take it otherwise than
on horseback. I have, too, a hereditary attachment to
the animal — not, I flatter myself, of the common jockey
cast, but because I regard him as the kindest and most
generous of the subordinate tribes. I hardly even except
the dogs; at least they are usually so much better treated,
that compassion for the steed should be thrown into the
scale when we weigh their comparative merits. My wife
(a foreigner) never sees a horse ill-used without asking
what that poor horse has done in his state of preëxist-
ence? I would fain hope they have been carters or
hackney-coachmen, and are only experiencing a retort of

the ill-usage they have formerly inflicted. What think you?"

It appears that Miss Seward had sent Scott some obscure magazine criticism on his Minstrelsy, in which the censor had condemned some phrase as naturally suggesting a low idea. The lady's letter not having been preserved, I cannot explain farther the sequel of that from which I have been quoting. Scott says, however: —

"I am infinitely amused with your sagacious critic. God wot, I have often admired the vulgar subtlety of such minds as can with a depraved ingenuity attach a mean or disgusting sense to an epithet capable of being otherwise understood, and more frequently, perhaps, used to express an elevated idea. In many parts of Scotland the word *virtue* is limited entirely to *industry*; and a young divine who preached upon the moral beauties of virtue was considerably surprised at learning that the whole discourse was supposed to be a panegyric upon a particular damsel who could spin fourteen spindles of yarn in the course of a week. This was natural; but your literary critic has the merit of going very far a-field to fetch home his degrading association."

To return to the correspondence with Ellis — Scott writes thus to him in July: "I cannot pretend immediately to enter upon the serious discussion which you propose respecting the age of ' Sir Tristrem; ' but yet, as it seems likely to strip Thomas the Prophet of the honors due to the author of the English Tristrem, I cannot help hesitating before I can agree to your theory; — and here my doubt lies. Thomas of Ercildoune, called the Rhymer, is a character mentioned by almost every Scottish historian, and the date of whose existence is almost as well known as if we had the parish register. Now, his great reputation, and his designation of *Rymour*, could only be derived from his poetical performances; and in what did these consist excepting in the Romance of ' Sir Tristrem,' mentioned by Robert de Brunne? I

hardly think, therefore, we shall be justified in assuming
the existence of an earlier *Thomas*, who would be, in
fact, merely the creature of our system. I own I am not
prepared to take this step, if I can escape otherwise from
you and M. de la Ravaillere — and thus I will try it.
M. de la R. barely informs us that the history of Sir
Tristrem was known to Chretien de Troyes in the end of
the twelfth century, and to the King of Navarre in the
beginning of the thirteenth. Thus far his evidence goes,
and I think not one inch farther — for it does not establish the existence either of the metrical romance, as you
suppose, or of the prose romance, as M. de la R. much
more erroneously supposes, at that very early period. If
the *story* of Sir Tristrem was founded in fact, and if,
which I have all along thought, a person of this name
really swallowed a dose of cantharides intended to stimulate the exertions of his uncle, a petty monarch of Cornwall, and involved himself of course in an intrigue with
his aunt, these facts must have taken place during a very
early period of English history, perhaps about the time
of the Heptarchy. Now, if this be once admitted, it is
clear that the raw material from which Thomas wove his
web must have been current long before his day, and I
am inclined to think that Chretien and the King of Navarre refer, not to the special metrical romance contained
in Mr. Douce's fragments, but to the general story of
Sir Tristrem, whose love and misfortunes were handed
down by tradition as a historical fact. There is no difficulty in supposing a tale of this kind to have passed from
the Armoricans, or otherwise, into the mouths of the
French; as, on the other hand, it seems to have been
preserved among the Celtic tribes of the Border, from
whom, in all probability, it was taken by their neighbor,
Thomas of Ercildoune. If we suppose, therefore, that
Chretien and the King allude only to the general and
well-known *story* of Tristrem, and not to the particular
edition of which Mr. Douce has some fragments — (and

I see no evidence that any such special allusion to these fragments is made) — it will follow that *they* may be as late as the end of the thirteenth century, and that the Thomas mentioned in them may be *the* Thomas of whose existence we have historical evidence. In short, the question is, shall Thomas be considered as a landmark by which to ascertain the antiquity of the fragments, or shall the *supposed* antiquity of the fragments be held a sufficient reason for *supposing* an earlier Thomas? For aught yet seen, I incline to my former opinion, that those fragments are coeval with the *ipsissimus Thomas*. I acknowledge the internal evidence, of which you are so accurate a judge, weighs more with me than the reference to the King of Navarre; but, after all, the extreme diffi- culty of judging of style, so as to bring us within sixty or seventy years, must be fully considered. Take notice, I have never pleaded the matter so high as to say, that the Auchinleck MS. contains the very words devised by Thomas the Rhymer. On the contrary, I have always thought it one of the spurious copies in *queint Inglis*, of which Robert de Brunne so heavily complains. But this will take little from the curiosity, perhaps little from the antiquity, of the romance. Enough of Sir T. for the present. — How happy it will make us if you can fulfil the expectation you hold out of a northern expedition. Whether in the cottage or at Edinburgh, we will be equally happy to receive you, and show you all the lions of our vicinity. Charlotte is hunting out music for Mrs. E., but I intend to add *Johnson's* collection, which, though the tunes are simple, and often bad sets, contains much more original Scotch music than any other."

About this time, Mr. and Mrs. Ellis, and their friend Douce, were preparing for a tour into the North of Eng- land; and Scott was invited and strongly tempted to join them at various points of their progress, particularly at the Grange, near Rotherham, in Yorkshire, a seat of the

Earl of Effingham. But he found it impossible to escape again from Scotland, owing to the agitated state of the country. — On returning to the cottage from an excursion to his Sheriffship, he thus resumes: —

TO GEORGE ELLIS, ESQ.

LASSWADE, August 27, 1803.

DEAR ELLIS, — My conscience has been thumping me as hard as if it had studied under Mendoza, for letting your kind favor remain so long unanswered. Nevertheless, in this it is, like Launcelot Gobbo's, but a hard kind of conscience, as it must know how much I have been occupied with Armies of Reserve, and Militia, and Pikemen, and Sharpshooters, who are to descend from Ettrick Forest to the confusion of all invaders. The truth is, that this country has for once experienced that the pressure of external danger may possibly produce internal unanimity; and so great is the present military zeal, that I really wish our rulers would devise some way of calling it into action, were it only on the economical principle of saving so much good courage from idle evaporation. — I am interrupted by an extraordinary accident, nothing less than a volley of small shot fired through the window, at which my wife was five minutes before arranging her flowers. By Camp's assistance, who run the culprit's foot like a Liddesdale bloodhound, we detected an unlucky sportsman, whose awkwardness and rashness might have occasioned very serious mischief — so much for interruption. — To return to Sir Tristrem. As for Mr. Thomas's *name*, respecting which you state some doubts,[1] I request you to attend to the following particulars: In the first place, surnames were of very late introduction into Scotland, and it would be difficult to show that they became in general a hereditary

[1] Mr. Ellis had hinted that " *Rymer* might not more necessarily indicate an actual poet, than the name of *Taylor* does in modern times an actual knight of the thimble."

distinction, until after the time of Thomas the Rhymer; previously they were mere personal distinctions peculiar to the person by whom they were borne, and dying along with him. Thus the children of *Alan Durward* were not called *Durward*, because they were not *Ostiarii*, the circumstance from which he derived the name. When the surname was derived from property, it became naturally hereditary at a more early period, because the distinction applied equally to the father and the son. The same happened with *patronymics*, both because the name of the father is usually given to the son; so that Walter Fitzwalter would have been my son's name in those times as well as my own; and also because a clan often takes a sort of general patronymic from one common ancestor, as Macdonald, etc., etc. But though these classes of surnames become hereditary at an early period, yet, in the natural course of things, epithets merely personal are much longer of becoming a family distinction.[1] But I do not trust, by any means, to this general argument; because the charter quoted in the Minstrelsy contains written evidence, that the epithet of *Rymour* was peculiar to our Thomas, and was dropped by his son, who

[1] The whole of this subject has derived much illustration from the recent edition of the *Ragman's Roll*, a contribution to the Bannatyne Club of Edinburgh by two of Sir Walter Scott's most esteemed friends, the Lord Chief Commissioner Adam and Sir Samuel Shepherd. That record of the oaths of fealty tendered to Edward I, during his Scotch usurpation, furnishes, indeed, very strong confirmation of the views which the editor of *Sir Tristrem* had thus early adopted concerning the origin of surnames in Scotland. The landed gentry, over most of the country, seem to have been generally distinguished by the surnames still borne by their descendants — it is wonderful how little the land seems to have changed hands in the course of so many centuries. But the towns' people have, with few exceptions, designations apparently indicating the actual trade of the individual; and in many instances, there is distinct evidence that the plan of transmitting such names had not been adopted; for example, Thomas the Tailor is described as son of Thomas the Smith, or *vice versâ*. The chief magistrates of the burghs appear, however, to have been, in most cases, younger sons of the neighboring gentry, and have of course their hereditary designations. This singular document, so often quoted and referred to, was never before printed *in extenso*.

designs himself simply, *Thomas of Erceldoune, son of Thomas the Rymour of Erceldoune;* which I think is conclusive upon the subject. In all this discussion, I have scorned to avail myself of the tradition of the country, as well as the suspicious testimony of Boece, Dempster, etc., grounded probably upon that tradition, which uniformly affirms the name of Thomas to have been Learmont or Leirmont, and that of the Rhymer a personal epithet. This circumstance may induce us, however, to conclude that some of his descendants had taken that name — certain it is that his castle is called Leirmont's Tower, and that he is as well known to the country people by that name, as by the appellation of the Rhymer.

Having cleared up this matter, as I think, to every one's satisfaction, unless to those resembling not Thomas himself, but his namesake the Apostle, I have, secondly, to show that my Thomas is the *Tomas* of Douce's MS. Here I must again refer to the high and general reverence in which Thomas appears to have been held, as is proved by Robert de Brunne; but above all, as you observe, to the extreme similarity betwixt the French and English poems, with this strong circumstance, that the *mode* of telling the story approved by the French minstrel, under the authority of his Tomas, is the very mode in which my Thomas has told it. Would you desire better sympathy?

I lately met by accident a Cornish gentleman, who had taken up his abode in Selkirkshire for the sake of fishing — and what should his name be but *Caerlion?* You will not doubt that this interested me very much. He tells me that there is but one family of the name in Cornwall, or as far as ever he heard, anywhere else, and that they are of great antiquity. Does not this circumstance seem to prove that there existed in Cornwall a place called Caerlion, giving name to that family? Caerlion would probably be *Castrum Leonense*, the chief town of Liones, which in every romance is stated to have been Tristrem's

country, and from which he derived his surname of Tristrem *de Liones*. This district, as you notice in the notes
on the *Fabliaux*, was swallowed up by the sea. I need
not remind you that all this tends to illustrate the *Caer-
lioun* mentioned by Tomas, which I always suspected to
be a very different place from Caerlion on Uske — which
is no seaport. How I regret the number of leagues
which prevented my joining you and the sapient Douce,
and how much ancient lore I have lost. Where I have
been, the people talked more of the praises of Ryno and
Fillan (not Ossian's heroes, but two Forest greyhounds
which I got in a present) than, I verily believe, they
would have done of the prowesses of Sir Tristrem, or of
Esplandian, had either of them appeared to lead on the
levy *en masse*. Yours ever,   W. SCOTT.

Ellis says in reply —

MY DEAR SCOTT: I must begin by congratulating you on Mrs.
Scott's escape; Camp, if he had had no previous title to immor-
tality, would deserve it, for his zeal and address in detecting
the stupid marksman, who, while he took aim at a bird on a
tree, was so near shooting your fair " bird in bower." If there
were many such shooters, it would become then a sufficient excuse for the reluctance of Government to furnish arms indiffer-
ently to all volunteers. In the next place, I am glad to hear
that you are disposed to adopt my channel for transmitting the
tale of Tristrem to Chretien de Troye. The more I have
thought on the subject, the more I am convinced that the Nor-
mans, long before the Conquest, had acquired from the Britons
of Armorica a considerable knowledge of our old British fables,
and that this led them, after the Conquest, to inquire after such
accounts as were to be found in the country where the events
are supposed to have taken place. I am satisfied, from the
internal evidence of Geoffrey of Monmouth's History, that it
must have been fabricated in Bretagne, and that he did, as he
asserts, only *translate* it. Now, as *Marie*, who lived about a
century later, *certainly* translated also from the Breton a series
of lays relating to Arthur and his knights, it will follow that
the first poets who wrote *in France*, such as Chretien, etc.,

must have acquired their knowledge of our traditions from Bretagne. Observe, that the pseudo-Turpin, who is supposed to have been anterior to Geoffrey, and who, on that supposition, cannot have borrowed from him, mentions, among Charlemagne's heroes, Hoel (the hero of Geoffrey also), "de quo canitur cantilena usque ad hodiernum diem." Now, if Thomas was able to establish his story as the most *authentic*, even by the avowal of the French themselves, and if the *sketch* of that story was previously known, it must have been because he wrote in the country which his hero was supposed to have inhabited; and on the same grounds the Norman minstrels here, and even their English successors, were allowed to fill up, with as many circumstances as they thought proper, the tales of which the Armorican Bretons probably furnished the first imperfect outline.

What you tell me about your Cornish fisherman is very curious; and I think with you that little reliance is to be placed on our Welsh geography — and that Caerlion on Uske is by no means *the* Caerlion of Tristrem. Few writers or readers have hitherto considered sufficiently, that from the moment when Hengist first obtained a settlement in the Isle of Thanet, that settlement became *England*, and all the rest of the country became *Wales;* that these divisions continued to represent different proportions of the island at different periods; but that Wales, during the whole Heptarchy, and for a long time after, comprehended the whole western coast very nearly from Cornwall to Dunbretton; and that this whole tract, of which the eastern frontier may be easily traced for each particular period, preserved most probably to the age of Thomas a community of language, of manners, and traditions.

As your last volume announces your Lay, as well as Sir Tristrem, as *in the press*, I begin, in common with all your friends, to be uneasy about the future disposal of your time. Having nothing but a very active profession, and your military pursuits, and your domestic occupations, to think of, and Leyden having monopolized Asiatic lore, you will presently be quite an idle man! You are, however, still in time to learn Erse, and it is, I am afraid, very necessary that you should do so, in order to stimulate my laziness, which has hitherto made no progress whatever in Welsh.   Your ever faithful,   G. E.

P. S. — *Is Camp married yet?*

Ellis had projected some time before this an edition of the Welsh Mabinogion,[1] in which he was to be assisted by Mr. Owen, the author of the Welsh and English Dictionary, Cambrian Biography, etc.

"I am very sorry," Scott says (September 14), "that you flag over those wild and interesting tales. I hope, if you will not work yourself (for which you have so little excuse, having both the golden talents and the golden leisure necessary for study), you will at least keep Owen to something that is rational — I mean to *iron horses*, and *magic cauldrons*, and *Bran the Blessed*, with the music of his whole army upon his shoulders, and, in short, to something more pleasing and profitable than old apophthegms, triads, and 'blessed burdens of the womb of the isle of Britain.' Talking of such burdens, Camp has been regularly wedded to a fair dame in the neighborhood; but notwithstanding the Italian policy of locking the lady in a stable, she is suspected of some inaccuracy; but we suspend judgment, as Othello ought in all reason to have done, till we see the produce of the union. As for my own employment, I have yet much before me; and as the beginning of letting out ink is like the letting out of water, I dare say I shall go on scribbling one nonsense or another to the end of the chapter. People may say this and that of the pleasure of fame or of profit as a motive of writing. I think the only pleasure is in the actual exertion and research, and I would no more write upon any other terms than I would hunt merely to dine upon hare-soup. At the same time, if credit and profit came unlooked for, I would no more quarrel with them than with the soup. I hope this will find you and Mrs. Ellis safely and pleasantly settled.

"— By the way, while you are in his neighborhood, I hope you will not fail to inquire into the history of the

---

[1] The *Mabinogion* have at last been translated, and are now in the course of publication, in a very beautiful form, by the Lady Charlotte Guest. (1839.)

valiant Moor of Moorhall and the Dragon of Wantley.
As a noted burlesque upon the popular romance, the
ballad has some curiosity and merit.

Ever yours,   W. S."

Mr. Ellis received this letter where Scott hoped it
would reach him, at the seat of Lord Effingham; and he
answers, on the 3d of October: —

The beauty of this part of the country is such as to indemnify the traveller for a few miles of very indifferent road, and
the tedious process of creeping up and almost sliding down a
succession of high hills ; — and in the number of picturesque
landscapes by which we are encompassed, the den of the dragon
which you recommended to our attention is the most superla-
tively beautiful and romantic. You are, I suppose, aware that
this same den is the very spot from whence Lady Mary Wortley Montagu wrote many of her early letters ; and it seems that
an old housekeeper, who lived there till last year, remembered
to have seen her, and dwelt with great pleasure on the various
charms of her celebrated mistress ; so that its wild scenes have
an equal claim to veneration from the admirers of wit and gallantry, and the far-famed investigators of remote antiquity.
With regard to the original Dragon, I have met with two different traditions. One of these (which I think is preserved by
Percy) states him to have been a wicked attorney, a relentless
persecutor of the poor, who was at length, fortunately for his
neighbors, ruined by a lawsuit which he had undertaken against
his worthy and powerful antagonist Moor of Moorhall. The
other legend, which is current in the Wortley family, states him
to have been a most formidable drinker, whose powers of inglu-
tition, strength of stomach, and stability of head, had procured
him a long series of triumphs over common visitants, but who
was at length fairly drunk dead by the chieftain of the opposite
moors. It must be confessed that the form of the den, a cavern
cut in the rock, and very nearly resembling a wine or ale cellar,
tends to corroborate this tradition ; but I am rather tempted to
believe that both the stories were invented *après coup*, and that
the supposed dragon was some wolf or other destructive animal,
who was finally hunted down by Moor of Moorhall, after doing

considerable mischief to the flocks and herds of his superstitious neighbors.

The present house appears to have grown to its even now moderate size by successive additions to a very small *logge* (lodge), built by " a gentle knight, Sir Thomas Wortley," in the time of Henry VIII., for the pleasure, as an old inscription in the present scullery testifies, of " listening to the Hartes bell." Its site is on the side of a very high rocky hill, covered with oaks (the weed of the country), and overhanging the river Don, which in this place is little more than a mountain torrent, though it becomes navigable a few miles lower at Sheffield. A great part of the road from hence (which is seven miles distant) runs through forest ground, and I have no doubt that the whole was at no distant period covered with wood, because the modern improvements of the country, the result of flourishing manufactories, have been carried on almost within our own time in consequence of the abundance of coal which here breaks out in many places even on the surface. On the opposite side of the river begin almost immediately the extensive moors which strike along the highest land of Yorkshire and Derbyshire, and following the chain of hills, probably communicated not many centuries ago with those of Northumberland, Cumberland, and Scotland. I therefore doubt whether the general face of the country is not better evidence as to the nature of the monster than the particular appearance of the cavern ; and am inclined to believe that Moor of Moorhall was a hunter of wild beasts, rather than of attorneys or hard drinkers.

You are unjust in saying that I flag over the Mabinogion ; I have been very constantly employed upon my preface, and was proceeding to the last section when I set off for this place — so you see I am perfectly exculpated, and all over as white as snow. Anne being a true aristocrat, and considering purity of blood as essential to lay the foundation of all the virtues she expects to call out by a laborious education of a true son of Camp — she highly approves the strict and even prudish severity with which you watch over the morals of his bride, and expects you, inasmuch as all the good knights she has read of have been remarkable for their incomparable beauty, not to neglect that important requisite in selecting her future guardian. We possess a vulgar dog (a pointer), to whom it is intended to commit

the charge of our house during our absence, and to whom I
mean to give orders to repel by force any attempts of our neighbors during the times that I shall be occupied in preparing
hare-soup; but Fitz-Camp will be *her* companion, and she trusts
that you will strictly examine him while yet a varlet, and only
send him up when you think him likely to become a true knight.
Adieu — mille choses.   G. E.

Scott tells Ellis in reply (October 14), that he was
"infinitely gratified with his account of Wortley Lodge
and the Dragon," and refers him to the article "Kem-
pion," in the Minstrelsy, for a similar tradition respecting an ancestor of the noble house of Somerville. The
reader can hardly need to be reminded that the gentle
knight Sir Thomas Wortley's love of hearing the deer
bell was often alluded to in Scott's subsequent writings.
He goes on to express his hope, that next summer will
be "a more propitious season for a visit to Scotland.
The necessity of the present occasion," he says, "has
kept almost every individual, however insignificant, to
his post. God has left us entirely to our own means of
defence, for we have not above one regiment of the line
in all our ancient kingdom. In the mean while, we are
doing the best we can to prepare ourselves for a contest,
which, perhaps, is not far distant. A beacon light, com-
municating with that of Edinburgh Castle, is just erecting in front of our quiet cottage. My field equipage is
ready, and I want nothing but a pipe and a *schnurbartchen* to convert me into a complete hussar.[1] Charlotte,
with the infantry (of the household troops, I mean), is to
beat her retreat into Ettrick Forest, where, if the Tweed
is in his usual wintry state of flood, she may weather out

---

[1] *Schnurbartchen* is German for mustachio. It appears from a page of
an early note-book previously transcribed, that Scott had been sometimes
a smoker of tobacco in the first days of his light-horsemanship. He had
laid aside the habit at the time when this letter was written; but he
twice again resumed it, though he never carried the indulgence to any
excess.

a descent from Ostend. Next year I hope all this will be over, and that not only I shall have the pleasure of receiving you in peace and quiet, but also of going with you through every part of Caledonia in which you can possibly be interested. Friday se'ennight our corps takes the field for ten days — for the second time within three months — which may explain the military turn of my epistle.

"Poor Ritson is no more. All his vegetable soups and puddings have not been able to avert the evil day, which, I understand, was preceded by madness. It must be worth while to inquire who has got his MSS., — I mean his own notes and writings. The Life of Arthur, for example, must contain many curious facts and quotations, which the poor defunct had the power of assembling to an astonishing degree, without being able to combine anything like a narrative, or even to deduce one useful inference — witness his Essay on Romance and Minstrelsy, which reminds one of a heap of rubbish, which had either turned out unfit for the architect's purpose, or beyond his skill to make use of. The ballads he had collected in Cumberland and Northumberland, too, would greatly interest me. If they have fallen into the hands of any liberal collector, I dare say I might be indulged with a sight of them. Pray inquire about this matter.

"Yesterday Charlotte and I had a visit which we owe to Mrs. E. A rosy lass, the sister of a bold yeoman in our neighborhood, entered our cottage, towing in a monstrous sort of bull-dog, called emphatically Cerberus, whom she came on the part of her brother to beg our acceptance of, understanding we were anxious to have a son of Camp. Cerberus was no sooner loose (a pleasure which, I suspect, he had rarely enjoyed) than his father (*supposé*) and he engaged in a battle which might have been celebrated by the author of the Unnatural Combat, and which, for aught I know, might have turned

out a combat à *l'outrance*, if I had not interfered with
a horse-whip, instead of a baton, as *juge de Camp*. The
odds were indeed greatly against the stranger knight —
two fierce Forest greyhounds having arrived, and, contrary to the law of arms, stoutly assailed him. I hope to
send you a puppy instead of this redoubtable Cerberus.
Love to Mrs. E.   W. S."

After giving Scott some information about Ritson's
literary treasures, most of which, as it turned out, had
been disposed of by auction shortly before his death, Mr.
Ellis (10th November) returns to the charge about Tristrem and True Thomas. "You appear," he says, "to
have been for some time so military, that I am afraid the
most difficult and important part of your original plan,
namely, your History of Scottish Poetry, will again be
postponed, and must be kept for some future publication.
I am, at this moment, much in want of two such assistants
as you and Leyden. It seems to me, that if I had some
local knowledge of that wicked Ettrick Forest, I could
extricate myself tolerably — but as it is, although I am
convinced that my general idea is tolerably just, I am
unable to guide my elephants in that quiet and decorous
step-by-step march which the nature of such animals
requires through a country of which I don't know any
of the roads. My comfort is, that you cannot publish
Tristrem without a preface, — that you can't write one
without giving me some assistance, — and that you must
finish the said preface long before I go to press with my
Introduction."

This was the Introduction to Ellis's Specimens of Ancient English Romances, in which he intended to prove,
that as Valentia was, during several ages, the exposed
frontier of Roman Britain towards the unsubdued tribes
of the North, and as two whole legions were accordingly
usually quartered there, while one besides sufficed for
the whole southern part of the island, the manners of
Valentia, which included the district of Ettrick Forest,

must have been greatly favored by the continued residence of so many Roman troops. "It is probable, therefore," he says, in another letter, "that the civilization of the northern part became gradually the most perfect. That country gave birth, as you have observed, to Merlin, and to Aneurin, — who was probably the same as the historian Gildas. It seems to have given education to Taliessin — it was the country of Bede and Adonnan."

I shall not quote more on this subject, as the reader may turn to the published essay for Mr. Ellis's matured opinions respecting it. To return to his letter of November 10, 1803, he proceeds: "And now let me ask you about The Lay of the Last Minstrel. That, I think, may go on as well in your tent, amidst the clang of trumpets and the dust of the field, as in your quiet cottage — perhaps indeed still better — nay, I am not sure whether a *real* invasion would not be, as far as your poetry is concerned, a thing to be wished."

It was in the September of this year that Scott first saw Wordsworth. Their common acquaintance, Stoddart, had so often talked of them to each other, that they met as if they had not been strangers; and they parted friends.

Mr. and Miss Wordsworth had just completed that tour in the Highlands, of which so many incidents have since been immortalized, both in the poet's verse and in the hardly less poetical prose of his sister's Diary. On the morning of the 17th of September, having left their carriage at Rosslyn, they walked down the valley to Lasswade, and arrived there before Mr. and Mrs. Scott had risen. "We were received," Mr. Wordsworth has told me, "with that frank cordiality which, under whatever circumstances I afterwards met him, always marked his manners; and, indeed, I found him then in every respect — except, perhaps, that his animal spirits were somewhat higher — precisely the same man that you knew him in

later life; the same lively, entertaining conversation, full
of anecdote, and averse from disquisition; the same unaffected modesty about himself; the same cheerful and
benevolent and hopeful views of man and the world. He
partly read and partly recited, sometimes in an enthusiastic style of chant, the first four cantos of The Lay of
the Last Minstrel; and the novelty of the manners, the
clear picturesque descriptions, and the easy glowing
energy of much of the verse, greatly delighted me."

After this he walked with the tourists to Rosslyn, and
promised to meet them in two days at Melrose. The
night before they reached Melrose they slept at the little
quiet inn of Clovenford, where, on mentioning his name,
they were received with all sorts of attention and kindness, — the landlady observing that Mr. Scott, "who was
a very clever gentleman," was an old friend of the house,
and usually spent a good deal of time there during the
fishing season; but, indeed, says Mr. Wordsworth,
"wherever we named him, we found the word acted as
an *open sesamum;* and I believe, that in the character
of the *Sheriff's* friends, we might have counted on a
hearty welcome under any roof in the Border country."

He met them at Melrose on the 19th, and escorted
them through the Abbey, pointing out all its beauties,
and pouring out his rich stores of history and tradition.
They then dined and spent the evening together at the
inn; but Miss Wordsworth observed that there was some
difficulty about arranging matters for the night, "the
landlady refusing to settle anything until she had ascertained from *the Sheriff himself* that he had no objection
to sleep in the same room with *William*." Scott was
thus far on his way to the Circuit Court at Jedburgh,
in his capacity of Sheriff, and there his new friends again
joined him; but he begged that they would not enter the
court, "for," said he, "I really would not like you to see
the sort of figure I cut there." They did see him casually, however, in his cocked hat and sword, marching

in the Judge's procession to the sound of one cracked trumpet, and were then not surprised that he should have been a little ashamed of the whole ceremonial. He introduced to them his friend William Laidlaw, who was attending the court as a juryman, and who, having read some of Wordsworth's verses in a newspaper, was exceedingly anxious to be of the party, when they explored at leisure, all the law-business being over, the beautiful valley of the Jed, and the ruins of the Castle of Fernieherst, the original fastness of the noble family of Lothian. The grove of stately ancient elms about and below the ruin was seen to great advantage in a fine, gray, breezy autumnal afternoon; and Mr. Wordsworth happened to say, "What life there is in trees!"—"How different," said Scott, "was the feeling of a very intelligent young lady, born and bred in the Orkney Islands, who lately came to spend a season in this neighborhood! She told me nothing in the mainland scenery had so much disappointed her as woods and trees. She found them so dead and lifeless, that she could never help pining after the eternal motion and variety of the ocean. And so back she has gone, and I believe nothing will ever tempt her from *the wind-swept Orcades* again."

Next day they all proceeded together up the Teviot to Hawick, Scott entertaining his friends with some legend or ballad connected with every tower or rock they passed. He made them stop for a little to admire particularly a scene of deep and solemn retirement, called *Horne's Pool*, from its having been the daily haunt of a contemplative schoolmaster, known to him in his youth; and at Kirkton he pointed out the little village schoolhouse, to which his friend Leyden had walked six or eight miles every day across the moors, "when a poor barefooted boy." From Hawick, where they spent the night, he led them next morning to the brow of a hill, from which they could see a wide range of the Border mountains, Ruberslaw, the Carter, and the Cheviots; and lamented

that neither their engagements nor his own would permit
them to make at this time an excursion into the wilder
glens of Liddesdale, "where," said he, "I have strolled
so often and so long, that I may say I have a home in
every farmhouse." "And, indeed," adds Mr. Wordsworth, "wherever we went with him, he seemed to know
everybody, and everybody to know and like him." Here
they parted — the Wordsworths to pursue their journey
homeward by Eskdale — he to return to Lasswade.

The impression on Mr. Wordsworth's mind was, that
on the whole he attached much less importance to his
literary labors or reputation than to his bodily sports,
exercises, and social amusements; and yet he spoke of his
profession as if he had already given up almost all hope
of rising by it; and some allusion being made to its
profits, observed that "he was sure he could, if he chose,
get more money than he should ever wish to have from
the booksellers." [1]

This confidence in his own literary resources appeared
to Mr. Wordsworth remarkable — the more so, from the
careless way in which its expression dropt from him. As
to his despondence concerning the Bar, I confess his *fee-
book* indicates much less ground for such a feeling than
I should have expected to discover there. His practice
brought him, as we have seen, in the session of 1796–97,
£144 10s.; — its proceeds fell down, in the first year of
his married life, to £79 17s.; but they rose again, in
1798–99, to £135 9s.; amounted, in 1799–1800, to £129
13s.; in 1800–1, to £170; in 1801–2, to £202 12s.; and
in the session that had just elapsed (which is the last included in the record before me), to £228 18s.

On reaching his cottage in Westmoreland, Wordsworth

[1] I have drawn up the account of this meeting from my recollection
partly of Mr. Wordsworth's conversation — partly from that of his sister's
charming *Diary*, which he was so kind as to read over to me on the 16th
May, 1836. [Dorothy Wordsworth's *Recollections of a Tour made in Scotland, 1803*, was first published in full in 1874, under the editorship of Principal Shairp.]

addressed a letter to Scott, from which I must quote a few sentences. It is dated Grasmere, October 16, 1803. "We had a delightful journey home, delightful weather, and a sweet country to travel through. We reached our little cottage in high spirits, and thankful to God for all his bounties. My wife and child were both well, and as I need not say, we had all of us a happy meeting. . . . We passed Branxholme — your Branxholme, we supposed — about four miles on this side of Hawick. It looks better in your poem than in its present realities. The situation, however, is delightful, and makes amends for an ordinary mansion. The whole of the Teviot and the pastoral steeps about Mosspaul pleased us exceedingly. The Esk below Langholm is a delicious river, and we saw it to great advantage. We did not omit noticing Johnnie Armstrong's Keep; but his hanging place, to our great regret, we missed. We were, indeed, most truly sorry that we could not have you along with us into Westmoreland. The country was in its full glory — the verdure of the valleys, in which we are so much superior to you in Scotland, but little tarnished by the weather, and the trees putting on their most beautiful looks. My sister was quite enchanted, and we often said to each other, What a pity Mr. Scott is not with us! . . . I had the pleasure of seeing Coleridge and Southey at Keswick last Sunday. Southey, whom I never saw much of before, I liked much: he is very pleasant in his manner, and a man of great reading in old books, poetry, chronicles, memoirs, etc., etc., particularly Spanish and Portuguese. . . . My sister and I often talk of the happy days that we spent in your company. Such things do not occur often in life. If we live we shall meet again; that is my consolation when I think of these things. Scotland and England sound like division, do what ye can; but we really are but neighbors, and if you were no farther off, and in Yorkshire, we should think so. Farewell. God prosper you, and all that belongs to you.

Your sincere friend, for such I will call myself, though slow to use a word of such solemn meaning to any one,   W. WORDSWORTH."

The poet then transcribes his noble Sonnet on Neidpath Castle, of which Scott had, it seems, requested a copy. In the MS. it stands somewhat differently from the printed edition; but in that original shape Scott always recited it, and few lines in the language were more frequently in his mouth.[1]

I have already said something of the beginning of Scott's acquaintance with "the Ettrick Shepherd." Shortly after their first meeting, Hogg, coming into Edinburgh, with a flock of sheep, was seized with a sudden ambition of seeing himself in type, and he wrote out that same night Willie and Katie, and a few other ballads, already famous in the Forest, which some obscure bookseller gratified him by printing accordingly; but they appear to have attracted no notice beyond their original sphere. Hogg then made an excursion into the Highlands, in quest of employment as overseer of some extensive sheep-farm; but, though Scott had furnished

[1] [More than a year later, Wordsworth sent to Scott a copy of *Yarrow Unvisited*, saying of the poem: " You will find a few stanzas, which I hope (for the subject at least) will give you some pleasure. I wrote them, not without a view of pleasing you, soon after our return from Scotland. . . . They are in the same sort of metre as the *Leader Haughs*." Scott says in his reply: " I am very much flattered by your choosing Yarrow for the subject of the verses sent me, which shall not pass out of my own hand, nor be read except to those worthy of being listeners. At the same time, I by no means admit your apology, however ingeniously and artfully stated, for not visiting the bonnie holms of Yarrow, and certainly will not rest till I have prevailed upon you to compare the ideal with the real stream. . . . There are some good lines in the old ballad, the hunted hare, for instance, who mourns that she must leave fair Leaderhaugh, and cannot win to Yarrow. And this from early youth has given my bosom a thrill when sung or repeated.

' For many a place stands in hard case,
    Where blithe folks kend nae sorrow ;
'Mongst Homes that dwelt on Leader side,
    And Scotts that lived on Yarrow.' "

Familiar Letters, vol. i. p. 28.]

him with strong recommendations to various friends, he
returned without success. He printed an account of his
travels, however, in a set of letters in the Scots Magazine, which, though exceedingly rugged and uncouth, had
abundant traces of the native shrewdness and genuine
poetical feeling of this remarkable man. These also
failed to excite attention; but, undeterred by such disap-
pointments, the Shepherd no sooner read the third volume of the Minstrelsy, than he made up his mind that
the Editor's "Imitations of the Ancients" were by no
means what they should have been. "Immediately," he
says, in one of his many Memoirs of himself, "I chose
a number of traditional facts, and set about imitating
the manner of the ancients myself." These imitations
he transmitted to Scott, who warmly praised the many
striking beauties scattered over their rough surface. The
next time that Hogg's business carried him to Edinburgh,
he waited upon Scott, who invited him to dinner in Castle Street, in company with William Laidlaw, who happened also to be in town, and some other admirers of the
rustic genius. When Hogg entered the drawing-room,
Mrs. Scott, being at the time in a delicate state of health,
was reclining on a sofa. The Shepherd, after being presented, and making his best bow, forthwith took possession of another sofa placed opposite to hers, and stretched
himself thereupon at all his length; for, as he said afterwards, "I thought I could never do wrong to copy the
lady of the house." As his dress at this period was precisely that in which any ordinary herdsman attends cattle
to the market, and as his hands, moreover, bore most
legible marks of a recent sheep-smearing, the lady of the
house did not observe with perfect equanimity the novel
usage to which her chintz was exposed. The Shepherd,
however, remarked nothing of all this — dined heartily
and drank freely, and, by jest, anecdote, and song, afforded plentiful merriment to the more civilized part of
the company. As the liquor operated, his familiarity

increased and strengthened; from "Mr. Scott," he advanced to "Sherra," and thence to "Scott," "Walter," and "Wattie," — until, at supper, he fairly convulsed the whole party by addressing Mrs. Scott as "Charlotte."

The collection entitled The Mountain Bard was eventually published by Constable, in consequence of Scott's recommendation, and this work did at last afford Hogg no slender share of the popular reputation for which he had so long thirsted. It is not my business, however, to pursue the details of his story. What I have written was only to render intelligible the following letter: —

TO WALTER SCOTT, ESQ., ADVOCATE, CASTLE STREET, EDINBURGH.

ETTRICK-HOUSE, December 24, 1803.

DEAR MR. SCOTT, — I have been very impatient to hear from you. There is a certain affair of which you and I talked a little in private, and which must now be concluded, that naturally increaseth this.

I am afraid that I was at least half-seas over the night I was with you, for I cannot, for my life, recollect what passed when it was late ; and, there being certainly a small vacuum in my brain, which, when empty, is quite empty, but is sometimes supplied with a small distillation of intellectual matter — this must have been empty that night, or it never could have been taken possession of by the fumes of the liquor so easily. If I was in the state in which I suspect that I was, I must have spoke a very great deal of nonsense, for which I beg ten thousand pardons. I have the consolation, however, of remembering that Mrs. Scott kept in company all or most of the time, which she certainly could not have done, had I been very rude. I remember, too, of the filial injunction you gave at parting, cautioning me against being ensnared by the loose women in town. I am sure I had not reason enough left at that time to express either the half of my gratitude for the kind hint, or the utter abhorrence I inherit at those seminaries of lewdness.

You once promised me your best advice in the first lawsuit in which I had the particular happiness of being engaged. I am now going to ask it seriously in an affair, in which, I am sure, we will both take as much pleasure. It is this : I have as many songs beside me, which are certainly the *worst* of my productions, as will make about one hundred pages close printed, and about two hundred, printed as the Minstrelsy is. Now, although I will not proceed without your consent and advice, yet I would have you to understand that I expect it, and have the scheme much at heart at present. The first thing that suggested it, was their extraordinary repute in Ettrick and its neighborhood, and being everlastingly plagued with writing copies, and promising scores which I never meant to perform. As my last pamphlet was never known, save to a few friends, I wish your advice what pieces of it are worth preserving. The Pastoral I am resolved to insert, as I am Sandy Tod. As to my manuscripts, they are endless ; and as I doubt you will disapprove of publishing them wholesale, and letting the good help off the bad, I think you must trust to my discretion in the selection of a few. I wish likewise to know if you think a graven image on the first leaf is any recommendation ; and if we might front the songs with a letter to you, giving an impartial account of my manner of life and education, and, which if you pleased to transcribe, putting He for I. Again, there is no publishing a book without a patron, and I have one or two in my eye, and of which I will, with my wonted assurance to you, give you the most free choice. The first is Walter Scott, Esq., Advocate, Sheriff-depute of Ettrick Forest, which, if permitted, I will address you in a dedication singular enough. The next is Lady Dalkeith, which, if you approved of, you must become the Editor yourself ; and I shall give you my word for it, that neither word nor sentiment in it shall offend the most delicate ear. You will not be in the least jealous, if, alongst with my services to you, I present my kindest compliments to the sweet little lady whom you call Charlotte. As for Camp and Walter (I beg pardon for this preëminence), they will not mind them if I should exhaust my eloquence in compliments. Believe me, Dear Walter, your most devoted servant,

JAMES HOGG.

The reader will, I doubt not, be particularly amused with one of the suggestions in this letter ; namely, that

Scott should transcribe the Shepherd's narrative *in for*
of his life and education, and merely putting "He" fo
"I," adopt it as his own composition.   James, however
would have had no hesitation about offering a simila
suggestion either to Scott, or Wordsworth, or Byron, a
any period of their renown.   To say nothing about mod
esty, his notions of literary honesty were always exceed
ingly loose; but, at the same time, we must take int
account his peculiar notions, or rather no notions, as t
the proper limits of a joke.

Literature, like misery, makes men acquainted witl
strange bedfellows.   Let us return from the worth
Shepherd of Ettrick to the courtly wit and scholar o
Sunning Hill.   In the last quoted of his letters, he ex
presses his fear that Scott's military avocations migh
cause him to publish the Tristrem unaccompanied by hi
Essay on the History of Scottish Poetry.   It is need
less to add that no such Essay ever was completed; but
have heard Scott say that his plan had been to begin witl
the age of Thomas of Ercildoune, and bring the subjec
down to his own, illustrating each stage of his progres
by a specimen of verse — imitating every great master'
style, as he had done that of the original Sir Tristrem ir
his *Conclusion*.   Such a series of pieces from his hanc
would have been invaluable, merely as bringing out i
a clear manner the *gradual* divarication of the two grea
dialects of the English tongue; but seeing by his Verse
on a Poacher, written many years after this, in pro
fessed imitation of Crabbe, with what happy art he coul
pour the poetry of his own mind into the mould of an
other artist, it is impossible to doubt that we have los
better things than antiquarian illumination by the non
completion of a design in which he should have embrace
successively the tone and measure of Douglas, Dunbar
Lindesay, Montgomerie, Hamilton, Ramsay, Fergusson
and Burns.

The Tristrem was now far advanced at press.   H

says to Ellis, on the 19th March, 1804, "As I had a world of things to say to you, I have been culpably, but most naturally, silent. When you turn a bottle with its head downmost, you must have remarked that the extreme impatience of the contents to get out all at once greatly impedes their getting out at all. I have, however, been forming the resolution of sending a grand packet with Sir Tristrem, who will kiss your hands in about a fortnight. I intend uncastrated copies for you, Heber, and Mr. Douce, who, I am willing to hope, will accept this mark of my great respect and warm remembrance of his kindness while in London. — Pray send me without delay the passage referring to *Thomas* in the French ' Hornchild.' Far from being daunted with the position of the enemy, I am resolved to carry it at the point of the bayonet, and, like an able general, to attack where it would be difficult to defend. Without metaphor or parable, I am determined, not only that my Tomas *shall* be the author of Tristrem, but that he shall be the author of Hornchild also. I must, however, read over the romance, before I can make my arrangements. Holding, with Ritson, that the copy in *his* collection is translated from the French, I do not see why we should not suppose that the French had been originally a version from our Thomas. The date does not greatly frighten me, as I have extended Thomas of Ercildoune's life to the threescore and ten years of the Psalmist, and consequently removed back the date of Sir Tristrem to 1250. The French translation might be written for that matter within a few days after Thomas's work was completed — and I can allow a few years. He lived on the Border, already possessed by Norman families, and in the vicinity of Northumberland, where there were many more. Do you think the minstrels of the Percies, the Vescies, the Morells, the Grais, and the De Vaux, were not acquainted with honest Thomas, their next door neighbor, who was a poet, and wrote excellent tales — and, more-

over, a *laird*, and gave, I dare be sworn, good dinners?
And would they not anxiously translate, for the amusement of their masters, a story like Hornchild, so intimately connected with the lands in which they had settled? And do you not think, from the whole structure
of Hornchild, however often translated and retranslated,
that it must have been originally of northern extraction?
I have not time to tell you certain suspicions I entertain
that Mr. Douce's fragments are the work of one Raoull
de Beauvais, who flourished about the middle of the thirteenth century, and for whose accommodation principally
I have made Thomas, to use a military phrase, *dress
backwards* for ten years."

All this playful language is exquisitely characteristic
of Scott's indomitable adherence to his own views. But
his making *Thomas dress backwards* — and resolving
that, if necessary, he *shall be* the author of Hornchild,
as well as Sir Tristrem — may perhaps remind the reader
of Don Quixote's method of repairing the headpiece
which, as originally constructed, one blow had sufficed to
demolish; — "Not altogether approving of his having
broken it to pieces with so much ease, to secure himself
from the like danger for the future, he made it over
again, fencing it with small bars of iron within, in such
a manner, that *he rested satisfied of its strength — and,
without caring to make a fresh experiment on it, he approved and looked upon it as a most excellent helmet.*"

Ellis having made some observations on Scott's article
upon Godwin's Life of Chaucer, which implied a notion
that he had formed a regular connection with the Edinburgh Review, he in the same letter says, "I quite
agree with you as to the general conduct of the Review,
which savors more of a wish to display than to instruct;
but as essays, many of the articles are invaluable, and
the principal conductor is a man of very acute and universal talent. I am not regularly connected with the
work, nor have I either inclination or talents to use the

critical scalping knife, unless as in the case of Godwin,
where flesh and blood succumbed under the temptation.
I don't know if you have looked into his tomes, of which
a whole edition has vanished — I was at a loss to know
how, till I conjectured that, as the heaviest materials to
be come at, they have been sent on the secret expedition,
planned by Mr. Phillips and adopted by our sapient
Government, for blocking up the mouth of our enemy's
harbors.   They should have had my free consent to take
Phillips and Godwin, and all our other lumber, literary
and political, for the same beneficial purpose.   But in
general, I think it ungentlemanly to wound any person's
feelings through an anonymous publication, unless where
conceit or false doctrine strongly calls for reprobation.
Where praise can be conscientiously mingled in a larger
proportion than blame, there is always some amusement
in throwing together our ideas upon the works of our
fellow-laborers, and no injustice in publishing them.   On
such occasions, *and in our way*, I may possibly, once or
twice a year, furnish my critical friends with an article."

Sir Tristrem was at length published on the 2d of
May, 1804, by Constable, who, however, expected so
little popularity for the work that the edition consisted
only of 150 copies.   These were sold at a high price (two
guineas), otherwise they would not have been enough to
cover the expenses of paper and printing.   Mr. Ellis,
and Scott's other antiquarian friends, were much dissat-
isfied with these arrangements; but I doubt not that
Constable was a better judge than any of them.   The
work, however, partook in due time of the favor attending its editor's name.   In 1806, 750 copies were called
for; and 1000 in 1811.   After that time Sir Tristrem
was included in the collective editions of Scott's poetry;
but he had never parted with the copyright, merely allowing his general publishers to insert it among his other
works, whenever they chose to do so, as a matter of courtesy.   It was not a performance from which he had ever

anticipated any pecuniary profit, but it maintained at least, if it did not raise, his reputation in the circle of his fellow-antiquaries; and his own Conclusion, in the manner of the original romance, must always be admired as a remarkable specimen of skill and dexterity.

As to the arguments of the Introduction, I shall not in this place attempt any discussion.[1] Whether the story of Tristrem was first told in Welsh, Armorican, French, or English verse, there can, I think, be no doubt that it had been told in verse, with such success as to obtain very general renown, by Thomas of Ercildoune, and that the copy edited by Scott was either the composition of one who had heard the old Rhymer recite his lay, or the identical lay itself. The introduction of Thomas's name in the third person, as not the author, but the author's authority, appears to have had a great share in convincing Scott that the Auchinleck MS. contained not the original, but the copy of an English admirer and contemporary. This point seems to have been rendered more doubtful by some quotations in the recent edition of Warton's History of English Poetry; but the argument derived from the enthusiastic exclamation "God help Sir Tristrem the knight — he fought for England!" still remains; and stronger perhaps even than that, in the opinion of modern philologists, is the total absence of any Scottish or even Northumbrian peculiarities in the diction.

All this controversy may be waived here. Scott's object and delight was to revive the fame of the Rhymer, whose traditional history he had listened to while yet an infant among the crags of Smailholme. He had already celebrated him in a noble ballad;[2] he now devoted a vol-

---

[1] The critical reader will find all the learning on the subject brought together with much ability in the Preface to *The Poetical Romances of Tristan*, in French, in Anglo-Norman, and in Greek, composed in the Twelfth and Thirteenth Centuries — Edited by Francisque Michel, 2 vols., London, 1835.

[2] See the *Minstrelsy* (Edition 1833), vol. iv. p. 110. [Also *Poetical Works*, Cambridge Edition, pp. 32-37.]

ume to elucidate a fragment supposed to be substantially his work; and we shall find that thirty years after, when the lamp of his own genius was all but spent, it could still revive and throw out at least some glimmerings of its original brightness at the name of Thomas of Ercildoune.[1]

[1] See *Castle Dangerous*, chap. v.

CHAPTER XIII

1804–1805

IT has been mentioned, that in the course of the preceding summer, the Lord-Lieutenant of Selkirkshire complained of Scott's military zeal as interfering sometimes with the discharge of his shrieval functions, and took occasion to remind him, that the law, requiring every Sheriff to reside at least four months in the year within his own jurisdiction, had not hitherto been complied with. It appears that Scott received this communication with some displeasure, being conscious that no duty of any importance had ever been neglected by him; well knowing that the law of residence was not enforced in the cases of many of his brother sheriffs; and, in fact, ascribing his Lord-Lieutenant's complaint to nothing but a certain nervous fidget as to all points of form, for which that respectable nobleman was notorious, as well became, perhaps, an old High Commissioner to the General Assembly of the Kirk. Scott, however, must have been found so clearly in the wrong, had the case been submitted to the Secretary of State, and Lord Napier conducted the correspondence with such courtesy, never failing to allege as a chief argument the pleasure which it would afford himself and the other gentlemen of Selkirkshire to have more of their Sheriff's society, that, while it would have been highly imprudent to persist, there could be no mortification in yielding. He flattered himself that his active habits would enable him to maintain his connection with the Edinburgh Cavalry as usual; and, perhaps, he also flattered himself, that residing for the summer in Selkirkshire would not interfere more seriously with his business as a barrister, than the occupation of the cottage at Lasswade had hitherto done.

While he was seeking about, accordingly, for some "lodge in the Forest," his kinsman of Harden suggested that the tower of Auld Wat might be refitted, so as to serve his purpose; and he received the proposal with enthusiastic delight. On a more careful inspection of the localities, however, he became sensible that he would be practically at a greater distance from county business of all kinds at Harden, than if he were to continue at Lasswade. Just at this time, the house of Ashestiel, situated on the southern bank of the Tweed, a few miles from Selkirk, became vacant by the death of its proprietor, Colonel Russell, who had married a sister of Scott's mother, and the consequent dispersion of the family. The young laird of Ashestiel, his cousin, was then in India; and the Sheriff took a lease of the house and grounds, with a small farm adjoining. On the 4th May, two days after the Tristrem had been published, he says to Ellis, "I have been engaged in travelling backwards and forwards to Selkirkshire upon little pieces of business, just important enough to prevent my doing anything to purpose. One great matter, however, I have achieved, which is, procuring myself a place of residence, which will save me these teasing migrations in future, so that, though I part with my sweet little cottage on the banks of the Esk, you will find me this summer in the very centre of the ancient Reged, in a decent farmhouse overhanging the Tweed, and situated in a wild pastoral country." And again, on the 19th, he thus apologizes for not having answered a letter of the 10th: "For more than a month my head was fairly tenanted by ideas, which, though strictly pastoral and rural, were neither literary nor poetical. *Long sheep* and *short sheep*, and *tups* and *gimmers*, and *hogs* and *dinmonts*, had made a perfect sheepfold of my understanding, which is hardly yet cleared of them.[1] — I hope Mrs. Ellis will clap a bridle on her imagination. Ettrick Forest boasts finely shaped hills and clear romantic streams; but, alas, they are bare, to wildness, and denuded of the beautiful natural wood with which they were formerly shaded. It is mortifying to see that, though wherever the sheep are excluded, the copse has immediately sprung up in abundance, so that enclosures only are wanting to restore the wood wherever it might be useful or ornamental, yet hardly a proprietor has attempted to give it fair play for a resurrection. . . . You see we reckon positively on you — the more because our arch-critic Jeffrey tells me that he met you in London, and found you still inclined for a northern trip. All our wise men in the north are rejoiced at the prospect of seeing George Ellis. If you delay your journey till July, I shall then be free of the

---

[1] Describing his meeting with Scott in the summer of 1801, James Hogg says: " During the sociality of the evening, the discourse ran very much on the different breeds of sheep, that curse of the community of Ettrick Forest. The original black-faced Forest breed being always called *the short sheep*, and the Cheviot breed *the long sheep*, the disputes at that period ran very high about the practicable profits of each. Mr. Scott, who had come into that remote district to preserve what fragments remained of its legendary lore, was rather bored with everlasting questions of the long and the short sheep. So at length, putting on his most serious, calculating face, he turned to Mr. Walter Bryden, and said, ' I am rather at a loss regarding the merits of this *very* important question. How long must a sheep actually measure to come under the denomination of *a long sheep* ? ' Mr. Bryden, who, in the simplicity of his heart, neither perceived the quiz nor the reproof, fell to answer with great sincerity. ' It 's the woo' [wool], sir — it 's the woo' that makes the difference. The lang sheep ha'e the short woo', and the short sheep ha'e the lang thing, and these are just kind o' names we gi'e them, like.' Mr. Scott could not preserve his grave face of strict calculation : it went gradually awry, and a hearty guffaw " [*i. e.*, horselaugh] " followed. When I saw the very same words repeated near the beginning of the *Black Dwarf*, how could I be mistaken of the author ? " — Autobiography prefixed to Hogg's *Altrive Tales*.

Courts of Law, and will meet you upon the Border, at whatever side you enter."

The business part of these letters refers to Scott's brother Daniel, who, as he expresses it, "having been bred to the mercantile line, had been obliged by some untoward circumstances, particularly an imprudent connection with an artful woman, to leave Edinburgh for Liverpool, and now to be casting his eyes towards Jamaica." Scott requests Ellis to help him if he can, by introducing him to some of his own friends or agents in that island; and Ellis furnishes him accordingly with letters to Mr. Blackburn, a friend and brother proprietor, who appears to have paid Daniel Scott every possible attention, and soon provided him with suitable employment on a healthy part of his estates. But the same low tastes and habits which had reduced the unfortunate young man to the necessity of expatriating himself, recurred after a brief season of penitence and order, and continued until he had accumulated great affliction upon all his family.

On the 10th of June, 1804, died, at his seat of Rosebank, Captain Robert Scott, the affectionate uncle whose name has often occurred in this narrative.[1] "He was," says his nephew to Ellis, on the 18th, "a man of universal benevolence and great kindness towards his friends, and to me individually. His manners were so much tinged with the habits of celibacy as to render them peculiar, though by no means unpleasingly so, and his profession (that of a seaman) gave a high coloring to the whole. The loss is one which, though the course of nature led me to expect it, did not take place at last without considerable pain to my feelings. The arrangement of his affairs, and the distribution of his small fortune among

---

[1] In the obituary of the *Scots Magazine* for this month I find: "Universally regretted, Captain Robert Scott of Rosebank, a gentleman whose life afforded an uniform example of unostentatious charity and extensive benevolence."

his relations, will devolve in a great measure upon me.
He has distinguished me by leaving me a beautiful little
villa on the banks of the Tweed, with every possible convenience annexed to it, and about thirty acres of the
finest land in Scotland. Notwithstanding, however, the
temptation that this bequest offers, I continue to pursue
my Reged plan, and expect to be settled at Ashestiel in
the course of a month. Rosebank is situated so near the
village of Kelso as hardly to be sufficiently a country
residence; besides, it is hemmed in by hedges and
ditches, not to mention Dukes and Lady Dowagers, which
are bad things for little people. It is expected to sell to
great advantage. I shall buy a mountain farm with the
purchase-money, and be quite the Laird of the Cairn and
the Scaur."

Scott sold Rosebank in the course of the year for
£5000; his share (being a ninth) of his uncle's other
property amounted, I believe, to about £500; and he
had besides a legacy of £100 in his quality of trustee.
This bequest made an important change in his pecuniary
position, and influenced accordingly the arrangements of
his future life. Independently of practice at the Bar,
and of literary profits, he was now, with his little patrimony, his Sheriffship, and about £200 per annum arising
from the stock ultimately settled on his wife, in possession of a fixed revenue of nearly, if not quite, £1000
a year.

On the 1st of August he writes to Ellis from Ashestiel:
"Having had only about a hundred and fifty things to
do, I have scarcely done anything, and yet could not give
myself leave to suppose that I had leisure to write letters.
1st, I had this farmhouse to furnish from sales, from
brokers' shops, and from all manner of hospitals for incurable furniture. 2dly, I had to let my cottage on the
banks of the Esk. 3dly, I had to arrange matters for
the sale of Rosebank. 4thly, I had to go into quarters
with our cavalry, which made a very idle fortnight in the

midst of all this business. Last of all, I had to superintend a removal, or what we call a *flitting*, which, of all
bores under the cope of Heaven, is bore the most tremendous. After all these storms, we are now most comfort-
ably settled, and have only to regret deeply our disappointment at finding your northern march blown up.
We had been projecting about twenty expeditions, and
were pleasing ourselves at Mrs. Ellis's expected surprise
on finding herself so totally built in by mountains, as I
am at the present writing hereof. We are seven miles
from kirk and market. We rectify the last inconvenience by killing our own mutton and poultry; and as to
the former, finding there was some chance of my family
turning pagans, I have adopted the goodly practice of
reading prayers every Sunday, to the great edification of
my household. Think of this, you that have the happiness to be within two steps of the church, and commiser-
ate those who dwell in the wilderness. I showed Charlotte yesterday *the Catrail*, and told her that to inspect
that venerable monument was one main object of your
intended journey to Scotland. She is of opinion that
ditches must be more scarce in the neighborhood of
Windsor Forest than she had hitherto had the least idea
of."

Ashestiel will be visited by many for his sake, as long
as Waverley and Marmion are remembered. A more
beautiful situation for the residence of a poet could not
be conceived. The house was then a small one, but,
compared with the cottage at Lasswade, its accommodations were amply sufficient. You approached it through
an old-fashioned garden, with holly hedges, and broad,
green, terrace walks. On one side, close under the windows, is a deep ravine, clothed with venerable trees, down
which a mountain rivulet is heard, more than seen, in its
progress to the Tweed. The river itself is separated
from the high bank on which the house stands only by a
narrow meadow of the richest verdure. Opposite, and

all around, are the green hills. The valley there is narrow, and the aspect in every direction is that of perfect pastoral repose. The heights immediately behind are those which divide the Tweed from the Yarrow; and the latter celebrated stream lies within an easy ride, in the course of which the traveller passes through a variety of the finest mountain scenery in the south of Scotland. No town is within seven miles but Selkirk, which was then still smaller and quieter than it is now; there was hardly even a gentleman's family within visiting distance, except at Yair, a few miles lower on the Tweed, the ancient seat of the Pringles of Whytbank, and at Bowhill, between the Yarrow and Ettrick, where the Earl of Dalkeith used occasionally to inhabit a small shooting-lodge, which has since grown into a magnificent ducal residence. The country all around, with here and there an insignificant exception, belongs to the Buccleuch estate; so that, whichever way he chose to turn, the bard of the clan had ample room and verge enough, and all appliances to boot, for every variety of field sport that might happen to please his fancy; and being then in the prime vigor of manhood, he was not slow to profit by these advantages. Meantime, the concerns of his own little farm, and the care of his absent relation's woods, gave him healthful occupation in the intervals of the chase; and he had long, solitary evenings for the uninterrupted exercise of his pen; perhaps, on the whole, better opportunities of study than he had ever enjoyed before, or was to meet with elsewhere in later days.

When he first examined Ashestiel, with a view to being his cousin's tenant, he thought of taking home James Hogg to superintend the sheep-farm, and keep watch over the house also during the winter. I am not able to tell exactly in what manner this proposal fell to the ground. In January, 1804, the Shepherd writes to him: "I have no intention of waiting for so distant a prospect as that of being manager of your farm, though I

have no doubt of our joint endeavor proving successful,
nor yet of your willingness to employ me in that capacity.
His Grace the Duke of Buccleuch hath at present a farm
vacant in Eskdale, and I have been importuned by friends
to get a letter from you and apply for it. You can
hardly be conscious what importance your protection hath
given me already, not only in mine own eyes, but even
in those of others. You might write to him, or to any
of the family you are best acquainted with, stating that
such and such a character was about leaving his native
country for want of a residence in the farming line." I
am very doubtful if Scott — however willing to encounter
the risk of employing Hogg as his own *grieve* or bailiff
— would have felt himself justified at this, or indeed at
any time, in recommending him as the tenant of a considerable farm on the Duke of Buccleuch's estate. But I
am also quite at a loss to comprehend how Hogg should
have conceived it possible, at this period, when he certainly had no capital whatever, that the Duke's Cham-
berlain should agree to accept him for a tenant, on any
attestation, however strong, as to the excellence of his
character and intentions. Be that as it may, if Scott
made the application which the Shepherd suggested, it
failed. So did a negotiation which he certainly did enter
upon about the same time with the late Earl of Caernar-
von (then Lord Porchester), through that nobleman's
aunt, Mrs. Scott of Harden, with the view of obtaining
for Hogg the situation of bailiff on one of his Lordship's
estates in the west of England; and such, I believe, was
the result of several other attempts of the same kind with
landed proprietors nearer home. Perhaps the Shepherd
had already set his heart so much on taking rank as a
farmer in his own district, that he witnessed the failure
of any such negotiations with indifference. As regards
the management of Ashestiel, I find no trace of that proposal having ever been renewed.

In truth, Scott had hardly been a week in possession

of his new domains, before he made acquaintance with a character much better suited to his purpose than James Hogg ever could have been. I mean honest Thomas Purdie, his faithful servant — his affectionately devoted humble friend from this time until death parted them. Tom was first brought before him, in his capacity of Sheriff, on a charge of poaching, when the poor fellow gave such a touching account of his circumstances, — a wife, and I know not how many children, depending on his exertions — work scarce and grouse abundant, — and all this with a mixture of odd sly humor, — that the Sheriff's heart was moved. Tom escaped the penalty of the law — was taken into employment as shepherd, and showed such zeal, activity, and shrewdness in that capacity, that Scott never had any occasion to repent of the step he soon afterwards took, in promoting him to the position which had been originally offered to James Hogg.

It was also about the same time that he took into his service as coachman Peter Mathieson, brother-in-law to Thomas Purdie, another faithful servant, who never afterwards left him, and still survives his kind master. Scott's awkward management of the little phaeton had exposed his wife to more than one perilous overturn, before he agreed to set up a close carriage, and call in the assistance of this steady charioteer.

During this autumn Scott formed the personal acquaintance of Mungo Park, the celebrated victim of African discovery. On his return from his first expedition, Park endeavored to establish himself as a medical practitioner in the town of Hawick, but the drudgeries of that calling in such a district soon exhausted his ardent temper, and he was now living in seclusion in his native cottage at Fowlsheils on the Yarrow, nearly opposite Newark Castle. His brother, Archibald Park (then tenant of a large farm on the Buccleuch estate), a man remarkable for strength both of mind and body, introduced the trav

eller to the Sheriff. They soon became much attached to
each other; and Scott supplied some interesting anecdotes
of their brief intercourse to Mr. Wishaw, the editor of
Park's posthumous Journal, with which I shall blend a
few minor circumstances, gathered from him in conversation long afterwards. "On one occasion," he says, "the
traveller communicated to him some very remarkable
adventures which had befallen him in Africa, but which
he had not recorded in his book." On Scott's asking the
cause of this silence, Mungo answered, "That in all
cases where he had information to communicate, which
he thought of importance to the public, he had stated the
facts boldly, leaving it to his readers to give such credit
to his statements as they might appear justly to deserve;
but that he would not shock their faith, or render his travels
more marvellous, by introducing circumstances, which,
however true, were of little or no moment, as they related
solely to his own personal adventures and escapes." This
reply struck Scott as highly characteristic of the man;
and though strongly tempted to set down some of these
marvels for Mr. Wishaw's use, he on reflection abstained
from doing so, holding it unfair to record what the adventurer had deliberately chosen to suppress in his own narrative. He confirms the account given by Park's biographer, of his cold and reserved manners to strangers;
and, in particular, of his disgust with the *indirect* questions which curious visitors would often put to him upon
the subject of his travels. "This practice," said Mungo,
"exposes me to two risks; either that I may not understand the questions meant to be put, or that my answers
to them may be misconstrued;" and he contrasted such
conduct with the frankness of Scott's revered friend, Dr.
Adam Ferguson, who, the very first day the traveller
dined with him at Hallyards, spread a large map of
Africa on the table, and made him trace out his progress
thereupon, inch by inch, questioning him minutely as to
every step he had taken. "Here, however," says Scott,

"Dr. F. was using a privilege to which he was well entitled by his venerable age and high literary character, but
which could not have been exercised with propriety by
any common stranger."

Calling one day at Fowlsheils, and not finding Park
at home, Scott walked in search of him along the banks
of the Yarrow, which in that neighborhood passes over
various ledges of rock, forming deep pools and eddies
between them. Presently he discovered his friend standing alone on the bank, plunging one stone after another
into the water, and watching anxiously the bubbles as
they rose to the surface. "This," said Scott, "appears
but an idle amusement for one who has seen so much
stirring adventure." "Not so idle, perhaps, as you
suppose," answered Mungo: "This was the manner in
which I used to ascertain the depth of a river in Africa
before I ventured to cross it — judging whether the attempt would be safe, by the time the bubbles of air took
to ascend." At this time Park's intention of a second
expedition had never been revealed to Scott; but he instantly formed the opinion that these experiments on
Yarrow were connected with some such purpose.

His thoughts had always continued to be haunted with
Africa. He told Scott, that whenever he awoke suddenly
in the night, owing to a nervous disorder with which he
was troubled, he fancied himself still a prisoner in the
tent of Ali; but when the poet expressed some surprise
that he should design again to revisit those scenes, he
answered, that he would rather brave Africa and all its
horrors, than wear out his life in long and toilsome rides
over the hills of Scotland, for which the remuneration
was hardly enough to keep soul and body together.

Towards the end of the autumn, when about to quit
his country for the last time, Park paid Scott a farewell
visit, and slept at Ashestiel. Next morning his host
accompanied him homewards over the wild chain of hills
between the Tweed and the Yarrow. Park talked much

of his new scheme, and mentioned his determination to tell his family that he had some business for a day or two in Edinburgh, and send them his blessing from thence, without returning to take leave. He had married, not long before, a pretty and amiable woman; and when they reached the *Williamhope ridge,* "the autumnal mist floating heavily and slowly down the valley of the Yarrow" presented to Scott's imagination "a striking emblem of the troubled and uncertain prospect which his undertaking afforded." He remained, however, unshaken, and at length they reached the spot at which they had agreed to separate. A small ditch divided the moor from the road, and, in going over it, Park's horse stumbled, and nearly fell. "I am afraid, Mungo," said the Sheriff, "that is a bad omen." To which he answered, smiling, "*Freits* (omens) follow those who look to them." With this expression Mungo struck the spurs into his horse, and Scott never saw him again. His parting proverb, by the way, was probably suggested by one of the Border ballads, in which species of lore he was almost as great a proficient as the Sheriff himself; for we read in Edom o' Gordon, —

> "Them look to freits, my master dear,
> Then freits will follow them."

I must not omit that George Scott, the unfortunate companion of Park's second journey, was the son of a tenant on the Buccleuch estate, whose skill in drawing having casually attracted the Sheriff's attention, he was recommended by him to the protection of the family, and by this means established in a respectable situation in the Ordnance department of the Tower of London; but the stories of his old acquaintance Mungo Park's discoveries had made such an impression on his fancy, that nothing could prevent his accompanying him on the fatal expedition of 1805.

The brother of Mungo Park remained in Scott's neighborhood for some years, and was frequently his compan-

ion in his mountain rides. Though a man of the most
dauntless temperament, he was often alarmed at Scott's
reckless horsemanship. "The de'il 's in ye, Sherra," he
would say; "ye 'll never halt till they bring you hame
with your feet foremost." He rose greatly in favor, in
consequence of the gallantry with which he assisted the
Sheriff in seizing a gypsy, accused of murder, from amidst
a group of similar desperadoes, on whom they had come
unexpectedly in a desolate part of the country.

To return to The Lay of the Last Minstrel: Ellis,
understanding it to be now nearly ready for the press,
writes to Scott, urging him to set it forth with some
engraved illustrations — if possible, after Flaxman, whose
splendid designs from Homer had shortly before made
their appearance. He answers, August 21: "I should
have liked very much to have had appropriate embellishments. Indeed, we made some attempts of the kind, but
they did not succeed. I should fear Flaxman's genius
is too classic to stoop to body forth my Gothic Borderers.
Would there not be some risk of their resembling the
antique of Homer's heroes, rather than the iron race of
Salvator? After all, perhaps, nothing is more difficult
than for a painter to adopt the author's ideas of an imaginary character, especially when it is founded on traditions
to which the artist is a stranger. I should like at least
to be at his elbow when at work. I wish very much I
could have sent you the Lay while in MS., to have had
the advantage of your opinion and corrections. But
Ballantyne galled my kibes so severely during an unusual
fit of activity, that I gave him the whole story in a sort
of pet both with him and with it. . . . I have lighted
upon a very good amanuensis for copying such matters
as the Lay le Frain, etc. He was sent down here by
some of the London booksellers in a half-starved state,
but begins to pick up a little. . . . I am just about to
set out on a grand expedition of great importance to my
comfort in this place. You must know that Mr. Plum-

mer, my predecessor in this county, was a good antiquary, and left a valuable collection of books, which he
entailed with the estate, the first successors being three
of his sisters, at least as old and musty as any Caxton or
Wynkyn de Worde in his library. Now I must contrive
to coax those watchful dragons to give me admittance into
this garden of the Hesperides. I suppose they trouble
the volumes as little as *the* dragon did the golden pippins;
but they may not be the more easily soothed on that
account. However, I set out on my *quest*, like a *preux
chevalier*, taking care to leave Camp, for dirtying the
carpet, and to carry the greyhounds with me, whose appearance will indicate that hare-soup may be forthcoming
in due season. By the way, did I tell you that Fitz-
Camp is dead, and another on the stocks? As our stupid
postman might mistake *Reged*, address, as per date,
Ashestiel, Selkirk, by Berwick."

I believe the spinsters of Sunderland Hall proved very
generous dragons; and Scott lived to see them succeeded
in the guardianship of Mr. Plummer's literary treasures
by an amiable young gentleman of his own name and
family. The half-starved amanuensis of this letter was
Henry Weber, a laborious German, of whom we shall
hear more hereafter. With regard to the pictorial embellishments contemplated for the first edition of The Lay
of the Last Minstrel, I believe the artist in whose designs the poet took the greatest interest was Mr. Mas-
querier, now of Brighton, with whom he corresponded at
some length on the subject; but his distance from that
ingenious gentleman's residence was inconvenient, and
the booksellers were probably impatient of delay, when
the MS. was once known to be in the hands of the
printer.

There is a circumstance which must already have struck
such of my readers as knew the author in his latter days,
namely, the readiness with which he seems to have communicated this poem, in its progress, not only to his own

familiar friends, but to new and casual acquaintances.
We shall find him following the same course with his
Marmion — but not, I think, with any of his subsequent
works. His determination to consult the movements of
his own mind alone in the conduct of his pieces was
probably taken before he began the Lay; and he soon
resolved to trust for the detection of minor inaccuracies
to two persons only — James Ballantyne and William
Erskine. The printer was himself a man of considerable
literary talents: his own style had the incurable faults
of pomposity and affectation, but his eye for more venial
errors in the writings of others was quick, and, though
his personal address was apt to give a stranger the impression of insincerity, he was in reality an honest man, and
conveyed his mind on such matters with equal candor
and delicacy during the whole of Scott's brilliant career.
In the vast majority of instances he found his friend ac-
quiesce at once in the propriety of his suggestions; nay,
there certainly were cases, though rare, in which his
advice to alter things of much more consequence than a
word or a rhyme was frankly tendered, and on deliberation adopted by Scott. Mr. Erskine was the referee
whenever the poet hesitated about taking the hints of the
zealous typographer; and his refined taste and gentle
manners rendered his critical alliance highly valuable.
With two such faithful friends within his reach, the
author of the Lay might safely dispense with sending his
MS. to be revised even by George Ellis.

Before he left Ashestiel for the winter session, the
printing of the poem had made considerable progress.
Ellis writes to him on the 10th November, complaining
of bad health, and adds: "Tu quid agis? I suppose
you are still an inhabitant of Reged, and being there, it
is impossible that your head should have been solely
occupied by the ten thousand cares which you are likely
to have in common with other mortals, or even by the
Lay, which must have been long since completed, but

must have started during the summer new projects sufficient to employ the lives of half-a-dozen patriarchs.
Pray tell me all about it, for as the present state of my
frame precludes me from much activity, I want to enjoy
that of my friends." Scott answers from Edinburgh:
"I fear you fall too much into the sedentary habits incident to a literary life, like my poor friend Plummer, who
used to say that a walk from the parlor to the garden
once a day was sufficient exercise for any rational being,
and that no one but a fool or a fox-hunter would take
more. I wish you could have had a seat on Hassan's
tapestry, to have brought Mrs. Ellis and you soft and
fair to Ashestiel, where, with farm mutton at 4 P. M.,
and goat's whey at 6 A. M., I think we could have re-
established as much *embonpoint* as ought to satisfy a
poetical antiquary. As for my country amusements, I
have finished the Lay, with which and its accompanying
notes the press now groans; but I have started nothing
except some scores of hares, many of which my gallant
greyhounds brought to the ground."

Ellis had also touched upon a literary feud then raging
between Scott's allies of the Edinburgh Review, and the
late Dr. Thomas Young, illustrious for inventive genius,
displayed equally in physical science and in philological
literature. A northern critic, whoever he was, had
treated with merry contempt certain discoveries in natural philosophy and the mechanical arts, more especially
that of the undulating theory of light, which ultimately
conferred on Young's name one of its highest distinctions.
"He had been for some time," says Ellis, "lecturer at
the Royal Institution; and having determined to publish
his lectures, he had received from one of the booksellers
the offer of £1000 for the copyright. He was actually
preparing for the press, when the bookseller came to him,
and told him that the ridicule thrown by the Edinburgh
Review on some papers of his in the Philosophical Transactions had so frightened the whole *trade* that he must

request to be released from his bargain. This consequence, it is true, could not have been foreseen by the
reviewer, who, however, appears to have written from
feelings of private animosity; and I still continue to
think, though I greatly admire the good taste of the literary essays, and the perspicuity of the dissertations on
political economy, that an apparent want of candor is too
generally the character of a work which, from its independence on the interests of booksellers, might have been
expected to be particularly free from this defect." Scott
rejoins, "I am sorry for the very pitiful catastrophe of
Dr. Young's publication, because, although I am altogether unacquainted with the merits of the controversy,
one must always regret so very serious a consequence of
a diatribe. The truth is that these gentlemen reviewers
ought often to read over the fable of the boys and frogs,
and should also remember it is much more easy to destroy
than to build, to criticise than to compose. While on
this subject, I kiss the rod of my critic in the Edinburgh,
on the subject of the price of Sir Tristrem; it was not my
fault, however, that the public had it not cheap enough,
as I declined taking any copy-money, or share in the
profits; and *nothing*, surely, was as reasonable a charge
as I could make."

On the 30th December he resumes: "The Lay is now
ready, and will probably be in Longman and Rees's
hands shortly after this comes to yours. I have charged
them to send you a copy by the first conveyance, and
shall be impatient to know whether you think the entire
piece corresponds to that which you have already seen.
I would also fain send a copy to Gifford, by way of introduction. My reason is that I understand he is about to
publish an edition of Beaumont and Fletcher, and I think
I could offer him the use of some miscellaneous notes,
which I made long since on the margin of their works.[1]

[1] It was his *Massinger* that Gifford had at this time in hand. His *Ben
Jonson* followed, and then his *Ford*. Some time later, he projected edi-

Besides, I have a good esteem of Mr. Gifford as a manly English poet, very different from most of our modern versifiers. — We are so fond of Reged, that we are just going to set out for our farm in the middle of a snow-storm; all that we have to comfort ourselves with is, that our march has been ordered with great military talent — a detachment of minced pies and brandy having preceded us. In case we are not buried in a snow-wreath, our stay will be but short. Should that event happen, we must wait the thaw."

Ellis, not having as yet received the new poem, answers, on the 9th January, 1805, "I look daily and with the greatest anxiety for the Last Minstrel — of which I still hope to see a future edition decorated with designs à la *Flaxman*, as the Lays of Homer have already been. I think you told me that Sir Tristrem had not excited much sensation in Edinburgh. As I have not been in London this age, I can't produce the contrary testimony of our metropolis. But I can produce one person, and that one worth a considerable number, who speaks of it with rapture, and says, ' I am only sorry that Scott has not (and I am sure he has not) told us the whole of his creed on the subject of Tomas, and the other early Scotch Minstrels. I suppose he was afraid of the critics, and determined to say very little more than he was able to establish by incontestable proofs. I feel infinitely obliged to him for what he has told us, and I have no hesitation in saying that I consider Sir T. as by far the most interesting work that has as yet been published on the subject of our earliest poets, and, indeed, such a piece of literary antiquity as no one could have, *a priori*, supposed to exist.' This is Frere — our ex-ambassador for Spain, whom you would delight to know, and who would delight

---

tions, both of *Beaumont and Fletcher* and of *Shakespeare :* but, to the grievous misfortune of literature, died without having completed either of them. We shall see presently what became of Scott's Notes on *Beaumont and Fletcher*.

to know you. It is remarkable that *you* were, I believe, the *most ardent* of all the admirers of his old English version of the Saxon Ode;[1] and he is, *per contra*, the warmest panegyrist of your *Conclusion*, which he can repeat by heart, and affirms to be the very best imitation of old English at present existing. I think I can trust you for having concluded the Last Minstrel with as much spirit as it was begun — if you have been capable of anything unworthy of your fame amidst the highest mountains of Reged, there is an end of all inspiration."

Scott answers, "Frere is so perfect a master of the ancient style of composition, that I would rather have his suffrage than that of a whole synod of your vulgar antiquaries. The more I think on *our* system of the origin of Romance, the more simplicity and uniformity it seems to possess; and though I adopted it late and with hesitation, I believe I shall never see cause to abandon it. Yet I am aware of the danger of attempting to *prove*, where proofs are but scanty, and probable suppositions must be placed in lieu of them. I think the Welsh antiquaries have considerably injured their claims to confidence, by attempting to detail very remote events with all the accuracy belonging to the facts of yesterday. You will hear one of them describe you the cut of Llywarch Hen's beard, or the whittle of Urien Reged, as if he had trimmed the one, or cut his cheese with the other. These high pretensions weaken greatly our belief

---

[1] " I have only met, in my researches into these matters," says Scott in 1830, " with one poem, which, if it had been produced as ancient, could not have been detected on internal evidence. It is the *War Song upon the Victory at Brunnanburgh*, translated from the Anglo-Saxon into Anglo-Norman, by the Right Hon. John Hookham Frere. See Ellis's *Specimens of Ancient English Poetry*, vol. i. p. 32. The accomplished editor tells us, that this very singular poem was intended as an imitation of the style and language of the fourteenth century, and was written during the controversy occasioned by the poems attributed to Rowley. Mr. Ellis adds, ' The reader will probably hear with some surprise, that this singular instance of critical ingenuity was the composition of an Eton schoolboy.'" — *Essay on Imitations of the Ancient Ballad*, p. 19.

in the Welsh poems, which probably contain real treasures. 'T is a pity some sober-minded man will not take the trouble to sift the wheat from the chaff, and give us a good account of their MSS. and traditions. Pray, what is become of the Mabinogion? It is a proverb, that children and fools talk truth, and I am mistaken if even the same valuable quality may not sometimes be extracted out of the tales made to entertain both. I presume, while we talk of childish and foolish tales, that the Lay is already with you, although, in these points, *Long-manum est errare*. Pray inquire for your copy."

In the first week of January, 1805, the Lay was published; and its success at once decided that literature should form the main business of Scott's life.

In his modest Introduction of 1830, he had himself told us all that he thought the world would ever desire to know of the origin and progress of this his first great original production. The present Memoir, however, has already included many minor particulars, for which I believe no student of literature will reproach the compiler. I shall not mock the reader with many words as to the merits of a poem which has now kept its place for nearly a third of a century; but one or two additional remarks on the history of the composition may be pardoned.

It is curious to trace the small beginnings and gradual development of his design. The lovely Countess of Dalkeith hears a wild rude legend of Border *diablerie*, and sportively asks him to make it the subject of a ballad. He had been already laboring in the elucidation of the "quaint Inglis" ascribed to an ancient seer and bard of the same district, and perhaps completed his own sequel, intending the whole to be included in the third volume of the Minstrelsy. He assents to Lady Dalkeith's request, and casts about for some new variety of diction and rhyme, which might be adopted without impropriety in a closing strain for the same collection. Sir John

Stoddart's casual recitation, a year or two before, of Coleridge's unpublished Christabel, had fixed the music of that noble fragment in his memory; and it occurs to him, that by throwing the story of Gilpin Horner into somewhat of a similar cadence, he might produce such an echo of the later metrical romance, as would serve to connect his *Conclusion* of the primitive Sir Tristrem with his imitations of the common popular ballad in the Gray Brother and Eve of St. John. A single scene of feudal festivity in the hall of Branksome, disturbed by some pranks of a nondescript goblin, was probably all that he contemplated; but his accidental confinement in the midst of a volunteer camp gave him leisure to meditate his theme to the sound of the bugle; — and suddenly there flashes on him the idea of extending his simple outline, so as to embrace a vivid panorama of that old Border life of war and tumult, and all earnest passions, with which his researches on the Minstrelsy had by degrees fed his imagination, until every the minutest feature had been taken home and realized with unconscious intenseness of sympathy; so that he had won for himself in the past another world, hardly less complete or familiar than the present. Erskine or Cranstoun suggests that he would do well to divide the poem into cantos, and prefix to each of them a motto explanatory of the action, after the fashion of Spenser in the Faery Queen. He pauses for a moment — and the happiest conception of the framework of a picturesque narrative that ever occurred to any poet — one that Homer might have envied — the creation of the ancient harper, starts to life. By such steps did The Lay of the Last Minstrel grow out of the Minstrelsy of the Scottish Border.

A word more of its felicitous machinery. It was at Bowhill that the Countess of Dalkeith requested a ballad on Gilpin Horner. The ruined castle of Newark closely adjoins that seat, and is now indeed included within its *pleasance*. Newark had been the chosen residence of the first Duchess of Buccleuch, and he accordingly shadows out his own beautiful friend in the person of her lord's ancestress, the last of the original stock of that great house; himself the favored inmate of Bowhill, introduced certainly to the familiarity of its circle in consequence of his devotion to the poetry of a bypast age, in that of an aged minstrel, "the last of all the race," seeking shelter at the gate of Newark, in days when many an adherent of the fallen cause of Stewart — his own bearded ancestor, *who had fought at Killiecrankie*, among the rest — owed their safety to her who

> " In pride of power, in beauty's bloom,
>   Had wept o'er Monmouth's bloody tomb."

The arch allusions which run through all these Introductions, without in the least interrupting the truth and graceful pathos of their main impression, seem to me exquisitely characteristic of Scott, whose delight and pride was to play with the genius which nevertheless mastered him at will. For, in truth, what is it that gives to all his works their unique and marking charm, except the matchless effect which sudden effusions of the purest heart-blood of nature derive from their being poured out, to all appearance involuntarily, amidst diction and sentiment cast equally in the mould of the busy world, and the seemingly habitual desire to dwell on nothing but what might be likely to excite curiosity, without too much disturbing deeper feelings, in the saloons of polished life? Such outbursts come forth dramatically in all his writings; but in the interludes and passionate parentheses of The Lay of the Last Minstrel we have the poet's own inner soul and temperament laid bare and throbbing before us. Even here, indeed, he has a mask, and he trusts it — but fortunately it is a transparent one.

Many minor personal allusions have been explained in the notes to the last edition of the Lay. It was hardly necessary even then to say that the choice of the hero had been dictated by the poet's affection for the living descendants of the Baron of Cranstoun; and now — none who have perused the preceding pages can doubt that he had dressed out his Margaret of Branksome in the form and features of his own first love. This poem may be considered as the "bright consummate flower" in which all the dearest dreams of his youthful fancy had at length found expansion for their strength, spirit, tenderness, and beauty.

In the closing lines —

> " Hush'd is the harp — the Minstrel gone;
> And did he wander forth alone?
> Alone, in indigence and age,
> To linger out his pilgrimage?
> No! — close beneath proud Newark's tower
> Arose the Minstrel's humble bower," etc.

— in these charming lines he has embodied what was, at the time when he penned them, the chief day-dream of Ashestiel. From the moment that his uncle's death placed a considerable sum of ready money at his command, he pleased himself, as we have seen, with the idea of buying a mountain farm, and becoming not only the "sheriff" (as he had in former days delighted to call himself), but "the *Laird* of the Cairn and the Scaur." While he was "laboring *doucement* at the Lay" (as in one of his letters he expresses it), during the recess of 1804, circumstances rendered it next to certain that the small estate of *Broadmeadows*, situated just over against the ruins of Newark, on the northern bank of the Yarrow, would soon be exposed to sale; and many a time did he ride round it in company with Lord and Lady Dalkeith,

> " When summer smiled on sweet Bowhill,"

surveying the beautiful little domain with wistful eyes, and anticipating that

> " *There* would he sing achievement high
> And circumstance of chivalry,
> Till the 'rapt traveller would stay,

> Forgetful of the closing day;
> And noble youths, the strain to hear,
> Forget the hunting of the deer;
> And Yarrow, as he rolled along,
> Bear burden to the Minstrel's song."

I consider it as, in one point of view, the greatest misfortune of his life that this vision was not realized; but the success of the poem itself changed "the spirit of his dream." The favor which it at once attained had not been equalled in the case of any one poem of considerable length during at least two generations: it certainly had not been approached in the case of any narrative poem since the days of Dryden. Before it was sent to the press it had received warm commendation from the ablest and most influential critic of the time; but when Mr. Jeffrey's reviewal appeared, a month after publication, laudatory as its language was, it scarcely came up to the opinion which had already taken root in the public mind. It, however, quite satisfied the author; and were I at liberty to insert some letters which passed between them in the course of the summer of 1805, it would be seen that their feelings towards each other were those of mutual confidence and gratitude. Indeed, a severe domestic affliction which about this time befell Mr. Jeffrey called out the expression of such sentiments on both sides in a very touching manner.[1]

I abstain from transcribing the letters which conveyed to Scott the private opinions of persons themselves eminently distinguished in poetry; but I think it just to state that I have not discovered in any of them — no, not even in those of Wordsworth or Campbell — a strain of approbation higher on the whole than that of the chief professional reviewer of the period. When the happy days of youth are over, even the most genial and gener-

---

[1] [Catherine Wilson, Jeffrey's first wife, died August 8. 1805. A touching letter, written August 19, from the bereaved husband, warmly thanking Scott for his kindness and sympathy, will be found in the *Familiar Letters*, vol. i. p. 30.]

ous of minds are seldom able to enter into the strains of
a new poet with that full and open delight which he
awakens in the bosoms of the rising generation about
him.   Their deep and eager sympathies have already
been drawn upon to an extent of which the prosaic part
of the species can never have any conception; and when
the fit of creative inspiration has subsided, they are apt
to be rather cold critics even of their own noblest appeals
to the simple primary feelings of their kind.   Miss Seward's letter, on this occasion, has been since included in
the printed collection of her correspondence; but perhaps
the reader may form a sufficient notion of its tenor
from the poet's answer — which, at all events, he will be
amused to compare with the Introduction of 1830 : —

TO MISS SEWARD, LICHFIELD.

EDINBURGH, 21st March, 1805.

MY DEAR MISS SEWARD, — I am truly happy that
you found any amusement in The Lay of the Last Minstrel.   It has great faults, of which no one can be more
sensible than I am myself.   Above all, it is deficient in
that sort of continuity which a story ought to have, and
which, were it to write again, I would endeavor to give
it.   But I began and wandered forward, like one in a
pleasant country, getting to the top of one hill to see a
prospect, and to the bottom of another to enjoy a shade;
and what wonder if my course has been devious and
desultory, and many of my excursions altogether unprofitable to the advance of my journey?   The Dwarf Page
is also an excrescence, and I plead guilty to all the cen-
sures concerning him.   The truth is, he has a history,
and it is this: The story of Gilpin Horner was told by
an old gentleman to Lady Dalkeith, and she, much diverted with his actually believing so grotesque a tale,
insisted that I should make it into a Border ballad.   I
don't know if ever you saw my lovely chieftainess — if
you have, you must be aware that it is *impossible* for any

one to refuse her request, as she has more of the angel in face and temper than any one alive; so that if she had asked me to write a ballad on a broomstick, I must have attempted it. I began a few verses, to be called The Goblin Page; and they lay long by me, till the applause of some friends whose judgment I valued induced me to resume the poem; so on I wrote, knowing no more than the man in the moon how I was to end. At length the story appeared so uncouth, that I was fain to put it into the mouth of my old Minstrel — lest the nature of it should be misunderstood, and I should be suspected of setting up a new school of poetry, instead of a feeble attempt to imitate the old. In the process of the romance, the page, intended to be a principal person in the work, contrived (from the baseness of his natural propensities, I suppose) to slink downstairs into the kitchen, and now he must e'en abide there.

I mention these circumstances to you, and to any one whose applause I value, because I am unwilling you should suspect me of trifling with the public in *malice prepense*. As to the herd of critics, it is impossible for me to pay much attention to them; for, as they do not understand what I call poetry, we talk in a foreign language to each other. Indeed, many of these gentlemen appear to me to be a sort of tinkers, who, unable to *make* pots and pans, set up for *menders* of them, and, God knows, often make two holes in patching one. The sixth canto is altogether redundant; for the poem should certainly have closed with the union of the lovers, when the interest, if any, was at an end. But what could I do? I had my book and my page still on my hands, and must get rid of them at all events. Manage them as I would, their catastrophe must have been insufficient to occupy an entire canto; so I was fain to eke it out with the songs of the minstrels. I will now descend from the confessional, which I think I have occupied long enough for the patience of my fair confessor. I am happy you

are disposed to give me absolution, notwithstanding all
my sins.

We have a new poet come forth amongst us — James
Grahame, author of a poem called The Sabbath, which I
admire very much. If I can find an opportunity, I will
send you a copy. Your affectionate humble servant,

WALTER SCOTT.

Mr. Ellis does not seem to have written at any length
on the subject of the Lay, until he had perused the article in the Edinburgh Review. He then says: "Though
I had previously made up my mind, or rather perhaps
because I had done so, I was very anxious to compare
my sentiments with those of the Edinburgh critic, and I
found that in general we were perfectly agreed, though
there are parts of the subject which we consider from very
different points of view. Frere, with whom I had not
any previous communication about it, agrees with me; and
trusting very much to the justice of his poetical feelings,
I feel some degree of confidence in my own judgment
— though in opposition to Mr. Jeffrey, whose criticism
I admire, upon the whole, extremely, as being equally
acute and impartial, and as exhibiting the fairest judgment respecting the work that could be formed by the
mere assistance of good sense and general taste, without
that particular sort of taste which arises from the study
of romantic compositions.

"What Frere and myself think, must be stated in the
shape of a *hypercriticism* — that is to say, of a review
of the reviewer. We say that The Lay of the Last Minstrel is a work *sui generis*, written with the *intention* of
exhibiting what our old romances do indeed exhibit in
point of fact, but incidentally, and often without the wish,
or rather contrary to the wish of the author; — namely,
the manners of a particular age; and that therefore, if it
does this truly, and is at the same time capable of keeping the steady attention of the reader, it is so far perfect.

This is also a poem, and ought therefore to contain a great deal of poetical merit. This indeed it does by the admission of the reviewer, and it must be admitted that he has shown much real taste in estimating the most beautiful passages; but he finds fault with many of the lines as careless, with some as prosaic, and contends that the story is not sufficiently full of incident, and that one of the incidents is borrowed from a merely local superstition, etc., etc. To this we answer — 1st, That if the Lay were intended to give *any* idea of the Minstrel compositions, it would have been a most glaring absurdity to have rendered the poetry as perfect and uniform as the works usually submitted to modern readers — and as in telling a story, nothing, or very little, would be lost, though the merely connecting part of the narrative were in plain prose, the reader is certainly no loser by the incorrectness of the smaller parts. Indeed, who is so unequal as Dryden? It may be said, that he was not intentionally so — but to be *very smooth* is very often to be *tame;* and though this should be admitted to be a less important fault than inequality in a common modern poem, there can be no doubt with respect to the necessity of subjecting yourself to the latter fault (if it is one) in an imitation of an ancient model. 2d, Though it is naturally to be expected that many readers will expect an almost infinite accumulation of incidents in a romance, this is only because readers in general have acquired all their ideas on the subject from the prose romances, which commonly contained a farrago of metrical stories. The *only* thing *essential* to a romance was, that it should be *believed* by the hearers. Not only tournaments, but battles, are indeed accumulated in some of our ancient romances, because tradition had of course ascribed to every great conqueror a great number of conquests, and the minstrel would have been thought deficient, if, in a warlike age, he had omitted any military event. But in other respects a paucity of incident is the general char-

acteristic of our Minstrel poems. 3d, With respect to
the Goblin Page, it is by no means necessary that the
superstition on which this is founded should be universally or even generally current. It is quite sufficient
that it should exist somewhere in the neighborhood of
the castle where the scene is placed; and it cannot fairly
be required, that because the goblin is mischievous, all
his tricks should be directed to the production of general
evil. The old idea of goblins seems to have been that
they were essentially active, and careless about the mischief they produced, rather than providentially malicious.

"We therefore (*i. e.*, Frere and myself) dissent from
all the reviewer's objections to these circumstances in the
narrative; but we entertain some doubts about the propriety of dwelling so long on the Minstrel songs in the
last canto. I say we *doubt*, because we are not aware of
your having *ancient authority* for such a practice; but
though the attempt was a bold one, inasmuch as it is not
usual to add a whole canto to a story which is already finished, we are far from wishing that you had left it unattempted. I must tell you the answer of a philosopher
(Sir Henry Englefield) to a friend of his who was criticis-
ing the obscurity of the language used in the Minstrel.
' I read little poetry, and often am in doubt whether I
exactly understand the poet's meaning; but I found,
after reading the Minstrel three times, that I understood it
all perfectly.' ' Three times?' replied his friend. ' Yes,
certainly; the first time I discovered that there was a
great deal of meaning in it; a second would have cleared
it all up, but that I was run away with by the beautiful
passages, which distracted my attention; the third time
I skipped over these, and only attended to the scheme
and structure of the poem, with which I am delighted.'
At this conversation I was present, and though I could
not help smiling at Sir Henry's mode of reading poetry,
was pleased to see the degree of interest which he took
in the narrative."

Mr. Morritt informs me that he well remembers the dinner where this conversation occurred, and thinks Mr. Ellis has omitted in his report the best thing that Sir Harry Englefield said, in answer to one of the *Dii Minorum Gentium*, who made himself conspicuous by the severity of his censure on the verbal inaccuracies and careless lines of the Lay. "My dear sir," said the Baronet, "you remind me of a lecture on sculpture, which M. Falconet delivered at Rome, shortly after completing the model of his equestrian statue of Czar Peter, now at Petersburg. He took for his subject the celebrated horse of Marcus Aurelius in the Capitol, and pointed out as many faults in it as ever a jockey did in an animal he was about to purchase. But something came over him, vain as he was, when he was about to conclude the harangue. He took a long pinch of snuff, and eyeing his own faultless model, exclaimed with a sigh, *Cependant, Messieurs, il faut avouer que cette vilaine bête là est vivante, et que la mienne est morte!* "

To return to Ellis's letter, I fancy most of my readers will agree with me in thinking that Sir Henry Englefield's method of reading and enjoying poetry was more to be envied than smiled at; and in doubting whether posterity will ever dispute about the "*propriety*" of the Canto which includes the Ballad of Rosabelle, and the Requiem of Melrose. The friendly *hypercritics* seem, I confess, to have judged the poem on principles not less pedantic, though of another kind of pedantry, than those which induced the *critic* to pronounce that its great prevailing blot originated in "those local partialities of the author," which had induced him to expect general interest and sympathy for such personages as his "Johnstones, Elliots, and Armstrongs." "Mr. Scott," said Jeffrey, "must either sacrifice his Border prejudices, or offend his readers in the other parts of the empire." It might have been answered by Ellis or Frere, that these Border clans figured after all on a scene at least as wide as the Troad;

and that their chiefs were not perhaps inferior, either in rank or power, to the majority of the Homeric kings; but even the most zealous of its admirers among the professed literators of the day would hardly have ventured to suspect that The Lay of the Last Minstrel might have no prejudices to encounter but their own. It was destined to charm not only the British empire, but the whole civilized world; and had, in fact, exhibited a more Homeric genius than any regular epic since the days of Homer.

"It would be great affectation," says the Introduction of 1830, "not to own that the author expected some success from The Lay of the Last Minstrel. The attempt to return to a more simple and natural poetry was likely to be welcomed, at a time when the public had become tired of heroic hexameters, with all the buckram and binding that belong to them in modern days. But whatever might have been his expectations, whether moderate or unreasonable, the result left them far behind; for among those who smiled on the adventurous minstrel were numbered the great names of William Pitt and Charles Fox. Neither was the extent of the sale inferior to the character of the judges who received the poem with approbation. Upwards of 30,000 copies were disposed of by the trade; and the author had to perform a task difficult to human vanity, when called upon to make the necessary deductions from his own merits, in a calm attempt to account for its popularity."

Through what channel or in what terms Fox made known his opinion of the Lay, I have failed to ascertain. Pitt's praise, as expressed to his niece, Lady Hester Stanhope, within a few weeks after the poem appeared, was repeated by her to Mr. William Stewart Rose, who, of course, communicated it forthwith to the author; and not long after, the Minister, in conversation with Scott's early friend the Right Hon. William Dundas, signified that it would give him pleasure to find some opportunity of advancing the fortunes of such a writer. "I remember," writes this gentleman, "at Mr. Pitt's table in 1805, the Chancellor asked me about you and your then situation, and after I had answered him, Mr. Pitt observed, ' He can't remain as he is,' and desired me to ' look to it.' He then repeated some lines from the Lay, describing the old harper's embarrassment when asked to play, and said, ' This is a sort of thing which I might have expected in painting, but could never have fancied capable of being given in poetry.' " [1]

It is agreeable to know that this great statesman and accomplished scholar awoke at least once from his supposed apathy as to the elegant literature of his own time.

The poet has under-estimated even the patent and tangible evidence of his success. The first edition of the Lay was a magnificent quarto, 750 copies; but this was soon exhausted, and there followed an octavo impression of 1500; in 1806, two more, one of 2000 copies, another of 2250; in 1807, a fifth edition, of 2000, and a sixth, of 3000; in 1808, 3550; in 1809, 3000 — a small edition in quarto (the ballads and lyrical pieces being then annexed to it) — and another octavo edition of 3250; in 1811, 3000; in 1812, 3000; in 1816, 3000; in 1823, 1000. A fourteenth impression of 2000 foolscap appeared in 1825; and besides all this, before the end of 1836, 11,000 copies had gone forth in the collected editions of his poetical works. Thus, nearly forty-four thousand copies had been disposed of in this country, and by the legitimate trade alone, before he superintended the edition of 1830, to which his biographical introductions were prefixed. In the history of British Poetry nothing had ever equalled the demand for The Lay of the Last Minstrel.

The publishers of the first edition were Longman and Co. of London, and Archibald Constable and Co. of

[1] Letter dated April 25, 1818, and indorsed by Scott, "*William Dundas — a very kind letter.*"

Edinburgh; which last house, however, had but a small share in the adventure. The profits were to be divided equally between the author and his publishers; and Scott's moiety was £169 6s. Messrs. Longman, when a second edition was called for, offered £500 for the copyright; this was accepted, but they afterwards, as the Introduction says, "added £100 in their own unsolicited kindness. It was handsomely given to supply the loss of a fine horse which broke down suddenly while the author was riding with one of the worthy publishers." This worthy publisher was Mr. Owen Rees, and the gallant steed, to whom a desperate leap in the coursing-field proved fatal, was, I believe, Captain, the immediate successor of Lenore, as Scott's charger in the volunteer cavalry; Captain was replaced by Lieutenant. The author's whole share, then, in the profits of the Lay came to £769 6s.

Mr. Rees's visit to Ashestiel occurred in the autumn. The success of the poem had already been decisive; and fresh negotiations of more kinds than one were at this time in progress between Scott and various booksellers' houses, both of Edinburgh and London.

CHAPTER XIV

1805

MR. BALLANTYNE, in his Memorandum, says, that
very shortly after the publication of the Lay, he found
himself obliged to apply to Mr. Scott for an advance of
money; his own capital being inadequate for the business which had been accumulated on his press, in consequence of the reputation it had acquired for beauty and
correctness of execution. Already, as we have seen,
Ballantyne had received "a liberal loan;" — "and now,"
says he, "being compelled, maugre all delicacy, to renew
my application, he candidly answered that he was not
quite sure that it would be prudent for him to comply,
but in order to evince his entire confidence in me, he was
willing to make a suitable advance to be admitted as a
third-sharer of my business." In truth, Scott now em-
barked in Ballantyne's concern almost the whole of the
capital which he had a few months before designed to

invest in the purchase of Broadmeadows. *Dis aliter visum.*

I have, many pages back, hinted my suspicion that he had formed some distant notion of such an alliance, as early as the date of Ballantyne's projected removal from Kelso to Edinburgh; and his Introduction to the Lay, in 1830, appears to leave little doubt that the hope of ultimately succeeding at the Bar had waxed very faint, before the third volume of the Minstrelsy was brought out in 1803. When that hope ultimately vanished altogether, perhaps he himself would not have found it easy to tell. The most important of men's opinions, views, and projects, are sometimes taken up in so very gradual a manner, and after so many pauses of hesitation and of inward retractation, that they themselves are at a loss to trace in retrospect all the stages through which their minds have passed. We see plainly that Scott had never been fond of his profession, but that, conscious of his own persevering diligence, he ascribed his scanty success in it mainly to the prejudices of the Scotch solicitors against employing, in weighty causes at least, any barrister supposed to be strongly imbued with the love of literature; instancing the career of his friend Jeffrey as almost the solitary instance within his experience of such prejudices being entirely overcome. Had Scott, to his strong sense and dexterous ingenuity, his well-grounded knowledge of the jurisprudence of his country, and his admirable industry, added a brisk and ready talent for debate and declamation, I can have no doubt that his triumph over the prejudices alluded to would have been as complete as Mr. Jeffrey's; nor in truth do I much question that, had one really great and interesting case been submitted to his sole care and management, the result would have been to place his professional character for skill and judgment, and variety of resource, on so firm a basis, that even his rising celebrity as a man of letters could not have seriously disturbed it. Nay, I think it quite possible, that had he been entrusted with one such case after his reputation was established, and he had been compelled to do his abilities some measure of justice in his own secret estimate, he might have displayed very considerable powers even as a forensic speaker. But no opportunities of this engaging kind having ever been presented to him — after he had persisted for more than ten years in sweeping the floor of the Parliament House, without meeting with any employment but what would have suited the dullest drudge, and seen himself termly and yearly more and more distanced by contemporaries for whose general capacity he could have had little respect — while, at the same time, he already felt his own position in the eyes of society at large to have been signally elevated in consequence of his extra-professional exertions — it is not wonderful that disgust should have gradually gained upon him, and that the sudden blaze and tumult of renown which surrounded the author of the Lay should have at last determined him to concentrate all his ambition on the pursuits which had alone brought him distinction. It ought to be mentioned, that the business in George's Square, once extensive and lucrative, had dwindled away in the hands of his brother Thomas, whose varied and powerful talents were unfortunately combined with some tastes by no means favorable to the successful prosecution of his prudent father's vocation; so that very possibly even the humble employment of which, during his first years at the Bar, Scott had at least a sure and respectable allowance, was by this time much reduced. I have not his fee-books of later date than 1803: it is, however, my impression from the whole tenor of his conversation and correspondence, that after that period he had not only not advanced as a professional man, but had been retrograding in nearly the same proportion that his literary reputation advanced.

We have seen that, before he formed his contract with

Ballantyne, he was in possession of such a fixed income as might have satisfied all his desires, had he not found his family increasing rapidly about him. Even as that was, with nearly if not quite £1000 per annum, he might perhaps have retired not only from the Bar, but from Edinburgh, and settled entirely at Ashestiel or Broadmeadows, without encountering what any man of his station and habits ought to have considered as an imprudent risk. He had, however, no wish to cut himself off from the busy and intelligent society to which he had been hitherto accustomed; and resolved not to leave the Bar until he should have at least used his best efforts for obtaining, in addition to his Shrievalty, one of those Clerkships of the Supreme Court at Edinburgh, which are usually considered as honorable retirements for advocates who, at a certain standing, finally give up all hopes of reaching the dignity of the Bench. "I determined," he says, "that literature should be my staff but not my crutch, and that the profits of my literary labor, however convenient otherwise, should not, if I could help it, become necessary to my ordinary expenses. Upon such a post an author might hope to retreat, without any perceptible alteration of circumstances, whenever the time should arrive that the public grew weary of his endeavors to please, or he himself should tire of the pen. I possessed so many friends capable of assisting me in this object of ambition, that I could hardly overrate my own prospects of obtaining the preferment to which I limited my wishes; and, in fact, I obtained, in no long period, the reversion of a situation which completely met them." [1]

The first notice of this affair that occurs in his correspondence is in a note of Lord Dalkeith's, February the 2d, 1805, in which his noble friend says, "My father desires me to tell you that he has had a communication with Lord Melville within these few days, and that he thinks *your business is in a good train, though not cer-*

[1] Introduction to *The Lay of the Last Minstrel* — 1830.

tain." I consider it as clear, then, that he began his negotiations concerning a seat at the clerk's table immediately after the Lay was published; and that their commencement had been resolved upon in the strictest connection with his embarkation in the printing concern of James Ballantyne and Company. Such matters are seldom speedily arranged; but we shall find him in possession of his object before twelve months had elapsed.

Meanwhile, his design of quitting the Bar was divulged to none but those immediately necessary for the purposes of his negotiation with the Government; and the nature of his connection with the printing company remained, I believe, not only unknown, but for some years wholly unsuspected, by any of his daily companions except Mr. Erskine.

The forming of this commercial connection was one of the most important steps in Scott's life. He continued bound by it during twenty years, and its influence on his literary exertions and his worldly fortunes was productive of much good and not a little evil. Its effects were in truth so mixed and balanced during the vicissitudes of a long and vigorous career, that I at this moment doubt whether it ought, on the whole, to be considered with more of satisfaction or of regret.

With what zeal he proceeded in advancing the views of the new copartnership, his correspondence bears ample evidence. The brilliant and captivating genius, now acknowledged universally, was soon discovered by the leading booksellers of the time to be united with such abundance of matured information in many departments, and, above all, with such indefatigable habits, as to mark him out for the most valuable workman they could engage for the furtherance of their schemes. He had, long before this, cast a shrewd and penetrating eye over the field of literary enterprise, and developed in his own mind the outlines of many extensive plans, which wanted nothing but the command of a sufficient body of able subalterns to be carried into execution with splendid success. Such of these as he grappled with in his own person were, with rare exceptions, carried to a triumphant conclusion; but the alliance with Ballantyne soon infected him with the proverbial rashness of mere mercantile adventure — while, at the same time, his generous feelings for other men of letters, and his characteristic propensity to overrate their talents, combined to hurry him and his friends into a multitude of arrangements, the results of which were often extremely embarrassing, and ultimately, in the aggregate, all but disastrous. It is an old saying, that wherever there is a secret there must be something wrong; and dearly did he pay the penalty for the mystery in which he had chosen to involve this transaction. It was his rule, from the beginning, that whatever he wrote or edited must be printed at that press; and had he catered for it only as author and sole editor, all had been well; but had the booksellers known his direct pecuniary interest in keeping up and extending the occupation of those types, they would have taken into account his lively imagination and sanguine temperament, as well as his taste and judgment, and considered, far more deliberately than they too often did, his multifarious recommendations of new literary schemes, coupled though these were with some dim understanding that, if the Ballantyne press were employed, his own literary skill would be at his friend's disposal for the general superintendence of the undertaking. On the other hand, Scott's suggestions were, in many cases, perhaps in the majority of them, conveyed through Ballantyne, whose habitual deference to his opinion induced him to advocate them with enthusiastic zeal; and the printer, who had thus pledged his personal authority for the merits of the proposed scheme, must have felt himself committed to the bookseller, and could hardly refuse with decency to take a certain share of the pecuniary risk, by allowing the time and method of his own payment to be regulated according to the employer's convenience. Hence, by degrees, was woven a web of entanglement from which neither Ballantyne nor his adviser had any means of escape, except only in that indomitable spirit, the mainspring of personal industry altogether unparalleled, to which, thus set in motion, the world owes its most gigantic monument of literary genius.

The following is the first letter I have found of Scott to his PARTNER. The Mr. Foster mentioned in the beginning of it was a literary gentleman who had proposed to take on himself a considerable share in the annotation of some of the new *editions* then on the carpet — among others, one of Dryden.

TO MR. JAMES BALLANTYNE, PRINTER, EDINBURGH.

ASHESTIEL, April 12, 1805.

DEAR BALLANTYNE, — I have duly received your two favors — also Foster's. He still howls about the expense of printing, but I think we shall finally settle. His argument is that you print too fine, *alias* too dear. I intend to stick to my answer, that I know nothing of the matter; but that settle it how you and he will, it must be printed by you, or can be no concern of mine. This gives you an advantage in driving the bargain. As to everything else, I think we shall do, and I will endeavor to set a few volumes agoing on the plan you propose.

I have imagined a very superb work. What think you of a complete edition of British Poets, ancient and modern? Johnson's is imperfect and out of print; so is Bell's, which is a Lilliputian thing; and Anderson's, the most complete in point of number, is most contemptible in execution both of the editor and printer. There is a scheme for you! At least a hundred volumes, to be published at the rate of ten a year. I cannot, however, be ready till midsummer. If the booksellers will give me a decent allowance per volume, say thirty guineas, I

shall hold myself well paid on the *writing* hand.   This is
a dead secret.

I think it quite right to let Doig[1] have a share of
Thomson;[2] but he is hard and slippery, so settle your
bargain fast and firm — no loop-holes!   I am glad you
have got some elbow-room at last.   Cowan will come to,
or we will find some fit place in time.   If not, we *must*
build — necessity has no law.   I see nothing to hinder
you from doing Tacitus with your correctness of eye, and
I congratulate you on the fair prospect before us.   When
you have time, you will make out a list of the debts to be
discharged at Whitsunday, that we may see what cash
we shall have in bank.   Our book-keeping may be very
simple — an accurate cash-book and ledger is all that is
necessary; and I think I know enough of the matter to
assist at making the balance sheet.

In short, with the assistance of a little cash I have no
doubt things will go on *à merveille*.   If you could take
a little pleasuring, I wish you could come here and see
us in all the glories of a Scottish spring.

Yours truly,   W. SCOTT.

Scott opened forthwith his gigantic scheme of the
British Poets to Constable, who entered into it with
eagerness.   They found presently that Messrs. Cadell
and Davies, and some of the other London publishers,
had a similar plan on foot, and after an unsuccessful
negotiation with Mackintosh, were now actually treating
with Campbell for the Biographical prefaces.   Scott proposed that the Edinburgh and London houses should join
in the adventure, and that the editorial task should be
shared between himself and his brother poet.   To this
both Messrs. Cadell and Mr. Campbell warmly assented;
but the design ultimately fell to the ground, in consequence of the booksellers refusing to admit certain works

---

[1] A bookseller in Edinburgh.
[2] A projected edition of the Works of the author of the *Seasons*.

which both Scott and Campbell insisted upon. Such, and from analogous causes, has been the fate of various similar schemes both before and since. But the public had no trivial compensation upon the present occasion, since the failure of the original project led Mr. Campbell to prepare for the press those Specimens of English Poetry which he illustrated with sketches of biography and critical essays, alike honorable to his learning and taste; while Scott, Mr. Foster ultimately standing off, took on himself the whole burden of a new edition, as well as biography, of Dryden. The body of booksellers meanwhile combined in what they still called a *general edition* of the English Poets, under the superintendence of one of their own Grub Street vassals, Mr. Alexander Chalmers.

Precisely at the time when Scott's poetical ambition had been stimulated by the first outburst of universal applause, and when he was forming those engagements with Ballantyne which involved so large an accession of literary labors, as well as of pecuniary cares and responsibilities, a fresh impetus was given to the volunteer mania in Scotland, by the appointment of the late Earl of Moira (afterwards Marquis of Hastings) to the chief military command in that part of the empire. The Earl had married, the year before, a Scottish Peeress, the Countess of Loudon, and entered with great zeal into her sympathy with the patriotic enthusiasm of her countrymen. Edinburgh was converted into a camp: independently of a large garrison of regular troops, nearly 10,000 fencibles and volunteers were almost constantly under arms. The lawyer wore his uniform under his gown; the shopkeeper measured out his wares in scarlet; in short, the citizens of all classes made more use for several months of the military than of any other dress; and the new commander-in-chief consulted equally his own gratification and theirs, by devising a succession of manœuvres which presented a vivid image of the art of war conducted on a large and scientific scale. In the *sham battles* and *sham sieges* of 1805, Craigmillar, Gilmerton, Braidhills, and other formidable positions in the neighborhood of Edinburgh, were the scenes of many a dashing assault and resolute defence; and occasionally the spirits of the mock combatants — English and Scotch, or Lowland and Highland — became so much excited that there was some difficulty in preventing the rough mockery of warfare from passing into its realities. The Highlanders, in particular, were very hard to be dealt with; and once, at least, Lord Moira was forced to alter at the eleventh hour his programme of battle, because a battalion of kilted fencibles could not or would not understand that it was their duty to be beat. Such days as these must have been more nobly spirit-stirring than even the best specimens of the fox-chase. To the end of his life, Scott delighted to recall the details of their countermarches, ambuscades, charges, and pursuits, and in all of these his associates of the Light Horse agree that none figured more advantageously than himself. Yet these military interludes seem only to have whetted his appetite for closet work. Indeed, nothing but a complète publication of his letters could give an adequate notion of the facility with which he already combined the conscientious magistrate, the martinet quartermaster, the speculative printer, and the ardent lover of literature for its own sake. A few specimens must suffice.

TO GEORGE ELLIS, ESQ.

EDINBURGH, May 26, 1805.

MY DEAR ELLIS, — Your silence has been so long and *opinionative*, that I am quite authorized, as a Border ballad-monger, to address you with a "Sleep you, or wake you?" What has become of the Romances? — which I have expected as anxiously as my neighbors around me have watched for the rain, which was to bring the grass, which was to feed the new-calved cows; and to as little purpose, for both Heaven and you have obstinately delayed your favors. After idling away the spring months at Ashestiel, I am just returned to idle away the summer here, and I have lately lighted upon rather an interesting article in your way. If you will turn to Barbour's Bruce (Pinkerton's edition, p. 66), you will find that the Lord of Lorn, seeing Bruce covering the retreat of his followers, compares him to Gow MacMorn (Macpherson's Gaul the son of Morni). This similitude appears to Barbour a disparagement, and he says, the Lord of Lorn might more mannerly have compared the King to Gadefeir de Lawryss, who was with the mighty Duke Betys when he assailed the forayers in Gadderis, and who in the retreat did much execution among the pursuers, overthrowing Alexander and Thelomier and Danklin, although he was at length slain; and here, says Barbour, the resemblance fails. Now, by one of those chances which favor the antiquary once in an age, a single copy of the romance alluded to has been discovered, containing the whole history of this Gadefeir, who had hitherto been a stumbling-block to the critics. The book was printed by Arbuthnot, who flourished at Edinburgh in the seventeenth century. It is a metrical romance, called The Buik of the Most Noble and Vauliant Conquerour, Alexander the Grit. The first part is called the Foray of Gadderis, an incident supposed to have taken place while Alexander was besieging Tyre; Gadefeir is one of the principal champions, and after exerting himself in the manner mentioned by Barbour, unhorsing the persons whom he named, he is at length slain by Emynedus, the Earl-Marshal of the Macedonian conqueror. The second part is called the Avowis of Alexander, because it introduces the oaths which he and others made to the peacock in the "chalmer of Venus," and gives an account of the mode in which they accomplished them. The third is the Great Battell of Effesoun, in which Porus makes a distinguished figure. This you are to understand is not *the* Porus of

India, but one of his sons. The work is in decided Scotch, and adds something to our ancient poetry, being by no means despicable in point of composition. The author says he translated it from the *Franch*, or *Romance*, and that he accomplished his work in 1438–39. Barbour must therefore have quoted from the French Alexander, and perhaps his praises of the work excited the Scottish translator. Will you tell me what you think of all this, and whether any transcripts will be of use to you? I am pleased with the accident of its casting up, and hope it may prove the forerunner of more discoveries in the dusty and ill-arranged libraries of our country gentlemen.

I hope you continue to like the Lay. I have had a flattering assurance of Mr. Fox's approbation, mixed with a censure of my eulogy on the Viscount of Dundee. Although my Tory principles prevent my coinciding with his political opinions, I am very proud of his approbation in a literary sense.

Charlotte joins me, etc., etc.   W. S.

In his answer Ellis says: —

"Longman lately informed me that you have projected a General Edition of our Poets. I expressed to him my anxiety that the booksellers, who certainly can ultimately sell what they please, should for once undertake something calculated to please intelligent readers, and that they should confine themselves to the selection of paper, types, etc. (which they possibly may understand), and by no means interfere with the literary part of the business, which, if popularity be the object, they must leave exclusively to you. I am talking, as you perceive, about your plan, without knowing its extent, or any of its details; for these, therefore, I will wait — after confessing that, much as I wish for a *corpus poetarum*, edited as you would edit it, I should like still better another Minstrel Lay by the last and best Minstrel; and the general demand for the poem seems to prove that the public are of my opinion. If, however, you don't feel disposed to take a second ride on Pegasus, why not undertake something far less *infra dig.* than a mere edition of our poets? Why not undertake what Gibbon once undertook — an edition of our historians? I have never been able to look at a volume of the Benedictine edition of the early French historians without envy."

Mr. Ellis appears to have communicated all his notions on this subject to Messrs. Longman, for Scott writes to Ballantyne (Ashestiel, September 5), "I have had a visit from Rees yesterday. He is anxious about a *corpus historiarum*, or full edition of the Chronicles of England, an immense work. I proposed to him beginning with Holinshed, and I think the work will be secured for your press. I congratulate you on Clarendon, which, under Thomson's direction, will be a glorious publication."[1]

The printing-office in the Canongate was by this time in very great request; and the letter I have been quoting contains evidence that the partners had already found it necessary to borrow fresh capital — on the personal security, it need not be added, of Scott himself. He says, "As I have full confidence in your applying the accommodation received from Sir William Forbes in the most convenient and prudent manner, I have no hesitation to return the bonds subscribed as you desire. This will put you in cash for great matters."

But to return. To Ellis himself he says: —

"I have had booksellers here in the plural number. You have set little Rees's head agog about the Chronicles, which would be an admirable work, but should, I think, be edited by an Englishman who can have access to the MSS. of Oxford and Cambridge, as one cannot trust much to the correctness of printed copies. I will, however, consider the matter, so far as a decent edition of Holinshed is concerned, in case my time is not otherwise taken up. As for the British Poets, my plan was greatly too liberal to stand the least chance of being

---

[1] An edition of Clarendon had been, it seems, contemplated by Scott's friend, Mr. Thomas Thomson.

adopted by the trade at large, as I wished them to begin
with Chaucer. The fact is, I never expected they would
agree to it. The Benedictines had an infinite advantage
over us in that *esprit de corps* which led them to set
labor and expense at defiance, when the honor of the
order was at stake. Would to God your English Uni-
versities, with their huge endowments and the number of
learned men to whom they give competence and leisure,
would but imitate the monks in their literary plans! My
present employment is an edition of John Dryden's
Works, which is already gone to press. As for riding
on Pegasus, depend upon it, I will never again cross him
in a serious way, unless I should by some strange accident reside so long in the Highlands, and make myself
master of their ancient manners, so as to paint them with
some degree of accuracy in a kind of *companion* to the
Minstrel Lay. . . . I am interrupted by the arrival of
two *gentil bachelors*, whom, like the Count of Artois,
I must despatch upon some adventure till dinner time.
Thank Heaven, that will not be difficult, for although
there are neither dragons nor boars in the vicinity, and
men above six feet are not only scarce, but pacific in
their habits, yet we have a curious breed of wild-cats
who have eaten all Charlotte's chickens, and against
whom I have declared a war at *outrance*, in which the
assistance of these *gentes demoiseaux* will be fully as
valuable as that of Don Quixote to Pentalopin with the
naked arm. So, if Mrs. Ellis takes a fancy for cat-skin
fur, now is the time."

Already, then, he was seriously at work on Dryden.
During the same summer, he drew up for the Edinburgh
Review an admirable article on Todd's edition of Spen-
ser; another on Godwin's Fleetwood; a third, on the
Highland Society's Report concerning the Poems of
Ossian; a fourth, on Johnes's Translation of Froissart;
a fifth, on Colonel Thornton's Sporting Tour; and a
sixth, on some cookery books — the two last being excel-

lent specimens of his humor. He had, besides, a constant succession of minor cares in the superintendence of
multifarious works passing through the Ballantyne press.
But there is yet another important item to be included in
the list of his literary labors of this period. The General
Preface to his Novels informs us, that "about 1805" he
wrote the opening chapters of Waverley; and the second
title, 'T is Sixty Years Since, selected, as he says, "that
the actual date of publication might correspond with the
period in which the scene was laid," leaves no doubt that
he had begun the work so early in 1805 as to contemplate
publishing it before Christmas.[1] He adds, in the same
page, that he was induced, by the favorable reception of
The Lady of the Lake, to think of giving some of his
recollections of Highland scenery and customs in prose;
but this is only one instance of the inaccuracy as to matters of date which pervades all those delightful Prefaces.
The Lady of the Lake was not published until five years
after the first chapters of Waverley were written; its
success, therefore, could have had no share in suggesting
the original design of a Highland novel, though no doubt
it principally influenced him to take up that design after
it had been long suspended, and almost forgotten. Thus
early, then, had Scott meditated deeply such a portraiture of Highland manners as might "make a sort of companion" to that of the old Border life in the Minstrel
Lay; and he had probably begun and suspended his
Waverley, before he expressed to Ellis his feeling that
he ought to reside for some considerable time in the
country to be delineated, before seriously committing
himself in the execution of such a task.

"Having proceeded," he says, "as far as I think the
seventh chapter, I showed my work to a critical friend,
whose opinion was unfavorable; and having then some

---

[1] I have ascertained, since this page was written, that a small part of
the MS. of *Waverley* is on paper bearing the watermark of 1805 — the
rest on paper of 1813.

poetical reputation, I was unwilling to risk the loss of it by attempting a new style of composition. I, therefore, then threw aside the work I had commenced, without either reluctance or remonstrance. I ought to add, that though my ingenuous friend's sentence was afterwards reversed, on an appeal to the public, it cannot be considered as any imputation on his good taste; for the specimen subjected to his criticism did not extend beyond the departure of the hero for Scotland, and consequently had not entered upon the part of the story which was finally found most interesting." A letter to be quoted under the year 1810 will, I believe, satisfy the reader that the first critic of the opening chapters of Waverley was William Erskine.

The following letter must have been written in the course of this autumn. It is in every respect a very interesting one; but I introduce it here as illustrating the course of his reflections on Highland subjects in general, at the time when the first outlines both of The Lady of the Lake and Waverley must have been floating about in his mind: —

TO MISS SEWARD, LICHFIELD.

ASHESTIEL [1805].

MY DEAR MISS SEWARD, — You recall me to some very pleasant feelings of my boyhood, when you ask my opinion of Ossian. His works were first put into my hands by old Dr. Blacklock, a blind poet, of whom you may have heard; he was the worthiest and kindest of human beings, and particularly delighted in encouraging the pursuits, and opening the minds, of the young people by whom he was surrounded. I, though at the period of our intimacy a very young boy, was fortunate enough to attract his notice and kindness; and if I have been at all successful in the paths of literary pursuit, I am sure I owe much of that success to the books with which he supplied me, and his own instructions. Ossian and

Spenser were two books which the good old bard put into my hands, and which I devoured rather than perused. Their tales were for a long time so much my delight, that I could repeat without remorse whole Cantos of the one and Duans of the other; and woe to the unlucky wight who undertook to be my auditor, for in the height of my enthusiasm I was apt to disregard all hints that my recitations became tedious. It was a natural consequence of progress in taste, that my fondness for these authors should experience some abatement. Ossian's poems, in particular, have more charms for youth than for a more advanced stage. The eternal repetition of the same ideas and imagery, however beautiful in themselves, is apt to pall upon a reader whose taste has become somewhat fastidious; and, although I agree entirely with you that the question of their authenticity ought not to be confounded with that of their literary merit, yet skepticism on that head takes away their claim for indulgence as the productions of a barbarous and remote age; and, what is perhaps more natural, it destroys that feeling of reality which we should otherwise combine with our sentiments of admiration. As for the great dispute, I should be no Scottishman if I had not very attentively considered it at some period of my studies; and, indeed, I have gone some lengths in my researches, for I have beside me translations of some twenty or thirty of the unquestioned originals of Ossian's poems. After making every allowance for the disadvantages of a literal translation, and the possible debasement which those *now* collected may have suffered in the great and violent change which the Highlands have undergone since the researches of Macpherson, I am compelled to admit that incalculably the greater part of the English Ossian must be ascribed to Macpherson himself, and that his whole introductions, notes, etc., etc., are an absolute tissue of forgeries.

In all the ballads I ever saw or could hear of, Fin and

Ossin are described as natives of Ireland, although it is not unusual for the reciters sturdily to maintain that this is a corruption of the text. In point of merit, I do not think these Gaelic poems much better than those of the Scandinavian Scalds; they are very unequal, often very vigorous and pointed, often drivelling and crawling in the very extremity of tenuity. The manners of the heroes are those of Celtic savages; and I could point out twenty instances in which Macpherson has very cunningly adopted the beginning, the names, and the leading incidents, etc., of an old tale, and dressed it up with all those ornaments of sentiment and sentimental manners, which first excite our surprise, and afterwards our doubt of its authenticity. The Highlanders themselves, recognizing the leading features of tales they had heard in infancy, with here and there a tirade really taken from an old poem, were readily seduced into becoming champions for the authenticity of the poems. How many people, not particularly addicted to poetry, who may have heard Chevy Chase in the nursery or at school, and never since met with the ballad, might be imposed upon by a new Chevy Chase, bearing no resemblance to the old one, save in here and there a stanza or an incident? Besides, there is something in the severe judgment passed on my countrymen — "that if they do not prefer Scotland to truth, they will always prefer it to inquiry." When once the Highlanders had adopted the poems of Ossian as an article of national faith, you would far sooner have got them to disavow the Scripture than to abandon a line of the contested tales. *Only* they all allow that Macpherson's translation is very unfaithful, and some pretend to say inferior to the original; by which they can only mean, if they mean anything, that they miss the charms of the rhythm and vernacular idiom, which pleases the Gaelic natives; for in the real attributes of poetry, Macpherson's version is far superior to any I ever saw of the fragments which he seems to have used.

The Highland Society have lately set about investigating, or rather, I should say, collecting materials to defend, the authenticity of Ossian. Those researches have
only proved that there were no real originals — using
that word as is commonly understood — to be found for
them. The oldest tale they have found seems to be that
of Darthula; but it is perfectly different, both in diction
and story, from that of Macpherson. It is, however, a
beautiful specimen of Celtic poetry, and shows that it
contains much which is worthy of preservation. Indeed
how should it be otherwise, when we know that, till about
fifty years ago, the Highlands contained a race of hereditary poets? Is it possible to think, that, among perhaps
many hundreds, who for such a course of centuries have
founded their reputation and rank on practising the art
of poetry, in a country where the scenery and manners
gave such effect and interest and imagery to their productions, there should not have been some who attained excellence? In searching out those genuine records of the
Celtic Muse, and preserving them from oblivion, with all
the curious information which they must doubtless contain, I humbly think our Highland antiquaries would
merit better of their country, than by confining their researches to the fantastic pursuit of a chimera.

I am not to deny that Macpherson's inferiority in other
compositions is a presumption that he did not actually
compose these poems. But we are to consider his advantage when on his own ground. Macpherson was a High-
lander, and had his imagination fired with the charms
of Celtic poetry from his very infancy. We know, from
constant experience, that most Highlanders, after they
have become complete masters of English, continue to
think in their own language; and it is to me demonstrable
that Macpherson *thought* almost every word of Ossian in
Gaelic, although he wrote it down in English. The
specimens of his early poetry which remain are also
deeply tinged with the peculiarities of the Celtic diction

and character; so that, in fact, he might be considered as a Highland poet, even if he had not left us some Earse translations (or originals of Ossian) unquestionably written by himself. These circumstances gave a great advantage to him in forming the style of Ossian, which, though exalted and modified according to Macpherson's own ideas of modern taste, is in great part cut upon the model of the tales of the Sennachies and Bards. In the translation of Homer, he not only lost these advantages, but the circumstances on which they were founded were a great detriment to his undertaking; for although such a dress was appropriate and becoming for Ossian, few people cared to see their old Grecian friend disguised in a tartan plaid and philibeg. In a word, the style which Macpherson had formed, however admirable in a Highland tale, was not calculated for translating Homer; and it was a great mistake in him, excited, however, by the general applause his first work received, to suppose that there was anything homogeneous betwixt his own ideas and those of Homer. Macpherson, in his way, was certainly a man of high talents, and his poetic powers as honorable to his country, as the use which he made of them, and I fear his personal character in other respects, was a discredit to it.

Thus I have given you with the utmost sincerity my creed on the great national question of Ossian; it has been formed after much deliberation and inquiry. I have had for some time thoughts of writing a Highland poem, somewhat in the style of the Lay, giving as far as I can a real picture of what that enthusiastic race actually were before the destruction of their patriarchal government. It is true, I have not quite the same facilities as in describing Border manners, where I am, as they say, more at home. But to balance my comparative deficiency in knowledge of Celtic manners, you are to consider that I have from my youth delighted in all the Highland traditions which I could pick up from the old

Jacobites who used to frequent my father's house; and this will, I hope, make some amends for my having less immediate opportunities of research than in the Border tales.

Agreeably to your advice, I have actually read over Madoc a second time, and I confess have seen much beauty which escaped me in the first perusal. *Yet* (which *yet*, by the way, is almost as vile a monosyllable as *but*) I cannot feel quite the interest I would wish to do. The difference of character which you notice, reminds me of what by Ben Jonson and other old comedians were called *humors*, which consisted rather in the personification of some individual passion or propensity, than of an actual individual man. Also, I cannot give up my objection, that what was strictly true of Columbus becomes an unpleasant falsehood when told of some one else. Suppose I was to write a fictitious book of travels, I should certainly do ill to copy exactly the incidents which befell Mungo Park or Bruce of Kinnaird. What was true of them would incontestably prove at once the falsehood and plagiarism of my supposed journal. It is not but what the incidents are natural — but it is their having already happened, which strikes us when they are transferred to imaginary persons. Could any one bear the story of a second city being taken by a wooden horse?

Believe me, I shall not be within many miles of Lichfield without paying my personal respects to you; and yet I should not do it in prudence, because I am afraid you have formed a higher opinion of me than I deserve: you would expect to see a person who had dedicated himself much to literary pursuits, and you would find me a rattle-skulled half-lawyer, half-sportsman, through whose head a regiment of horse has been exercising since he was five years old; half-educated — half-crazy, as his friends sometimes tell him; half everything, but *entirely* Miss Seward's much obliged, affectionate, and faithful servant, WALTER SCOTT.

His correspondence shows how largely he was exerting himself all this while in the service of authors less fortunate than himself. James Hogg, among others, continued to occupy from time to time his attention; and he assisted regularly and assiduously throughout this and the succeeding year Mr. Robert Jameson, an industrious and intelligent antiquary, who had engaged in editing a collection of ancient popular ballads before the third volume of the Minstrelsy appeared, and who at length published his very curious work in 1807. Meantime, Ashestiel, in place of being less resorted to by literary strangers than Lasswade cottage had been, shared abundantly in the fresh attractions of the Lay, and "booksellers in the plural number" were preceded and followed by an endless variety of enthusiastic "gentil bachelors," whose main temptation from the south had been the hope of seeing the Borders in company with their Minstrel. He still writes of himself as "idling away his hours;" he had already learned to appear as if he were doing so to all who had no particular right to confidence respecting the details of his privacy.

But the most agreeable of all his visitants were his own old familiar friends, and one of these has furnished me with a sketch of the autumn life of Ashestiel, of which I shall now avail myself. Scott's invitation was in these terms: —

TO JAMES SKENE, ESQ., OF RUBISLAW.

ASHESTIEL, 18th August, 1805.

DEAR SKENE, — I have prepared another edition of the Lay, 1500 strong, moved thereunto by the faith, hope, and charity of the London booksellers. . . . If you could, in the interim, find a moment to spend here, you know the way, and the ford is where it was; which, by the way, is more than I expected after Saturday last, the most dreadful storm of thunder and lightning I ever witnessed. The lightning broke repeatedly in our immediate vicinity, *i. e.*, betwixt us and the Peel wood. Charlotte resolved to die in bed like a good Christian. The servants said it was the preface to the end of the world, and I was the only person that maintained my character for stoicism, which I assure you had some merit, as I had no doubt that we were in real danger. It was accompanied with a flood so tremendous that I would have given five pounds you had been here to make a sketch of it. The little Glenkinnon brook was impassable for all the next day, and indeed I have been obliged to send all hands to repair the ford, which was converted into a deep pool. Believe me ever yours affectionately,

W. S.

Mr. Skene says: —

" I well remember the ravages of the storm and flood described in this letter. The ford of Ashestiel was never a good one, and for some time after this it remained not a little perilous. He was himself the first to attempt the passage on his favorite black horse Captain, who had scarcely entered the river when he plunged beyond his depth, and had to swim to the other side with his burden. It requires a good horseman to swim a deep and rapid stream, but he trusted to the vigor of his steady trooper, and in spite of his lameness kept his seat manfully. A cart bringing a new kitchen *range* (as I believe the grate for that service is technically called) was shortly after upset in this ugly ford. The horse and cart were with difficulty got out, but the grate remained for some time in the middle of the stream to do duty as a horse-trap, and furnish subject for many a good joke when Mrs. Scott happened to complain of the imperfection of her kitchen appointments."

Mr. Skene soon discovered an important change which had recently been made in his friend's distribution of his time. Previously it had been his custom, whenever professional business or social engagements occupied the middle part of his day, to seize some hours for study after he was supposed to have retired to bed. His physician suggested that this was very likely to aggravate his nervous headaches, the only malady he was subject to in the prime of his manhood; and, contemplating with steady eye a course not only of unremitting but of increasing industry, he resolved to reverse his plan, and carried his purpose into execution with unflinching energy. In short, he had now adopted the habits in which, with very slender variation, he ever after persevered when in the country. He rose by five o'clock, lit his own fire when the season required one, and shaved and dressed with great deliberation — for he was a very martinet as to all but the mere coxcombries of the toilet, not abhorring effeminate dandyism itself so cordially as the slightest approach to personal slovenliness, or even those "bed-gown and slipper tricks," as he called them, in which literary men are so apt to indulge. Arrayed in his shooting-jacket, or whatever dress he meant to use till dinner time, he was seated at his desk by six o'clock, all his papers arranged before him in the most accurate order, and his books of reference marshalled around him on the floor, while at least one favorite dog lay watching his eye, just beyond the line of circumvallation. Thus, by the time the family assembled for breakfast between nine and ten, he had done enough (in his own language) "*to break the neck of the day's work.*" After breakfast, a couple of hours more were given to his solitary tasks, and by noon he was, as he used to say, "his own man." When the weather was bad, he would labor incessantly all the morning; but the general rule was to be out and on horseback by one o'clock at the latest; while, if any more distant excursion had been proposed over night, he was ready to start on it by ten; his occasional rainy days of unintermitted study forming, as he said, a fund in his favor, out of which he was entitled to draw for accommodation whenever the sun shone with special brightness.

It was another rule, that every letter he received should be answered that same day. Nothing else could

have enabled him to keep abreast with the flood of communications that in the sequel put his good-nature to
the severest test — but already the demands on him in
this way also were numerous; and he included attention
to them among the necessary business which must be
despatched before he had a right to close his writing-box,
or, as he phrased it, "to say, *out damned spot*, and be
a gentleman." In turning over his enormous mass of
correspondence, I have almost invariably found some indication that, when a letter had remained more than a
day or two unanswered, it had been so because he found
occasion for inquiry or deliberate consideration.

I ought not to omit, that in those days Scott was far
too zealous a dragoon not to take a principal share in the
stable duty. Before beginning his desk-work in the
morning, he uniformly visited his favorite steed, and
neither Captain nor Lieutenant, nor the Lieutenant's
successor, Brown Adam (so called after one of the heroes
of the Minstrelsy), liked to be fed except by him. The
latter charger was indeed altogether intractable in other
hands, though in his the most submissive of faithful
allies. The moment he was bridled and saddled, it was
the custom to open the stable door as a signal that his
master expected him, when he immediately trotted to the
side of the *leaping-on-stone*, of which Scott from his
lameness found it convenient to make use, and stood
there, silent and motionless as a rock, until he was fairly
in his seat, after which he displayed his joy by neighing
triumphantly through a brilliant succession of curvet-
tings. Brown Adam never suffered himself to be backed
but by his master. He broke, I believe, one groom's
arm and another's leg in the rash attempt to tamper with
his dignity.

Camp was at this time the constant parlor dog. He
was very handsome, very intelligent, and naturally very
fierce, but gentle as a lamb among the children. As for
the more locomotive Douglas and Percy, he kept one

window of his study open, whatever might be the state of
the weather, that they might leap out and in as the fancy
moved them. He always talked to Camp as if he understood what was said — and the animal certainly did understand not a little of it; in particular, it seemed as if
he perfectly comprehended on all occasions that his master considered him as a sensible and steady friend — the
greyhounds as volatile young creatures whose freaks
must be borne with.

"Every day," says Mr. Skene, "we had some hours of
coursing with the greyhounds, or riding at random over the
hills, or of spearing salmon in the Tweed by sunlight: which
last sport, moreover, we often renewed at night by the help of
torches. This amusement of *burning the water*, as it is called,
was not without some hazard; for the large salmon generally
lie in the pools, the depths of which it is not easy to estimate
with precision by torchlight, — so that not unfrequently, when
the sportsman makes a determined thrust at a fish apparently
within reach, his eye has grossly deceived him, and instead of
the point of the weapon encountering the prey, he finds himself launched with corresponding vehemence heels over head
into the pool, both spear and salmon gone, the torch thrown out
by the concussion of the boat, and quenched in the stream,
while the boat itself has of course receded to some distance. I
remember the first time I accompanied our friend, he went
right over the gunwale in this manner, and had I not accidentally been close at his side, and made a successful grasp at the
skirt of his jacket as he plunged overboard, he must at least
have had an awkward dive for it. Such are the contingencies
of *burning the water*. The pleasures consist in being penetrated with cold and wet, having your shins broken against the
stones in the dark, and perhaps mastering one fish out of every
twenty you take aim at."

In all these amusements, but particularly in the *burning of the water*, Scott's most regular companion at this
time was John, Lord Somerville, who united with many
higher qualities a most enthusiastic love for such sports,
and consummate address in the prosecution of them.

This amiable nobleman then passed his autumns at his pretty seat of Alwyn, or the Pavilion, situated on the Tweed, some eight or nine miles below Ashestiel. They interchanged visits almost every week; and Scott did not fail to profit largely by his friend's matured and well-known skill in every department of the science of rural economy. He always talked of him, in particular, as his master in the art of planting.

The laird of Rubislaw seldom failed to spend a part of the summer and autumn at Ashestiel, as long as Scott remained there, and during these visits they often gave a wider scope to their expeditions.

"Indeed," says Mr. Skene, "there are few scenes at all celebrated either in the history, tradition, or romance of the Border counties, which we did not explore together in the course of our rambles. We traversed the entire vales of the Yarrow and Ettrick, with all their sweet tributary glens, and never failed to find a hearty welcome from the farmers at whose houses we stopped, either for dinner or for the night. He was their chief magistrate, extremely popular in that official capacity ; and nothing could be more gratifying than the frank and hearty reception which everywhere greeted our arrival, however unexpected. The exhilarating air of the mountains, and the healthy exercise of the day, secured our relishing homely fare, and we found inexhaustible entertainment in the varied display of character which the affability of *the Sheriff* drew forth on all occasions in genuine breadth and purity. The beauty of the scenery gave full employment to my pencil, with the free and frequent exercise of which he never seemed to feel impatient. He was at all times ready and willing to alight when any object attracted my notice, and used to seat himself beside me on the brae, to con over some ballad appropriate to the occasion, or narrate the tradition of the glen — sometimes, perhaps, to note a passing idea in his pocket-book; but this was rare, for in general he relied with confidence on the great storehouse of his memory. And much amusement we had, as you may suppose, in talking over the different incidents, conversations, and traits of manners that had occurred at the last hospitable fireside where we had mingled with the natives. Thus the minutes glided away until my sketch was complete, and then we mounted again with fresh alacrity.

"These excursions derived an additional zest from the uncertainty that often attended the issue of our proceedings; for, following the game started by the dogs, our unfailing comrades, we frequently got entangled and bewildered among the hills, until we had to trust to mere chance for the lodging of the night. Adventures of this sort were quite to his taste, and the more for the perplexities which on such occasions befell our attendant squires, — mine a lanky Savoyard, his a portly Scotch butler — both of them uncommonly bad horsemen, and both equally sensitive about their personal dignity, which the ruggedness of the ground often made it a matter of some difficulty for either of them to maintain, but more especially for my poor foreigner, whose seat resembled that of a pair of compasses astride. Scott's heavy lumbering *beauffetier* had provided himself against the mountain showers with a huge cloak, which, when the cavalcade were at gallop, streamed at full stretch from his shoulders, and kept flapping in the other's face, who, having more than enough to do in preserving his own equilibrium, could not think of attempting at any time to control the pace of his steed, and had no relief but fuming and *pesting* at the *sacré manteau*, in language happily unintelligible to its wearer. Now and then some ditch or turf-fence rendered it indispensable to adventure on a leap, and no farce could have been more amusing than the display of politeness which then occurred between these worthy equestrians, each courteously declining in favor of his friend the honor of the first experiment, the horses fretting impatient beneath them, and the dogs clamoring encouragement. The horses generally terminated the dispute by renouncing allegiance, and springing forward without waiting the pleasure of the riders, who had to settle the matter with their saddles as they best could.

"One of our earliest expeditions was to visit the wild scenery of the mountainous tract above Moffat, including the cascade of the Grey Mare's Tail, and the dark tarn called Loch Skene. In our ascent to the lake we got completely bewildered in the thick fog which generally envelopes the rugged features of that lonely region; and, as we were groping through the maze of bogs, the ground gave way, and down went horse and horsemen pell-mell into a slough of peaty mud and black water, out of which, entangled as we were with our plaids and floundering nags, it was no easy matter to get extricated. Indeed, unless we had prudently left our gallant steeds at a farmhouse below, and borrowed hill ponies for the occasion, the result might have been worse than laughable. As it was, we rose like the spirits of the bog, covered *cap-à-pie* with slime, to free themselves from which, our wily ponies took to rolling about on the heather, and we had nothing for it but following their example. At length, as we approached the gloomy loch, a huge eagle heaved himself from the margin and rose right over us, screaming his scorn of the intruders ; and altogether it would be impossible to picture anything more desolately savage than the scene which opened, as if raised by enchantment on purpose to gratify the poet's eye ; thick folds of fog rolling incessantly over the face of the inky waters, but rent asunder now in one direction, and then in another — so as to afford us a glimpse of some projecting rock or naked point of land, or island bearing a few scraggy stumps of pine — and then closing again in universal darkness upon the cheerless waste. Much of the scenery of Old Mortality was drawn from that day's ride.

" It was also in the course of this excursion that we encountered that amusing personage introduced into Guy Mannering as 'Tod Gabbie,' though the appellation by which he was known in the neighborhood was 'Tod Willie.' He was one of those itinerants who gain a subsistence among the moorland farmers by relieving them of foxes, polecats, and the like depredators — a half-witted, stuttering, and most original creature.

" Having explored all the wonders of Moffatdale, we turned ourselves towards *Blackhouse Tower*, to visit Scott's worthy acquaintances the Laidlaws, and reached it after a long and intricate ride, having been again led off our course by the greyhounds, who had been seduced by a strange dog that joined company, to engage in full pursuit upon the track of what we presumed to be either a fox or a roe-deer. The chase was protracted and perplexing, from the mist that skirted the hilltops ; but at length we reached the scene of slaughter, and were much distressed to find that a stately old he-goat had been the victim. He seemed to have fought a stout battle for his life, but now lay mangled in the midst of his panting enemies, who betrayed, on our approach, strong consciousness of delinquency and apprehension of the lash, which was administered accordingly to soothe the manes of the luckless Capricorn — though, after all, the dogs were not so much to blame in mistaking his game flavor, since the fogs must have kept him out of view till the last moment. Our visit to Blackhouse was highly interesting; — the excellent old tenant being still in life, and the whole family group presenting a perfect picture of innocent and simple happiness, while the animated, intelligent, and original conversation of our friend William was quite charming.

"Sir Adam Ferguson and the Ettrick Shepherd were of the party that explored Loch Skene and hunted the unfortunate he-goat.

"I need not tell you that Saint Mary's Loch, and the Loch of the Lowes, were among the most favorite scenes of our excursions, as his fondness for them continued to his last days, and we have both visited them many times together in his company. I may say the same of the Teviot and the Aill, Borthwick-water, and the lonely towers of Buccleuch and Harden, Minto, Roxburgh, Gilnockie, etc. I think it was either in 1805 or 1806 that I first explored the Borthwick with him, when on our way to pass a week at Langholm with Lord and Lady Dalkeith, upon which occasion the otter-hunt, so well described in Guy Mannering, was got up by our noble host; and I can never forget the delight with which Scott observed the enthusiasm of the high-spirited yeomen, who had assembled in multitudes to partake the sport of their dear young chief, well mounted, and dashing about from rock to rock with a reckless ardor which recalled the alacrity of their forefathers in following the Buccleuchs of former days through adventures of a more serious order.

"Whatever the banks of the Tweed, from its source to its termination, presented of interest, we frequently visited; and I do verily believe there is not a single ford in the whole course of that river which we have not traversed together. He had an amazing fondness for fords, and was not a little adventurous in plunging through, whatever might be the state of the flood, and this even though there happened to be a bridge in view. If it seemed possible to scramble through, he scorned to go ten yards about, and in fact preferred the ford; and it is to be remarked that most of the heroes of his tales seem to have been endued with similar propensities — even the White Lady of Avenel delights in the ford. He sometimes even attempted them on foot, though his lameness interfered considerably with his progress among the slippery stones. Upon one occasion of this sort I was assisting him through the Ettrick, and we had both got upon the same tottering stone in the middle of the stream, when some story about a *kelpie* occurring to him, he must needs stop and tell it with all his usual vivacity — and then laughing heartily at his own joke, he slipped his foot, or the stone shuffled beneath him, and down he went headlong into the pool, pulling me after him. We escaped, however, with no worse than a thorough drenching and the loss of his stick, which floated down the river, and he was as ready as ever for a similar exploit before his clothes were half dried upon his back."

About this time Mr. and Mrs. Scott made a short excursion to the lakes of Cumberland and Westmoreland, and visited some of their finest scenery, in company with Mr. Wordsworth. I have found no written narrative of this little tour, but I have often heard Scott speak with enthusiastic delight of the reception he met with in the humble cottage which his brother poet then inhabited on the banks of Grasmere; and at least one of the days they spent together was destined to furnish a theme for the verse of each, namely, that which they gave to the ascent of Helvellyn, where, in the course of the preceding spring, a young gentleman having lost his way and perished by falling over a precipice, his remains were discovered, three months afterwards, still watched by "a faithful terrier-bitch, his constant attendant during frequent rambles among the wilds."[1] This day they were

---

[1] See notice prefixed to the song —

> "I climbed the dark brow of the mighty Helvellyn," etc.,

in Scott's *Poetical Works*, vol. vi. p. 370 [Camb. Ed. p. 37] ; and compare the lines —

> " Inmate of a mountain dwelling,
> Thou hast clomb aloft, and gazed
> From the watch-towers of Helvellyn,
> Awed, delighted, and amazed," etc.

Wordsworth's *Poetical Works*, vol. iii. p. 96.

accompanied by an illustrious philosopher, who was also
a true poet — and might have been one of the greatest of
poets had he chosen; and I have heard Mr. Wordsworth
say that it would be difficult to express the feelings with
which he, who so often had climbed Helvellyn alone,
found himself standing on its summit with two such men
as Scott and Davy.

After leaving Mr. Wordsworth, Scott carried his wife
to spend a few days at Gilsland, among the scenes where
they had first met; and his reception by the company at
the wells was such as to make him look back with something of regret, as well as of satisfaction, to the change
that had occurred in his circumstances since 1797. They
were, however, enjoying themselves much there, when he
received intelligence which induced him to believe that a
French force was about to land in Scotland: the alarm
indeed had spread far and wide; and a mighty gathering
of volunteers, horse and foot, from the Lothians and the
Border country, took place in consequence at Dalkeith.
He was not slow to obey the summons. He had luckily
chosen to accompany on horseback the carriage in which
Mrs. Scott travelled. His good steed carried him to the
spot of rendezvous, full a hundred miles from Gilsland,
within twenty-four hours; and on reaching it, though,
no doubt to his disappointment, the alarm had already
blown over, he was delighted with the general enthusiasm
that had thus been put to the test — and, above all, by
the rapidity with which the yeomen of Ettrick Forest had
poured down from their glens, under the guidance of his
good friend and neighbor, Mr. Pringle of Torwoodlee.
These fine fellows were quartered along with the Edinburgh troop when he reached Dalkeith and Musselburgh;
and after some sham battling, and a few evenings of
high jollity, had crowned the needless muster of the beacon fires,[1] he immediately turned his horse again towards
the south, and rejoined Mrs. Scott at Carlisle.

[1] See note "Alarm of Invasion," *Antiquary*, chap. xlv.

By the way, it was during his fiery ride from Gilsland to Dalkeith, on the occasion above mentioned, that he composed his Bard's Incantation, first published six years afterwards in the Edinburgh Annual Register: —

> " The forest of Glenmore is drear,
> It is all of black pine and the dark oak tree," etc.,

and the verses bear the full stamp of the feelings of the moment.

Shortly after he was reëstablished at Ashestiel, he was visited there by Mr. Southey; this being, I believe, their first meeting. It is alluded to in the following letter — a letter highly characteristic in more respects than one: —

TO GEORGE ELLIS, ESQ., SUNNING HILL.

ASHESTIEL, 17th October, 1805.

DEAR ELLIS, — More than a month has glided away in this busy solitude, and yet I have never sat down to answer your kind letter. I have only to plead a horror of pen and ink with which this country, in fine weather (and ours has been most beautiful), regularly affects me. In recompense, I ride, walk, fish, course, eat and drink, with might and main, from morning to night. I could have wished sincerely you had come to Reged this year to partake her rural amusements; — the only comfort I have is, that your visit would have been over, and now I look forward to it as to a pleasure to come. I shall be infinitely obliged to you for your advice and assistance in the course of Dryden. I fear little can be procured for a Life beyond what Malone has compiled, but certainly his facts may be rather better told and arranged. I am at present busy with the dramatic department. This undertaking will make my being in London in spring a matter of absolute necessity.

And now let me tell you of a discovery which I have made, or rather which Robert Jameson has made, in copying the MS. of True Thomas and the Queen of Elf-

land, in the Lincoln Cathedral. The queen, at parting, bestows the gifts of harping and carping upon the
prophet, and mark his reply: —

> " To harp and carp, Tomas, where so ever ye gen —
> Thomas, take thou these with thee." —
> " Harping," he said, " ken I nane,
> For Tong is chefe of mynstrelsie."

If poor Ritson could contradict his own system of mate-
rialism by rising from the grave to peep into this MS.,
he would slink back again in dudgeon and dismay.
There certainly cannot be more respectable testimony
than that of True Thomas, and you see he describes the
tongue, or recitation, as the principal, or at least the
most dignified, part of a minstrel's profession.

Another curiosity was brought here a few days ago by
Mr. Southey, the poet, who favored me with a visit on his
way to Edinburgh. It was a MS. containing sundry
metrical romances, and other poetical compositions, in the
northern dialect, apparently written about the middle of
the fifteenth century. I had not time to make an analysis
of its contents, but some of them seem highly valuable.
There is a tale of Sir Gowther, said to be a Breton Lay,
which partly resembles the history of Robert the Devil,
the hero being begot in the same way; and partly that of
Robert of Sicily, the penance imposed on Sir Gowther
being the same, as he kept table with the hounds, and
was discovered by a dumb lady to be the stranger knight
who had assisted her father the emperor in his wars.
There is also a MS. of Sir Isanbras; *item* a poem called
Sir Amadas — not Amadis of Gaul, but a courteous
knight, who, being reduced to poverty, travels to conceal
his distress, and gives the wreck of his fortune to purchase the rites of burial for a deceased knight, who had
been refused them by the obduracy of his creditors. The
rest of the story is the same with that of Jean de Calais,
in the Bibliothèque Bleue, and with a vulgar ballad
called the Factor's Garland. Moreover there is a merry

tale of hunting a hare, as performed by a set of country clowns, with their mastiffs, and curs with "short legs and never a tail." The disgraces and blunders of these ignorant sportsmen must have afforded infinite mirth at the table of a feudal baron, prizing himself on his knowledge of the mysteries of the chase performed by these unauthorized intruders. There is also a burlesque sermon, which informs us of Peter and Adam journeying together to Babylon, and how Peter asked Adam *a full great doubtful question*, saying, "Adam, Adam, why didst thou eat the apple unpared?" This book belongs to a lady. I would have given something valuable to have had a week of it. Southey commissioned me to say that he intended to take extracts from it, and should be happy to copy, or cause to be copied, any part that you might wish to be possessed of; an offer which I heartily recommend to your early consideration. — Where dwelleth Heber the magnificent, whose library and cellar [1] are so superior to all others in the world? I wish to write to him about Dryden. Any word lately from Jamaica?

Yours truly,   W. S.

Mr. Ellis, in his answer, says: —

Heber will, I dare say, be of service to you in your present undertaking, if indeed you want any assistance, which I very much doubt; because it appears to me that the best edition which could now be given of Dryden would be one which should unite accuracy of text and a handsome appearance with good critical notes. *Quoad* Malone, — I should think Ritson himself, could he rise from the dead, would be puzzled to sift out a single additional anecdote of the poet's life; but to abridge Malone — and to render his narrative terse, elegant, and intelligible — would be a great obligation conferred on the purchasers (I will not say the readers, because I have doubts whether they exist in the plural number) of his very laborious

---

[1] Ellis had mentioned, in a recent letter, Heber's buying wines to the value of £1100 at some sale he happened to attend this autumn.

compilation. The late Dr. Warton, you may have heard, had a project of editing Dryden *à la* Hurd ; that is to say, upon the same principle as the castrated edition of Cowley. His reason was, that Dryden, having written for bread, became of necessity a most voluminous author, and poured forth more nonsense of indecency, particularly in his theatrical compositions, than almost any scribbler in that scribbling age. Hence, although his transcendent genius frequently breaks out, and marks the hand of the master, his comedies seem, by a tacit but general consent, to have been condemned to oblivion ; and his tragedies, being printed in such bad company, have shared the same fate. But Dr. W. conceived that, by a judicious selection of these, together with his fables and prose works, it would be possible to exhibit him in a much more advantageous light than by a republication of the whole mass of his writings. Whether the Doctor (who, by the way, was by no means scrupulously chaste and delicate, as you will be aware from his edition of Pope) had taken a just view of the subject, you know better than I ; but I must own that the announcement of a *general* edition of Dryden gave me some little alarm. However, if you can suggest the sort of assistance you are desirous of receiving, I shall be happy to do what I can to promote your views. . . . And so you are not disposed to *nibble* at the bait I throw out ! Nothing but " a decent edition of Holinshed " ? I confess that my project chiefly related to the later historical works respecting this country — to the union of Gall, Twisden, Camden, Leibnitz, etc., etc., leaving the Chronicles, properly so called, to shift for themselves. . . . I am ignorant when you are to be in Edinburgh, and in that ignorance have not desired Blackburn, who is now at Glasgow, to call on you. He has the best practical understanding I have ever met with, and I vouch that you would be much pleased with his acquaintance. And so for the present God bless you.   G. E.

Scott's letter in reply opens thus : —

I will not castrate John Dryden. I would as soon castrate my own father, as I believe Jupiter did of yore. What would you say to any man who would castrate

Shakespeare, or Massinger, or Beaumont and Fletcher?
I don't say but that it may be very proper to select correct passages for the use of boarding-schools and colleges,
being sensible no improper ideas can be suggested in
these seminaries, unless they are intruded or smuggled
under the beards and ruffs of our old dramatists. But
in making an edition of a man of genius's works for
libraries and collections, and such I conceive a complete
edition of Dryden to be, I must give my author as I find
him, and will not tear out the page, even to get rid of
the blot, little as I like it. Are not the pages of Swift,
and even of Pope, larded with indecency, and often of the
most disgusting kind, and do we not see them upon all
shelves and dressing-tables, and in all boudoirs? Is not
Prior the most indecent of tale-tellers, not even excepting La Fontaine, and how often do we see his works in
female hands? In fact, it is not passages of ludicrous
indelicacy that corrupt the manners of a people — it is
the sonnets which a prurient genius like Master Little
sings *virginibus puerisque* — it is the sentimental slang,
half lewd, half methodistic, that debauches the understanding, inflames the sleeping passions, and prepares
the reader to give way as soon as a tempter appears. At
the same time, I am not at all happy when I peruse some
of Dryden's comedies: they are very stupid, as well as
indelicate; sometimes, however, there is a considerable
vein of liveliness and humor, and all of them present
extraordinary pictures of the age in which he lived. My
critical notes will not be very numerous, but I hope to
illustrate the political poems, as Absalom and Achitophel,
The Hind and Panther, etc., with some curious annota-
tions. I have already made a complete search among
some hundred pamphlets of that pamphlet-writing age, and
with considerable success, as I have found several which
throw light on my author. I am told that I am to be
formidably opposed by Mr. Crowe, the Professor of
Poetry at Oxford, who is also threatening an edition of

Dryden. I don't know whether to be most vexed that some one had not undertaken the task sooner, or that Mr. Crowe is disposed to attempt it at the same time with me; — however, I now stand committed, and will not be *crowed* over, if I can help it. The third edition of the Lay is now in the press, of which I hope you will accept a copy, as it contains some trifling improvements or additions. They are, however, very trifling.

I have written a long letter to Rees, recommending an edition of our historians, both Latin and English; but I have great hesitation whether to undertake much of it myself. What I can, I certainly will do; but I should feel particularly delighted if you would join forces with me, when I think we might do the business to purpose. Do, Lord love you, think of this *grande opus*.

I have not been so fortunate as to hear of Mr. Blackburn. I am afraid poor Daniel has been very idly employed — *Cœlum non animum*. I am glad you still retain the purpose of visiting Reged. If you live on mutton and game, we can feast you; for, as one wittily said, I am not the hare with many friends, but the friend with many hares.   W. S.

Mr. Ellis, in his next letter, says: —

"I will not disturb you by contesting any part of your ingenious apology for your intended *complete* edition of Dryden, whose genius I venerate as much as you do, and whose negligences, as he was not rich enough to doom them to oblivion in his own lifetime, it is perhaps incumbent on his editor to transmit to the latest posterity. Most certainly I am not so squeamish as to quarrel with him for his immodesty on any moral pretence. Licentiousness in writing, when accompanied by wit, as in the case of Prior, La Fontaine, etc., is never likely to excite any *passion*, because every passion is serious; and the grave epistle of Eloisa is more likely to do moral mischief, and convey infection to love-sick damsels, than five hundred stories of Hans Carvel and Paulo Purgante; but whatever is in point

of expression vulgar — whatever disgusts the taste — whatever
might have been written by any fool, and is therefore unworthy
of Dryden — whatever might have been suppressed, without
exciting a moment's regret in the mind of any of his admirers
— *ought*, in my opinion, to be suppressed by any editor who
should be disposed to make an appeal to the public taste upon
the subject; because a man who was perhaps the best poet and
best prose writer in the language — but it is foolish to say so
much, after promising to say nothing. Indeed I own *myself*
guilty of possessing all his works in a very indifferent edition,
and I shall certainly purchase a better one whenever you put
it in my power. With regard to your competitors, I feel perfectly at my ease, because I am convinced that though you
should generously furnish them with all the materials, they
would not know how to use them: *non cuivis hominum con-
tingit* to write critical notes that any one will read."

Alluding to the regret which Scott had expressed some
time before at the shortness of his visit to the libraries
of Oxford, Ellis says, in another of these letters: —

" A library is like a butcher's shop: it contains plenty of
meat, but it is all raw; no person living (Leyden's breakfast
was only a *tour de force* to astonish Ritson, and I except the
Abyssinians, whom I never saw) can find a meal in it, till some
good cook (suppose yourself) comes in and says, ' Sir, I see
by your looks that you are hungry; I know your taste — be
patient for a moment, and you shall be satisfied that you have
an excellent appetite.' "

I shall not transcribe the mass of letters which Scott
received from various other literary friends whose assistance he invoked in the preparation of his edition of Dryden; but among them there occurs one so admirable,
that I cannot refuse myself the pleasure of introducing
it, more especially as the views which it opens harmonize
as remarkably with some, as they differ from others, of
those which Scott himself ultimately expressed respecting
the poetical character of his illustrious author: —

MY DEAR SCOTT, — . . . I was much pleased to hear of your engagement with Dryden : not that he is, as a poet, any great favorite of mine : I admire his talents and genius highly, — but his is not a poetical genius. The only qualities I can find in Dryden that are *essentially* poetical, are a certain ardor and impetuosity of mind, with an excellent ear. It may seem strange that I do not add to this, great command of language : *That* he certainly has, and of such language, too, as it is most desirable that a poet should possess, or rather that he should not be without. But it is not language that is, in the highest sense of the word, poetical, being neither of the imagination nor of the passions ; I mean the amiable, the ennobling, or the intense passions. I do not mean to say that there is nothing of this in Dryden, but as little, I think, as is possible, considering how much he has written. You will easily understand my meaning, when I refer to his versification of Palamon and Arcite, as contrasted with the language of Chaucer. Dryden had neither a tender heart nor a lofty sense of moral dignity. Whenever his language is poetically impassioned, it is mostly upon unpleasing subjects, such as the follies, vices, and crimes of classes of men or of individuals. That his cannot be the language of imagination, must have necessarily followed from this, — that there is not a single image from nature in the whole body of his works ; and in his translation from Virgil, wherever Virgil can be fairly said to have his *eye* upon his object, Dryden always spoils the passage.

But too much of this. I am glad that you are to be his editor. His political and satirical pieces may be greatly benefited by illustration, and even absolutely require it. A correct text is the first object of an editor ; then such notes as explain difficult or obscure passages ; and lastly, which is much less important, notes pointing out authors to whom the poet has been indebted, — not in the fiddling way of phrase here and phrase there (which is detestable as a general practice), — but where he has had essential obligations either as to matter or manner.

If I can be of any use to you, do not fail to apply to me. One thing I may take the liberty to suggest, which is, when you come to the fables, might it not be advisable to print the whole of the tales of Boccace in a smaller type in the original language? If this should look too much like swelling a book, I should certainly make such extracts as would show where Dryden has most strikingly improved upon, or fallen below, his original. I think his translations from Boccace are the best, at least the most poetical, of his poems. It is many years since I saw Boccace, but I remember that Sigismunda is not married by him to Guiscard — (the names are different in Boccace in both tales, I believe — certainly in Theodore, etc.) I think Dryden has much injured the story by the marriage, and degraded Sigismunda's character by it. He has also, to the best of my remembrance, degraded her still more by making her love absolute sensuality and appetite; Dryden had no other notion of the passion. With all these defects, and they are very gross ones, it is a noble poem. Guiscard's answer, when first reproached by Tancred, is noble in Boccace — nothing but this: *Amor può molto più che ne voi ne io possiamo.* This, Dryden has spoiled. He says first very well, " The faults of love by love are justified," and then come four lines of miserable rant, quite *à la Maximin.* Farewell, and believe me ever your affectionate friend,

WILLIAM WORDSWORTH.

CHAPTER XV

AFFAIR OF THE CLERKSHIP OF SESSION. — LETTERS TO
ELLIS AND LORD DALKEITH. — VISIT TO LONDON. —
EARL SPENCER AND MR. FOX. — CAROLINE, PRINCESS
OF WALES. — JOANNA BAILLIE. — APPOINTMENT AS
CLERK OF SESSION. — LORD MELVILLE'S TRIAL. —
SONG ON HIS ACQUITTAL

1806

WHILE the first volumes of his Dryden were passing
through the press, the affair concerning the Clerkship
of the Court of Session, opened nine or ten months before, had not been neglected by the friends on whose
counsel and assistance Scott had relied. In one of his
Prefaces of 1830, he briefly tells the issue of this negotiation, which he justly describes as "an important circumstance in his life, of a nature to relieve him from the
anxiety which he must otherwise have felt as one upon
the precarious tenure of whose own life rested the principal prospects of his family, and especially as one who
had necessarily some dependence on the proverbially capricious favor of the public." Whether Mr. Pitt's hint
to Mr. William Dundas, that he would willingly find an
opportunity to promote the interests of the author of the
Lay, or some conversation between the Duke of Buccleuch and Lord Melville, first encouraged him to this
direction of his views, I am not able to state distinctly;
but I believe that the desire to see his fortunes placed on
some more substantial basis was at this time partaken
pretty equally by the three persons who had the princi-

pal influence in the distribution of the Crown patronage in Scotland; and as his object was rather to secure a future than an immediate increase of official income, it was comparatively easy to make such an arrangement as would satisfy his ambition. George Home of Wedderburn, in Berwickshire, a gentleman of considerable literary acquirements, and an old friend of Scott's family, had now served as Clerk of Session for upwards of thirty years. In those days there was no system of retiring pensions for the worn-out functionary of this class, and the usual method was, either that he should resign in favor of a successor who advanced a sum of money according to the circumstances of his age and health, or for a coadjutor to be associated with him in his patent, who undertook the duty on condition of a division of salary. Scott offered to relieve Mr. Home of all the labors of his office, and to allow him, nevertheless, to retain its emoluments entire during his lifetime; and the aged clerk of course joined his exertions to procure a conjoint-patent on these very advantageous terms. Mr. Home resigned, and a new patent was drawn out accordingly; but, by a clerical inadvertency, it was drawn out solely in Scott's favor, no mention of Mr. Home being inserted in the instrument. Although, therefore, the sign-manual had been affixed, and there remained nothing but to pay the fees and take out the commission, Scott, on discovering this error, could not of course proceed in the business; since, in the event of his dying before Mr. Home, that gentleman would have lost the vested interest which he had stipulated to retain. A pending charge of pecuniary corruption had compelled Lord Melville to retire from office some time before Mr. Pitt's death; and the cloud of popular obloquy, under which he now labored, rendered it impossible that Scott should expect assistance from the quarter to which, under any other circumstances, he would naturally have turned for extrication from this difficulty. He therefore, as soon as the Fox and Grenville Cabinet had been nominated, proceeded to London, to make in his own person such representations as might be necessary to secure the issuing of the patent in the right shape.

It seems wonderful that he should ever have doubted for a single moment of the result; since, had the new Cabinet been purely Whig, and had he been the most violent and obnoxious of Tory partisans, neither of which was the case, the arrangement had been not only virtually, but, with the exception of an evident official blunder, formally completed; and no Secretary of State, as I must think, could have refused to rectify the paltry mistake in question, without a dereliction of every principle of honor. The seals of the Home Office had been placed in the hands of a nobleman of the highest character — moreover, an ardent lover of literature; — while the chief of the new Ministry was one of the most generous as well as tasteful of mankind; and accordingly, when the circumstances were explained, there occurred no hesitation whatever on their parts. "I had," says Scott, "the honor of an interview with Earl Spencer, and he in the most handsome manner gave directions that the commission should issue as originally intended; adding that, the matter having received the royal assent, he regarded only as a claim of justice what he would willingly have done as an act of favor." He adds: "I never saw Mr. Fox on this or any other occasion, and never made any application to him, conceiving, that in doing so, I might have been supposed to express political opinions different from those which I had always professed. In his private capacity, there is no man to whom I would have been more proud to owe an obligation — had I been so distinguished."[1]

In January, 1806, however, Scott had by no means measured either the character, the feelings, or the arrangements of great public functionaries, by the standard

[1] Introduction to *Marmion* — 1830.

with which observation and experience subsequently furnished him. He had breathed hitherto, as far as political questions of all sorts were concerned, the hot atmosphere of a very narrow scene — and seems to have pictured to himself Whitehall and Downing Street as only a wider stage for the exhibition of the bitter and fanatical prejudices that tormented the petty circles of the Parliament House at Edinburgh; the true bearing and scope of which no man in after-days more thoroughly understood, or more sincerely pitied. The variation of his feelings, while his business still remained undetermined, will, however, be best collected from the correspondence about to be quoted. It was, moreover, when these letters were written, that he was tasting for the first time the full cup of fashionable blandishment as a *London Lion;* nor will the reader fail to observe how deeply, while he supposed his own most important worldly interests to be in peril on the one hand, and was surrounded with so many captivating flatteries on the other, he continued to sympathize with the misfortunes of his early friend and patron, now hurled from power, and subjected to a series of degrading persecutions, from the consequences of which that lofty spirit was never entirely to recover.

TO GEORGE ELLIS, ESQ., SUNNING HILL.

EDINBURGH, January 25, 1806.

MY DEAR ELLIS, — I have been too long in letting you hear of me, and my present letter is going to be a very selfish one, since it will be chiefly occupied by an affair of my own, in which, probably, you may find very little entertainment. I rely, however, upon your cordial good wishes and good advice, though, perhaps, you may be unable to afford me any direct assistance without more trouble than I would wish you to take on my account. You must know, then, that with a view of withdrawing entirely from the Bar, I had entered into a transaction with an elderly and infirm gentleman, Mr. George Home, to be associated with him in the office which he holds as one of the Principal Clerks to our Supreme Court of Session; I being to discharge the duty gratuitously during his life, and to succeed him at his decease. This could only be carried into effect by a new commission from the Crown to him and me jointly, which has been issued in similar cases very lately, and is in point of form quite correct. By the interest of my kind and noble friend and chief, the Duke of Buccleuch, the countenance of Government was obtained to this arrangement, and the affair, as I have every reason to believe, is now in the Treasury. I have written to my solicitor, Alexander Mundell, Fludyer Street, to use every despatch in hurrying through the commission; but the news of to-day giving us every reason to apprehend Pitt's death, if that lamentable event has not already happened,[1] makes me get nervous on a subject so interesting to my little fortune. My political sentiments have been always constitutional and open, and although they were never rancorous, yet I cannot expect that the Scottish Opposition party, should circumstances bring them into power, would consider me as an object of favor: nor would I ask it at their hands. Their leaders cannot regard me with malevolence, for I am intimate with many of them; — but they must provide for the Whiggish children before they throw their bread to the Tory dogs; and I shall not fawn on them because they have in their turn the superintendence of the larder. At the same time, if Fox's friends come into power, it must be with Windham's party, to whom my politics can be no exception, — if the politics of a private individual ought at any time to be made the excuse for intercepting the bounty of his Sovereign, when it is in the very course of being bestowed.

The situation is most desirable, being £800 a year, besides being consistent with holding my sheriffdom;

[1] Mr. Pitt died January 23 two days before this letter was written.

and I could afford very well to wait till it opened to me by the death of my colleague, without wishing a most worthy and respectable man to die a moment sooner than ripe nature demanded. The duty consists in a few hours' labor in the forenoons when the Court sits, leaving the evenings and whole vacation open for literary pursuits. I will not relinquish the hope of such an establishment without an effort, if it is possible without dereliction of my principles to attain the accomplishment of it. As I have suffered in my professional line by addicting myself to the profane and unprofitable art of poem-making, I am very desirous to indemnify myself by availing myself of any prepossession which my literary reputation may, however unmeritedly, have created in my favor. I have found it useful when I applied for others, and I see no reason why I should not try if it can do anything for myself.

Perhaps, after all, my commission may be got out before a change of Ministry, if such an event shall take place, as it seems not far distant. If it is otherwise, will you be so good as to think and devise some mode in which my case may be stated to Windham or Lord Grenville, supposing them to come in? If it is not deemed worthy of attention, I am sure I shall be contented; but it is one thing to have a right to ask a favor, and another to hope that a transaction, already fully completed by the private parties, and approved of by an existing Administration, shall be permitted to take effect in favor of an unoffending individual. I believe I shall see you very shortly, unless I hear from Mundell that the business can be done for certain without my coming up. I will not, if I can help it, be flayed like a sheep for the benefit of some pettifogging lawyer or attorney. I have stated the matter to you very bluntly; indeed, I am not asking a favor, but, unless my self-partiality blinds me, merely fair play. Yours ever,

WALTER SCOTT.

TO WALTER SCOTT, ESQ., EDINBURGH.

BATH, 6th February, 1806.

MY DEAR SCOTT, — You must have seen by the lists of the new Ministry already published in all the papers, that, although the death of our excellent Minister has been certainly a most unfortunate event, in as far as it must tend to delay the object of your present wishes, there is no cause for your alarm on account of the change, excepting as far as that change is very extensive, and thus perhaps much time may elapse before the business of every kind which was in arrears can be expedited by the new Administration. There is no change of principle (as far as we can yet judge) in the new Cabinet — or rather the new Cabinet has no general political creed. Lord Grenville, Fox, Lord Lansdowne, and Addington were the four nominal heads of four distinct parties, which must now by some chemical process be amalgamated ; all must forget, if they can, their peculiar habits and opinions, and unite in the pursuit of a common object. How far this is possible, time will show ; to what degree this motley Ministry can, by their joint influence, command a majority in the House of Commons ; how far they will, *as a whole,* be assisted by the secret influence and power of the Crown ; whether, if not so seconded, they will be able to appeal some time hence to the people, and dissolve the Parliament — all these, and many other questions, will receive very different answers from different speculators. But in the mean time it is self-evident that every individual will be extremely jealous of the patronage of his individual department; that individually as well as conjointly, they will be cautious of provoking enmity ; and that a measure patronized by the Duke of Buccleuch is not very likely to be opposed by any member of such a Cabinet.

If, indeed, the object of your wishes were a sinecure, and at the disposal of the Chancellor (Erskine), or of the President of the Board of Control (Lord Minto), you might have strong cause, perhaps, for apprehension ; but what you ask would suit few candidates, and there probably is not one whom the Cabinet, or any person in it, would feel any strong *interest* in obliging to your disadvantage. But farther, we know that Lord Sidmouth is in the Cabinet, so is Lord Ellenborough, and these two are notoriously the *King's* Ministers. Now we may be very sure that they, or some other of the King's friends, will possess one department, which has no name, but is not the less real; namely, the supervision of the King's influence both here and in Scotland. I therefore much doubt whether there is any man in the Cabinet who, as Minister, has it in his power to prevent your attainment of your object. Lord Melville, we know, *was* in a great measure the representative of the King's personal influence in Scotland, and I am by no means sure that he is no longer so; but be that as it may, it will, I am well persuaded, continue in the hands of some one who has not been forced upon his Majesty as one of his confidential servants.

Upon the whole, then, the only consolation that I can confidently give you is, that what you represent as a *principal* difficulty is *quite imaginary*, and that your own political principles are exactly those which are most likely to be serviceable to you. I need not say how happy Anne and myself would be to see you (we shall spend the month of March in London), nor that, if you should be able to point out any means by which I can be of the slightest use in advancing your interests, you may employ me without reserve. I must go to the Pump-room for my glass of water — so God bless you.

Ever truly yours,   G. ELLIS.

TO GEORGE ELLIS, ESQ., BATH.

LONDON, February 20, 1806.

MY DEAR ELLIS, — I have your kind letter, and am infinitely obliged to you for your solicitude in my behalf. I have indeed been rather fortunate, for the gale which has shattered so many goodly argosies, has blown my little bark into the creek for which she was bound, and left me only to lament the misfortunes of my friends. To vary the simile, while the huge frigates, the Moira and Lauderdale, were fiercely combating for the dominion of the Caledonian main, I was fortunate enough to get on board the good ship Spencer, and leave them to settle their disputes at leisure. It is said to be a violent ground of controversy in the new Ministry, which of those two noble lords is to be St. Andrew for Scotland.

I own I tremble for the consequences of so violent a temper as Lauderdale's, irritated by long-disappointed ambition and ancient feud with all his brother nobles. It is a certain truth that Lord Moira insists upon his claim, backed by all the friends of the late Administration in Scotland, to have a certain weight in that country; and it is equally certain that the Hamiltons and Lauderdales have struck out. So here are people who have stood in the rain without doors for so many years, quarrelling for the nearest place to the fire, as soon as they have set their feet on the floor. Lord Moira, as he always has been, was highly kind and courteous to me on this occasion.

Heber is just come in, with your letter waving in his hand. I am ashamed of all the trouble I have given you, and at the same time flattered to find your friendship even equal to that greatest and most disagreeable of all trials, the task of solicitation. Mrs. Scott is *not* with me, and I am truly concerned to think we should be so near, without the prospect of meeting. Truth is, I had half a mind to make a run up to Bath, merely to break the spell which has prevented our meeting for these two years. But Bindley,[1] the collector, has lent me a parcel of books, which he insists on my consulting within the liberties of Westminster, and which I cannot find elsewhere, so that the fortnight I propose to stay will be fully occupied by examination and extracting. How long I may be detained here is very uncertain, but I wish to leave London on Saturday se'ennight. Should I be so delayed as to bring my time of departure anything near that of your arrival, I will stretch my furlough to the utmost, that I may have a chance of seeing you.

---

[1] James Bindley, Esq., famed for his rich accumulation of books, prints, and medals, held the office of a commissioner of Stamps during the long period of 53 years. He died in 1818, in his 81st year. At the sale of his library a collection of penny ballads, etc., in 8 volumes, produced £837.

and that you will feel emboldened, by the quan-
-inforcement which the radical heat shall have
to undertake your expedition to the *tramontane*
Reged this season. My time has been spent
here, and I should have liked very well to
-ined till you came up to town, had it not been
-e and bairns at home, whom I confess I am
-s to see. Accordingly I set off early to-mor-
-g — indeed I expected to have done so to-day,
-panion, Ballantyne, our Scottish Bodoni, was
-a violent diarrhœa, which, though his phy-
-d him it would serve his health in general,
-ly have contributed little to his accomplish-
-greeable companion in a post-chaise, which
very respectable. I own Lord Melville's
-ect me deeply. He, at least his nephew,
-atron, and gave me countenance and as-
had but few friends. I have seen when
-linburgh were thought by the inhabitants
-ar for Lord Melville to walk upon; and
with his power and influence gone, his
-e accounted by many, from whom he
-er thoughts, an embarrassment, if not
All this is very vile — it is one of the
Providence, as it were, industriously
-y, to let us see the ragged ends of the
-pose its most beautiful figures. God
-cies may be true, which I fear are
your kind heart than your experience
-es and the fate of fallen statesmen.
-s to Mrs. Ellis. Your next will find
WALTER SCOTT.

GEORGE ELLIS, ESQ.

ASHESTIEL, April 7, 1806.
— Were I to begin by telling you
not finding you in London, and at

Nothing is minded here but domestic politics, and if we
are not clean swept, there is no want of new brooms to
perform that operation. I have heard very bad news
of Leyden's health since my arrival here — such, indeed,
as to give room to apprehend the very worst. I fear he
has neglected the precautions which the climate renders
necessary, and which no man departs from with impu-
nity. Remember me kindly and respectfully to Mrs.
Ellis; and believe me ever yours faithfully,

WALTER SCOTT.

P. S. — Poor Lord Melville! how does he look? We
have had miserable accounts of his health in London. He
was the architect of my little fortune, from circumstances
of personal regard merely; for any of my trifling literary
acquisitions were out of his way. My heart bleeds when
I think on his situation —

> " Even when the rage of battle ceased,
> The victor's soul was not appeased." [1]

TO THE EARL OF DALKEITH.

LONDON, 11th February, 1806.
MY DEAR LORD, — I cannot help flattering myself —
for perhaps it is flattering myself — that the noble architect of the Border Minstrel's little fortune has been sometimes anxious for the security of that lowly edifice,
during the tempest which has overturned so many palaces
and towers. If I am right in my supposition, it will
give you pleasure to learn that, notwithstanding some
little rubs, I have been able to carry through the transaction which your Lordship sanctioned by your influence
and approbation, and that in a way very pleasing to my
own feelings. Lord Spencer, upon the nature of the
transaction being explained in an audience with which he
favored me, was pleased to direct the commission to be
issued, as an act of justice, regretting, he said, it had
not been from the beginning his own deed. This was

---

[1] These lines are from Smollett's *Tears of Scotland*.

doing the thing handsomely, and like an English nobleman. I have been very much fêted and caressed here,
almost indeed to suffocation, but have been made amends
by meeting some old friends. One of the kindest was
Lord Somerville, who volunteered introducing me to
Lord Spencer, as much, I am convinced, from respect
to your Lordship's protection and wishes, as from a desire to serve me personally. He seemed very anxious to
do anything in his power which might evince a wish to
be of use to your protégé. Lord Minto was also infinitely kind and active, and his influence with Lord
Spencer would, I am convinced, have been stretched to
the utmost in my favor, had not Lord Spencer's own
view of the subject been perfectly sufficient.

After all, a little literary reputation is of some use here.
I suppose Solomon, when he compared a good name to
a pot of ointment, meant that it oiled the hinges of the
hall-doors into which the possessors of that inestimable
treasure wished to penetrate. What a *good* name was
in Jerusalem, a *known* name seems to be in London. If
you are celebrated for writing verses or for slicing cu-
cumbers, for being two feet taller or two feet less than
any other biped, for acting plays when you should be
whipped at school, or for attending schools and institu-
tions when you should be preparing for your grave, your
notoriety becomes a talisman — an "Open Sesame" before which everything gives way — till you are voted a
bore, and discarded for a new plaything. As this is a
consummation of notoriety which I am by no means ambitious of experiencing, I hope I shall be very soon
able to shape my course northward, to enjoy my good
fortune at my leisure, and snap my fingers at the Bar
and all its works.

There is, it is believed, a rude scuffle betwixt our late
commander-in-chief and Lord Lauderdale, for the patronage of Scotland. If there is to be an exclusive administration, I hope it will not be in the hands of the latter.

Indeed, when one considers,
Sidmouth and Ellenborough
actual power of casting the ba
villites and four Foxites w
cannot think they will find
upon his Majesty any one t
like. I should therefore s
Andrew's Cross will be d
a little consolidated, *if th*
is much loose gunpowd
would make a fine e
effusions; I am infec
breathe, and cannot
state affairs. I hope
chief are now recove
has so turned out
of the family here,
the pleasure it wil
ship be so kind
grateful and resp
I have this day
office? I dine
before, lest it
in that quarte
or turning w

I am eve
ship's much

My
happy
at a d
us; a
to-m
that

springs,
tity of r
received,
region of
very gayly
have rema
for the wif
now anxiou
row mornin
but my com
afflicted with
sician assure
would certain
ments as an a
are otherwise
misfortunes aff
was my early p
sistance when I
the streets of E
almost too vulg
now I fear that,
presence would
has deserved oth
something worse.
occasions when
turns the tapestr
worsted which co
grant your proph
rather dictated by
of political enmiti
Kindest complimen
me in Edinburgh.

TO

My DEAR ELLIS,
all the regret I had a

being obliged to leave it before your return, this very
handsome sheet of paper, which I intend to cover with
more important and interesting matters, would be entirely occupied by such a Jeremiade as could only be
equalled by Jeremiah himself. I will therefore waive
that subject, only assuring you that I hope to be in London next spring, but have much warmer hopes of seeing
you here in summer. I hope Bath has been of service;
if not so much as you expected, try easy exercise in a
northward direction, and make proof of the virtues of
the Tweed and Yarrow. We have been here these two
days, and I have been quite rejoiced to find all my dogs,
and horses, and sheep, and cows, and two cottages full
of peasants and their children, and all my other stock,
human and animal, in great good health — we want nothing but Mrs. Ellis and you to be the strangers within
our gates, and our establishment would be complete on
the patriarchal plan. I took possession of my new office
on my return. The duty is very simple, consisting
chiefly in signing my name; and as I have five colleagues, I am not obliged to do duty except in turn, so
my task is a very easy one, as my name is very short.

My principal companion in this solitude is John Dryden. After all, there are some passages in his translations from Ovid and Juvenal that will hardly bear reprinting, unless I would have the Bishop of London [1] and
the whole corps of Methodists about my ears. I wish
you would look at the passages I mean. One is from
the fourth book of Lucretius; the other from Ovid's Instructions to his Mistress. They are not only double-
entendres, but good plain single-entendres — not only
broad, but long, and as coarse as the mainsail of a first-
rate. What to make of them I know not; but I fear
that, without absolutely gelding the bard, it will be indispensable to circumcise him a little by leaving out
some of the most obnoxious lines. Do, pray, look at the

[1] Dr. Porteous.

poems and decide for me. Have you seen my friend
Tom Thomson, who is just now in London? He has, I
believe, the advantage of knowing you, and I hope you
will meet, as he understands more of old books, old laws,
and old history, than any man in Scotland. He has
lately received an appointment under the Lord Register
of Scotland, which puts all our records under his immediate inspection and control, and I expect many valuable
discoveries to be the consequence of his investigation, if
he escapes being smothered in the cloud of dust which
his researches will certainly raise about his ears. I sent
your card instantly to Jeffrey, from whom you had doubtless a suitable answer.[1] I saw the venerable economist
and antiquary, Macpherson, when in London, and was
quite delighted with the simplicity and kindness of his
manners. He is exactly like one of the old Scotchmen
whom I remember twenty years ago, before so close a
union had taken place between Edinburgh and London.
The mail-coach and the Berwick smacks have done more
than the Union in altering our national character, sometimes for the better and sometimes for the worse.

I met with your friend, Mr. Canning, in town, and
claimed his acquaintance as a friend of yours, and had
my claim allowed; also Mr. Frere, — both delightful
companions, far too good for politics, and for winning
and losing places. When I say I was more pleased with
their society than I thought had been possible on so short
an acquaintance, I pay them a very trifling compliment
and myself a very great one. I had also the honor of
dining with a fair friend of yours at Blackheath, an
honor which I shall very long remember. She is an enchanting princess, who dwells in an enchanted palace,
and I cannot help thinking that her prince must labor
under some malignant spell when he denies himself her

---

[1] Mr. Ellis had written to Mr. Jeffrey, through Scott, proposing to draw
up an article for the *Edinburgh Review* on the *Annals of Commerce*, then
recently published by Mr. David Macpherson.

society. The very Prince of the Black Isles, whose bottom was marble, would have made an effort to transport himself to Montague House. From all this you will understand I was at Montague House.

I am quite delighted at the interest you take in poor Lord Melville. I suppose they are determined to hunt him down. Indeed, the result of his trial must be ruin from the expense, even supposing him to be honorably acquitted. Will you, when you have time to write, let me know how that matter is likely to turn? I am deeply interested in it; and the reports here are so various, that one knows not what to trust to. Even the common rumor of London is generally more authentic than the "from good authority" of Edinburgh. Besides, I am now in the wilds (alas, I cannot say *woods* and wilds), and hear little of what passes. Charlotte joins me in a thousand kind remembrances to Mrs. Ellis; and I am ever yours most truly,   WALTER SCOTT.

I shall not dwell at present upon Scott's method of conduct in the circumstances of an eminently popular author beleaguered by the importunities of fashionable admirers: his bearing, when first exposed to such influences, was exactly what it was to the end, and I shall have occasion in the sequel to produce the evidence of more than one deliberate observer.

Caroline, Princess of Wales, was in those days considered among the Tories, whose politics her husband had uniformly opposed, as the victim of unmerited misfortune, cast aside, from the mere wantonness of caprice, by a gay and dissolute voluptuary; while the Prince's Whig associates had espoused his quarrel, and were already, as the event showed, prepared to act, publicly as well as privately, as if they believed her to be among the most abandoned of her sex. I know not by whom Scott was first introduced to her little Court at Blackheath; but I think it was probably through Mrs. Hay-

man, a lady of her bedchamber, several of whose notes
and letters occur about this time in the collection of his
correspondence. The careless levity of the Princess's
manner was observed by him, as I have heard him say,
with much regret, as likely to bring the purity of heart
and mind, for which he gave her credit, into suspicion.
For example, when, in the course of the evening, she
conducted him by himself to admire some flowers in a
conservatory, and, the place being rather dark, his lameness occasioned him to hesitate for a moment in following her down some steps which she had taken at a skip,
she turned round, and said, with mock indignation, "Ah!
false and faint-hearted troubadour! you will not trust
yourself with me for fear of your neck!"

I find from one of Mrs. Hayman's letters, that on
being asked, at Montague House, to recite some verses
of his own, he replied that he had none unpublished
which he thought worthy of Her Royal Highness's attention, but introduced a short account of the Ettrick Shepherd, and repeated one of the ballads of the Mountain
Bard, for which he was then endeavoring to procure
subscribers. The Princess appears to have been interested by the story, and she affected, at all events, to be
pleased with the lines; she desired that her name might
be placed on the Shepherd's list, and thus he had at
least one gleam of royal patronage.

It was during the same visit to London that Scott first
saw Joanna Baillie, of whose Plays on the Passions he
had been, from their first appearance, an enthusiastic
admirer. The late Mr. Sotheby, the translator of
Oberon, etc., etc., was the friend who introduced him to
the poetess of Hampstead. Being asked very lately what
impression he made upon her at this interview — "I was
at first," she answered, "a little disappointed, for I was
fresh from the Lay, and had pictured to myself an ideal
elegance and refinement of feature; but I said to myself,
If I had been in a crowd, and at a loss what to do, I should

have fixed upon that face among a thousand, as the sure index of the benevolence and the shrewdness that would and could help me in my strait. We had not talked long, however, before I saw in the expressive play of his countenance far more even of elegance and refinement than I had missed in its mere lines." The acquaintance thus begun, soon ripened into a most affectionate intimacy between him and this remarkable woman; and thenceforth she and her distinguished brother, Dr. Matthew Baillie, were among the friends to whose intercourse he looked forward with the greatest pleasure when about to visit the metropolis.

I ought to have mentioned before, that he had known Mr. Sotheby at a very early period of life, that amiable and excellent man having been stationed for some time at Edinburgh while serving his Majesty as a captain of dragoons. Scott ever retained for him a sincere regard; he was always, when in London, a frequent guest at his hospitable board, and owed to him the personal acquaintance of not a few of their most eminent contemporaries in various departments of literature and art.

When the Court opened after the spring recess, Scott entered upon his new duties as one of the Principal Clerks of Session; and as he continued to discharge them with exemplary regularity, and to the entire satisfaction both of the Judges and the Bar, during the long period of twenty-five years, I think it proper to tell precisely in what they consisted, the more so because, in his letter to Ellis of the 25th January, he has himself (characteristically enough) understated them.

The Court of Session sits at Edinburgh from the 12th of May to the 12th of July, and again from the 12th of November, with a short interval at Christmas, to the 12th of March. The Judges of the Inner Court took their places on the Bench, in his time, every morning not later than ten o'clock, and remained according to the amount of business ready for despatch, but seldom for less than four or more than six hours daily; during which space the Principal Clerks continued seated at a table below the Bench, to watch the progress of the suits, and record the decisions — the cases, of all classes, being equally apportioned among their number. The Court of Session, however, does not sit on Monday, that day being reserved for the criminal business of the High Court of Justiciary; and there is also another blank day every other week, — the *Teind Wednesday*, as it is called, when the Judges are assembled for the hearing of tithe questions, which belong to a separate jurisdiction, of comparatively modern creation, and having its own separate establishment of officers. On the whole, then, Scott's attendance in Court may be taken to have amounted, on the average, to from four to six hours daily during rather less than six months out of the twelve.

Not a little of the Clerk's business in Court is merely formal, and indeed mechanical; but there are few days in which he is not called upon for the exertion of his higher faculties, in reducing the decisions of the Bench, orally pronounced, to technical shape; which, in a new, complex, or difficult case, cannot be satisfactorily done without close attention to all the previous proceedings and written documents, an accurate understanding of the principles or precedents on which it has been determined, and a thorough command of the whole vocabulary of legal forms. Dull or indolent men, promoted through the mere wantonness of political patronage, might, no doubt, contrive to devolve the harder part of their duty upon humbler assistants: but, in general, the office had been held by gentlemen of high character and attainments; and more than one among Scott's own colleagues enjoyed the reputation of legal science that would have done honor to the Bench. Such men, of course, prided themselves on doing well whatever it was their proper function to do; and it was by their example, not that of the drones who condescended to lean upon unseen and irresponsible inferiors, that Scott uniformly modelled his own conduct as a Clerk of Session. To do this required, of necessity, constant study of law-papers and authorities at home. There was also a great deal of really base drudgery, such as the authenticating of registered deeds, by signature, which he had to go through out of Court; he had, too, a Shrievalty, though not a heavy one, all the while upon his hands; — and, on the whole, it forms one of the most remarkable features in his history, that, throughout the most active period of his literary career, he must have devoted a large proportion of his hours, during half at least of every year, to the conscientious discharge of professional duties.

Henceforth, then, when in Edinburgh, his literary work was performed chiefly before breakfast; with the assistance of such evening hours as he could contrive to rescue from the consideration of Court papers, and from those social engagements in which, year after year, as his celebrity advanced, he was of necessity more and more largely involved; and of those entire days during which the Court of Session did not sit — days which, by most of those holding the same official station, were given to relaxation and amusement. So long as he continued Quartermaster of the Volunteer Cavalry, of course he had, even while in Edinburgh, some occasional horse exercise; but, in general, his town life henceforth was in that respect as inactive as his country life ever was the reverse. He scorned for a long while to attach any consequence to this complete alternation of habits; but we shall find him confessing in the sequel, that it proved highly injurious to his bodily health.

I may here observe, that the duties of his clerkship brought him into close daily connection with a set of gentlemen, most of whom were soon regarded by him with the most cordial affection and confidence. One of his new colleagues was David Hume (the nephew of the historian), whose lectures on the Law of Scotland are

characterized with just eulogy in the Ashestiel Memoir,
and who subsequently became a Baron of the Exchequer;
a man as virtuous and amiable, as conspicuous for masculine vigor of intellect and variety of knowledge.[1]   Another was Hector Macdonald Buchanan of Drummakiln,
a frank-hearted and generous gentleman, not the less
acceptable to Scott for the Highland prejudices which he
inherited with the high blood of Clanranald; at whose
beautiful seat of Ross Priory, on the shores of Loch Lo-
mond, he was henceforth almost annually a visitor — a
circumstance which has left many traces in the Waverley
Novels.   A third (though I believe of later appointment)
with whom his intimacy was not less strict, was the late
excellent Sir Robert Dundas of Beechwood, Bart.; and
a fourth was the friend of his boyhood, one of the dearest
he ever had, Colin Mackenzie of Portmore.   With these
gentlemen's families, he and his lived in such constant
familiarity of kindness, that the children all called their
fathers' colleagues *uncles*, and the mothers of their little
friends *aunts;* and, in truth, the establishment was a
brotherhood.

Scott's nomination as Clerk of Session appeared in the
same Gazette (March 8, 1806) which announced the in-
stalment of the Hon. Henry Erskine and John Clerk of
Eldin as Lord Advocate and Solicitor-General for Scotland.   The promotion, at such a moment, of a distinguished Tory might well excite the wonder of the Parliament House, and even when the circumstances were
explained, the inferior local adherents of the triumphant
cause were far from considering the conduct of their
superiors in this matter with feelings of satisfaction.
The indication of such humors was deeply resented by

[1] Mr. Baron Hume died at Edinburgh, 27th July, 1838, in his 82d year.
I had great gratification in receiving a message from the venerable man
shortly before his death, conveying his warm approbation of these Memoirs
of his friend. — (1839.)

his haughty spirit; and he in his turn showed his irritation in a manner well calculated to extend to higher quarters the spleen with which his advancement had been regarded by persons wholly unworthy of his attention. In short, it was almost immediately after a Whig Ministry had gazetted his appointment to an office which had for twelve months formed a principal object of his ambition that, rebelling against the implied suspicion of his having accepted something like a personal obligation at the hands of adverse politicians, he for the first time put himself forward as a decided Tory partisan.

The impeachment of Lord Melville was among the first measures of the new Government; and personal affection and gratitude graced as well as heightened the zeal with which Scott watched the issue of this, in his eyes, vindictive proceeding; but, though the ex-minister's ultimate acquittal was, as to all the charges involving his personal honor, complete, it must now be allowed that the investigation brought out many circumstances by no means creditable to his discretion; and the rejoicings of his friends ought not, therefore, to have been scornfully jubilant. Such they were, however — at least in Edinburgh; and Scott took his share in them by inditing a song, which was sung by James Ballantyne, and received with clamorous applauses, at a public dinner given in honor of the event on the 27th of June, 1806. I regret that this piece was inadvertently omitted in the late collective edition of his poetical works; but since such is the case, I consider myself bound to insert it here. However he may have regretted it afterwards, he authorized its publication in the newspapers of the time, and my narrative would fail to convey a complete view of the man if I should draw a veil over the expression, thus deliberate, of some of the strongest personal feelings that ever animated his verse.

HEALTH TO LORD MELVILLE.

AIR — *Carrickfergus.*

Since here we are set in array round the table,
  Five hundred good fellows well met in a hall,
Come listen, brave boys, and I'll sing as I'm able
  How innocence triumphed and pride got a fall.
      But push round the claret —
      Come, stewards, don't spare it —
With rapture you'll drink to the toast that I give.
      Here, boys,
      Off with it merrily —
MELVILLE forever, and long may he live!

What were the Whigs doing, when boldly pursuing,
  PITT banished Rebellion, gave Treason a string?
Why, they swore, on their honor, for ARTHUR O'CONNOR,
  And fought hard for DESPARD against country and king.
      Well, then, we knew, boys,
      PITT and MELVILLE were true boys,
And the tempest was raised by the friends of Reform.
      Ah, woe!
      Weep to his memory;
Low lies the pilot that weathered the storm!

And pray, don't you mind when the Blues first were raising,
  And we scarcely could think the house safe o'er our heads?
When villains and coxcombs, French politics praising,
  Drove peace from our tables and sleep from our beds?
      Our hearts they grew bolder
      When musket on shoulder,
Stepp'd forth our old Statesmen example to give.
      Come, boys, never fear,
      Drink the Blue grenadier —
Here's to old HARRY, and long may he live!

They would turn us adrift; though rely, sir, upon it —
  Our own faithful chronicles warrant us that
The free mountaineer and his bonny blue bonnet
  Have oft gone as far as the regular's hat.
      We laugh at their taunting,
      For all we are wanting
Is license our life for our country to give.
      Off with it merrily,
      Horse, foot, and artillery,
Each loyal Volunteer, long may he live!